Managing Bandwidth: Deploying QOS in Enterprise Networks

ISBN 0-13-011391-3

90000

9 780130 113917

The Prentice Hall PTR
Internet Infrastructure Series

Croll/Packman	*Managing Bandwidth: Deploying QOS in Enterprise Networks*
Doraswamy/Harkins	*IPSec: The New Security Standard for the Internet, Intranets, and Virtual Private Networks*
Luotonen	*Web Proxy Servers*
Rose/Strom	*Internet Messaging: From the Desktop to the Enterprise*

Managing Bandwidth: Deploying QOS in Enterprise Networks

Alistair Croll
Eric Packman

Prentice Hall PTR
Upper Saddle River, NJ 07458

http://www.phptr.com

Library of Congress Cataloging-in-Publication Date
Croll, Alistair.
    Managing bandwidth : deploying QOS in enterprise networks /
Alistair Croll, Eric Pack man.
       p.   cm. -- (Internet infrastructure series)
    Includes bibliographical references.
    ISBN 0-13-011391-3
    1. Computer networks--Management. 2. Telecomunnication--Traffic-Management.
    3. Business enterprises--Computer networks-Management. I. Packman, Eric. II. Title.
    III. Series: Prentice Hall PTR internet infrastructure series.
    TK5105.5.C76   1999   99-35921
    658.4'038--dc21

Editorial/Production Supervision: Joanne Anzalone
Acquisitions Editor: Mary Franz
Editorial Assistant: Noreen Regina
Marketing Manager: Lisa Konzelmann
Manufacuturing Manager: Alexis Heydt
Cover Design: Anthoy Gemmallaro
Cover Design Direction: Jerry Votta
Art Director: Gail Cocker-Bogusz

© 2000 Prentice Hall PTR
Prentice-Hall, Inc.
Upper Saddle River, NJ 07458

Prentice Hall books are widley used by permission by corporations and government agencies for training,
marketing, and resale. The publisher offers discounts on this book when ordered in bulk quantities.
For more information, contact:

Corporate Sales Department,
Prentice Hall PTR
One Lake Street
Upper Saddle River, NJ 07458
Phone: 800-382-3419; FAX: 201-236-7141
E-mail (Internet): corpsales@prenhall.com

Printed in the United States of America

10 9 8 7 6 5 4 3 2 1

ISBN 0-13-011391-3

Prentice-Hall International (UK) Limited, London
Prentice-Hall of Australia Pty. Limited, Sydney
Prentice-Hall Canada Inc., Toronto
Prentice-Hall Hispanoamericana, S.A., Mexico
Prentice-Hall of India Private Limited, New Delhi
Prentice-Hall of Japan, Inc., Tokyo
Prentical--Hall (Singapore) Pte. Ltd., Singapore
Editora Prentice-Hall do Brasil, Ltda., Rio de Janeiro

For my mother, who taught me the real meaning of communication.—AC

"The Linux Community"—EP

Contents

Part 5   371

Part 6   385

Introduction

Bandwidth is getting cheaper. Technical innovation in software, protocols, and hardware has pushed data networks to new heights of performance, while attacking costs aggressively. Fast links are available today for a fraction of what far slower connections cost a mere decade ago. While bandwidth may never be "too cheap to meter," as was promised for nuclear power, technological developments may make regulating bandwidth more like regulating the use of copy machines or pencils. Some day, it may hardly be worth the effort to monitor network usage except in cases of gross abuse, or as a fee-collection mechanism in lawyers' offices.

At the same time, new applications are placing increasing demands on the network. We invent new ways of using the network infrastructure as fast as we can deploy it. Networks are called upon to support myriad voice, video, and interactive applications alongside traditional data systems, each of which must run in concert with the objectives of the organization.

Now that the network is a part of the business infrastructure, we need control systems to make it toe the line. The network has to meet the same requirements as other parts of the company: increased effectiveness and reduced costs.

Increased effectiveness means faster customer service, quicker dissemination of information, and so on. It means access to more current information. It means clear, accurate communications systems that are integrated with the reliable operation of business-critical applications.

Reduced costs can come from more efficient use of existing resources, lower costs of expansion, or delayed expenditures. The ability of data networks to supplant other critical infrastructures, such as office or long-distance telephony, means that networks can reduce costs substantially. Careful management of costly wide-area-network (WAN) links can delay the inevitable bandwidth upgrades, further lowering the organization's expenses.

IT managers have only recently begun to think in business terms. For many IT organizations, the business objectives of the network are now becoming obvious. To succeed in an information age, companies must translate their business practices into network behaviors and information architectures, designing the network for specific business goals and objectives.

This book is about managing bandwidth and quality of service in enterprise networks. The discussion will take us into the realm of real-time classification and packet handling as well as into the systems and processes that are part of building and maintaining a bandwidth-managed network.

The Internet began with the premise that discrete chunks of data travel across a network of routers without the involvement of the end nodes. This meant that the sender and receiver were "smart" and the intermediate network was "dumb." This model allowed the Internet to grow at an amazing pace. Unfortunately, it also led to a service-poor network infrastructure in which the onus was on the end nodes to provide any of the services an application might need. Traffic might be lost, rerouted, or delayed during transmission, and it was left to the sender and receiver to sort things out. Unlike circuit-switched or packet-switched networks, routed networks like IP offer none of the determinism we need—in return for optimal use of available bandwidth.

As we introduce new applications onto IP networks, we place new demands on the network. We need high performance, low delay, and consistent behavior from a best-effort network so that we can deploy multimedia and mission-critical systems. Consequently, IP's simplicity is an obstacle to certain applications. Bandwidth management systems allow us to regulate the performance of a network and share bandwidth equitably across various applications and users.

At the same time, we don't want to sacrifice the simplicity that has brought us this far. Successful QOS solutions will be those that implement a few changes and have far-reaching effects. This book is about such solutions.

Consequently, IP's simplicity is an obstacle to certain applications. Bandwidth management systems allow us to regulate the performance of a network and share bandwidth equitably across various applications and users.

At the same time, we don't want to sacrifice the simplicity that has brought us this far. Successful QOS solutions will be those that implement a few changes and have far-reaching effects. This book is about such solutions.

Intended audience

This book covers the issues surrounding quality of service in enterprise networks and the Internet. It assumes some degree of knowledge about general networking concepts, and provides a foundation for understanding bandwidth management mechanisms. It is suited for a variety of readers, including:

- Network engineers, architects, and managers seeking a consolidated book from which to learn about Quality of Service (QOS) and policy-based networking.

- People charged with implementing QOS systems in products or applications, including product managers, sales engineers, and network system integrators.

- CIO's and senior IT managers who are responsible for assuring the competitive capability of their information systems and allocating budgets and personnel to the deployment of next-generation networking infrastructures.

Acknowledgments

The elegant design of networking protocols such as TCP has taken them far beyond their intended goals, and ushered in a new era of communication worldwide. The simplicity and elegance of these designs is to be applauded. We owe our thanks to the thousands of engineers who work to push the envelopes of networking in private companies and standards bodies worldwide. QOS is a complex and still subjective area. Rod Anderson, Lionel Gibbons, Elaine Lusher, Paul Mokapetris and Mark Roy helped with structure and technical insight and are responsible for substantial improvements and clarifications in the text.

Mary Franz is the most encouraging of editors, and the staff at Networkshop has been patient throughout the creation of this work. On a personal note, Alistair would like to thank Lionel for his support, patience, and pragmatic counsel over the years; Jen for her encouragement, concern, and frequent cups of tea; Ted and Kip for their unconditional companionship; and Becky, for her buoyant enthusiasm.

Any errors, omissions, or oversights are ours alone.

Recent Developments

The field of QOS is dynamic and constantly changing. To provide you with current information and links to relevant standards, we maintain a site dedicated to QOS work and standards at www.networkshop.ca/QOS.

PART 1

We begin the discussion of QOS by defining the problem. Quality of service means many things to many people. To understand the motivations and challenges that multiservice networks pose we must look at the way public and private networks have evolved. We divide this into the following sections:

- Defining the scope of bandwidth management

- Motivations for bandwidth management

- A history of networking usage

- Bandwidth today

Defining the scope of bandwidth management

The ultimate goal of bandwidth management is the assignment of appropriate carrying capacity within the network for every user and application.

This seemingly simple phrase hides a considerable amount of ambiguity and is open to subjective interpretation. In order to understand the issues and opportunities with which managed networks present us, we define the scope of bandwidth management. In the process, we'll look at class-, type-, and quality-of service; at differentiated and integrated services; and at different systems for assigning differentiated service to traffic.

Today's best-effort model for public and private networks is based on the ideas that traffic may be lost in transmission and that all traffic is created equal. By contrast, network services such as the public switched telephone network have separate channels for signaling traffic and voice traffic, and they guarantee a fixed capacity end to end with small, predictable delays.

As we rely on best-effort networks to carry concurrent voice, video, data, and interactive applications across a common network infrastructure, we must offer each of these traffic types the specific services and handling characteristics it requires.

Managing bandwidth is also good business sense: having control over network capacity allows you to better regulate the pace of network expansions and the addition of capacity in the organization. Managing bandwidth means controlling traffic levels in real time in order to make optimal use of scarce capacity.

In the first part of this book we will look at the technologies and trends that are driving service-level management, and we will glance back at a history of bandwidth-management systems. Our aim is to understand the needs of the various types of traffic that travel across modern networks.

Characteristics of a bandwidth-managed network

The ultimate goal of bandwidth management is the assignment of **appropriate carrying capacity within the network for every user and application**. Let's look at this statement in detail.

"Appropriate" capacity means the right data rate, the proper delay, and the right level of change in delay. Offering every application a 10-millisecond end-to-end delay is a great idea, but "appropriate" also means cost effective. If backups can run late at night over slow links, then using an expensive high-performance video link for them is wasteful.

"Within the network" means that a network has differentiated services to offer. If a network is to provide more than one sort of service, then it must be able to identify different types of traffic and handle them in different ways. Classification and handling can result in a coarse differentiation, such as using two circuits with different latencies, or a very granular one, such as dynamically negotiating throughput and delay on a session-by-session basis.

"For every user and application" implies that the network has user- and application-based identification systems. Today's networking devices work with addresses and interfaces, so a bandwidth-managed network needs to determine user and application information from addressing information using a variety of network services such as user-based logins. This represents a significant shift away from a low-level addressing perspective and toward a view of the network based on users and services as the networking infrastructure starts to offer so-called "policy" capabilities.

A bandwidth-managed network is able to offer distinct characteristics based on the kinds of traffic it handles. Traffic can be classified by application, user, or even "external" factors such as time of day, date, or level of network congestion. While today's technology won't enable us to build a perfectly manageable network, we can take steps to build a network that can offer varying degrees of service and to deploy the system of directories and authentication points that will govern allocation of these services.

Imagine an engineering company that must communicate between two offices, one in North America and one in Europe. The WAN link between the offices is a bottleneck, and a number of applications use the link to exchange everything from new software or hardware specifications to human-resources data.

At certain times of the year, different applications will be important to the organization's success. The human-resources and payroll information is vital at tax time, and software builds must cross the Atlantic quickly during periods of engineering integration. So different applications have different levels of *mission criticality* to the organization.

Some of the traffic is generated by traditional, store-and-forward applications that are not real time. Applications such as file transfers and e-mail are generally able to survive varying delays in the network. The information they convey may be critical to the business, but it will still be valid and useful if it is delayed for a few hundred milliseconds. We might say that delivery of this information is less *delay sensitive* from a narrow perspective. Overall, the file transfers must be completed—but it is generally acceptable for them to encounter some delay in order for real-time traffic to arrive quickly.

The company also does collaborative engineering on computer-aided-design (CAD) systems. It is experimenting with interactive whiteboard tools and is considering using voice-over-IP to reduce its long-distance charges. These applications, unlike files and e-mail, don't function properly if they encounter delays. They need higher priority of transmission relative to store-and-forward traffic, and each application has a different level of delay sensitivity and of mission criticality (Figure 1–1).

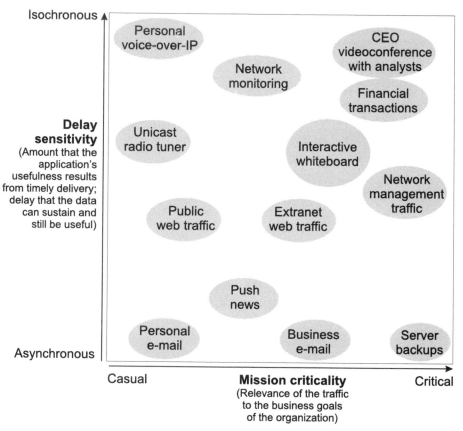

Figure 1–1   A comparison of application delay sensitivity and criticality in an enterprise

Mission criticality depends on the organization's business goals. A map of urgency and importance for a service provider might look substantially different from that for an engineering company, since the provider's objectives are to encourage users to stay online[1] and play video games.[2] The ISP and the enterprise IT manager would both agree that interactive games are delay sensitive, because after some level of delay the game becomes unplayable. Both would also agree that e-mail is not delay sensitive, since an additional delay of a few seconds does not render the mail system useless. They would, however, disagree strongly on the mission criticality of the two (Figure 1–2).

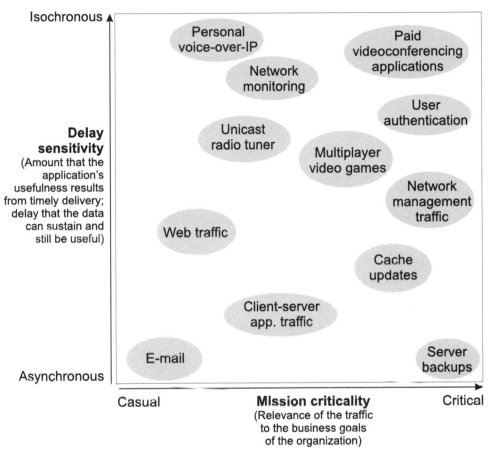

Figure 1–2   A comparison of application delay sensitivity and criticality in an ISP

Bandwidth management is increasingly important for distributed companies. These firms often use common carriers that bill for bandwidth on a per-bit basis and are much more expensive than privately owned networks. A reduction in costs is a powerful driver, and it's easier to make a business case for the deployment of new equipment or new technologies if a business will recover the cost in the near future. Private WAN costs are a function of distance and link speed, and are less often used by distributed companies.

Link speed also affects the importance of bandwidth management. If a company doesn't need speed and has very long distances in its WAN mesh, it may be *less* concerned about bandwidth management than a company that has many local loop connections and high traffic volumes, since slow, long links may be cheaper than fast, short ones. On a more pragmatic note, if your WAN budget is fixed and you need to squeeze more capacity from your WAN, your only option may be to manage the bandwidth. Managing bandwidth properly will also postpone the need for additional bandwidth, making it a suitable alternative to increased WAN capacity.

Translating the relative priorities of mission criticality and delay sensitivity into real network configurations can be a challenge. There are many ways to identify and shape traffic so that it behaves commensurate with business objectives, including traffic prioritization, smoothing traffic flows, discarding unwanted or excessive transmissions, and throttling applications. Each of these mechanisms needs to be linked to the business model so that, for example, human-resources traffic doesn't get in the way of vital software builds during a critical product release, and videoconferencing continues to work. These kinds of rules are grouped under the overburdened notion of "network policy."

Typically a network manager changes network behavior by altering parameters on a device manually, using a management console. Such a change is called an "administrative configuration." If the change is repeated across a range of devices automatically and it involves the creation of specific services, then the process is known as "provisioning."

Traffic urgency is generally consistent for a particular type of application. Most videoconferencing applications have similar needs, as do most file transfers. Consequently, a simple association of application types with relative priorities that can be configured administratively on an individual device or provisioned for a specific service can administer some degree of quality of service (QOS). A truly dynamic policy system is needed only when extrinsic factors such as time of day, identity of the sender, or on-the-fly allocations of capacity, are part of the set of rules by which network traffic must abide. In this respect, policy-based networking is a form of dynamic provisioning.

Because network bandwidth is a scarce resource, devices can be said to *enforce* the use of network capacity. Enforcers attempt to deliver optimal bandwidth allocation, delay, variance in delay, and so on. Enforcing devices can send different kinds of traffic across different paths in the network, or they can treat traffic differently as it passes through them, using queues, packet filters, firewalls, and so on.

In addition to handling criticality and delay sensitivity, we may want to regulate a third dimension: traffic load. Some kinds of traffic—for example, voice—have very little impact on the network (a voice stream can easily fit in 8 Kbps of network capacity with some loss of quality); others, such as video, fill a network for a sustained period of time. Knowing the relative importance, urgency, and traffic burden of an application will tell us much about running it in a network.

Sidebar

Stock-trading application in the LAN

A financial company runs a stock-trading application. It is a traditional client-server model, properly architected for use on a network. It is resilient to delays, and it functions even when the network is congested. At first glance, it imposes little burden on the network and has little delay sensitivity; it would survive a delay as long as transmissions were not lost.

But the nature of the business—instant stock transactions in which a delay of a second can mean a change of thousands of dollars—is such that the application's traffic has become urgent. The company is concerned about timeliness of the *information*, not just the effect of delay on the application. The information is delay sensitive, but the application *per se* is not.

It is vital that we keep delay sensitivity of information distinct from delay sensitivity of an application. Different business models have different outside needs that may make a traditional application urgent. These are often the networks in which policy makes the most sense. For these companies, business as usual dictates at least a two-class network in which every other kind of traffic plays second fiddle to the vital, core application. These firms are familiar with the impact of delay from an information perspective. They experience a need for bandwidth management long before they introduce delay-sensitive applications into their networks.

In practice, the early adopters of policy may not be the ones who are deploying the latest interactive communication tools. Rather, they are the ones who've had to tread lightly on their network for fear of breaking the core of their business. Bandwidth management gives them the tools to create a multiservice network that affords core business applications the protection they need.

> Stock traders, hospitals, and companies that rely on legacy systems for mission-critical data can all profit from a differentiated-service network for applications they run today.

Rolling your own: How close to the edge do you want to live?

Need bandwidth management? You can have it today, if you're willing to work at it.

The tools to manage new networking technologies typically lag behind the technologies themselves. With the development of virtual LAN (VLAN) technology, for example, it was 12 to 18 months before comprehensive VLAN management applications began to emerge. Early adopters of new technologies are forced to adopt user-intensive procedures for the integration of products.

To further muddy the management waters, quality-of-service (QOS) parameters are complex. IT must monitor bandwidth reservations, application response times, traffic classification, and the status of various packet-shaping tools. Recent developments in virtual addressing and dynamic multihomed links make transmitting, interpreting, and acting upon management information intimidating at the very least.

With the convergence of most networks on IP, a variety of application-, network-, link-, and session-layer services have emerged. Services like the Dynamic Host Configuration Protocol (DHCP), Dynamic VLAN Configuration Protocol (DVCP), IP Control Protocol (IPCP), and Domain Name Service (DNS) provision network addressing dynamically. This dynamic information must be relayed to enforcers throughout the network.

You can deploy QOS systems manually today by creating custom access lists and filters on your network devices. You may run into additional problems, however, because a hand-crafted QOS system will introduce additional delays into your normal administrative processes. Moves, adds, and changes will require that the access lists of various devices be altered to accommodate the new nodes, applications, and users in the network. Incorporating DHCP, DNS, DVCP, and IPCP into a policy system poses significant problems, since the linkages between the disparate bodies of information that each service uses simply aren't there today.

There is hope, however. Directory technologies and integrated network-configuration services may help link the behavior of enforcing devices to the users and applications with which a policy system works.

Alphabet soup: QOS, COS, integrated and differentiated services

We'll delve into the details of traffic handling and classification in later sections. Before we look at the motivations for bandwidth management, let's consider the fundamental philosophies underlying current technical thinking about quality of service in networks.

The terminology for bandwidth management is complex. There were initially two big camps for bandwidth management: class of service and quality of service (COS and QOS, respectively).[3] COS chopped the network into a few discrete categories of service; QOS, on the other hand, allowed negotiation of specific network services dynamically through bandwidth reservation. Both camps felt that the "best-effort" model of today made some kinds of applications unusable.

As you might imagine, a COS-based network with a few discrete classes of service is far simpler to create than a complete QOS system. A reasonably small number of classes may not be sufficient for the many different applications that will appear in the coming years, each of which will have specific needs. On the other hand, increasing the number of classes undermines the simplicity of a COS model.

Many standard bodies offer both COS and QOS standards. QOS models include the Integrated Services (IntServ) group in the Internet Engineering Task Force (IETF) and the ATM forum's QOS work. COS models include the Differentiated Services (DiffServ) group in the IETF, the 802.1p/Q extensions to 802.1D in the IEEE, and the user-network interface (LUNI 2.0) extension work in the ATM forum.

QOS models

QOS signaling occurs via the Resource Reservation Protocol (RSVP) and the negotiation of ATM service contracts. Each of these tries to get a guarantee of network behavior by negotiating characteristics for the circuit or flow explicitly. The Integrated Services approach assumes a relatively small number of guaranteed traffic flows, which consume a portion of the bandwidth otherwise allocated to best-effort traffic. These guaranteed flows enjoy preferential treatment in terms of queuing, the likelihood of packet loss, the round-trip time, and the apparent capacity of the various links along the path.

IntServ assumes that there are two major types of traffic: *adaptive*, in which the application adjusts to the capacity of the network, and *rate controlled*, in which the applications generate a relatively constant rate of traffic regardless of network capacity.

COS models

COS signaling resides in the header of each packet of data. This tells devices the class to which the packet belongs. In a COS world, traffic might be classified as "best effort" or "multimedia," for example. It might also be marked as "suitable for discard" or in need of higher levels of security. Rather than determining how to handle traffic as capacity is needed, behaviors for a given class of traffic are provisioned ahead of time; it is the association of packets or flows with a particular class that happens at run-time.

At its simplest, COS is a way of deciding how to act when two packets arrive at a device from different source ports and must be forwarded to the same destination port, or when ingress capacity exceeds egress capacity. COS tells the device which class to favor under such congestion— through either a simple priority scheme or more sophisticated ratios of forwarding by traffic class.

COS is actually more complex than indicated by this simple view of congestion management. A class of service may be "shaped" or throttled back even when excess capacity exists. In addition, some classes of traffic may be handled in other ways—for example, you may want a particular application to be encrypted. Most of the COS uses that we will cover, however, relate to the anticipation and avoidance of congestion, and the relative priorities of different applications in the face of scarce bandwidth.

Classifying traffic

In an IntServ world, the sender asks the network for permission to send a certain kind of traffic. When a QOS system is asked to treat a flow of traffic in a distinct manner, it looks at the capacity available to satisfy this request and the right of the sender to make the request. Assuming the capacity exists and the sender has permission, the network delivers the agreed-upon service.

COS works by associating traffic with a particular class based on traffic characteristics. Classification can take place on the transmitting device, where there is the greatest amount of information on the nature of the application or the identity of the user. It can also occur at the core of the network and on the LAN/WAN interface. As we shall see, classification at each of these locations offers benefits and drawbacks.

A COS-capable device understands that a tagged packet was "entitled" to a certain class by a preceding device. Since network resources are scarce and the COS values are set by a sender, the actual selection of appropriate COS values must be performed in a trustworthy manner. This may mean performing a *policing* function before admitting traffic to a particular class, or relying on trusted network devices, rather than unreliable end nodes, to mark traffic as belonging to a particular class.

As this book goes to press, the concepts of integrated and differentiated services have consolidated into an overall need for differentiated services on networks. Mechanisms that control the allocation of network capacity are now referred to as "QOS," a term that recognizes a need for several classes of service end-to-end alongside some degree of reservation within individual administrative domains.

Fixing bottlenecks

Many current deployments of QOS management focus on a specific link or a congested segment of the network, such as the LAN/WAN boundary or the server farm. Since the addition of WAN links is both the most costly and the fastest-growing activity in IT worldwide,[4] this makes sense. IT has implemented solutions at these critical junctures in the network to deal with the twin demons of growing demand and expensive bandwidth.

How real is this?

ATM QOS is well accepted for specific applications such as committed-bit-rate links within ISPs or backbones of campus networks, where data multiplexing is important. It is also key to the delivery of toll-quality voice in telephone carrier network cores today. Unfortunately, issues with billing and dynamic service negotiation have slowed the deployment of dynamic QOS negotiation between service providers and enterprises.

RSVP is a promising technology for negotiating network services, but many network architects feel that it will not scale effectively in a busy WAN core like the Internet. Current routers lack the capacity to handle the huge number of flows within a network core unless the flows are combined into aggregate flows. While RSVP's complexity may limit it to the edge of the network, emerging systems such as Multi-Protocol Label Switching (MPLS) offer the promise of service negotiation with flow aggregation and may solve the scaling problems.

IP Type of Service (IPTOS) information has existed for many years, but until recently the information in this portion of every IP header was ignored. IPTOS is promising because of its simplicity and broad compatibility—most routers support it—but discussions about the next-generation prioritization schemes that will use this field have hampered reliable adoption. We'll look at this emerging standard, called DiffServ, in coming chapters.

Media-layer class-of-service systems such as 802.1p, differentiated PPP, and differentiated Frame Relay, are promising because they're simple enough to implement between devices immediately. On the other hand, they lack the end-to-end functionality that will win them broad adoption.

Comparing reservation, network COS, and media COS

We've covered a lot of ground so far, and we'll look at all of these topics in more detail in the coming pages. Understanding the difference between end-to-end reservation, network-level prioritization, and media-level prioritization is critical to understanding QOS. Since the bandwidth-management world is filled with analogies, we'll use one to illustrate.

A reservation analogy

Imagine that you live in New York and you have an urgent meeting in Los Angeles. You call ahead to have the taxi company send their fastest car. You also plan your drive to the airport and contact the police to ensure that traffic will be OK. You arrange for security to clear you quickly and for the plane to depart as soon as you arrive. You get the airline to fly faster than usual, and you even call ahead to have a porter meet you with your luggage.

While this tailored reservation sounds rather nice, implementing it is obviously impractical. The coordination that would have to occur between the various organizations and administrative bodies is unimaginable, and it's simply not economical for each to offer this degree of personalization. On the other hand, the reservation may not require you to call someone at each step of your trip in turn. When a step of the trip approves both your right to a level of service and the availability of that service, the agent at that step could forward your request to the next step in the path.

In practice, reservation systems are even more complex. In our analogy, you call ahead to each service along your trip—asking the cab driver whether he can take you, and whether the traffic flow is good enough for him to get you there in a certain time. You call the airline to check for a seat and flying time. You call the porter to see if he's around, and if he can carry your bags fast enough. You're not just checking for your right to use these services. You're also determining whether they can be offered to suit your needs. If *any one* of them says, "no" to your request, you're out of luck—you have to start calling again, with a different request, until an end-to-end trip is planned. On the up side, though, once you've negotiated a trip, you know with certainty exactly how long it will take. The stops along your way also know when to expect you.

This is a reservation model, similar to RSVP. It works on a flow-by-flow basis, dynamically negotiating reservations as they are needed. A high-level view of this model is illustrated in Figure 1–3.

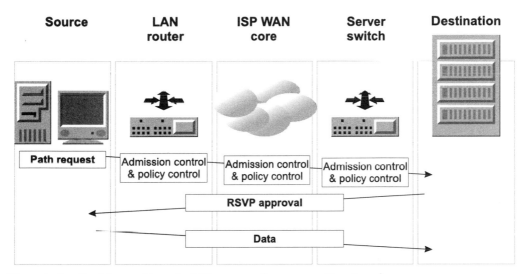

Figure 1–3   End-to-end bandwidth reservation on an IP network

If you are already familiar with the workings of RSVP, you may know that you actually write down the various stops you'll make in your journey, how many bags you're carrying, the time you'd like to arrive, and the variance from that time that you can tolerate. You then send this list to your host in Los Angeles, and have your host make the reservations. To the weary traveler, such an arrangement is not an unwelcome prospect! We'll cover RSVP in more detail later in the text.

A network class-of-service analogy

Instead of a reservation system, imagine that the various transportation providers along the way all recognize a special card that identifies VIP travelers. Showing this card to security, cabbies, shuttle-bus drivers, and airplane attendants makes them all leap into action to speed you on your way. The VIP card works across planes, taxis, busses, and porters. Unfortunately, everyone has to agree to recognize it. A single cab driver who has not signed up for the card program can delay your entire trip.

The priority and type-of-service fields in a standard IP header are an example of an end-to-end VIP card model. Since every routed network node understands IP, the stage is set for a consistent end-to-end signaling mechanism. This model is shown in Figure 1–4.

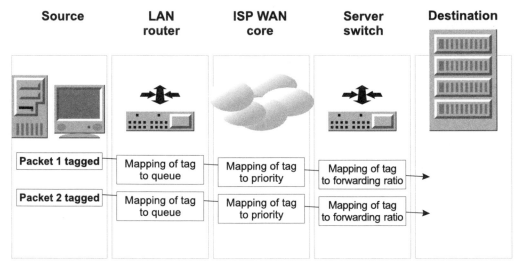

Figure 1–4   End-to-end network-layer class-of-service across a network

This may seem simple, but it's handled today only by the layer-3-aware devices (generally the routers).[5] Devices that do *not* support IPTOS will forward traffic normally, but without any kind of preferential treatment. This means that you can't know ahead of time what your trip will be like and when you'll arrive. To use our analogy, by calling ahead you'd discover that the airline did not offer priority seating. If you relied on a network-layer tagging system, you'd find out when you got to the check-in counter—too late to try and make other arrangements. Furthermore, it may not be in the interest of each organization along your trip to afford you preferential treatment—billing for such a system would be complex indeed.

A media-layer class-of-service analogy

There's another way to approach this problem. Each stage of your journey could talk to its neighbors on your behalf, informing them of any special needs you might have. As you leave the taxi, the driver hands you an airport priority card. Upon clearing security, you're given a card to get on the airplane quickly. Upon landing, the airplane gives you a VIP card for the rental car company, and so on.

In this case, each component of the system need be aware only of its immediate neighbors' capabilities. The airport security system knows the airlines and the local taxi companies. The airline knows the airports and the rental car companies. There's an additional demand on each stop along your trip, because in addition to knowing how to handle *you*, each step has to *map* the way it handles you to the adjacent services along your way. On the other hand, the local cab driver may not participate in our earlier end-to-end VIP card analogy, but he probably knows the person who runs the taxi stand at the local airport.

This model is analogous to prioritizing at the media layer, mapping the priorities of adjacent media on either side of a device. In such a media-layer system, end-to-end priority occurs because each device knows the features of its link layers and can associate QOS information from each of them. Figure 1–5 shows this model.

802.1p, ATM available-bit-rate (ABR) queue simulation, differentiated frame relay, and ATM QOS are examples of media that can differentiate traffic. No standard for this mapping currently exists, although work on implementing differentiated services with the Common Open Policy Service (COPS) may pave the way.

Media-layer mapping can take advantage of specific media characteristics. In a network-layer class of service model, media properties may be ignored when traffic passes through the IP layer. It's possible that some kind of improved service (such as curbside pickup) would have been better for a traveler because of the way the plane and the car work; a network-layer model forces them into one of several discrete groups for simplification. Link-layer optimizations are overlooked in "lowest common denominator" models. Since a few discrete classes must work for all instances, specific efficiencies where two modes of transport join are simply not available.

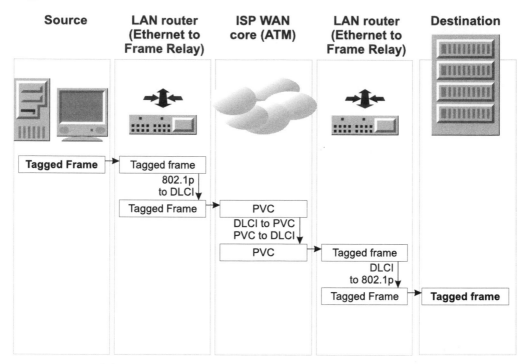

Figure 1–5   Link-layer mapping across multiple media for priority

If IP information is the only factor used in associating two links, some media-specific capabilities that might have been associated could be overlooked. For example, both Frame Relay and ATM offer explicit congestion-signaling mechanisms, while IP does not. A router that joined ATM and Frame Relay would have no way of representing the information within the IP datagram itself, so congestion signaling might be lost.

Hybrid models of prioritization

For a final analogy, consider a tour guide. It may be a lot of work for you to speak to people at each step of your journey. You'd much rather call a travel coordinator in Los Angeles who would set up the appropriate services on your behalf by choosing, for example, a taxi or a limousine, depending on the transport to which you were entitled. The local tour operator knows local traffic conditions and weather and can provide you with a rough estimate of your journey through the city.

A tour operator is analogous to a set of services known as a subnet bandwidth manager. This is a system that will allow routers to characterize their adjacent media layers, exposing the media capacity to the routing decisions so that you don't have to talk to the media layers directly.

Back to reality

We've seen analogies for QOS reservation (calling ahead), network-layer classification (end-to-end VIP cards), media-mapped prioritization (each step talking to its neighbors), and subnet bandwidth management (tour operators speaking on behalf of local transportation). Each has its own strengths and weaknesses.

For example, if networks are to offer end-to-end QOS, rather than best effort, then the rules and classifications that they enforce must be both *pervasive* and *consistent*. That is, they must come from a common source that is readily available. Directory servers can offer access to a centralized, replicated set of information that provides such consistency; as such, many QOS management systems available today rely on directory services and industry initiatives for schema structure.

Each model faces challenges. IPTOS has no model for trust or accountability—which means that everyone will claim they're "gold" travelers. Similarly, media-mapping and subnet bandwidth managers must deal with so many modes of transport that they will often give up and resort to some lowest common denominator that's less than optimal.

A managed QOS network also needs monitoring capabilities and service-level management tools that allow IT to run things on a day-to-day basis. IT must verify network behavior, plan for expansion, and charge bandwidth and network services back to the users or applications that request them. Real-time feedback mechanisms are built into many of the QOS mechanisms we will discuss, allowing the network to adapt to changing levels of congestion.

Clearly, there had better be some good reasons for all of this bandwidth management.

Endnotes

1. Admittedly, service providers in North America generally derive their revenue from monthly fees rather than from connect time. Nevertheless, a satisfying online experience (for example, one in which interactive gaming is not interrupted by delay) is more likely to retain a customer's business, so it is in the service provider's best interests to treat delay-sensitive traffic with a high priority in order to remain profitable.

2. The concepts of "importance" and "urgency" have been around in the field of time management for some time, where they were championed by Steven Covey in his *7 Habits of Highly Effective People*. Importance is similar to mission criticality; urgency parallels delay sensitivity.

3. The term "type of service" is sometimes used as an equivalent to "class of service." Others use it to describe the different behaviors that a service (such as a Web server) will afford to specific users, depending on their privileges. We use the term TOS to describe the type-of-service bits in an IP header.

4. Scott Mace, "Breaking Bandwidth Bottlenecks," *Byte Magazine*, May 1998.

5. Some recently announced switches can inspect the layer-3 TOS information even though they perform forwarding based on layer-2 addressing information.

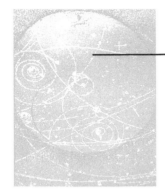

Motivations for bandwidth management

If we're going to invest time and effort in the creation of a differentiated-service network, there had better be good reasons to do so. Fortunately, there are many such reasons. In this chapter, we explore the motivations for deploying QOS systems, and look at the benefits and drawbacks of so-called "managed" bandwidth versus the "big" bandwidth approach of simply throwing capacity at congestion problems. We also look at some of the technical shifts that make QOS possible.

There are, of course, many good reasons for managing the QOS capabilities of a network.

Saving money

In a converged network—one in which latency-sensitive voice, bandwidth-hungry video, and business-critical data must coexist—some degree of control will be needed to keep things running smoothly, even with virtually infinite bandwidth. But managed bandwidth on WAN links can deliver cost savings because of WAN link pricing.

Voice-over-IP solutions can dramatically cut long-distance spending. By directing calls between branch offices across an IP link instead of a traditional long-distance circuit, IP-enabled PBX systems can leverage intranet capacity and reduce costs.

Protecting legacy traffic

Do you need bandwidth management to protect critical traffic or ensure response in a data-only network? There is a broad spectrum of traffic criticality. It may be easy to understand why routing protocols, such as Open Shortest Path First (OSPF), are more important than push news services like Pointcast. On the other hand, it is less clear whether you should separate repetitive, automatic service advertisements such as Service Advertisement Protocol (SAP) traffic from store-and-forward e-mail traffic. Furthermore, if bandwidth is cheap and abundant, then as long as the mission-critical and network-critical data gets through, does it really matter what else happens?

Paving the way for new technology

The need to regulate bandwidth does not stem solely from the relative priority of traffic. Many of the network protocols we use today were designed to support relatively robust client-server applications, such as file transfer or text messages to a human. New flow types—peer-to-peer, manager-agent—and the inclusion of latency- or jitter-sensitive applications in modern desktop operating systems require bandwidth regulation and management across both LAN and WAN infrastructures to support multiservice networks.

Do we need true QOS end-to-end?

At the most fundamental level, a network can differentiate traffic by prioritizing it—deciding which of any two packets is sent first. Differentiation is a sophisticated and powerful tool that delivers class-of-service enforcement so that a network is "better than best effort" for some kinds of traffic. Differentiated services, by themselves, cannot respond to a request for specific latency, bandwidth, or jitter characteristics.

On the other hand, a "true" QOS network allocates network services to users or applications in ways that are rigidly adhered to. Imagine that a videoconferencing application requests a 200-millisecond latency, with a constant 64-Kbps data stream, across a network. A QOS network would evaluate this request and set aside a fixed portion of the network across a sufficiently low-latency path—or refuse the request. A better-than-best-effort network would put the packets (identified as videoconferencing) into the appropriate queues and circuits across the network. If the network had been architected in such a way that the particular combination of queues, circuits, and devices delivered a delay of 200 milliseconds or less, then the two would be effectively identical.

In a world where LAN bandwidth is cheap and switched networking cores are delivering tiny delays, the additional complexity needed to guarantee performance seems wasted. It's rather like buying expensive insurance for an extremely rare event—the disaster never comes, and you wonder if you've wasted your money. Architecting a network to deliver specific levels of service dynamically is a complex, costly, and strategic process. So why not simply design the capacity into the architecture rather than using explicit reservations as needed?

Network managers are already buying and adding reservation-capable devices to their networks. Unfortunately, at the time of this writing the use of dynamic reservation features on an end-to-end basis is rare at best. Similarly, the deployment of policy-based management systems is lagging for anything but niche applications. Even with QOS on the intranet, there is no assurance of QOS capabilities on public networks or the Internet. Most current applications for QOS occur in the "last mile": ISDN or dialup traffic shaping, Asymmetric digital subscriber loop (ADSL) circuits, or T1 links from Internet backbones into the campus LAN or office. One major international ISP has ten times the capacity it needs on its backbone, with a spare ATM PVC trunk to handle overflow traffic—and while its devices offer QOS capabilities, it has yet to enable them.

Complete QOS systems are rare. Integration among multiple vendors is weak and makes negotiation across multiple devices for common traffic-handling characteristics uncertain. Political disputes among administrators further complicate things. So QOS systems today are limited to fixing "problem points" where bandwidth becomes congested or application performance declines, rather than delivering pervasive end-to-end systems.

The good news, as we shall see, is that proper network architecture and a network that can offer different kinds of traffic behaviors may be good enough.

IT's new role

Demand for WAN bandwidth is growing faster than supply. On the LAN, bandwidth is substantially cheaper, but upgrade costs must still be accounted for and allocated. As more and more departments and applications rely on network infrastructures for their basic business practices, corporate networks begin to resemble a market economy, with IT as the service provider to the organization. In market economies, vendors typically seek differentiation to better address the specific needs of their market segment. In networking, similar rules apply. IT must be able to offer differentiated services to its customers in order to target their needs and command the appropriate prices. To be fair, a company's IT has somewhat of a monopoly—but must remain competitive and accountable to avoid being bypassed by other parts of the organization.

IT has a traditional role of network management. The advent of converged networks means that videoconferences, the PBX, and groupware of all kinds now fall onto the network manager's lap. Multilevel networks can offer a broader utility by segmenting available network capacity into discrete chunks for specific applications. Some network managers may find themselves operating the company's telephone systems and handling the booking of virtual meeting rooms in the very near future, and managed bandwidth is an enabling technology behind these developments.

IT's new role as an internal ISP is made more difficult by its inability to properly account for the "soft" costs of an underperforming network. High latency or low performance may hamper employee productivity or cause frustration and rejection of new systems. For example, if the network crashes frequently and affects desktops, then users will save their files more often. If the brief delay of saving a file is multiplied by hundreds of employees, its impact can be a significant one—but try to put it in a spreadsheet, and your CFO will laugh out loud.

Is bandwidth management necessary?

A fundamental question an IT manager must ask before embarking on the deployment of a bandwidth-managed network is whether the total cost of managing the network is lower than the cost of throwing bandwidth at congestion problems. The decision has been termed the "big bandwidth/managed bandwidth" debate, and it is hotly contested. Pundits on one side espouse the virtues of laissez-faire networking while others tout complete control of network resources.[1]

We now present both sides of the argument for your consideration—although, as you may gather from the subject of this book, we fall into the managed-bandwidth camp.

The argument for big bandwidth

Managing bandwidth in detail is an extremely complicated task. Handling the myriad requests for response time, jitter, and capacity with dimensions of application, user, time-of-day, congestion, and link type is so complicated, in fact, that it's *always* cheaper to throw faster boxes at the problem on the LAN and leave it to someone else on the WAN.

The stuff's just not ready

True QOS—an end-to-end guarantee of network behavior—requires a degree of cooperation between end-node and network devices that does not exist today. If end nodes and applications take control of the network's resources, network managers are at the mercy of application developers or users smart enough to hack their registry.

Ease of management (none!)

There is one big argument for throwing bandwidth at networks: it's cheaper than the alternative.

By throwing cheap LAN bandwidth at the problem, you save your most precious commodities—time and skilled network operators. A purchase of a fast switch is a known, one-time investment. Even though network use is growing, we'll always have faster boxes to throw at the problem. Gigabit LAN cores and high-speed optical WAN circuits will work so fast that all applications will work fine on them.

Moore's law and bandwidth

Network devices run on processors. According to Moore's famous prediction, at least until the year 2010 this will mean that the available computing power per dollar for these devices will double every 18 months. Interestingly, UUNET's capacity is also increasing at this rate. The doubling rate for LAN technology is a little less than 12 months at the moment with the introduction of Arcnet, 10BaseT Ethernet, Fast Ethernet, and now Gigabit Ethernet.

Desktops, of course, also run on processors. A slow desktop relies on a fast server to perform the majority of the calculations in delivering screen content. An example is older "interactive" applications that relied on a server farm to make high-resolution stills, then played them back on the desktop (Myst and Riven did this; Riven fills five CD-ROMs with stunning, painstakingly rendered images).

By contrast, games like Unreal and Tomb Raider render their images real-time on the desktop. Each ships on a single CD and doesn't fill it with images—but each needs a Pentium II with a dedicated graphics coprocessor to run well. The same is true of Java applets that generate complex sounds: the size of the applet is far smaller than the size of the sound that it produces. In another example from gaming, multiplayer software uses predictive-motion models to provide smooth action even when network congestion delays information on the positioning of other players on the network. Rather than transferring things, we're transferring *descriptions* of the things and leaving the re-creation of them up to the desktop.

As the end station is better able to generate content locally, the size of transmissions may drop. Animated GIFs on Web sites are larger than the client-side-rendered animations of Macromedia's Flash, but Flash images are far larger and more detailed. So Moore's law may actually reduce the cost and ease the burden of networking by empowering end nodes. More end-system CPU power means better compression on the end system and so on.

It is unclear who will win the race between network capacity and processing power. In some cases, you can trade processing for bandwidth; as processing gets cheaper every day, substituting it for bandwidth may make sense. On the other hand, technology is creating new ways of moving bits around faster than Moore's law is creating processing. The capacities of new signaling methods such as wave-division multiplexing (WDM) will fundamentally alter the ratio of processing cost to bandwidth cost—whatever the case, big bandwidth is on its way. Simply riding the "speed wave" of faster and faster deployment is enough to solve bandwidth problems more cost effectively than by deploying complex QOS systems.

The argument for managed bandwidth

Throwing bandwidth at the problem is naïve. It discounts the impact of network failures, the delays in deploying capacity broadly, and the effects of application bandwidth hunger in coming years. Without controls, even a network of enormous bandwidth can still be overrun by miscreant applications. If a network cannot be throttled to some degree, managers cannot ensure the proper service of mission-critical applications.

Perceived shortages

Bandwidth comes in discrete steps. Protocol design, LAN capacity, and WAN costs are all responsible for this. Bandwidth must be managed to handle these changes in capacity smoothly: IT needs to maintain consistent network performance while leveraging cheap LAN and WAN technologies as they emerge.

TCP/IP traffic and its growing role in the LAN contributes to the perceived shortage. (While this text assumes a basic knowledge of TCP/IP, we've included a brief description of how it works and the aspects of the protocol that are relevant to bandwidth management in Appendix A.) TCP/IP wasn't initially designed for real-time networks or LANs. Instead, it was conceived for store-and-forward client-server systems and "loosely interactive" systems like telnet and tn3270, where guarantees of delivery were more important than constant levels of delay. While constant-bit-rate and time-division-multiplexed networks introduce a constant stream of information into the network, TCP/IP networks are characterized by sudden bursts of traffic, coming close to the network interface's carrying capacity.

The arrival of network capacity in discrete chunks is another cause of perceived shortages. New applications emerge, and new networking infrastructures are deployed. The two seldom seem to happen at the same time. Client-server technology gave rise to networks suited for client-server traffic. Peer-to-peer networks have created a different traffic flow, driving new networking systems. Similarly, traffic is shifting toward store-and-forward multimedia and real-time traffic.

Network upgrades occur by an order of magnitude or some relatively large fraction thereof. We smooth these changes aggregating slower links until a faster one comes along. On the WAN, we bundle multiple point-to-point connections into multilink (MLPPP); LAN architectures combine multiple Ethernet connections into trunked Fast Ethernet. We do this because we can't wait for or can't afford bigger pipes, and this need is driven by our applications.

Saying that speed is available today ignores the delay between the creation of these new technologies and their deployment in corporate networks. In many cases, a software fix or bandwidth management of a particularly troublesome part of the network may be enough to resolve today's crisis; budgeting for a strategic upgrade to new hardware is time consuming and impractical. While it's easy to look at all the wonderful features in new networking equipment, it's hard to deploy these same features in your network as soon as they appear in research labs or on the market.

On the LAN, there has been a progression through 10BaseT, switched 10BaseT, Fast Ethernet, and now Gigabit Ethernet. A similar curve exists for WAN links, ranging from 56/64-Kbps links through T1, T3, OC-3, OC-12, and on to OC-192 and beyond. The LAN bandwidth step curve is shown in Figure 2–1.

During times of overcapacity, network expansion is hard to justify. As a result, most of us aren't lucky enough to enjoy a proactive deployment of capacity. We'd like to rely on service-level monitoring or predictive analysis tools, but it is usually an interruption in network services or upcoming crises that justify major deployments.

Because "big" bandwidth comes in big chunks, we may need a mechanism for metering it out more smoothly to soften the step curves, depending on the cost of upgrades. Bandwidth management through queues, reservation, and prioritization is such a mechanism. With a managed network, we can deploy our own "logical capacity" atop the network infrastructure to reduce the impact of bandwidth shortage.

The perceived shortage of bandwidth exists on the WAN as well, partly for **economic reasons**. Telephone companies have traditionally priced their circuits in a way that allows them to amortize the high capital outlay of their switches across many users and long periods of time. Telephone-company pricing structures create a disparity between the available bandwidth and the actual price of bandwidth—from which the company extracts profit and capital for the next wave of bandwidth. Faced with deregulation and the challenge of parallel networks from startups, telephone companies are defending their local loop ownership vigorously. It is to their advantage to charge what the market will bear for bandwidth rather than to expose the actual cost of WAN capacity.

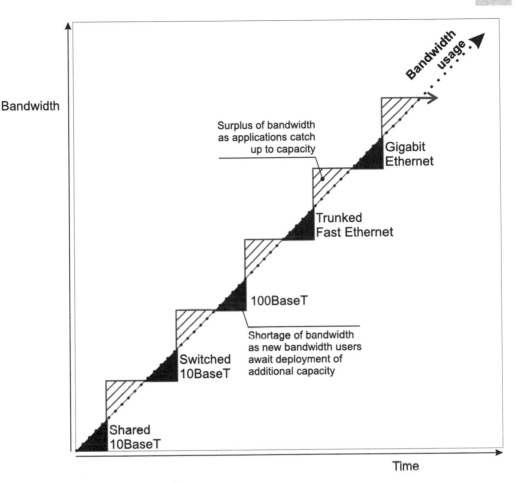

Figure 2–1   The LAN bandwidth step curve

How much damage can one user do?

There was a time when to really hurt a network, you had to know how. Moving large amounts of information across network links meant knowing cryptic commands. By contrast, today anyone can accidentally save a 100-MB file to a network drive, or attach a large video clip to an e-mail, without realizing the impact of what they're doing. Some people believe that the biggest threat to a business network comes from within the business itself—in the form of Dancing Baby screen savers, electronic greeting cards, unsuspected viruses in macro languages that tie up mail systems, casual multimedia file transfers, and from push content.[2] The GUI has put the tools to break a network into the hands of every computer operator and hidden the effects from them. Without systems for regulating bandwidth, networks and their managers are at the mercy of innocent users.

Integrating with security

A major objection to managed bandwidth is the administrative burden that it imposes on IT. The main reason for this is that the capacity and policy decisions a network makes require integration with back-end systems. Setting up specific mappings between traffic types and handling characteristics can be complex. In fact, it may be so hard to deploy a good back-end identification infrastructure that network managers avoid doing it for just QOS regulation.

On the other hand, the need for network security is unavoidable, and user-identification and traffic-classification tools are needed for good enterprise security. There's no way to get around security by "throwing bandwidth at it." If a company deploys a comprehensive security system, they'll have laid the foundation for QOS management because they'll have brought together the required databases, directories, and classification systems. Once the network can identify users and applications pervasively, much of the QOS infrastructure is already in place. The deployment of security systems may be a back door for the addition of managed-bandwidth services with only a small incremental administrative burden.

The highway analogy and wanting to drive in the commuter lane

A classic "managed bandwidth" argument is the jealousy factor. Few people are aware of the commuter lane until they're stuck in traffic, with passenger-laden cars speeding past them. The same applies for networks: once prioritization exists, everyone will want some. Creating high-performance network capacity will mean that developers are able to integrate more multimedia content. The developers will be less conscious of network impact. Today, a 100-Mbps Ethernet network with reasonably powerful computers at each end can transfer information faster than a hard drive. Web designers building pages that work well on the LAN but fail on the Internet are a good example of this—they're "spoiled" for bandwidth, and their poorly designed sites further slow the network.

On the other hand, application developers may find that their applications are seen as "high-cost" network citizens because they use a higher, more expensive priority than is needed. Once billing and accounting mechanisms can tie high-priority traffic back to the applications that gen-erate it and the prices that service providers charge for it, applications will have to become accountable for the traffic they generate.

It's not just capacity

New networks aren't just forwarding more information—they're forward-ing different *kinds* of information. This information includes voice, video, and interactive traffic that needs specific handling from the network. Two-way traffic is conversational and can't handle delay. Audio traffic doesn't handle discard well. Video traffic consumes substantial amounts of bandwidth and responds poorly to variance in latency. While faster networking equipment may address total bandwidth, it does not necessar-ily address other aspects of network service that an application may need.

Inevitability of multiservice applications

Just as Windows 95 brought a whole slew of users into the IP fold, Win-dows 98 has done the same for users of interactive, real-time applications. Out of the box, it includes Winsock 2.0 along with COS-aware applica-tions such as NetMeeting.

In 1993, users running an Intel-based computer with a Microsoft operating system had to install a third-party stack or change to Windows for Workgroups and install two disks' worth of IP drivers to run IP-based applications. They then had to manually configure a number of parame-ters such as address, DNS server, and host name. Windows 95 radically simplified this by including TCP/IP and DHCP support, much as Win-dows 98 can make interactive network applications immediately available by including support for COS signaling and compression schemes.

The release of a new operating system can drastically alter the net-work in ways that network managers can't anticipate. None of us can fore-see the next "killer application" that will spur networking on, the volumes of traffic it will generate, and the nature of that traffic. It's hard to tell how much is too much—but once we run out of capacity, we'll all want the tools in place to prioritize traffic. It's rather like building fallout shelters in our back yards just in case.

It's not just the WAN

The big-vs.-managed-bandwidth argument rages on the LAN rather than on the WAN. Most people agree that managing costly WAN traffic is wise. If you take a close look at WAN prioritization, however, you realize that classification of WAN traffic must often occur on or near the end system, making it in part a LAN issue.

Determining the nature of traffic in the middle of a stream (i.e., on a WAN router) is difficult, and it is getting worse for several reasons:

- Sniffing the port number of a TCP stream tends to reveal little. For example, RealAudio, a time-critical streamed multimedia application, travels across TCP port 80 which is also used for non-time-critical bulk-data Web traffic. We call this "popular port gravity."

- Applications like FTP and the Real Time Streaming Protocol (RTSP) use nonfixed port numbers, negotiated dynamically. Tracking dynamically allocated port numbers requires processor-intensive, protocol-specific traffic sniffing and statefulness. We call this "the jumping port problem."

- Packets can be encrypted, either as part of a Virtual Private Network (VPN) tunnel or for privacy, thus concealing the traffic's true port numbers. The two main candidates for this are voice traffic and VPN tunnels containing non-IP payloads that are generally more time sensitive or broadcast constrained (AppleTalk, IPX, and SNA). We call this "tunnel opacity."

Some degree of prioritization must therefore happen on a device that can identify users and applications. Protocols at layers 2 and 3 exist to allow end systems to tag the traffic for proper downstream handling. End stations can also reserve bandwidth across the network, so in situations where the end node knows best, managed bandwidth on LAN or end station is a prerequisite for a managed WAN.

So, what's the conclusion?

As you can see, there are valid points to both the "big" and "managed" bandwidth arguments. The reality is that it's acceptable to throw bandwidth at a problem when it is cost effective to do so.

In general, a happy medium between "big" and "managed" bandwidth is best. Embrace the cheap, fast networks that are available today. At the same time, ensure that the devices you buy can manage traffic through end-system classification and support for differentiated traffic handling.

Technologies that enable multiservice networks

A number of recent developments in networking and telecommunications technology are driving the need for bandwidth management. They include the use of voice on data circuits, the broad deployment of real-time applications, packetization technologies, the capabilities of smarter networking equipment, the deployment of mission-critical applications on best-effort networks, and the desire to reduce network costs.

Voice on data circuits and faster local loops: The beginning of convergence

Have you noticed the number of times your local telephone company has renumbered the telephone system lately? Designers of traditional telephone exchanges weren't ready for the amazing number of second lines that people wanted.

For that matter, the designers of the phone switches weren't ready for the long-hold local calls that Internet surfers place, either. Data traffic will soon outstrip voice traffic on long-distance networks.[3] With a number of emerging long-distance carriers deploying voice-over-IP solutions, the preponderance of data will only increase. To some extent, the amazing growth of the Internet is due to the availability of excess capacity on the public switched telephone network, and that excess capacity is nearly gone.

New systems to bypass phone switches are now being installed as traditional public switched telephone network (PSTN) circuits become saturated. Digital subscriber loop (DSL) systems take advantage of unused frequencies in the existing telephone wires; cable modems use an alternate piece of copper. Both circumvent the traditional PBX switches used to carry voice traffic, overcoming the limitations of the circuit-switched voice infrastructure.

On a packet-based network, chunks of traffic intermingle. Packets can be aggregated to make them more efficient. Packet-based simulation of circuits makes it possible to maximize the capacity a network link can offer by increasing the number of "circuits" available in a given amount of bandwidth.

The economics of a packet-based network are compelling enough to warrant huge amounts of research and capital expenditure by global telecommunications giants. Circuits are inefficient—most traditional voice circuits reserve 64 Kbps of bandwidth for information that can be squeezed into 8 Kbps of data with little discernible loss in speech quality.

How much cheaper is a data circuit? This depends a great deal on how fast the link must be, how far it should run, the technology it relies on, and the country in which it is deployed. For example, in 1998, a U.S. intracity T1 link cost US$300 a month; in Canada, a comparable link was approximately US$600 a month.

The flexibility of packet-based networks is also driving their rapid deployment in traditional circuit-switched environments. Routed, packet-based services are destination independent, making them more ubiquitous than the traditional permanent virtual circuits (PVCs) and leased lines that companies rely on for interoffice communications. IP services are easier to administer and better suited to an extranet model of interrelated business.

Looking forward, networking equipment will be designed for data. Already, Qwest has rolled out a North American long-distance backbone based on fast, cheap IP devices and is using software to simulate voice circuits. Because of the difference between packet-based switches and voice-circuit switches, data switches offer unavoidable price-performance benefits over their voice-only brethren. This is driving many different kinds of traffic onto multiservice, packet-based backbones.

Of course, cheaper equipment, broader availability, and greater technical innovation in the data world aren't the only factors driving this convergence. The raw cost of maintaining parallel networks—one for voice, one for video, one for data—and managing the interfaces between them is one that corporations cannot bear forever.

Convergence refers to the combination of voice, video, and data on a single network link through the insertion of voice or video samples into packets, frames, or cells. The trick of making a packet-based, connectionless network such as the Internet simulate a circuit-switched, predictable phone or video infrastructure is at the root of most bandwidth-management and QOS problems. We'll look at this concept of *convergence* in more detail later. For now, it is important to recognize that converged networks will be the focus of major network deployments in the coming years.

A move to public networks

There are three basic wide-area network services a company can use. *Private networks* include leased lines, rented trunking, and satellite links. *Public circuits* include Frame Relay and X.25, as well as some specific deployments of ATM. Finally, *public routed networks* consist of a private link to a service provider, but no guarantee of capacity once traffic enters the Internet backbone.

The pricing structure between private, public circuit, and routed networks is radically different. In a private network environment, the subscriber pays by the month for a fixed capacity between two fixed points. In a public switched network, the user pays for traffic sent, as well as call or session establishment in some systems.

If you make light use of WAN data, it may make sense to go with X.25 or Frame Relay. If your company's monthly usage fees with these networks would be higher than the cost for a leased line, then you should opt for the leased line. With the emergence of new traffic-shaping technologies, you have at your disposal a set of traffic-regulation tools that will allow you to manage the use of WAN links in either case. Traffic regulation either reduces the WAN traffic to the light levels at which a public network is appropriate, or shapes private link traffic so that increases in the data rate of the link are delayed or avoided.

In a public, routed network the user pays for an access rate to an uncertain end-to-end bandwidth. As senders on a best-effort network, the users know only the capacity between themselves and the service provider. They don't know the capacity from that service provider to the many destinations that their traffic will visit during the month. The provider is in no position to offer guarantees on a service basis unless the user's destination is within the ISP's administrative scope of control.

The shift from private, point-to-point links to switched circuits and best-effort routed networks is a key enabler for multiservice networks. An organization can deploy multiple link types to multiple destinations, relying on the distinct handling characteristics and economics of each to support the needs of various traffic types.

The availability of real-time applications in operating systems and browsers

Modern desktops offer the computing power and peripherals to support animation, audio playback, and voice digitization without any changes. Two-way conferencing and interactive application sharing are a part of many operating systems, and plug-ins for browsers allow users to view a range of media formats.

For the pessimistic IT manager, this means that users are running unsanctioned traffic on the network. A more optimistic outlook might be that this means the only hardware change the company must endure to run new applications is in the network.

Whatever the outcome, these new hardware platforms, applications, and operating-system features increase demand for capacity—since they generate more traffic—and make users more aware of the health of the network. A delayed file transfer was hard for a user to notice. By contrast, a delayed video frame is easily detected. The growing demands on and increasingly visible behavior of the network are driving the deployment of smarter boxes.

Smarter networking equipment

Today's networking equipment can offer service classification or bandwidth reservation for guaranteed performance and delivery of traffic. Where we once had many separate wires, today we see only one. Fast software is able to simulate multiple concurrent networks across a single physical link, and to do so in a way that optimizes the available bandwidth by offering surplus capacity to less important traffic when appropriate while satisfying delay-sensitive application requirements. Traffic that isn't well suited for intermingling—real-time and store-and-forward, high-volume constant-bit-rate and bursty short packets, and so on—can coexist on differentiated logical links where it might not have survived in a pure best-effort environment.

The bottom line is that today's devices can offer differentiation. Different devices are differently suited for converged network traffic. A traditional phone switch carries many streams of isochronous data very well, but does so at a high cost per bit. An Ethernet hub, on the other hand, carries multiple streams of time-sensitive traffic poorly, but is extremely economical in terms of price for capacity.

Connection-oriented technologies like ATM and Frame Relay are more suited to carrying time-dependent, first-in-first-out traffic like voice; end nodes need only digitize it and switch it across a circuit, and handling tends to be more deterministic. ATM, for example, already defines how to handle voice traffic in some detail. Many vendors already ship voice-over-ATM solutions that offer specific voice capabilities such as echo cancellation and silence compression.

Many Frame Relay Access Devices (FRADs) offer built-in voice features as well, although the limited deployment of new Frame Relay networks (compared to FR over ATM) has slowed adoption of these products. In May 1997, the voice-over Frame standard FRF.11 defined voice interoperability, including interoperable prioritization—the missing piece for deployment of differentiated Frame Relay circuits by carriers.

The way ATM devices work mimics the functionality of a voice PBX. The ATM access node combines the incoming voice information from a PBX and then splits it into cells for transmission across the data network. Just as workgroup switches in a wiring closet aggregate data for transmission across the corporate backbone, so voice-over-circuit systems prepare data for the transmission at the periphery and forward it with known performance characteristics in the core.

Other deployments that will make networks smarter include the following:

- **Local loop technologies** such as ADSL and cable modems broaden the range of converged network applications

- **Smart voice bandwidth management** is finally being released from the standards bodies. Voice technologies include H.323 gateways that map voice-over-IP to traditional phone switches, Integrated and Differentiated services, and media-based prioritization

- **Integration with telephony directories** and switch management systems such the X.500 directory front-ended by the Lightweight Directory Access Protocol (LDAP) make plugging private phone networks into the public network easier than ever

Sidebar ▬▬▬▬▬▬▬▬▬▬▬▬▬▬▬▬▬▬▬▬▬▬

How important is this voice stuff anyway?

The term *voice-over-IP* (*VoIP*) refers to a set of routing, switching, prioritization, encoding, directory, and compression technologies that deliver voice-grade connectivity across an IP-based packet network. The VoIP market is huge. Improvements in circuitry, including custom-built Application-Specific Integrated Circuits (ASICs) to minimize the encoding and decoding of voice traffic, will reduce the unacceptable delays that today's products introduce into a conversation. Vendors are announcing "layer-5" switches that interleave constant-bit-rate traffic regularly and parse application control channels, aiming their offerings at the telephony market. Some estimates claim $1.8B US by 2001, and voice-over-IP products are coming to market from carrier switch vendors, networking vendors, and more.

With this amount of capital involved, vendors of carrier equipment, network components, and PBX systems are themselves converging on this space aggressively. The next networking device you buy will probably have voice capabilities built in—making the decision to converge your voice, video, and data networks a far easier one.

As devices offer improved capabilities and better-defined interfaces between the telephony and the data worlds, a number of business opportunities have arisen that will fuel the voice-over-IP market. The need for interaction between a Web customer and an online store's sales personnel is fueling a spending spree into research on concurrent voice and data across public infrastructures. Call-center and help-desk systems want to move callers into a shared data environment where support costs can be lowered and turnaround time for problem resolution is reduced. At the same time, distributed organizations are seeking more than just messaging as a way of interacting with telecommuting, mobile, and remote workers.

Mission-critical applications

Part of the IT manager's job is to architect a network such that congestion will seldom, if ever, occur. Traditionally, the IT manager installed all the systems on the network, and thus intuitively had a pretty good idea of what the traffic levels were and what kinds of traffic the network would handle. In modern networks, however, protocols like Windows' peer-to-peer networking are easy enough for the average user to set up without the assistance (or knowledge) of the IT staff. Consequently, the IT director's "intuitive understanding" of traffic patterns in the LAN is vanishing. If the IT director has less knowledge about traffic levels on the LAN, poor performance from congestion can more easily occur.

The good news here is that new protocols and smarter routers allow the network manager to reserve "slices" of the LAN bandwidth for mission-critical applications. For example, if peer-to-peer windows traffic starts to saturate the network and causes mission-critical LAN traffic such as SNA to break, the IT director can lessen the problem by always reserving a slice of the LAN for SNA traffic only. Similarly, LAN routers may be configured with an access list that guarantees some percentage of the router's traffic will consist of SNA, Data Link Switching (DLSw), or tn3270 protocols that are used to communicate with mainframes if legacy traffic is threatened.

The conflict between legacy and real-time traffic—an argument about the relative priorities of different types of information—is driving the deployment of networking hardware that can also be used to differentiate application priority.

Keeping costs down in on-demand services

On a point-to-point WAN link, managing bandwidth is straightforward. Network managers have known for years that by simply ensuring dial-on-demand circuits are only forwarding necessary traffic, long-distance charges can be substantially reduced.

What's not so apparent is that a new wave of services from carriers will offer "pay-as-you-go" bandwidth on IP networks, as well as multiservice link-layer circuits. These services will support switched or routed point-to-point circuits with the capacity and response times needed to perform interactive video sessions. If these on-demand links are easily available to all corporate users, WAN costs could skyrocket. Consequently, bandwidth management is essential to curtail spending at the LAN/WAN edge in the coming years.

Using virtual private networks is another example of how IT can cut costs dramatically. By replacing leased lines or public switched network links with VPNs over routed networks, managers can set up dynamic tunnels across the public network infrastructure. However, in order for the links to perform adequately, the managers must take certain steps:

- Ensure that the VPN tunnel end-points are able to negotiate type-of-service and precedence information with your service provider

- Ensure that the appropriate security measures (authentication and encryption) don't introduce unacceptable tunnel setup or latency into the connection

- Properly configure backup systems that can deliver deterministic performance (such as a dedicated dial circuit) in the case of heavy public-network congestion

Whatever your situation, properly managed bandwidth can reduce the costs of running a network. At its most fundamental, bandwidth management is about using the network you have today in an optimal manner so that you can delay the inevitable upgrades until absolutely necessary.

There are many reasons for managing bandwidth, including wanting to protect legacy traffic, saving money, and paving the way for new technology. You may not need full end-to-end reservation systems to reap some of the benefits of a differentiated network. LAN and WAN costs are dropping, and class-of-service systems may be sufficient.

The debate about whether bandwidth management is necessary at all on the LAN still rages. You may want to deploy QOS in order to smooth perceived network shortages, control accidental or intentional misuse of network capacity, or shield your organization from lagging network infrastructure. You may also be able to deploy QOS atop your security deployment efforts. Whatever the case, you must consider the operational costs of QOS before rushing headlong into a deployment.

A number of factors are driving the move to a converged network. They include the move toward public-switched and routed WANs; technologies for integrating voice, video, and data; new device capabilities; and a range of real-time applications within operating systems.

Endnotes

1. The "big" and "managed" bandwidth argument was formally recognized by David Passmore of Net Reference, who delivered a compelling first-person argument with himself at Networld + Interop in Atlanta, Georgia, in late 1998.

2. From a 1998 keynote address by Cabletron, Inc., which quoted a *Computerworld* survey of network managers' greatest threats to networks.

3. According to K. G. Coffman and Andrew Odlyzko in *The Size and Growth Rate of the Internet,* "if current trends continue, and there seems to be no reason they should not, data traffic will overtake voice traffic around the year 2002, and will be going primarily over the public Internet." This study is available online at `http://www.firstmonday.dk/issues/issue3_10/coffman/index.html`.

A history of networking usage

Today's best-effort, client-server networks evolved from rigidly controlled, tightly managed mainframes in which network performance was under the irrevocable control of a central computer. The pendulum of network control is now swinging back towards earlier models as business-critical applications go live. At the same time, the ubiquity that a best-effort network and coarse, open standards have wrought leads to more and more types of traffic rolling the bandwidth dice. How did we get here? This chapter looks at the ways in which networks have been used and the resulting traffic characteristics.

To understand the directions that networking is taking today, we need to look back at some of the trends and systems that were deployed in the past.

How things change

At one time, computing horsepower was scarce and bandwidth (relatively speaking) was abundant—primarily because processing power was so centralized that communication took place between the processor and its printers and terminals. Back then, the real bottlenecks were the punched-card readers and keypunch operators, and the processors churned all night.

Of course, back then, IBM thought that 26 computers would suffice for the entire world.

As computing power grew and the importance of the desktop in computer networks changed, bandwidth became the bottleneck. Packet processing emerged as a way to optimize the use of expensive bandwidth with cheap minicomputers. We now have more computing power on our desks—not to mention larger hard drives and bigger monitors with more colors—than the mainframes of old. The increased capacity of modern computing devices has in many cases saturated network links.

In recent years, slow shared links have migrated through Ethernet, Fast Ethernet, trunked Fast Ethernet, and now Gigabit Ethernet. Dense wave-division multiplexing promises to deliver a hundred concurrent OC-48 links to WAN providers. High-speed local-loop connections such as ADSL, cable modems, and 10BaseS will also improve edge access.

The people who run networks today ride a perilous step-curve. As abundant bandwidth begets bandwidth-hungry applications, and bandwidth-hungry applications in turn drive the need for more bandwidth, network managers must teeter between costly overprovisioning and crippling bandwidth shortages.

Early master-slave computer systems

The first networks assumed a central "master," such as a mainframe, and dumb terminals, as shown in Figure 3–1.

Since the central device was the only "intelligent" device on the network, there was a single, final authority on network utilization—hence no contention for bandwidth. Delays occurred, to be sure, but they were

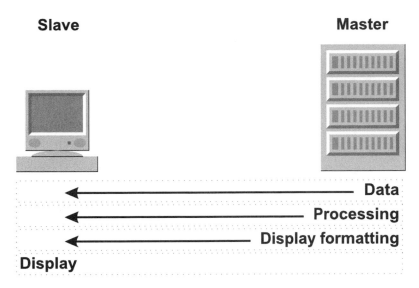

Slave   **Master**

Figure 3–1   Traffic flow in early master-slave computing

processor delays—network latency remained relatively static. Terminals didn't generate traffic without the involvement of the central computer. More importantly, the links between the terminals and their mainframe used time-division multiplexing (TDM). A portion of available bandwidth was set aside for each terminal, regardless of whether or not it was turned on. IBM's Structured Network Architecture (SNA), the protocol that many mainframes use, has a physical layer that is continuously clocked by a central controller. Each terminal is polled at a regular interval, as seen in Figure 3–2.

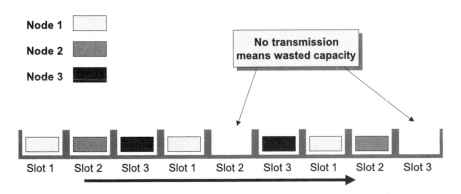

Figure 3–2   Time-division multiplexing

In early networks this made for a wonderfully predictable, albeit inefficient, connection. If only one employee from a staff of hundreds was using the network, she would get *exactly* the same performance from the network as she would when everyone was at work. The system assumes that only the central controller is smart enough to manage the network.

Many older WAN systems (such as X.25) assume dumb end nodes and core switching intelligence and handle flow control within the network itself. In these models, end systems have no way of requesting differentiated services other than by calling the network administrator and asking for the service to be reprovisioned.

The arrival of the LAN

Business adoption of computing proved to be the downfall of network determinism. As more and more companies sought the benefits of computers for their organizations, technologies emerged that could offer cheaper networking. Cheaper technologies brought networks to the masses, which in turn led to the creation of a wide range of applications for networks. The economics of the packet proved too much for time-division-based networks.

Because of the sheer number of nodes connected to the business network, it didn't make sense to have reserved portions of dedicated links from every point to every other possible point. Instead, packet-based networks emerged. If the master-slave model is like having telephone lines permanently connected from every person to everyone else, packet-based networks resemble the postal service.

To send a stream of information that was larger than a single packet, protocols appeared that could simulate a point-to-point session. The best known of these is IP's counterpart, the Transmission Control Protocol (TCP).[1] TCP provides the point-to-point connectivity and congestion awareness that IP lacks. The elegant design of TCP has been one of the main reasons that the Internet gets slow on Friday nights—but doesn't stop altogether. A packet-based system is illustrated in Figure 3–3.

In packet-based networks, senders began to control the rate at which they introduced information into the network. Academic institutions began to train a wave of computer engineers who adopted a communal approach to developing standards and technologies. The communal attitude is still found in the Internet Engineering Task Force's love of "loose consensus and working code." At the same time, public routed

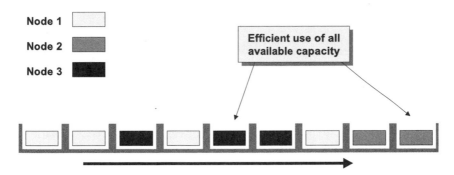

Figure 3–3   Packets make efficient, irregular use of available bandwidth

networks—available primarily to students and teachers—were an incubator for new kinds of networking. The Internet's military beginnings were quickly usurped by university users, and cheap minicomputers from companies like DEC and Wang sprang up.

In early LAN environments, the main function of the LAN was still access to the mainframes and minicomputers, and this gradually grew to include file sharing and printing. Relatively simple terminals were connected to powerful servers, and the bulk of the processing was still done on the central computer. But the democracy of the packet was still at work.

The mission-critical business network

The first companies to adopt networking as a key part of their business were those whose core practices emphasized the movement of information in a reliable manner. Airlines, banks, and insurance companies saw amazing benefits from deploying electronic systems that could replace and expedite their paperwork. These companies were breaking new ground; they needed the handholding that only a big system developer could offer.

Companies like UNIVAC, IBM, Burroughs, and Sperry provided the design, application development, operating systems, hardware, and networks for many of these early adopters. In order to reduce confusion and improve reliability, IBM's model was regimented and deterministic. It consisted of centrally controlled applications that relied heavily on physical security. Network links were predictable, running SNA and eventually using systems such as token ring and X.25 (and later, Frame Relay). The system ran only a small number of applications, each of which was carefully aimed at the goals of the business.

Distributing centralized applications

As the end nodes grew in power, it made sense to distribute the responsibility for networking out to the end systems. Local processing of information on desktops was a possibility, and application developers began to write programs for personal computers. These computers were able to make decisions about the condition of the network rather than waiting passively to be polled by a central controller—and could decide for themselves when to introduce traffic.

The wrong way: The LAN as a hard drive

At the same time as big companies were leveraging networks, application developers had been writing standalone programs on the newly developed Personal Computers. With slow, cheap networks available to small and medium-sized businesses, a shift was underway. Companies that had formerly been denied the benefits of a shared computer system because of their size rushed to share their applications. The programs weren't customized the way they had been on a minicomputer or mainframe, but they were good enough. Spreadsheets, word processing, and databases were all possible. Figure 3–4 shows how this system allocated processing and storage.

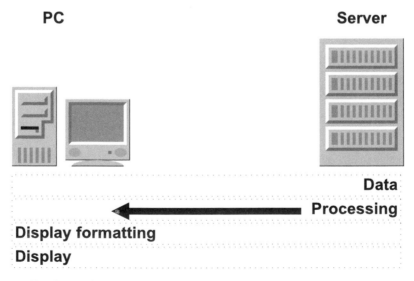

Figure 3–4   Traffic flow when using servers as remote hard drives

As applications became crucial to the business, employees wanted to share the information within them quickly. Doing so presented several problems to application developers, and they initially used the networks the wrong way. They "networked" their applications, dragging them kicking and screaming onto the LAN. Under pressure to share their programs with groups of users, many simply relied on the network as a file system. They stored all of the *data* centrally, and then each PC copied the information locally before working with it. Copying data to the client for processing presented a number of problems, including sharing violations and integration of data—and it brought the LAN to its knees.

The "proper way" to network an application is by using a client-server model. Client-server architectures, in which the client formulates a request and sends it to the server for processing, seem natural today. For example, if an SQL user wishes to search for "customer X" on the corporate database, he will send a short "give me customer X" message to the server. The server performs the lookup and responds with the appropriate record. By contrast, in a poorly designed database system the user will open the database file on the file server and download the entire file until she finds the record matching "customer X." The latter model consumes vast amounts of network capacity and processor time.

While this example is generally confined to smaller business environments, the problem is a common one: poorly architected applications can overlook fundamental networking systems, generating an excessive amount of traffic unless somehow controlled.

Client-server models

Fortunately, application developers were able to adopt a model in which not only information, but also some processor-intensive calculations, were performed centrally. Instead of all the work being done on the central computer and the PC being a dumb end node (the master-slave model), the PC was able to take an active role in the application. Figure 3–5 shows a client-server model.

In client-server networks, traffic patterns are still centralized and predictable to some degree. Information tends to flow from the end node to the center of the network—be it a mainframe, a minicomputer, or a simple file server—as shown in Figure 3–6.

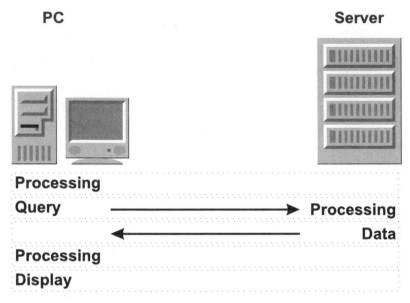

Figure 3–5   Traffic flow with a client-server application

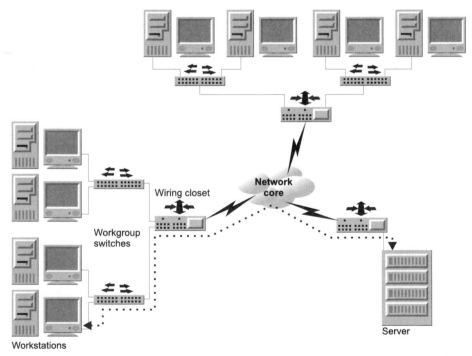

Figure 3–6   Traffic patterns in a traditional client-server environment

All this was about to change. As end systems gained excess computing power and applications became network aware, they began to initiate communications among themselves. The majority of traffic still flowed from the big machines (the servers) to the small ones, but traffic patterns altered drastically.

Client-server networking is ubiquitous. Rather than being assigned to a specific central computer, a client is free to request information from many servers throughout the network, be they near or far. Accordingly, corporate information was often distributed and replicated across the various geographic sites at which clients would need it in order to save on WAN costs and improve performance. The flows were less predictable as application developers began to "stretch" their client muscles.

Client software also began to standardize. The advent of the Internet drove the broad adoption of common client applications, especially Web browsers. Moreover, Web access wasn't limited to business usage—personal sites, from sports to pornography, are more commonly accessed than business sites.

As you might imagine, people who were accustomed to dedicated, deterministic master-slave networking resisted the best-effort, chaotic client-server model. In spite of this resistance, the economics of a multivendor interoperable network meant that packet-based networks like the Internet became broadly available at relatively low costs. The need to merge legacy mainframe applications with new systems and the desire to make mainframe information available to a broader audience finally wore down the master-slave proponents' resolve, and they moved away from central polling with the introduction of Web front ends and packet-network-friendly protocols.

The managed-chaos business network

In the face of such change, many networks are becoming loosely managed chaos. Managed chaos isn't necessarily a bad thing; it's more a recognition of the dynamic nature of a network. Such networks are common in places where security and performance cannot be tightly managed, such as academic environments.

Several elements make up a "managed-chaos" network:

- Distributed clients coupled with secure servers get information to the right people. End users may be local, remote, or mobile; server-side security is relied upon to guarantee privacy.

- The underlying assumption is that the media are fundamentally insecure; any privacy will be offered with network protocol security or secure sockets.

- The network is an open field for applications. The only truly differentiated traffic is the network-control information that keeps the network running.

- The network is best effort, which underscores a fundamental problem in bandwidth management. A fundamentally untrusted network must offer the same service to everyone until the user's privileges are known. The user is known only after it has authenticated with a server—at which point, initial network protocols and configurations are in place.

Along with file-system access, messaging and printing within the workgroup made up most network traffic in the early 1990s. The advent of the corporate intranet and adoption of a client-server model built around the Web browser has shifted traffic patterns significantly. Hotmail has shown us that users are willing to subject their recipients to advertising and to sacrifice features like local storage in order to attain the simplicity of a centralized mail system and a common interface. It's far easier to support a database with a Web front end than to support distributed SQL clients on multiple platforms.

This transition means that the mobility of users is offset by the centralization of intranet applications. Large files and personal content will be retained on the mobile desktop, but group information will be centralized and front-ended with widely available interfaces such as the Web.

Peer-to-peer networks

With these shifts in traffic flows throughout a network and the increasing number of server-capable platforms connected to the Internet, many networks include some degree of peer-to-peer traffic.

Most operating systems can run a web and an FTP server. Most can also share files and printers with a few mouse clicks. Consequently, a number of peer-to-peer relationships exist within nearly any network, as shown in Figure 3–7. Peer-to-peer traffic is localized, hard to regulate, and wreaks havoc on traditional network architectures. If any desktop can potentially be a server, then every workgroup hub may be connected to the most popular site on your network.

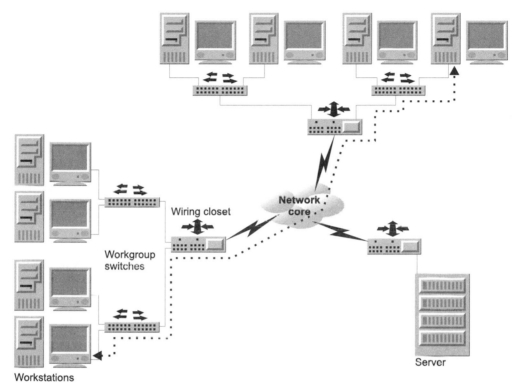

Figure 3–7   Traffic patterns in a peer-to-peer model

The good news is that this kind of traffic still makes up a small portion of a network's total traffic today. A more realistic traffic pattern is one in which information flows from an end node to both peer nodes and known servers—but the servers are part of an intranet, an extranet, or the Internet itself. The only difference between servers is their reachability: the intranet server is inside the firewall, and the extranet server may be accessible only through some kind of secure link or virtual private network. All are used as part of the distributed business. A hybrid peer/client model is shown in Figure 3–8.

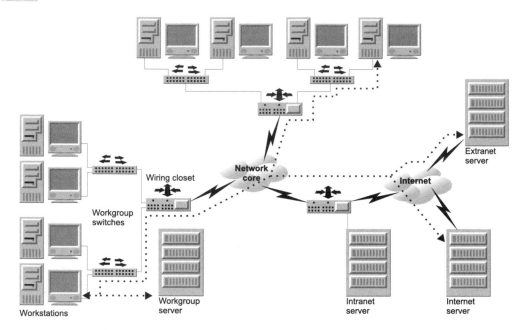

Figure 3–8   Traffic patterns in today's hybrid peer/client-server environment

Manager-agent networks

A step away from client-server traffic is the manager-agent network. A fundamental problem with a client-server network is that only the client can initiate communications. In many applications, however, the server can maintain information on the client and may wish to update or alter information it has previously transmitted. These "stateful" servers need a mechanism for communicating with their clients in an unsolicited manner, as shown in Figure 3–9.

A number of recent protocols, including push systems, the Common Open Policy Service (COPS), SQL triggers, and the Diameter authentication and authorization protocol, are examples of manager-agent applications. Some recent developments in persistent queries for databases are also manager-agent. We'll look at COPS and Diameter in more detail later.

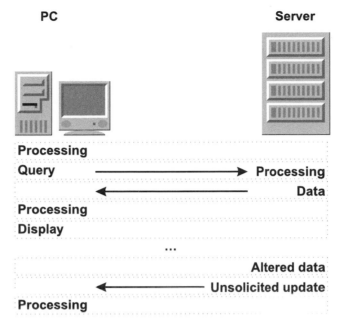

Figure 3–9   Traffic flow in a manager-agent system

Endnotes

1. The reader is referred to Appendix A for a more complete discussion of TCP.

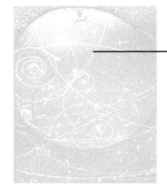

Bandwidth today

After a varied evolution, today's networks are converging. Multiple traffic types are converging on a few protocols and ports; at the same time, new network architectures and topologies allow traffic management with unprecedented levels of performance and scalability. The next-generation business network leverages innovations in WAN service, local loop technology, and mobility to "virtually centralize" information without sacrificing broad availability.

With all these changes afoot, what do we have to look forward to?

The next-generation business network

Tomorrow's network will be purpose-built for business. The fabric of the network—from the architecture and fundamental technologies to the configurations of the devices themselves—will be tuned to the essential business processes that drive profits. Where the benefits of combining the network are incontrovertible, we'll see a migration toward convergence, and users will be free to deploy their own applications within rough guidelines on a workgroup basis.

Figure 4–1 shows a network where capacity is sliced into multiple discrete tiers, with the top tier being reservable by qualified users or applications.

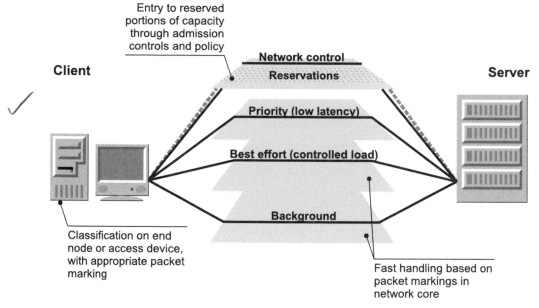

Figure 4–1   A multitier business network

Business traffic will come first, and the network will include support for mobile users across dialup links or access VPNs. To keep it all running smoothly, we'll have token- or certificate-based security in place, and the management of the network will be focused on applications and users.

We will also see a major change from interfaces and addresses to applications and users. This shift will be fueled by the increasing use of portal sites as application platforms rather than just links, as well as by the deployment of dynamic configuration systems that make plug-and-play mobility possible.

The WAN and bandwidth

A new generation of carriers is leading the race to deploy big pipes in the WAN. While this fiber is already running at an impressive 155 Mbps, technologies like dense wave-division multiplexing (DWDM) will boost this to 10 Gbps. Instead of a fivefold increase in capacity, this is a five *hundredfold* increase.

WDM circuits stack multiple OC-48 and OC-192 signals in today's deployments. As of the second half of 1998, a WDM circuit carried 4 to 10 of these links, but factors of a hundred are promised in the near future. In late 1997, Qwest had nearly 4000 miles of OC-48 synchronous optical network (SONET) links with OC-3 drops, with plans for growth to five times that by the end of the decade.

Other vendors aren't far behind. Worldcom has stated plans to have 20,000 route miles of OC-3, migrating to OC-48 in the core, by the end of the decade. UUNET's plans call for a 1000 percent annual growth in data-access capacity, and the company tripled its entire network during 1997.[1] LCI had 8000 route miles by the end of 1997, based largely on ATM and SONET.

The advent of Metropolitan-Area Networks (MANs) built atop optical technologies is making it even easier for companies to tap into fat pipes. Local loop speeds are finally catching up as the innovation in the WAN core trickles out to consumers. In 1996, cable modems were in commercial trials in several U.S. states; by February of 1997, modems were commercially available in San Diego. Within 6 months, over 200,000 houses were ready to receive the service and 4000 customers had signed up. Traffic speeds of 10 Mbps to the home and 1.5 Mbps from the home were not uncommon at a cost of less than $50 US. In Canada, at the time of this writing, Rogers Cable offers similar data rates for $39 a month (approximately $25 US).

These new links introduce consumers to compellingly cheaper price/performance levels and in turn urge them to experiment with more demanding applications. Already, some Canadian high-speed local-loop providers have begun to limit the length of sustained real-time streaming traffic that they will allow on their networks.[2]

While WAN bandwidth is growing at an incredible pace, demand continues to outstrip supply. AT&T was unable to meet orders for T1 links in 1997—and by early 1998 this inability had shifted to OC-3. What's more, local carriers are slow to deploy fast pipes into the core because of the challenge posed to their pricing systems.

Hardware upgrades aren't instantaneous, of course: WAN bandwidth is still expensive for most of us.

Virtual centralization

Changes in the way networks are built—and the way we work—are altering the role of the WAN. New technologies that can increase the performance of links to the home, together with rising numbers of distributed, "nomadic" workers, are forcing IT to reconsider the notions of centralization. While centralized information is good for control, historically it's been bad for performance, reliability, and distributed access.

Some examples of new technologies that have emerged to support a distributed, nomadic organization in which information is centralized but access is pervasive include the following:

- **Application proxies** that allow you to connect to a local device that in turn connects you to the actual information. Proxy servers are typically used to insulate a LAN from the WAN. If a company has a proxy gateway instead of (or in addition to) a router to the WAN, then clients on the LAN can ask the proxy server to get a specific URL on their behalf. Proxies are like an insulating layer, since the local client and the remote server never talk directly. Proxies have three main benefits: protection of LAN nodes from the WAN, improved control over users' surfing habits, and the ability to store a copy of requested information so they needn't retrieve it a second time.

- **Mirroring** of information in many places on a network reduces the need to go across the WAN for information and improves the response time that users experience. Mirroring involves keeping multiple copies of information at various sites and backing them up across the WAN periodically using a process called *replication*. Mirrored information is somewhat dated but is appropriate for many applications.

- **Referral** is a technique by which an authority within the network returns a pointer to another authority when it is unable to answer a query itself. A directory, for example, might refer a client to another directory server that has a specific piece of information. Distributed load-balancing tools and smart DNS servers perform this kind of function, allowing portions of a large body of information to be distributed geographically or logically.

- **Caching** information locally, similar to mirroring, means reducing WAN usage and improving response time. A cache generally checks to make sure that information is current periodically, so it can be configured to be more accurate than a mirror. In other words, a cache is selective about the content it stores, based on what it's been asked for in the past. Caches are often a part of a proxy system.

Who'll go first?

With faster pipes, new applications, and a legacy of business-critical information buried in corporate servers, the protocols on which the Internet was founded are at the breaking point. As a result of its broad popularity, IP is called upon to simulate point-to-point links, deterministic circuits, broadcast media, and many other applications for which it was not intended (but did not preclude).

At the same time, the Internet we have today is unequaled. Since enhancements to IP such as IPv6 will require substantial refitting of much of the Internet, the industry is building a number of mechanisms into devices and applications to leverage the pervasiveness and ubiquity of today's IP without breaking it.

In North America, cheap networking equipment and deregulated WAN communications mean that while many customers will buy the smart equipment that can help IP deliver QOS, they may be less eager to turn on these features. The first users will be those who, for whatever reason, are at the breaking point:

- A critical business application (such as an alarm system on a nuclear reactor)

- A time-sensitive business model (such as stock trading)

- A converged network (such as an integrated call center or distance telelearning)

- Bandwidth-hungry applications that must be insulated from important traffic during congestion (such as medical imaging systems)

Other factors

A number of other changes in the way we use information affect the state of networking today.

Multicast versus personalization

Early network protocols were unicast (meaning point-to-point) or broadcast (meaning sender-to-everyone). Today's networks generally rely on broadcast traffic for discovery of resources or for advertising services; most other traffic is unicast.

Multicast traffic is a form of "controlled broadcast" in which a sender transmits to multiple receivers. Rather than communicating with each receiver individually, however, the multicast sender transmits a single stream of information and the *network* copies it for each user as appropriate. Multicast greatly reduces the load on both the sender and the WAN links. Multicast traffic is efficient and sensible. By aggregating identical traffic that is being transmitted to specific subsets of the network, a multicast application can reduce bandwidth usage significantly.

The content providers on the Internet have other plans. The Holy Grail of advertising is individually targeted messages—and this personalization is at odds with multicast. If everyone watches the same multicast programming, then individually targeted messaging is impossible. At the same time, if everyone watches a personal version of the multicast programming, then the network becomes congested.

There's a compromise here. Content manipulators are appearing[3] that function above layer 4 in the stack, altering the presentation of information and combining multicast traffic with personalized content (Figure 4–2).

These kinds of systems are generally sold to media brokers and online content providers, but the role of a "presentation-layer router" in the enterprise should not be overlooked. For everything from code updates to HR information, a split multicast/unicast model like this one will play a major role in networking tomorrow.

Multiple platforms, single content

Now that Personal Digital Assistants (PDAs) and hybrid TV/Web displays are common, many different platforms can display the same content in different ways (Figure 4–3). For example, a stream of voice, video, and data information may journey across a network link for presentation on text-based systems, video screens, and speakers. The stream might include

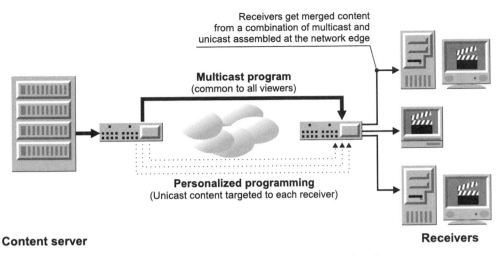

Figure 4–2   Combining multicast programming with personalized content

additional data: pricing an encoded audio download for one-time audi-
tioning is different from buying the right to store it in an online jukebox,
but the content is similar, so authorization information may be needed
alongside content.

As the breadth of networked devices increases, we will have to deal with
another level of prioritization complexity. Aggregate streams of data may
contain information of varying urgency and importance. Their transmis-

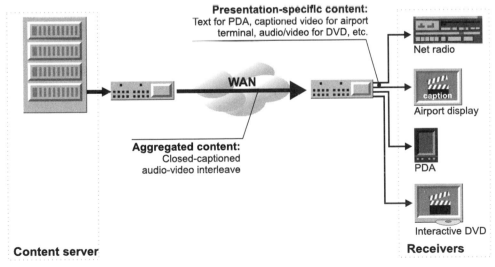

Figure 4–3   Formatting content streams based on target display platform

sion across the shared portion of the network will have to be at the levels needed for the highest-priority content, since closed-captioning data must arrive as the corresponding picture is being shown. After extraction from the common stream, however, each individual component of the aggregate information may be prioritized differently by the receiver.

Moving up the stack

Underlying many of the trends we've looked at is the notion that we're moving up the stack. As more and more internetworking functions are rolled into hardware, an array of "over IP" products are emerging. Tunnels, voice, video, session balancing, and encryption all happen at layer 4 or higher. Now that the underlying IP infrastructure is in place, the hot markets and new products in the networking arena exist between layers 4 and 7 of the OSI reference model.

This change has important implications for the designers of networks. The "other convergence" is a convergence on IP as a development platform for enabling technologies. Just as choosing a computer platform affects the longevity of the system and the applications you can run on it, so choosing the right IP infrastructure (and the right enabling media layers) affects your ability to deploy applications across it.

As the "over IP" applications battle for market share, and the market for their products grows with IP deployment, prices will drop and features will increase. More features over IP will in turn fuel a greater demand for the network. So the commoditization of IP and the migration up the stack by networking vendors make the right underlying infrastructure more important than ever.

"IP over everything" means that while IT can fairly safely choose a network transport to consolidate their networks, they will now have to scan emerging IP services with a critical eye to understand their value to—and impact on—the network.

Endnotes

1. Note that for more recent information, numbers will be available for the aggregate MCI/Worldcom/UUNET capacity, since the companies have now merged.

2. One may debate, however, whether blocking streamed video traffic is a matter of limiting network usage, or rather an attempt to reduce competition between data transfer and many local loop companies' other businesses of voice calls or cable television programming. Clearly, everything-over-IP makes the unbundling of local loop services relatively simple to achieve.

3. Redbox is an example of such a company.

PART 2

As our study of the QOS problem has shown us, we are chiefly concerned with enabling specific business applications and allowing traffic with differing needs to coexist relatively peacefully. In the second part of this book, we will look at the ways in which network performance can be described, and the specific needs of different classes of traffic such as voice, video, and data.

We divide this into the following sections:

- Understanding traffic performance characteristics
- The needs of different traffic types

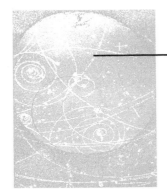

Understanding traffic performance characteristics

The way in which a network handles traffic can be characterized through a set of metrics such as latency, jitter, and reliability. Networks introduce delay from network congestion, server congestion, and the inherent delays of the protocols that are used. These metrics are the *lingua franca* of QOS networks.

Traffic management and the creation of a multiservice network is extremely complex. To understand it, we need to begin with a general understanding of the network behavior that various applications require to function correctly. Applications are of two main types:

- applications that generate *elastic* traffic—that is, the application would rather wait for reception of traffic in the correct order, without loss, than display incoming information at a constant rate (such as an e-mail)

- applications that generate *inelastic* traffic—that is, timeliness of information is more important to the application than zero loss, and traffic that arrives after a certain delay is essentially useless (such as interactive video)

In an IP-based network, applications run across user data protocol (UDP) or TCP connections. TCP guarantees delivery, doing so through some overhead and session-layer sequencing of traffic. It also throttles back transmission rates to behave gracefully in the face of network congestion. By contrast, UDP is connectionless—no guarantee of delivery is made, and sequencing of information is left to the application itself.

Most elastic applications use TCP for transmission; many inelastic applications use UDP as a real-time transport. Inelastic applications are often those that demand a preferential class of service or some form of reservation to behave properly. However, many of the mechanisms that networking devices use (such as traffic discard or TCP session control) are less effective on UDP-based traffic, since it does not offer some of TCP's self-regulation.

In order to regulate network capacity, the network must classify traffic and then handle it in some way. The classification and handling may happen on a single device consisting of both classifiers and queues or routes. In a larger network, however, it is likely that classification will happen at the periphery where devices can recognize application needs, with handling occurring at the core where congestion occurs. The signaling between classifying devices and handling devices can come in a number of ways, including IPTOS, 802.1p, Frame Relay discard eligibility, RSVP, and ATM QOS circuit selection. We'll look at each of these in more detail in the coming chapters.

Classification can occur based on a variety of information sources such as protocol content, RSVP flows, media identifiers, the application that generated the traffic, or extrinsic factors such as time of day or congestion levels.

Similarly, handling can be performed in a number of ways:

- Through traffic shaping (traffic arrives, it is placed in a queue, its forwarding is regulated, and excess traffic is discarded)

- Through various queuing mechanisms (first-in-first-out, priority, weighting, and class-based queuing)

- Through throttling using various flow-control algorithms such as TCP rate control

- Through the selective discard of traffic to notify transmitters of congestion

Handling can also result in packet marking for sending instructions to downstream devices that will shape the traffic. A marked packet cannot always be trusted, because people will want better service than they are entitled to. Consequently, a network administrator has two alternatives when a packet is marked. If her network permits the packet and bills accordingly, a billing mechanism must be in place. If her network reclassifies the packet when it enters her network's trust domain, suboptimal handling may occur because of processor-intensive delays and the fact that her devices will ignore any potentially useful information from the transmitter.

Finally, handling can be performed via route or session selection based on appropriate protocol metrics such as latency, hop count, number of connections, response time, or reliability.

Sources of delay

The way traffic is handled can be characterized by a number of parameters, such as round-trip delay, variance in delay (jitter), packet loss, peak throughput, and so on. The main reason that inelastic applications don't generally work well over IP-based networks is latency, and the change in latency that traffic queuing can produce.

There are three components of latency—delay introduced by the **internetwork**, delay introduced by the **protocol**, and delay introduced by the **turnaround of information**.

Internetwork delay

Internetwork delay is constant when the capacity of the network exceeds the information across the network—it is the aggregate of link delays and device delays. In order to improve this best-case delay preferentially—for example, to improve performance of videoconferencing—an alternate path across the network must be used. We can call the selection of paths based on traffic need "QOS-based routing."

Internetwork delay grows when the traffic introduced into the network exceeds the network's capacity. The network can be thought of as a storage buffer that holds excess traffic until it can be transmitted. A properly built network has more capacity than the expected average data rate in order to clear bursts of congestion quickly. Building networks so that they handle the maximum burst rate is called overengineering, and it is generally unaffordable to do so.

In other words, if you're the only car in your lane on a highway, you can go as fast as your car will drive. Sadly, we can't afford to build one lane per car. We therefore build highways with enough lanes to "clear" rush-hour congestion reasonably quickly. The highway may be built to handle more than the average level of traffic, but at rush hour, delays abound. Overprovisioning a network is like building a highway to handle above-average traffic loads; overengineering the network is like building one lane per car so that congestion never occurs.

The change in delay that an internetwork introduces when traffic load exceeds capacity is directly related to the fullness of the buffers on the various devices a packet must cross. But simply knowing buffer size won't tell you what you need to know about delay, since different kinds of traffic get through the buffers at different rates.

Protocol delay

Different protocols have inherent delays, either because of the way they work or because of the way they interact with the network.

- Compression or encryption schemes introduce computational delay.

- Ethernet's Carrier Sense Multiple Access/Collision Detect (CSMA-CD) algorithm relies on probabilistic "gaps" in transmission within a broadcast domain; more traffic means fewer gaps, which can theoretically mean infinite delay in transmission.

- TCP/IP detects dropped or delayed packets and infers congestion, causing it to slow down. Queues and buffers can hide congestion from the transmitting device, making the sender less able to detect congestion until queues are saturated and traffic is being discarded.

- In many modern server applications, retrieval of a piece of information is in fact achieved through a number of concurrent connections. A Web page, for example, contains the HTML code and the various graphical elements needed to construct the page; additional HTML pages may be needed to assemble a complex frame. While some of the content may take a short amount of time to retrieve—or may be stored locally in the browser's cache—all of the query's components must be retrieved to properly display the information. Many of these retrievals may involve their own TCP setup and teardown, increasing the impact of protocol delays.

The specific ways in which protocols interact with queuing and discard mechanisms in the network as well as the layers above and below them make bandwidth management somewhat of a black art.

Information turnaround

The delay that occurs between receipt of a network request and effective response—the delay that a server's internal processes introduce into total round-trip delay—is a major factor that is often overlooked by network engineers. The total response time experienced by end users is the one that shapes their opinion of the network's performance. Information turnaround delays are generally a function of server load, which comes from many sources:

- The server's CPU may be occupied by other processing and unable to service all queries promptly.

- The request may require computationally intensive processing, such as running interpreted scripts in real time.

- The server may be able to service and process the query promptly, but a back-end system such as a database lookup may take a long time.

Load-balancing systems provide some relief from server delays. These can come from rudimentary round-robin schemes, or from sophisticated load-balancers that share the load equitably across many servers.[1] Such devices can also improve the availability of servers in case of failure and redirect clients to a geographically closer server to reduce the internetwork delay. They may even classify and tag return traffic for preferential handling. Such systems are essential to an end-to-end QOS system: Simply put, if the server is slow, the network may still be blamed.

Traffic performance characteristics[2]

Many applications generate traffic that needs some degree of performance guarantee to behave correctly (such as interactive multimedia). Other applications are less "fussy," either because the function they serve does not involve humans (file transfer) or because a variance in performance is acceptable (telnet). To support these kinds of traffic, a number of philosophies have emerged in networking.

The differentiated-services philosophy is that a small number of distinct network behaviors is sufficient to support this range of applications. The integrated-services philosophy holds that some sort of guarantee, rather than just differential classification, is needed to offer true time-sensitive application support for things like constant-bit-rate video.

It is a basic assumption of integrated services that traffic entering the network for guaranteed handling must be subject to some kind of regulation—an admission control. Otherwise, everyone would request guarantees and exceed the capacity of the network, rendering it unable to offer reservations to legitimate users.

In an ideal world, unlimited network capacity with a reliable, short delay would be available to every user and application that wanted it. Outside the lab, this is not the case. To understand the rocky terrain of modern network media, we must first consider the factors that can undermine freely available, high-performance network capacity.

Two major factors affect the ability of the network to service a user: oversubscription and error rates. As we shall see, oversubscription is an increasingly important problem in a multiservice network, while network errors are less and less important with today's highly reliable transmission mechanisms.

Oversubscription

When a network is not oversubscribed, there is no immediate cause for bandwidth management. All traffic can pass through the network without appreciable delay in excess of what is imposed by the equipment and transmission medium itself.

Delays occur for several reasons:

- Traffic is buffered because inbound links carry more traffic than outbound links can handle.

- Traffic is discarded because buffers are nonexistent or full and is retransmitted.

- Traffic is sent across an alternate, slower route because primary connections are full.

In a bursty network like the Internet, devices are regularly oversubscribed, even when their *average* traffic rate is well below the capacity of the network infrastructure, as a part of good network design. The queuing needed to smooth out this burstiness introduces latency.

Overprovisioning avoids conditions of congestion most of the time. As end nodes increase the rate at which they can introduce traffic into a network, some degree of buffering will be necessary with even the fastest LAN links. Besides, if a network never becomes oversubscribed, this may be a sign that you are paying for too much bandwidth.

A trade-off is in order, then, between the cost of a network delay and the cost of unused bandwidth. This is illustrated in Figure 5–1. Recall that on a LAN, the cost of unused bandwidth is virtually nothing—costs are fixed, incurring neither monthly nor per-packet charges. On a WAN circuit, the amount of overprovisioning that is appropriate will vary dramatically.

On a LAN, faster network links dramatically reduce the duration of network congestion. Consider that a 1-gigabyte file across a private, full-duplex link should theoretically take 17.5 minutes to transmit over 10BaseT. The same file can cross a 100BaseT link in 1.7 minutes, and a Gigabit Ethernet (GE) link in around 10.5 seconds. A fast server at the time of this writing will generally generate about 4 MByte/second transmitting this file, using a reasonably quick IP implementation.[3] With a GE, the connection isn't saturated. The file transfer would take approximately 3.5 minutes at that data rate. A rough comparison of burst durations is shown in Figure 5–2.

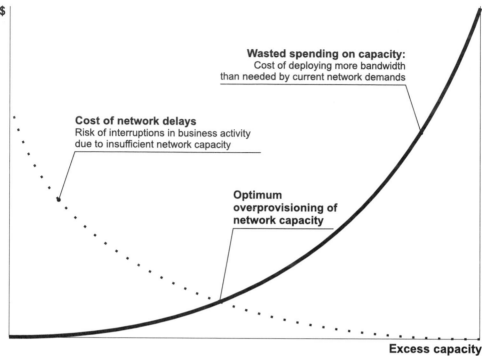

Figure 5–1   The trade-off between capacity and cost

Your network may be so overprovisioned that current LAN traffic never causes enough delay to adversely affect time-sensitive applications like interactive voice or streamed multimedia; if so, then configuring managed LAN bandwidth immediately is unnecessary and simple monitoring will suffice. If the network capacity exceeds the ability of a host to introduce traffic into the network, congestion will not occur.

Lack of real capacity

Most networks today are single-tier. In other words, they offer a level playing field to all traffic. When a link becomes congested or oversubscribed, it drops packets. In some cases this discard can result in an explicit notification to the transmitter (for example, in an X.25 network). In other cases the discard is "silent," and higher-layer mechanisms must manage data integrity. For example, a TCP sender would time out and resend data presumed missing. Some networks offer buffering capabilities that allow bursty data to enter the network quickly, but any time spent in a buffer is a source of additional delay.

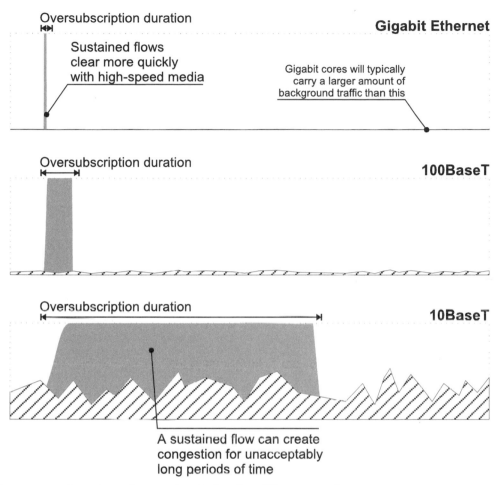

Figure 5–2   Duration of oversubscription for different media

Lack of reservable capacity

By contrast, multitier or reservable networks can set aside a portion of their bandwidth for a specific kind of traffic, either statically or on a dynamic, negotiated basis. In this case, a network may refuse admission and discard traffic even when not oversubscribed, simply because a particular application's assigned portion of the capacity is oversubscribed. The latter is termed *proactively* shaping traffic.

Additional complexity emerges when each node in a link has an algorithm by which it prioritizes traffic. Prioritization may occur through implicit traffic information (such as 802.1p or IPTOS bits in the packet header) or through explicit rules that have been assigned by a network administrator (such as "SAP is more important than Pointcast for people in accounting"). In a simple priority queue, lower-priority network "tiers" give way to higher-priority tiers; traffic in high-priority queues is more predictable and deterministic, but low-priority traffic may encounter increasingly erratic behavior. In other words, predicting how low-priority data will be handled means knowing what the high-priority traffic conditions are like.

Error rates

Most networks discard errored packets. The difference between a network error and a discard due to oversubscription is not always obvious. With today's forward error correction and highly reliable WAN links, errors are scarce enough that it is seldom worth introducing explicit signaling methods to notify transmitters of errors at the link layer. Modern optical networks are typically engineered to better than a 10^{-12} bit-error-rate (one error every trillion bits) and often perform at better than a 10^{-14} bit-error-rate. When discards occur, they are usually a way for the network to inform the sender and receiver of congestion.

Retransmission

Discarded packets will result in retransmission. Packets may be discarded because of a failed checksum (errored) or because of router buffer shortages due to oversubscription. Retransmission can be signaled on a node-by-node basis (X.25) or on a sender-receiver basis (Frame Relay). It can be communicated explicitly (X.25 and Frame Relay) or inferred based on sequencing information (TCP). Retransmission can be the responsibility of the application if the underlying network protocols do not offer guaranteed delivery.

Retransmission in different kinds of networks will have different levels of impact on network performance.

X.25 retransmission

Early networks experienced a far higher rate of errors and were designed accordingly. X.25, for example, relies on a transmit-and-acknowledge mechanism between individual switches in the network. The network itself implements flow control between each switch, as shown in Figure 5–3.

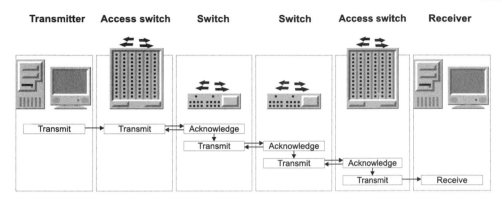

Figure 5–3   X.25 signaling of traffic receipt

This kind of step-by-step approach leads to delays as each step transmits the information, waits for a confirming response, and verifies that the information has been successfully transmitted. While inefficient in networks with low error rates, it is well suited for unreliable networks, since the loss is discovered immediately and retransmitted between the two switches. In X.25, then, the impact of an error and a retransmission is less significant—but the amount of error correction built into the system is "overkill" for modern networks.

Frame Relay retransmission

Frame Relay networks are essentially X.25 networks with these systems removed; improved performance through faster transmission and reduced protocol overhead is a consequence of more reliable links.

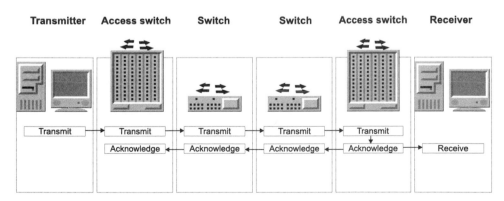

Figure 5–4   Frame relay signaling of traffic receipt

As Figure 5–4 shows, a Frame Relay circuit signals receipt only at the end points of the link. Once the packet has been switched across the network successfully, the receiver sends an acknowledgment to the transmitter. Retransmission results in increased delays, since the error is only discovered once the receiver has looked at the information—but this delay is more than made up for in a highly reliable network when compared with X.25.

TCP retransmission

TCP was conceived as a connection-oriented protocol for internetworks. Because it had to work over a variety of media whose reliability and error rate were unknown, it had to offer error correction and delivery guarantee services (Figure 5–5).

Unreliable networks have a great deal of impact on the performance of a TCP connection. TCP decides how much data to introduce into the network—and consequently, the performance of the link—based on the response time and discard levels of the packets it sends. Packet loss and retransmission in a TCP environment will have an effect not only on the delay of the lost packet, but also on the sender's perception of network capacity.

Application-based retransmission

If a network runs a custom application that does not employ some sort of feedback and throttling system, then it is a candidate for retransmission congestion. Retransmission congestion can occur when a LAN applica-

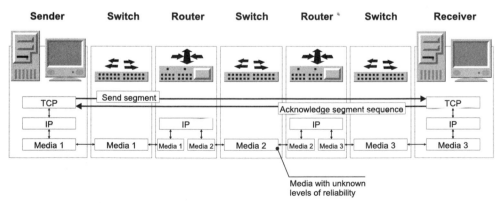

Figure 5–5   TCP delivers end-to-end sequencing and delivery guarantees in a connectionless network with heterogeneous media types

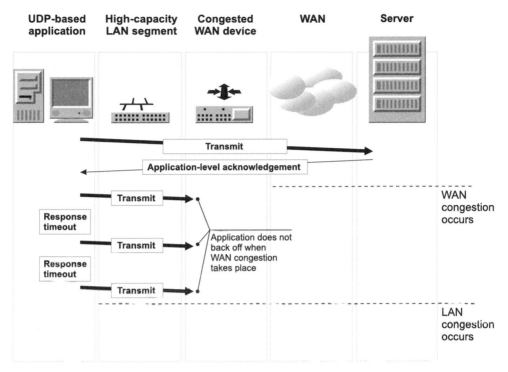

Figure 5–6   Application retransmission without discard detection and backoff can multiply congestion problems

tion that had plentiful bandwidth (and therefore ran smoothly) encounters a slow link (such as a frame relay circuit to a remote office or a dialup connection from a mobile user).

If a custom application uses UDP-based communications to send transactions between client and server, the developer must implement some kind of flow control or backoff capability. Backoff functionality will avoid flooding the LAN segment with retransmissions when the WAN link is slow, as is the case in Figure 5–6.

Capacity

To understand the amount of information a network can carry, and the speed with which it can deliver that information to its destination, we must first be explicit about what the information is. Generally, transmission is measured in bits per second or packets per second. Both are somewhat misleading, as they tend to ignore the nature of the application itself.

Application bandwidth calculation

Let's look at a key frame from a videoconferencing application. The application takes a grid of color information from a camera at one end of a link and transmits it to another machine on which the information is used to color a corresponding raster grid. The information that is transmitted varies in a number of protocol-specific and application-specific ways:

The **packet overhead** is the "wasted" data in the traffic that is used to signal a path through the network. In our example, this might include the layer-2 Ethernet header, layer-3 IP header, and application-specific information such as frame sequencing or caller ID.

Frame size is another consideration. Depending on the number of columns and rows in the transmitted image, the number of pixels will vary. Small changes in frame size may cause larger variance due to packet fragmentation. If the frame "spills over" into another packet, packet overhead will increase accordingly. Such fragmentation will probably have a minimal impact, but the delay that occurs from packetization and compression may be more significant.

Frame rate, or the number of frames per second (FPS), describes how often the image is refreshed. Our eyes detect flicker below approximately 24 frames a second; a lower FPS reduces bandwidth consumption at the expense of image quality or smoothness of movement.

Color depth is the number of possible color values that a pixel can take. Whereas static images can be *dithered* (blended) to generate the illusion of more colors from fewer, dithering a moving image can cause unattractive artifacts in the picture. Additional color depth incurs additional bandwidth usage; an 8-bit (256-color) video is a third of the size of a 24-bit (16 million color) video.

Performing **traffic compression** is mathematically intensive, and so compression delay can be significant. In most cases, a reduction in the volume of data sufficiently outweighs the delay from compression to make it worthwhile on the WAN. Hardware is now available to compress traffic quickly. As such, compression latency is less of an issue than it once was.

A more pragmatic form of compression latency is the delay that occurs when a **differential compression** scheme (one that transmits only the changed pixels in a moving image from frame to frame) is used. Differential compression is common in video, and because the amount of change from frame to frame varies, video traffic which might otherwise have a constant bit rate may in fact vary over time. The jumpiness in image formation that can happen when a camera's position is suddenly shifted is a product of compression delay.

Sustainability of the network service

Traditional client-server or interactive user applications are extremely "bursty"; that is, their average bandwidth utilization varies greatly compared to their peak utilization. A Web download consists of a small request packet from the client to the server, followed by a larger response from the server to the client—and then, from the network's perspective, an interminable pause while the human reads the information. This is a "short" hold time from the network's perspective.

By contrast, applications such as voice and streamed multimedia have long "hold times." They can range from a few minutes to several hours, and their data rate may be variable or constant. Voice traffic has a relatively constant usage of bandwidth; multimedia traffic may vary more widely, based on the type of content and compression. A phone call lasts for minutes rather than the seconds needed to get a Web page, and while the page is being read, it does not consume bandwidth; a streamed video link may be maintained for hours while watching a film.

Link hold time is a function of the application that is generating the traffic. When home computers began to use modems to reach online services or the Internet, telephone switches that had been built around the five-minute call collapsed under the weight of hour-long online sessions.

Some networking components simulate a long-hold session through spoofing. If a session is established across a series of links and one hop of that link doesn't sustain long hold times, then the devices at either end of the weak link will tear down and reestablish the connection as needed. Link spoofing is common in dial-on-demand applications.

Many LAN-based applications assume a network that can deliver long hold times, and spoofing is a common mechanism for tricking them into thinking that the link exists and allowing them to function across a WAN connection. Real hold time may not be the same as the duration of the application's network usage, but link spoofing may reduce network responsiveness, since short-hold connections need to be reestablished when they have become idle and disconnected.

In Frame Relay, sustainability is known as a Committed Information Rate, (CIR). A CIR is a "promise of minimum bandwidth" over their network. In 1997, Bellsouth and Pacific Bell both offered a CIR of zero, meaning that they wouldn't promise any given minimum. In general, this is not a problem and you'll get the minimum throughput for which you've contracted. If you order a T1 link and ask for a Frame Relay PVC with CIR of 56 Kbps, then you can usually burst at higher rates—but all the carrier will guarantee is 56 Kbps worth of bandwidth.

If you use a 56-Kbps line driver across a 56-Kbps link, with a CIR of 56 Kbps, then you can't burst at higher than your data rate, since your physical layer won't allow it. There's no bit-rate magic going on here—you can burst at higher rates if and only if your line equipment and line are capable of better performance. If you have an ISDN B channel, and you want to burst at higher than 64k, your only choice is to add more B channels.

Carriers that *do* support CIR properly will usually tag all frames above your CIR as "loss-permitted," and they will be dropped as soon as there's contention anywhere in the link.

Burst capacity

Some networks offer the ability to exceed the agreed-upon capacity of a link for a certain amount of time. The burst capacity of a network is the maximum throughput that the network will accept for relatively brief, unsustained periods. Generally, burst capacity will exceed the sustainable capacity of the link.

No line can burst above the maximum bit rate of the physical connection. You can, however, purchase a T1 from an ISP and get 128k worth of bandwidth at 128k pricing with the option to occasionally burst at higher than 128k rates because your physical-layer bit rate supports it. Load on a line is based on averages; the ISP wants to be sure that you don't exceed average data rate for which you pay. In other words, if you buy a 5-Mbps link and burst at 10 Mbps for an hour followed by an hour of silence, your service provider will object—based on how often they sample your link usage. The averaging interval can affect your ability to burst for a sustained period while remaining within your service contract.

ATM and Frame Relay protocols reside atop a physical layer. For example, ATM and Frame Relay can run over DS-0, T1, T3, DS-3, and so on. The useful ranges for these two protocols can be complex to understand:

- Neither protocol has a maximum or minimum bit rate built into the specifications, but they only make sense at certain speeds.

- ATM is commonly used at DS-3 and above. It is occasionally used on T1 and T3 links but is relatively unpopular—at these speeds ATM largely benefits the provider, who is able to better regulate the injection of traffic into the network.

• Frame Relay is software intensive, and since most hardware high-level data link control (HDLC) chipsets don't go beyond 45 Mbps, this is generally the peak rate for a Frame Relay service. In North America, commercial Frame Relay vendors generally don't offer speeds in excess of a T1, opting instead for leased lines for that level of traffic.

Instead, consider that the only things that *really* matter to your WAN service are the cost, the level of service to which the provider is willing to commit, and the protocol or connection to the service. With today's IP ubiquity, media are simply a means for sending IP datagrams. The complexity of the service level agreement will grow as providers offer differentiated services, but these three factors remain the fundamentals of WAN link selection.

Constant and variable bit rates

ATM links send 53-byte cells across a circuit; the cells are *multiplexed* according to their bit rate. We will deal briefly with ATM service types and parameters later; a more detailed description of ATM is beyond the scope of this text.

A network link that offers constant throughput regardless of the amount that is needed is known as a Constant Bit Rate (CBR) link. CBR links are "ideal" links: They provide a deterministic network service with a predictable data rate. They do so at great expense, however; in order to guarantee constant handling of traffic, they forward "null" data when there is none to send. CBR is roughly the same as the centrally clocked models of older WANs.

Nevertheless, CBR links are ideal for voice and video transmissions where variance in the network link is unacceptable. They simulate a point-to-point, dedicated connection over a shared network. The IntServ model is trying to approximate CBR links when it offers a "guaranteed" service across a network path.

Variable Bit Rate (VBR) links provide a varying level of throughput, as their name implies. They are more suited for data applications where unpredictable network capacity can be tolerated; their lack of determinism is offset by the increased economy that they offer by letting other traffic use their "empty" space. In the ATM world, two other bit-rate types are available: Available Bit Rate (ABR) and Unspecified Bit Rate (UBR). We'll look at both in the coming pages; in particular, ABR offers Diff-Serv-like opportunities for traffic regulation.

Delay (latency)

The performance metric with which network managers are most familiar is total average latency. As converged networks lower our tolerance for network delay, the individual components of latency will come under increasing scrutiny. The overall delay across a network is in fact a function of hardware latency, access delay, transmission delay, and round-trip processing.

Hardware latency

In today's high-speed networks, hardware latency is minimal. There will always be some degree of delay from the transmission of information; a 100-ms lag in transmitting across the Atlantic is reasonable simply because of speed-of-light constraints. But it takes only *20 microseconds* for a packet to traverse a so-called "wire speed" networking component, and fiber optics are reducing even negligible WAN delays as they move from the speed of electrons to the speed of light. For point-to-point connections, the busy network administrator does not generally need to concern himself with this aspect of performance.

Access delay

In local-area networks and shared WAN networks, there is often an unpredictable delay in accessing the medium. For a token-based network such as Token Ring, this is a function of the time the transmitting node must wait for the right to transmit—in the form of the token—and it can be roughly estimated with an understanding of the network topology. For Ethernet, it's more complicated.

Sidebar

Ethernet networks and access delay

Ethernet networks employ a carrier-sense-multiple-access/collision detect (CSMA/CD) mechanism. With such a model, the maximum possible access delay is infinite in a constantly congested network: The node must wait for the network to become available.

The infinite-access-delay problem is theoretical and shouldn't be seen in proper network deployments. Switching also addresses access delay. As Ethernet networks become switched at the edge, the sender never detects another transmission, and end stations are free to transmit immediately. It will then be up to the workgroup switch to either buffer the data or discard the traffic if upstream capacity is unavailable.

Managing access delay is an easy step to take in preparing for next-generation applications and converged networking. By deploying full-duplex switched Ethernet to the desktop, the CSMA/CD constraints of the end node are effectively bypassed. If you are not fortunate enough to have switching to the desktop, then you need to maintain a level of congestion that is significantly lower than the theoretical maximum capacity of the network in order to ensure relatively quick access to the media.

So can a congested, shared Ethernet segment block a user's traffic indefinitely? If one node is transmitting an extremely large file, will other devices be unable to access the network? The short answer is no. CSMA/CD is a "listen before you speak" method of sharing wire. A part of this is a fairness clause in the specification called the Inter Packet Gap (IPG) that says speakers must "pause for breath" occasionally. Ten-megabit Ethernet uses a 9.6-microsecond forced silence period after sending a packet. At the end of this silence, other stations can seize control of the link and send a packet. The period of 9.6 microseconds is the time it takes to send 96 bits over thick coaxial cable at 10 MHz with a defined maximum distance between any two nodes.

The 100Base-T CSMA/CD Media Access Control layer uses the same 96-bit interpacket gap (IPG) rule used at 10 Mbps. At 100 Mbps, ten times faster than regular Ethernet, the interpacket gap time between packets shrinks by a factor of ten. It is the same number of bits, but the bits are moving faster. Consequently, in Fast Ethernet the IPG is 0.96 ms.

When two stations are conversing on a full-duplex network, there are no collisions. If a third node tries to send traffic, there will still probably be no collisions, because the newcomer will transmit at the end of the IPG. As more nodes appear, there is a statistical probability per packet that any two stations will try to transmit a packet at the same time. If such a collision happens, the two transmitting stations wait for an individually random length of time and then retransmit. The randomness is used to ensure that they don't begin retransmitting simultaneously.

According to the Ethernet specification, the more times a packet collides during transmission, the longer the random wait time will be. After 15 failed retransmissions, the sender drops the packet, leaving it to higher-layer protocols to retransmit the information. This allows them to learn of the link-layer condition, allowing them to respond accordingly.

Collision detection is a function of delay and distance, since distance affects how long it takes for a pair of senders to collide in the worst case. Cable delays for most kinds of Ethernet traffic are about .005 microseconds per meter, whereas hubs, receivers, transceivers, and similar devices range from 0.1 to about 1.9 microseconds. In other words, a low-quality hub is the same as 114 meters of 10BaseT copper cable. (See Table 5–1.)

Table 5–1   Delay for various Ethernet media and apparatus[4]

Media	Delay
Local repeater	0.65 microseconds
Fiber optic repeater	1.55 microseconds
Multiport repeater	1.55 microseconds
Multiport transceiver	0.10 microseconds
Standard transceiver	0.86 microseconds
Fiber optic transceiver	0.20 microseconds
Twisted pair transceiver	0.27 microseconds
Concentrator	1.90 microseconds
10Base5 coaxial cable	0.00433 microseconds per meter

Table 5–1   Delay for various Ethernet media and apparatus[4] (Continued)

Media	Delay
10Base2 coaxial cable	0.00514 microseconds per meter
Shielded twisted pair (STP)	0.0057 microseconds per meter
Unshielded twisted pair (UTP)	0.0057 microseconds per meter
Fiber optic	0.005 microseconds per meter
Attachment unit interface (AUI)	0.00514 microseconds per meter

The farther away two nodes are on an Ethernet segment, the longer it will take for them to realize they are talking at the same time. To control the number of collisions, the time it takes to transmit the shortest legal frame must be less than the total time it takes to cross the network. The rationale here is actually simple: A sender should never be able to "get out" an entire frame without its colliding with another frame if one is transmitted simultaneously.

The higher the data rate of the network, the more bits a sender can "get out." This means that faster shared media must have shorter wires. A 10BaseT network has a collision domain of 2000 meters (but apparatus must also be factored in). The time it takes for electricity to travel twice this distance is the time it takes to send the smallest Ethernet frame at 10 Mbps. A 100BaseT network has a collision domain of 200 meters; a Gigabit Ethernet domain should therefore have a collision domain of 20 meters.

This may seem like a moot point: nobody makes Gigabit Ethernet hubs, and we're talking about collisions on a largely hypothetical shared domain. If the GE ports are all switched, full-duplex links, no collisions will occur. The GE standard contains two mechanisms for making the collision domain longer, just in case somebody decides to make a GE hub.

The first mechanism is to increase the minimum frame to 512 bytes, which means it takes longer to get out a frame. This in turn allows a greater maximum length than the 20-meter limitation. The second mechanism is to allow a node to burst multiple frames up to about 9018 bytes (a technique that is also used in Appletalk). The bursting compensates for the minimum-frame-size penalty on the network. These techniques boost the collision domain to nearly 200 meters while still permitting a good transmission rate.

Because of the larger burst size, GE is a good choice for server-to-server communications and will deliver peak performance when high-traffic servers are connected directly to the gigabit core with GE network interfaces.

Transmission delay

Most of the delay that traffic experiences in a modern network is a result of transmission delay. As traffic travels along a network, it will traverse intermediate nodes. The delay that a node produces may be caused by the current processor load of that node, or by buffer levels, or even by the number of packet filters and access lists the node needs to apply to traffic. Collectively, this is known as intermediate node delay.

Transmission delay can be caused in many ways, such as the following:

- Packet fragmentation, where adjacent networks have different maximum transmission units, and an incoming packet must be broken into two or more shorter packets

- Software delay, when forwarding information must be determined before transmission can continue

- Buffer hold times, which occur in order to smooth oversubscription elsewhere in the network

- Queuing of lower priority packets while higher priority traffic is forwarded

A certain amount of delay is inevitable. Even in a telephone call over traditional phone circuits, each central office that the call traverses introduces some degree of latency. Satellite links can add from 200 milliseconds to *two seconds* onto a data stream. For this reason the TCP transmissions over satellite link are often adjusted with a window size of over 64 KB to allow many packets in transmission without acknowledgments.

Time sensitivity

At first glance, a network that can offer the needed capacity with an acceptable delay would seem to be suitable for a given application. In practice, it is the *variability* of the delay that matters most for many time-sensitive applications.

Take, for example, a network that offers a consistent delay of a whole second end to end. The network may be unacceptable for two-way interactive voice because of the 2-second delay of a round-trip packet. On the other hand, a streamed video application works just fine. The 1-second delay on the receiving end means that the viewer sees images a second after they are sent, but since the entire video has a constant lag, there is no perceptible difference in image quality.

Now consider the same network, but assume instead that it has a variable delay. Sometimes the streamed video's bits arrive rapidly, with only 20 milliseconds' delay. Sometimes, they take an entire 2 seconds. What should the wise application developer do? Conventional wisdom holds that a buffer sufficient to support the largest possible delay for the duration of the session will allow the application to insulate the viewer from the network. This buffer must be accompanied by clever protocol mechanisms which might signal congestion, throttle the video's output, and discard frames in order to stay in sync with the transmitting end. A predictable delay will reduce software overhead and improve performance by reducing the "worst-case" buffers. Consequently, *variability of latency is of more concern to the inelastic users of a multiservice network than simple latency.*

In some extreme cases, network managers report that variable delay can reduce the effectiveness of legacy data applications. For example, an organization whose employees are accustomed to the predictable lag of a deterministic mainframe-based application on an SNA network may have "learned" that an excessive delay means they should restart their terminal. Once this application migrates to a best-effort, packet-based network, its behavior becomes detrimental. When the network is slow, they restart their desktop computers, wasting time and possibly even creating additional traffic during the start-up sequence with DHCP and network login scripts.

Jitter is caused by several factors, which are similar to the delay sources listed above.

Physical delay variance

Most networks provide a constant level of delay. Older systems might vary transmission speeds over very long lengths, but modern networks include better error correction and shielding, preventing physical variance. Nevertheless, mode partition noise and dispersion will introduce jitter in high-speed optical links.

Access delay variability

Access variability is the change in the delay with which an application is able to gain the right to transmit. In a bursty CSMA/CD network, access delay variability is high; for unshared links, it will be less so. Reducing the variability in media access is one reason to deploy switching to the desktop in anticipation of voice-over-IP or interactive applications.

Network delay variability

When a network is congested, queue depth and retransmission due to discards are two major sources of delay. Queue depths change with the level of congestion. Retransmissions due to discarded packets increase as network devices attempt to signal transmitters about congestion. Consequently, the variability in network delay is the major cause of jitter in networks. Adjusting queue and admission controls, as well as using prioritization of urgent traffic to bypass long queues, are the best ways to overcome this sort of delay.

Session-establishment variability

When an application creates a session across a network, a series of setup acknowledgments must take place. Depending on factors such as server load or discard rate, this sequence may experience an unpredictable delay to the start of the network service. Session-establishment variability is seldom an issue for the timely delivery of isochronous traffic once the session is established, however.

One way to resolve such a problem is to ensure that your servers, like your network, are relatively uncongested. Implementing a load-balancing front end can help with this problem by directing each client's traffic to the most available server. Proper design of the networking stack can also guarantee that session establishment is given a priority on the system.

As an application's traffic makes its way across a network, it must contend with delay, jitter, packet loss, and changing network capacity. Delay comes from the network itself, the computers at either end of the link, and the inherent inefficiencies of the protocols used. Jitter results from varying queue depths across many devices, as well as from packet loss and retransmission.

Depending on the nature of the application, the levels of jitter, latency, capacity, and retransmission may prevent it from functioning correctly in a best-effort environment. As a result, QOS must be introduced into the network fabric to support different network characteristics for different users or applications.

Endnotes

1. An excellent study of load-balancing systems is available from Acuitive, inc. at `www.acuitive.com`.

2. The following discussion assumes a working knowledge of TCP. While a proper treatment of the subject is beyond the scope of this text, a basic background is available in Appendix A.

3. Testing on a Pentium-II/350 with a 100-Mbps PCI network card, including reading information from a hard drive optimized for transmission, running Red Hat Linux 5.1.

4. From various sources, including `http://wwwhost.ots.utexas.edu/ethernet/10quickref/ch7qr_7.html`.

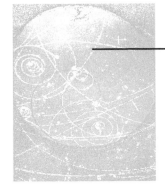

The needs of different traffic types

Traffic can be grouped into four coarse categories. Conversational traffic needs synchronization between sender and receiver, and latency is an important consideration for such systems. Streamed traffic can use large buffers to overcome loss or variance in delay, but constant changes in jitter will exhaust deep buffers. Informationally delay-sensitive traffic comes from a "robust" application whose *payload* cannot be delayed, such as a stock trade or credit card verification. The remainder of the traffic fits the traditional best-effort model. When these kinds of traffic coexist on a network, we call that network a converged network.

Armed with an understanding of the characteristics that a network can have when it transmits data, we can now consider the specific demands that various applications place on a network. We can make some rough statements about the needs and behaviors of different traffic types that will help us classify them into distinct classes of service. Those that require special attention may benefit from some degree of reservation, which can be achieved administratively or dynamically. Administrative reservation means setting a portion of the link aside, using the device's configuration; dynamic reservation happens at run time, as part of a system such as RSVP. Table 6–1 summarizes different application types and their handling needs.

Table 6–1   Different application types and the network services they require

	Bandwidth needs	Hold time (session duration)	Burstiness	Latency sensitivity	Jitter sensitivity
Voice	Low	Low	Low	High	Medium
Streamed video	High	High	Low	Low	High
Interactive video	High	High	Medium	High	High
Shared application	Low–medium	Medium	High	Medium	Low
Data	Low–medium	Low–medium	High	Low	Low

Before we look at how the network identifies and handles these different traffic types, we will consider the specific needs of each.

Sidebar

User robustness

One aspect of delay that can't be easily measured is the user's expectations. Before the days of automatic teller machines, a bank customer's expectation of delay in withdrawing money was some 10 minutes. Today, if the machine takes more than 30 seconds to give you your money, you're likely to call the bank's support number. Similarly, people evolve an understanding of how to cope with slower systems.

A user running an application created in a Windows-based GUI environment has an expectation of response time. An SQL client, for example, may look just like any other desktop dialog box. If the SQL server is congested or unavailable, users may not know how to handle the problem. By contrast, users are accustomed to Web browsers being slow; they will probably understand how to wait and how to reload a page. The Web browser affords them cues about the progress of their transfer—sliding bars, flying stars, or orbiting lights, imaginatively known as "throbers."

So, while accounting traffic accessed by an SQL client and by a Web client might be equally important to the organization, they may not have the same *urgency*— because of the humans involved and their expectations.

Voice

Voice traffic requires relatively little bandwidth, and it is not compressed differentially. It is sensitive to loss (which appears in the form of "static" or gaps in conversation), so minor overall delays that can correct loss are acceptable, to a degree. Voice traffic has a relatively constant, low bit rate when sending. Consequently, message sizes are relatively small (between 44 and 200 bytes), as this allows rapid transmission of low traffic volumes. Voice also consists of up to 60 percent silence; for pauses in a conversation to sound natural, the receiver must often play back low-level static to reassure the listener that the line has not gone dead.

If voice applications waited around for 1500 bytes of traffic (a large IP datagram), for example, then a 16-Kbps voice stream would fit into 1.365 packets—meaning that the sender would transmit only 1.365 packets a second.[1]

One of the main reasons for using a packetized network (rather than just recreating the telephone network with reserved IP links everywhere) is to optimize bandwidth by sharing the link. This occurs in traditional phone circuits as well, albeit less flexibly. A normal phone link runs at 64 Kbps (known as G.711). International links often economize by using a 64-Kbps link to carry two 32-Kbps circuits (known as G.726). The use of 32-Kbps circuits doesn't affect sound quality much, but some links go so far as to aggregate four circuits onto a link. These 16-Kbps circuits create a perceptible, but acceptable, degradation in sound quality. Voice-over-IP systems typically run between 4 and 15 Kbps per circuit, making them comparable to a cheap transatlantic link.

The best voice-over-IP compression systems we have today (G.729 and G.723.1) introduce 20 to 40 milliseconds at the transmitting end; jitter buffering adds somewhere under 100 milliseconds at the receiving end. By contrast, traditional isochronous telephone switch circuits introduce traffic into the network the instant it is sampled—at a constant bit rate.

Consequently, even with an excellent network the inherent packetization, compression, and jitter-smoothing functions on the end nodes use up nearly all the delay that a human ear will tolerate for "local call" quality voice. Network latency must be carefully regulated indeed, or you may find that you are the only person in the organization actually *using* the VoIP solution because of poor sound quality.

Sidebar

Can my network handle voice?

How fast does a network have to be to support voice traffic effectively? Effective throughput of interactive, low-volume traffic is a function not only of round-trip delay, but also of the percentage and pattern of packet loss, the variance in delay, and the throughput of the connection.

• The delay affects human perception of the call itself. Mouth-to-ear delays of under 250 milliseconds are generally acceptable for voice-over IP. A local phone offers a delay between 10 and 30 milliseconds, with a 56-Kbps audio stream and no variance in latency (also known as jitter). A transatlantic call offers the same characteristics, with a 100–200 millisecond delay.

• Pattern of packet loss, as well as percentage of loss, is important. Losing a packet every minute is no cause for alarm; losing two packets in a row may indicate a real problem.

• We control variance in delay through buffering at the receiver. Jitter tolerances are stringently specified for telephone circuits, and with 125-microsecond frame buffers in many phone switches jitter is tightly controlled. Buffering introduces additional delay. For buffers to be useful they must correct jitter—so they are largely wasted on low-variance networks.

• Throughput is important because it affects the frequency response, sampling rate, and resulting sound quality of the phone call itself.

• If voice is delayed more than about 150 milliseconds, speakers begin to interrupt one another or give negative impressions because of their slow response.

We present some sample voice connections, and their characteristics, in Table 6–2.

Table 6–2   Comparison of various voice connection characteristics

Connection	Packet loss	Audio stream	Latency	Jitter (% variance in latency)
Normal phone line, local call	0%	56 Kbps	10–30 msec	0%
Undersea transatlantic link	0%	56 Kbps	100–200 msec	0%
Typical GSM (digital wireless) connection	5–15%	13 Kbps	100–300 msec	50%
Internet telephone application (assumes good ISP and dialup modem)	5–20%	20 Kbps	120–240 msec	150%
Unacceptable Internet telephone application	10–35%	20 Kbps	100–300 msec	300%

Voice traffic typically travels over UDP rather than TCP. The retransmission of voice packets—which TCP does automatically—delays the delivery of those packets and the ones that follow them in a voice stream. Listeners don't usually detect voice packet loss if less than 5 percent of data is discarded; consequently, UDP allows the application to sacrifice guaranteed delivery in return for low delay.

Compression and latency

Isochronous traffic is the product of sampling and digitizing an analog signal at a fixed, highly precise frequency. Packetization is the trick of dividing serialized data into discrete chunks, sending them across a wire, and extracting them at the other end unharmed, as shown in Figure 6–1.

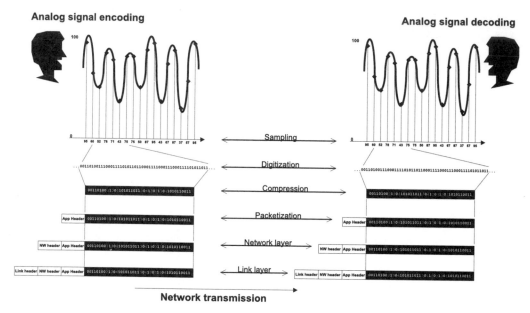

Figure 6–1   The process of sampling, transmitting, and reassembling a voice sample

The efficiency of the simulated circuit can be expressed as a ratio of the packet overhead to the payload. If we send a small payload, we use the network inefficiently. If each header is 40 bytes, and each payload is 40 bytes, we're limiting the effective transmission rate of useful data to 50 percent. If we were to send each sample as soon as it arrived (for example, a stream of 1-byte packets), we'd generate a huge amount of traffic for a relatively small amount of content. However, if we sent a large payload (say, 1500-byte packets), we couldn't transmit the entire packet until the last sampled datum was added to it.

With a large payload, if we waited a minute to send what we'd sampled of a conversation, then the listener might experience a minute-long delay. Similarly, a single lost packet would cause a minute of silence. Choosing the right ratio of payload to header is critical and can vary according to network conditions and application type.

Packetization is an important source of delay that occurs because a device that is to perform compression or transmission must wait until sufficient information has been received to be compressed. Compression algorithms work by looking at a large chunk of data in order to identify "compressible" sequences of similar data. Generally, the larger the "table" used in compression is, the better the compression ratio. However, a sender can look at a long sequence of packets and build a good table so that each individual packet is compressed better.

The packetization delay varies with the payload of the packet (i.e., the number of bytes that make up a sample, into which the traffic will be inserted) and the rate of the sampled traffic. For example, ATM has a payload of 48 bytes with a 5-byte header. The first byte that arrives for insertion into an ATM cell must wait for 47 other bytes to arrive, after which the header is added.

Imagine that an application samples voice traffic at 64 Kbps—commonly referred to as "toll quality" because this is the actual throughput of a telephone-company circuit. This means that at 8 bits per sample, there are 8,000 samples every second. Therefore, for 47 bytes to be sampled, the time required will be 47/8000, or about 5.8 ms. Consequently, data will arrive at an ATM device and will experience at least 5.8 ms delay. This is the delay from the time the first piece of data is received until the time the last arrives (48 bytes at 64 Kbps). Only once the entire source has been received can the packet be transmitted. Each time data must be assembled into a chunk like this, delay occurs.

Packetization delay is analogous to a bus that must wait until all its seats are full before departing. If a constant stream of passengers arrives, the first passenger must nevertheless wait until a busload of others have arrived before the bus can leave.

The delay is acceptable to passengers only if the bus travels fast enough to make up for the time the first person sat waiting—otherwise each person would be better off traveling via some other vehicle that took fewer passengers. Of course, the local bus dispatcher (the network administrator) would like to have as few busses as possible in order to meet budget goals. The number of "passengers" on a voice bus is far smaller than the number of passengers on a video-conferencing bus, because there are far more video passengers in a video session and the bus fills more quickly.

Sidebar

Link compression and packetization

Link-layer compression is commonly used to optimize slow links such as modem, PPP, or ISDN connections. These links often have a round-trip time (RTT) of more than 100 milliseconds, largely because of the serial delay from the computer to the terminal adapter or modem and the subsequent PPP reprocessing. ISDN-to-Ethernet connections typically range from 20 to 40 milliseconds RTT.[2] A typical modem will suffer 20 to 40 milliseconds of increased round-trip delay from compression; for a typical ISDN terminal adapter, delay due to compression will be about 4–5 milliseconds. The packetization delay from an Ethernet network to an ISDN basic-rate-interface (BRI) link seldom exceeds 1 millisecond.

The added benefit of increased bandwidth that results from compression can result in faster transmission rates by upper network layers, which may offset the corresponding delay in an ISDN environment. Two modem-attached users communicating voice traffic across the Internet will incur an additional 40–80 milliseconds of delay if compression is enabled on the modems.

Note that PPP stacks often use Van Jacobsen (VJ) header compression, which lessens the delay introduced by the PPP stack by replacing most of the TCP/IP information with a symbol that represents the TCP headers. The optimization happens entirely in software, between the two PPP stacks, and can reduce the propagation delay for TCP connections by about 10 milliseconds for a 28.8-Kbps modem.

Packetization delay means that, at its simplest, you will get better performance for gaming over the Internet (low bandwidth, latency sensitive) if you turn off modem compression and turn on header compression. VJ compression will have no effect, however, on UDP traffic, which is commonly used for interactive gaming and multimedia streaming.

The effects of compression can be summarized in two simple observations. Compression generates an increase in delay due to compression processing and a decrease in bandwidth due to compression overhead. At the same time, it generates a reduction in delay and increase in bandwidth due to shorter packets. Slow links and clever compression, therefore, generally make compression worthwhile.

Overcoming packetization delay with multiplexing

Packetization delay at the network layer can to some extent be resolved by multiplexing several short bursts of conversation into each packet or cell, lowering the size of the individual samples and increasing the frequency with which they are sent. By including small samples of multiple streams into a single larger cell or packet we can reduce the packetization delay that each traffic stream encounters. Multiplexing within the packet is akin to having several kinds of passengers board the bus at once, so that it can leave more often.

Multiplexing carries a penalty, of course. In order to cleanly combine and separate distinct streams of application information, we need to perform additional signaling.

The ATM adaptation layer handles multiplexing of conversation samples automatically. Consequently, ATM is often used for efficient WAN circuits carrying latency-sensitive applications. Fragmentation and reassembly is feasible for PBX-to-PBX communications, but it does little to improve individual client traffic on an end-to-end network link. Sample multiplexing works well when a distribution point (for example, an interface between an IP backbone and a traditional PBX) can carry the traffic serially across the final circuit to the user.

Another technique for reducing the effects of packetization delay is to employ a session algorithm that meters traffic as it arrives for transmission and transmits packets that aren't full if some kind of timer expires. In our analogy, this is like telling the bus to leave when it is still half-empty, if a certain amount of time has passed. Maximum-delay algorithms like this generate a higher header-to-payload ratio and require either packet padding (to maintain a constant packet size) or variable-length packets. Padding and variable-length packets can both introduce some degree of processing delay. For applications that have a substantially varying bit rate, this technique can improve perceived response time. Handling the variable-length packets may also require additional computation or signaling.

Sidebar

Some compression schemes

Application-specific compression schemes can be tailored to their intended usage.

• Regularly shaped, monotone images compress well with run-length encoding

• Photographs and gradients can be processed algorithmically

• Moving images are compressed differentially

• Voice traffic employs mathematical processing that takes advantages of certain characteristics of human speech.

Simple compression techniques such as run-length encoding (Figure 6–2) are used to pare down Web pages today. GIF files use compression (called Lempel-Ziv Welch), and their size is greatly reduced when their content consists of repetitive bands of the same color.

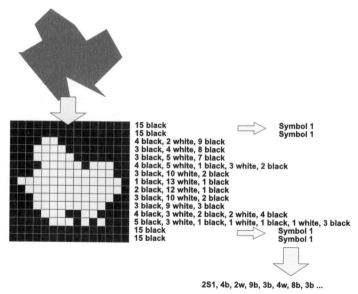

Figure 6–2   Run-length encoding of an irregular shape

Depending on the regularity of the compressed shape, a simple run-length encoding can itself be encoded, leading to even greater compression (Figure 6–3). Repeated passes also work in compressing data for transmission. The more we know about the "shape" of the traffic—its nature, the ranges of signals, and so on—the more efficient a compression algorithm we can apply to it.

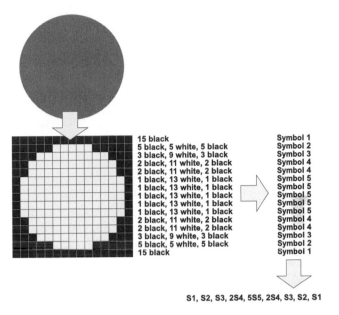

15 black	Symbol 1
5 black, 5 white, 5 black	Symbol 2
3 black, 9 white, 3 black	Symbol 3
2 black, 11 white, 2 black	Symbol 4
2 black, 11 white, 2 black	Symbol 4
1 black, 13 white, 1 black	Symbol 5
1 black, 13 white, 1 black	Symbol 5
1 black, 13 white, 1 black	Symbol 5
1 black, 13 white, 1 black	Symbol 5
1 black, 13 white, 1 black	Symbol 5
2 black, 11 white, 2 black	Symbol 4
2 black, 11 white, 2 black	Symbol 4
3 black, 9 white, 3 black	Symbol 3
5 black, 5 white, 5 black	Symbol 2
15 black	Symbol 1

S1, S2, S3, 2S4, 5S5, 2S4, S3, S2, S1

Figure 6–3   Run-length encoding of a regular shape

Better image quality—higher resolution or greater color depth—requires more information. It is generally less compressible in this way as well; images that require many hues tend to be organic and therefore less regularly colored. Instead, photographic compression uses mathematical processing of the image information by sampling areas of the image and storing information on color variance from the center of each area. A variance-based system assumes that photographic images have few harsh lines and many smooth gradients of similar hue, saturation, or brightness. The JPEG format relies on this kind of algorithmic compression to reduce the size of noncontiguous image blocks.

The more a sender knows about the shape of the information, the better it is able to optimize it for transmission. This is true not only for two-dimensional images, but also for multimedia such as video: Knowing the previous image means the sender only has to transmit changes.

Static images consist of three dimensions: vertical position, horizontal position, and color depth. With animation, the fourth dimension of time is introduced. Video compression is generally differential, based on the notion that images don't change all at once. Differential compression allows a large, relatively unchanging image to be transmitted over a relatively small quantity of network capacity. A normal, uncompressed television image can consume more than 6 Mbps of the network; differential compression can move this reasonably well to several 64-Kbps streams.

Human voice consists largely of silence and generates sounds in specific frequencies. Voice-compression schemes rely on some mathematical processing, as well as the multiplexing of many voice circuits, to take advantage of the gaps in speech. The level of sampling needed to transmit voice efficiently is far less than that needed for high-fidelity musical transmission—a fact to which anyone who has listened to hold music on a GSM phone will attest.

The choice of content and compression type in electronic media has played an important factor in the online world and can reduce delays in your organization's Internet and intranet usage. As caching systems, faster local loops, and client-side content generation become more common, however, choice of content format is less and less important.

Video

Video traffic can be classified into two groups: interactive ("conversational") video and streamed one-way video ("playback"). Video sessions are often delivered over the WAN using multiple bonded switched connections—for example, multiple ISDN links. In order to address the widest possible market, makers of videoconferencing applications design their products to work with a variety of data rates from a simple modem link (56 Kbps) to a T1 or more (1.544 Mbps).

A typical video application might rely on a TCP control channel and two UDP data channels—one for voice and one for data. Classification of a videoconferencing session will therefore be complex, requiring devices to recognize the relationship between the control channel and the related data channels. Control-channel traffic may have to be prioritized to allow devices to adjust their data transmissions when the control channel signals congestion, for example.

Uncompressed video traffic runs at a constant bit rate. The high price of WAN circuits and the significant impact of broadcast-quality video means that most video traffic is actually variable bit rate because of compression. VBR video will generally use the largest possible packet size to send information, so each datagram will be the size of the maximum transmission unit (MTU). On the other hand, constant-bit-rate traffic has a high bit rate and low variability.

Differentially compressed traffic consists of key frames that describe the entire image and intermediate frames that describe changes, or deltas, from the original key frame. An unhindered stream of differentially compressed video shows bursts of traffic at each key frame, and relatively less traffic for intermediate frames, as illustrated in Figure 6–4.

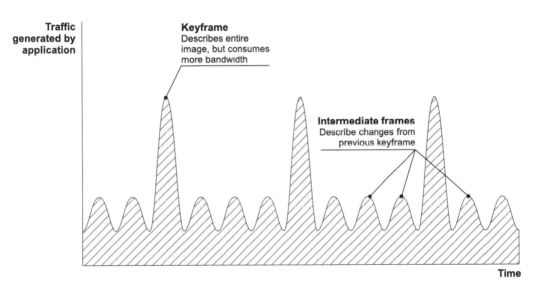

Figure 6–4   Key frames and intermediate frames on an uncongested network

Key frames allow the receiver to "sync up" periodically so that the sender and receiver don't get too much out of state. As a network becomes congested, packets are buffered, queued, or discarded. Different pieces of the video image are delivered at different times, and the receiver must store them to assemble a completed image. Some traffic may arrive earlier than expected, while other packets may arrive later. As Figure 6–5 shows, some packets will even arrive so late that they are useless—the frame for which they contain information has already been displayed.

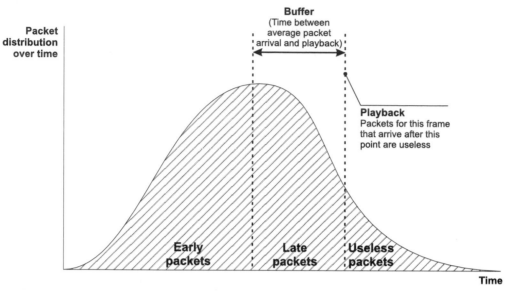

Figure 6–5   Distribution of packet arrival and average buffer delay

This means that, for high-volume (i.e., key) frames when congestion exists, some packets may arrive so late they are discarded by the receiver. Delay in packet delivery results in "clipping" of the key frames, degrading the image as seen in Figure 6–6.

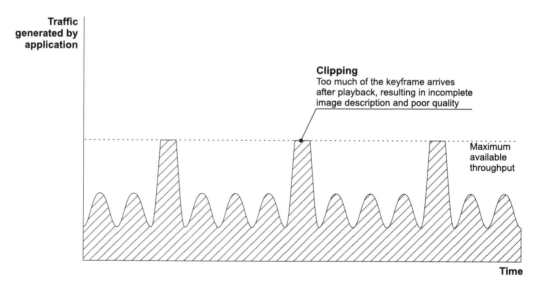

Figure 6–6   Clipping of key frames when available throughput is limited

The effects of this clipping can be reduced by changing the application's parameters so that the size of key frames is smaller (by reducing display size or color depth) or by increasing the delay between receipt of traffic and playback. If you alter the key-frame size, the picture will take longer to converge when the image changes significantly, but there will be less jumpiness or static in the transmission (Figure 6–7). Increasing the delay between receipt and playback will introduce more latency into the image.

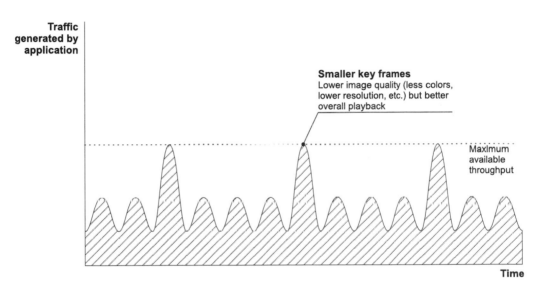

Figure 6–7   Adjusting frame size to compensate for reduced throughput

In practical deployment, capacity varies constantly. This makes it harder for a sender and receiver to evaluate the capacity of the network enough to properly select frame size, color depth, and buffer settings in a best-effort network. True QOS attempts to resolve this by setting aside a guaranteed portion of bandwidth for some degree of determinism through either a "controlled load," where network delay will be within a predictable range, or a "guarantee," where network delay and variance will remain relatively static.

Interactive conversation

Human factors play a significant role in the tolerance for delay. Users have a set of expectations about the behavior of a two-way voice session; as a result, they will be frustrated by latency. Such an expectation is less likely to exist today for videoconferencing. So for hearing, delay and jitter control are vital.

When we discuss "conversation," we mean an interaction between impatient humans. This is often voice traffic, but many data applications are becoming conversational. Shared whiteboard and concurrent working systems that let distributed groups run the same application must offer a suitable response time as they share files. This is the case even when a separate circuit (such as a phone line) is employed for voice. These systems are latency sensitive but less concerned with jitter, because they emphasize timely playback.

Human factors play a part in some typical data applications as well. Latency can manifest itself in hard-to-measure ways. For example, a slow link may cause meeting productivity to slip as employees try to troubleshoot the problem. It may also waste time because users are distracted by the unusual effects of the delay itself—a fact to which anyone who has waved a hand during a videoconference will attest!

The converged network

We call a network that can satisfy the requirements of latency, jitter, capacity, reliability, and hold times that the various application types impose a *converged* network. It has certain characteristics.

Common wiring

A converged network shares wiring among many applications and traffic types. Generally, this will be Category 5 twisted pair cabling, allowing a 10-Mbps link to migrate to 100 Mbps in the future. An excellent case can be made for the consolidation of voice and data onto a single wiring plant for purely operational reasons. We achieve not only a savings in the elimination of the cable plant itself, but also a reduction of the plant as moves, adds, and changes occur.

Common protocols in the stack

A converged network brings together several kinds of traffic. It also relies on a common set of protocols to serve as a "rallying point" around which applications and services can be built. For the foreseeable future, because of its broad adoption and rich variety of applications, the common protocol is IP.

Switching to the edge

Switched ports reduce the effects of congestion on media-access delays, making them ideal for low-latency applications such as voice. What's more, with security a growing concern, switching reduces the risk that a company's sensitive data can be seen by a hacker. From a QOS perspective, switched-to-the-desktop network architectures allow circuit simulation end to end by the network layer.

High-forwarding core

In order to achieve the benefits of a "proprietary" fast core while making the capacity available to many administrative domains, a public addressing and routing scheme must map to a private circuit addressing mechanism. These "route-then-switch" mechanisms include systems such as Cisco's Tag Switching and the Ipsilon Flow Management Protocol (IFMP), whose legacies can be seen in the IETF's Multi-Protocol Label Switching (MPLS). A publicly accessible, high-performance core such as MPLS is sometimes referred to as "layer 2.5," since it has the characteristics of a media layer within the network but presents a layer-3 interface to adjacent devices.

The core of a converged network emphasizes forwarding of traffic over granular classification. The core will manage relatively few discrete classifiers (such as 802.1p values, MPLS headers, ATM QOS characteristics, and IPTOS or precedence information). It will employ proprietary methods for speeding up traffic within the administrative domain, and less optimized standard methods for doing so across domains or in a multivendor environment.

Application integration

Rather than just carrying several separate traffic types on a wire, a converged network merges several data types into novel hybrids. Some examples are provided in Table 6–3.

Table 6–3   Examples of hybrid, multimedia applications on a converged network

Streamed Video	Narrated presentations			
Interactive Video	Mixed-media conference call	Telelearning with Q&A		
Shared application	Group white-boarding	Application training with video & simulation	Concurrent design	
Data	Real-time support on Web site	Television with custom stock ticker	Distributed review meetings	Team content creation
	Voice	**Streamed video**	**Interactive video**	**Shared application**

For example, an e-mail application may include the ability to leave voicemail; a one-way streamed video system may support lower-bandwidth interactive video for questions. The rise of such *cross-media* applications is a key driver for the deployment of a next-generation network infrastructure.

Sidebar

A sample converged network: The call center

A call center is a perfect example of an application that can benefit immediately from convergence. Two kinds of traffic are key to the operation of the center: voice traffic from callers and data traffic pertaining to customer-support and product-information issues. More importantly, there are compelling benefits to the marriage of the two: knowing something about the caller makes it easier to find the right information quickly, improving customer satisfaction. Switching call destinations at the time that a support call is escalated—along with the appropriate information—can be achieved through custom applications and tight integration with networking components.

Integrated voice/data systems are available already. For example, Integrated Device Technology's Click2Talk system[3] lets Web developers tie hyperlinks to telephone calls, allowing sales or support personnel to contact Web visitors directly. The only convergence here is in the integration of call placement across parallel links (data and phone network), but if the applications are accepted by companies, the reasons for converging traffic will become even stronger.

There is a shared set of wires between the various players in the system. There is also a possibility that more applications—support videos, hand-holding via voice while a customer browses online information, and the like—will become important to the center as time goes by.

Most environments in which a converged network offers tangible benefits share these characteristics. Generally, there will be more than one type of traffic, a strong benefit to the marriage of the traffic types, common wiring, and potential deployment of still more traffic types.

Practical uses for converged networks

Let's take a closer look at the convergence of voice and data. Converging different traffic types does not mean that every computer in the company is also a telephone; rather, convergence happens in specific locations where the benefits of a common infrastructure outweigh the costs of management.

A voice-over-IP network may use IP-enabled handsets with Ethernet interfaces to reduce the amount of redundant wiring in the network. This is a phone-to-phone voice-over-IP solution. By contrast, the telephone switches at each branch office might distinguish between internal and external calls, using reserved capacity on the data network for calling between offices. This is a PBX-to-PBX network. The cornerstone of such a solution is a Voice-over-IP gateway that can manage the various connections, as well as the circuit-to-packet encoding of call traffic for transmission across the data network.

PBX-to-PBX systems may offer additional features such as off-net calling (in which a user at one location can access the PBX at another in order to place an outside local call at the remote site) as well as advanced, computer-controlled call handling and conferencing.

Obstacles to convergence

Uptake of converged networks has lagged, however. Despite some compelling evidence for the move to common wiring and integrated traffic, companies are slow to deploy converged technology immediately.

Human factors

Humans are creatures of habit. We are accustomed to reaching for the telephone, sitting back when watching the television, and dialing on a keypad that feels "just so." Several vendors of computer-telephony integration (CTI) products have adopted a user interface that mimics an answering machine, despite the fact that answering machines are often confusing and complex to users. Such mimicry is done simply so that the vendor can leverage the affordances we've learned about such devices.

Successful implementations will mimic or leverage existing systems where possible. This may mean a familiar phone handset attached to the computer. It might even consist of re-use of the PBX, but with convergence of signaling across the WAN using a gateway. Similarly, an integrated application might send e-mail with a voice attachment that could be forwarded to a traditional voice mailbox.

If it ain't broke, don't fix it

Most organizations are reasonably satisfied with the functionality of their systems today, and the perceived risk of deploying a critical phone system may outweigh any potential for cost savings in the short term. The introduction of "dual-mode" equipment that functions as a VoIP gateway and a traditional telephone exchange switch, or of plain-old-telephone-system (POTS)/IP handsets, may overcome this kind of reticence.

Forklift upgrades

Changing our hardware is never easy. Recent budgets have emphasized security, remote access, Internet connectivity, and timely bug fixes such as Y2K and three-nine end-of-file problems. Until switched links to desktops, multimedia interfaces on workstations, classification-capable end nodes, and priority-capable cores gradually percolate out into the network infrastructure, deploying converged applications requires a major overhaul. As devices with QOS capabilities make their way into the network in the course of regular upgrades, it becomes increasingly more affordable to implement converged networks without requiring the massive upgrades that were previously necessary.

Management complexity

A final obstacle is the potential complexity of this sort of system. Managing the relative mission criticality and delay sensitivity of each of these applications, for a range of users and to a range of destinations, is difficult. It requires a degree of integration with IP services and directories, as well as an ease of use, that today's management platforms do not deliver. While vendors are working diligently to reduce the complexity and improve the ease-of-use of these systems, IT's pragmatic experience with other, less-than-successful solutions is a major deterrent to deployment.

Fortunately, industry initiatives and cheap bandwidth will probably allow us to deploy a "good enough" converged solution in the near future.

The real world

The pragmatic reader may make a rather blunt observation that without end-to-end QOS, applications that *need* end-to-end QOS will not be deployed. The chicken-and-egg argument is a valid one; many converged applications have been hindered by the lack of services in underlying networks, and without such applications end-to-end QOS is not in demand.

Endnotes

1. A number of technical papers on voice encoding are available from various vendors. They include "Impact and Performance of Lucent's Internet Telephony Server (ITS) over IP Networks" (`http://www.lucent.com/enterprise/internet-its-e/documentation.html#white`); "Voice/Fax over IP" from Nortel Networks" (`http://www.micom.com/WhitePapers/index.html`); and "The Market for Internet Telephony" (`http://www.deltathree.com/company/press/whitepaper.asp`).

2. Results are from Networkshop's testing of a variety of vendors' modems, including the Gandalf 5242i bridge on one B-channel at 20 milliseconds and the 3Com NetBuilder Remote Office at 40 milliseconds. Propagation delay and latency may be a result of complex software or specific configuration, so these estimates should be considered anecdotal.

3. `http://www.net2phone.com` or `http://www.click2talk.com`

Armed with an understanding of the QOS problem and the levels of network service that various applications require in order to function properly, we can consider how our networks must accommodate their needs. We divide this into the following sections:

- An introduction to traffic management

- Classification and identification of traffic, as well as complications to classification

- Handling the traffic, both within a device and across a network path

- Server-side delay considerations

- Directory infrastructures and policy systems needed to manage QOS

- Monitoring service levels in the network

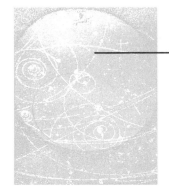

An introduction to traffic management

Traffic management systems consist of a set of high-level rules that are propagated out to enforcement points using a policy system. At a high level, the network classifies traffic, handles it appropriately, polices traffic to ensure it is conforming to expected norms, and monitors the effects of changes it has made to its configuration. On a more strategic level, these same functions must also occur. IT managers need to classify traffic within their organization and evaluate its relative importance. They must also design networks that can offer the differentiation this traffic needs. Finally, they must track the effects of their changes to learn from them.

A QOS management system can be created in a number of ways:

• You can deploy point products with similar behaviors at specific places in the network where they will do the most good—and rely on overprovisioning to make best effort good enough. This is not a "system" *per se*, but it may deliver an appropriate level of QOS depending on your needs.

• You can set QOS configurations locally, so that each device classifies traffic and enforces its own set of rules. In this case, you must ensure rule consistency across devices. Maintaining consistent rules for large numbers of devices is a major burden that may prove too substantial an obstacle until reliable management tools such as directories are in place.

• You can make the end systems and access routers perform local classification and mark the packets for preferential downstream handling (IPTOS byte, 802.1p). Having edge devices perform classification shares the workload but requires that the "classifying" and "handling" devices infer exactly the same meaning from a particular classification.

• You can rely on a system of reservation, in which senders request specific handling across a circuit or flow. Creating dedicated links across a network path means introducing signaling awareness and decision making into devices, but network behavior becomes far more predictable.

All traffic processing, including service-level management, involves the two steps of *classification* and *handling*. There are many ways to classify and handle traffic, as we shall see.

• Different devices may classify traffic based on different criteria such as IPTOS, IP precedence, 802.1p, circuit number, user identity, or group membership.

• Different devices may have different ways of handling traffic, such as separate network paths, differing numbers of queues, or different queuing algorithms.

— Cisco Systems supports 6 queues in its Internet Operating System (IOS) release 11.1

— 3Com Corporation supports 2 queues in layer-2 switches and 4 queues in layer-3 switches

— Nortel Networks supports multiple priority levels in its layer-3 switching products

— Windows desktops can assign 8 levels of priority in Ethernet, and 8 in IP

— Most routers can offer customized packet interleaving, simulating any number of queues

— ATM implementations generally offer 4 types of circuits, ranging from reserved circuits to best-effort circuits

A policy system

A general model for understanding the classification, decision making, and handling of traffic across a network is useful in discussing specific implementations and applications. A system of classification and handling across multiple devices is known as a *policy architecture*, because it elevates network decisions from complex detail to general rules known as policies. Many networking vendors have proposed policy architectures, and Internet drafts and standards suggest common terminology and general systems for networking policies.

At the lowest level, devices look at traffic and try to categorize it, then handle it in different ways based on that classification. In a system, classification and handling rules must reach the network devices in a scalable, trustworthy, highly available manner. These rules may change, depending on a number of factors such as time of day, network congestion, or operator intervention.

At its most general, a policy-based network's components consist of real-time traffic handlers, decision makers, and information stores (Figure 7–1). The handlers apply rules handed to them by the decision-making components, which in turn retrieve the information they need from various data repositories. The rules are called *policies*, and the act of passing information out to these devices from a central authority is policy distribution. Acting on these rules is called *enforcement*. A sample policy trans-action might be as follows:

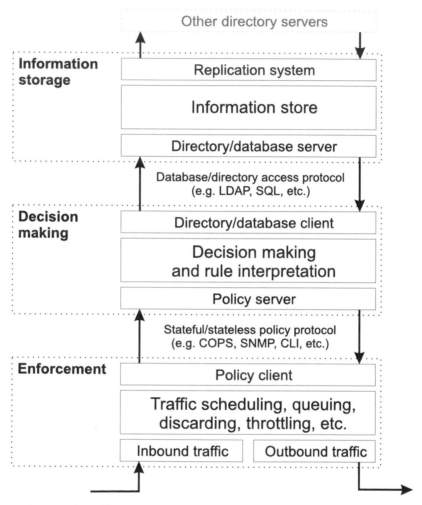

Figure 7–1   A generic policy system

1. A packet arrives at a QOS-capable device.

2. The packet is classified by looking at some of its characteristics—layer-2 and -3 media information, source and destination address, or TCP port, for example. The classification can occur administratively (i.e., someone preconfigured a set of criteria that match traffic) or in real time (i.e., the network has negotiated

some kind of reservation or preferential treatment for traffic of a certain type).

3. The device tries to determine how to handle the traffic of this type by consulting its local rules, but it does not know how. It therefore asks a policy server to decide on its behalf, using a stateful protocol (such as COPS) to register itself and request guidance.

4. The policy server uses a data-access protocol (such as LDAP) to get more detailed information about the packet from a data repository—for example, by determining the sender's identity based on MAC or IP address.

5. The data repositories, meanwhile, have been exchanging information among themselves whenever situations change or administrators change the content or configuration of the network.

6. The data repository replies to the policy server with the needed information, which the policy server uses to formulate a rule about how the device should handle traffic that fits this classification.

7. The policy server updates the device with the new information via the COPS session, and the device can therefore handle the traffic in the appropriate manner. It forwards the traffic according to the handling it has been told is appropriate, and it may cache the classification and handling rules to speed up further transactions.

This model is an oversimplification. Specifically, in most cases where performance is critical, the classifiers and handling information would already be pushed out to the devices in anticipation of traffic. If each device requested information from a central authority every time a new packet appeared, we'd have very slow networks indeed. For this reason, devices register with a server when they first initialize, and the server propagates new configurations out to the device when circumstances change.

The functions of our generic policy system would be distributed among a replicated directory, policy servers, and enforcing devices. We will return to review the notion of a policy architecture later, once we have laid the foundation for traffic classification, policing, and handling.

On the desktop, Microsoft's Windows 2000 allows application designers to create network-aware applications that can signal traffic priority and negotiate reserved paths through a network.

In the wiring closet, switching is replacing shared segments, allowing queuing and prioritization of traffic as well as broadcast containment and the creation of dynamic segments based on user identity or protocol type.

On the LAN/WAN edge or **in the server farm**, routers are offering queuing algorithms that give some applications precedence while rationing enough of the remaining capacity among other, less important, traffic.

End-to-end, bandwidth reservation systems are negotiating reserved routed paths (RSVP) or alternate switched paths (MPLS) across expensive WAN links and congested LAN segments

In the WAN switch, circuits with varying priority or capacity from traditional Frame Relay Circuits, as well as ATM QOS and ABR queue simulation, are allowing carriers to offer differentiated services to their customers.

A policy system might configure a wide range of devices. From the desktop to the WAN core, companies are turning on and installing new capabilities that allow networking components to play an active role in the regulation of traffic.

Networks enforce bandwidth constraints by handling individual packets differently. Doing so requires a number of signaling systems to identify traffic and communicate the rules about how it is to be handled.

The way a device handles traffic is known as its *per-hop behavior*. The aggregate of link delays and per-hop behaviors makes up the *path behavior*. The path behavior can be used by applications and networking software to set transmission parameters, frame rates, screen sizes, and so on.

A high-level view: Classify, handle, police, and monitor

Classifying the traffic

All traffic contains identifying properties at various layers of the protocol stack (Figure 7–2). While we confine our discussion here to the Internet Protocol, it is important to realize that much of this applies equally to other protocol types.

Despite the myriad classifications that a device can apply to a packet, most systems implement classification in one of two ways:

- They associate certain identifiers with specific behaviors, which is done by mapping explicit tags in the packet to service levels that the device can deliver. For example, a router might inspect the 3 bits of

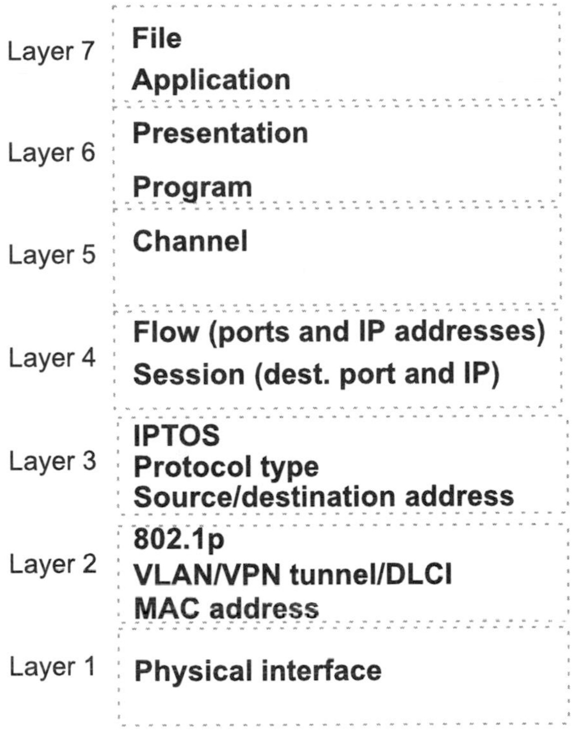

Layer 7	**File** **Application**
Layer 6	**Presentation** **Program**
Layer 5	**Channel**
Layer 4	**Flow (ports and IP addresses)** **Session (dest. port and IP)**
Layer 3	**IPTOS** **Protocol type** **Source/destination address**
Layer 2	**802.1p** **VLAN/VPN tunnel/DLCI** **MAC address**
Layer 1	**Physical interface**

Figure 7–2   Types of traffic classification and the OSI 7-layer model

the IP header that identify priority, and associate the packet with one of eight queues. The association of a class with a handling mechanism is known as "mapping," because it forms a relationship between a specific value and a per-hop behavior.

• They assume a "default" service level for all traffic, then look at specific exception conditions. For example, a router with a firewall forwards traffic with a generic service level unless it finds a specific match for the traffic type, in which case it applies a different packet-interleaving ratio. We can call this an access-list approach.

Mapping works well if the priority is to be configured across a number of devices that will provide consistent handling. In other words, if you have a switched LAN, then mapping Ethernet priorities to 2 or 4 queues will create a multiservice network, once all devices are configured in this way. Generally, such a system is less well equipped to deal with per-user behavior, relying instead on traffic tagging or packet coloring on the end stations.

On a boundary device (such as a firewall or LAN/WAN interface) an access-list approach works well instead. The typical configuration of a perimeter device such as a firewall is well suited to the defaults-and-exceptions model, since firewalls generally behave this way in any event. Access router firewalls are also optimized for packet inspection rather han forwarding for speed, because they are servicing a comparatively slow WAN link. Furthermore, all traffic must traverse the node on its way to the WAN, which makes consistency with other networking devices lcss important than in a switched LAN core.

Default mappings and access lists are not mutually exclusive, however. Next-generation policy devices will combine the two into a multiservice device that has default mappings of classifiers to handlers, and exceptions for specific circumstances.

Policing the classifications

Bandwidth is precious. Tagging traffic on the end station is useful, but policy requests should be validated to ensure that the network's users are behaving properly. Without a policing function in a policy system, the network is exposed to potential abuses.

The policing function is one of inspecting policy rules and verifying that they are being obeyed. Policing can include a comparison of priority tags to user permissions and application priorities, or it can involve a comparison of service levels to established SLAs. Policing is a second level of classification that occurs by a more trusted device than the one that performed the initial classification.

Because users have complete control of their desktops in most companies, end-node classification cannot always be trusted. Proper configuration of monitoring tools will allow you to identify possible suspects whose traffic is significantly different from the "typical" traffic profile on the network. If you have sufficient control of the desktop within the organization, tools such as the Windows Policy Editor may let you lock down the registry access that users need to fiddle with these configurations. In general, unchecked modification of priorities by an end station is not viable from a security standpoint. While current systems provide no standard means for validating end-node configuration, checksums and authentication that will force end nodes to behave are on the horizon.

Handling traffic

A traffic-handling system must offer differentiated services without noticeable delay. For high-performance networking applications, a switch must be able to classify traffic and forward it without slowing the traffic down appreciably.

"Noticeable delay" is variable. For a low-speed WAN link, sophisticated classification of packets can be performed with a great deal of granularity without slowing down the traffic. Conversely, a router between two Gigabit Ethernet (GE) segments must perform classification and handling in microseconds. Buffering discrepancies between disparate link types—such as aggregating workgroup switch 10-Mbps links into a shared 100-Mbps uplink to the campus backbone—requires sufficient memory to smooth out bursty traffic by buffering it so that the network doesn't become choked with retransmissions.

A device's ability to handle traffic is a function of its hardware and software features. With today's fast, cheap processors, a networking device that interfaces to a slow link (such as a T1) is not the bottleneck—it can simulate multiple queues in software. For wire-speed handling at Fast Ethernet or Gigabit Ethernet speeds, queues must generally be designed into the system's hardware.

Bandwidth congestion occurs at these slow-link boundaries, and good traffic management can fix the problem. Software-based handling is sufficient for LAN-WAN interfaces, since they forward traffic at comparatively slow speeds. Unfortunately, network peering points—the places at which service providers exchange information—are sources of additional delay in many networks. Clearly, enterprises can do little to regulate this kind of congestion, other than trying to stay within a single service provider.

There are generally two types of traffic restriction—handling queues on the device, or modifying rate-control and sliding-window flow-control information to change behavior on the end nodes. Throttles work by putting traffic into queues, where it is admitted into the bandwidth-constrained link according to queuing algorithms. Rate-control and sliding-window control systems modify sender behavior. Sliding-window controllers alter the values of TCP windows to restrict admission from end nodes into the network. Purveyors of throttling systems criticize rate-control or sliding-window systems, pointing to the variance in Internet protocols as a proof that such systems may become proprietary and that they apply only to flow-controlled protocols like TCP. Similarly, rate-control vendors criticize throttles by observing that they can create additional overhead on the network and are less efficient.

Higher-layer systems (those that work on network or session protocols) are by definition protocol specific; an IPTOS system will not help your DECNet application flow more smoothly. On the other hand, lower-layer systems like Ethernet switches (which handle both IP and DECNet traffic) cannot generally classify traffic at higher layers, so they rely more heavily on clients to classify network traffic.

Sophisticated traffic handlers allocate excess bandwidth and oversubscription according to still more rules. Important applications that are exceeding their permitted traffic limits may use a portion of the "general use" bandwidth if excess capacity exists. Furthermore, if a reserved portion of bandwidth is unused, it may be available to otherwise unqualified applications.

Monitoring the effects of a policy

Monitoring the effects of traffic management is challenging. The network may (rightly) treat an intrusive test protocol differently from the application you're trying to study. You may ping a link and get different queue treatment or a different path than that assigned to a video stream if congested. Even if your ping *is* handled in the same way, "probe" type measurements don't detect queue behavior well. What's more, the applications themselves often won't let you see response times; an agent on the end node is the best way to monitor activity.

Perhaps more importantly, administrative domains and internetwork politics will get in the way of end-to-end analysis across multiple domains—which is precisely where QOS is most desirable. Industry initiatives are underway to respond to these problems, but they're not ready yet—so administrators are faced with relying on trusty tools like ping and traceroute, as well as application round-trip measurement.

Current network-monitoring tools generally do not report sufficient information to identify individual streams of traffic without putting the network devices into debug or promiscuous mode. For this reason, monitoring negotiated QOS is challenging. In an RSVP network, a policy server is the most "aware" node in the network, because it knows about all QOS policy-control assignments and has all admission decisions reported to it. Unfortunately, policy-server monitoring and reporting systems are in their infancy. In fact, the first deployment of RSVP uses only admission control—each node makes its own local decisions without consulting a central decision point such as a policy server.

Some vendors have defined MIBs for multiservice networks that will allow management systems to monitor the behavior of discrete classes of traffic. The challenge here is to separate "background" traffic from important traffic. In a multiservice network, a congested link may be misleading; if business-critical traffic is uninterrupted and the remainder of available bandwidth is used for low-priority or unimportant traffic (i.e., Pointcast, video games), then the network is efficiently apportioned.

Stepping back from QOS deployment: A strategic perspective

The techniques we'll look at happen in real time. Classifications and perhaps behaviors change as traffic flows are established and torn down. It is nevertheless important to consider the architectural strategy of the organization.

Neither traffic prioritization, nor throttling, nor the deployment of multiple circuits will overcome poor network design. An improperly architected network will suffer from outages, routing flaps, points of oversubscription and of excess capacity, and costly inefficiencies. What's more, measuring the effect of policies in a network is nearly impossible without an understanding of the network architectures—a ping may report a different latency than the one experienced by true videoconferencing traffic. To complicate matters, determining proper network architecture may be difficult with a changing mix of applications and less-than-complete knowledge about how the network is actually used.

Real-time traffic handling is a useful way of managing oversubscription and reducing latency on a per-packet or per-flow basis to handle planned exceptions or congestion. Managing QOS begins with a strategy for performance management beyond the individual classification and handling of traffic on each box. It begins with proper network architecture. The ultimate goal of bandwidth management must be to reduce the real-time classification, throttling, and retransmission that needs to occur.

This can be achieved by identifying trends in network capacity early on and adjusting network design to mitigate the trends' effects before they cause an unwanted delay. Also, the organizational response time—the time it takes IT to correct a problem—is often as important as the packet response time. While classification and handling of network traffic is at the root of deploying a multilayer network, it is important not to neglect the network-management processes and organizational systems that can maintain network operations.

Identifying the traffic at a strategic level

The information that flows through an organization has varying levels of importance to a business. Outside of the IT department, however, most people do not realize that they *can* assign different priorities to different kinds of information. Strategic management of traffic is a political shift within the organization; IT must take a more active role in understanding the business processes upon which the company is dependent.

At the outset, it is wise to pick a small subset of the information on the network. Find the most important piece of the company—the trading application or order-entry system, for example. Then work with the departments that manage the content of those systems, and make them aware of the multiservice capabilities you can implement. Set priorities on the network devices accordingly; this may mean interaction between the managers of the network, PC's, and servers.

Critical traffic generally will be a specific application (for example, SAP) or will center around a specific platform (for example, a server cluster). You can use port numbers or flows to identify traffic on a tactical level, but when working at the strategic level you must try to understand the long-term implications of the application. Is it likely to grow to encompass voice? Will it become real-time conversational? Will workgroup collaboration be a factor? Is the system likely to migrate to an extranet (meaning encryption and harder classification) or a well-known interface such as a Web server (meaning a change from port to flow)?

Begin to track these critical business flows. Trend them, and share the trends with the relevant managers in order to anticipate and plan for network expansion—or the reduction of competing traffic, if appropriate. At the strategic level, there may be alternatives to the real-time handling and classification.

Regulating traffic is not the only strategic option. By implementing local mirroring and caching, you may be able to reduce congestion. Similarly, replication of important information using directories may lessen the burden on WAN links.

Handling the traffic at a strategic level

Deploying classifiers and handlers can hide poor strategic design of the network. If the architecture of your existing LAN is not suited to the applications you run, bandwidth management may be able to correct some of your problems, albeit suboptimally.

One important shift, as we have seen, is the move from a routed core to a switched core. Routers served a purpose of broadcast containment in the LAN, nicely dividing it up into clean subnets of 256 nodes. With broadcast throttling and automated addressing systems making these issues less and less important, a switched network core makes more sense. Routers are still essential—but with so much traffic running on IP and IP over Ethernet, layer-3 switches are sufficient for the majority of traffic. Because they are software based and can be modified to understand stateful application signaling, traditional routers are good at handling stateful traffic. They also excel at integration with legacy LANs such as DECNet.

What's most important is that the network architecture matches the application need. A call center will require switching to the desktop to handle concurrent voice and video; a distributed organization may need multicast capabilities, for example, because the president's weekly briefings hold the company's personnel together. Look at the information flows, then at how your network handles them. From this, design the ideal infrastructure. Then plan a gradual migration beginning with inflection points—the places in the network where a small change has a great deal of effect in terms of cost, performance, or user satisfaction. Classic candidates for such makeovers include server forms, LAN/WAN interfaces, and high-volume segments for CAD/CAM or visualization work.

Monitoring the effects at a strategic level

Deploying a multiservice network means changing the ways in which you assess the health of the information infrastructure. Measuring traffic levels across a given link won't give you the per-application information you need. Instead, you need trend analysis and application-specific monitoring. Historical trend analysis can be readily adapted to a differentiated services network. Most trending tools offer grouping features; by grouping types of traffic according to the classifier mappings that exist on network devices, you can understand how "business critical" or "background" traffic is changing over time. By comparing real-time usage to these historical trends and measuring growth or decline against business objectives, you can plan for network growth.

Planning a multiservice network at a strategic level isn't much different from planning a traditional network. You simply have a new set of requirements (real-time, low-latency) and a new set of tools (prioritization, queuing, switching-to-the-desktop) to meet these requirements. On the other hand, the *political* ramifications of a multiservice network are significant. Now, different users can get different treatment, and it falls to the network administrator to act as arbiter among the various factions within the company. Armed with an understanding of the true business objectives, you will be equipped to make defensible decisions and ensure that the network behaves according to the goals of the organization rather than according to political whim.

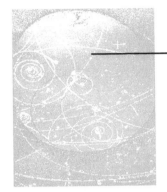

Classification— identifying the traffic

Traffic is classified according to a number of attributes in the protocol stream, as well as by the state of the application that generated the traffic. There are many obstacles to highly granular classification, from packet encryption to scalability and security concerns. Depending on the circumstances of the organization, classification can occur at many locations in the network.

Now that we've taken a high-level look at the classification and handling of traffic in a network, we'll delve into the specific technologies that exist to classify traffic in device.

Classification is the identification of traffic. Through classification, a network devices may discover the transmitting and receiving nodes, the packet coloring that has been applied by other devices, the application, the user, and even the function being performed (purchasing versus browsing, for example.) In general, classification is performed at a specific location according to a comparison with traffic contents. Indirect information not carried in the packet itself—such as "user identity"—is obtained through lookups to network authorities.

As a network designer working with today's equipment, you can choose either fast classification or granular classification. Detailed classifications that involve lookups before traffic is forwarded introduce delays that are unacceptable on a packet-by-packet basis. A high-level classification such as user identity at session setup may be acceptable if the session is being authenticated anyway, or if the hold time of the session is significant compared to the delay. In other words, a user lookup to retrieve a small GIF from a Web site makes no sense; a lookup before playing a 2-hour-long streamed video session is fine.

Classification is performed on a packet-by-packet basis (looking at traffic characteristics and acting in a certain way) or on a session-by session basis (the transmitter negotiates end-to-end before sending). Packet-by-packet classification can be based on traditional access-list information such as source address, destination address, and port number. It can also be based on a relatively small number of "tags" like 802.1p or IPTOS.

We've seen the three biggest enemies of classification (popular-port gravity, the jumping-port problem, and tunnel opacity). All of these prevent a classifier from determining the true nature of the application that generated the traffic by looking at information within the packet itself.

Where on the network does classification make sense?

Classification can occur at a number of places in the network. Some devices may classify traffic, but not handle it differently; others may handle it based on packet coloring from upstream classifiers, but not otherwise classify it. Some devices may perform both classification and handling.

Network cores are less well suited to granular classification for a variety of reasons:

- As we approach the network core, the capacity of a link increases. The core of a LAN backbone may run at gigabit speeds; in a WAN environment, OC-3 and OC-12 are matched by faster routers and greater fiber capacity.

- The core of the network is less suited to the needs of the end systems. In an internetwork, there is no guarantee that the managers of the network core will know what traffic is urgent for you (making box-by-box classification difficult). Nor may they know whether you are entitled to improved performance (making negotiated reservations unlikely.)

- The number of discrete source and destination addresses (flows) that the devices will see in the core increases. Most workgroup switches in today's network see traffic going to or from users in that workgroup. A rule based on the address of someone in that group can be stored on the device, and there will be relatively few rules as a result. In the core of the network, however, thousands or even millions of rules would need to be assigned in order to deliver the same level of classification granularity. Consequently, we sacrifice granularity for raw performance as we move toward the core. We select a simple common denominator such as the 8 levels of priority in the IP precedence fields that exist both at the edge of the network and in the core.

- Granularity vanishes in the core. The use of classless interdomain routing (CIDR) to advertise contiguous blocks of addresses efficiently makes it harder to deliver personalized settings in the core. A node at 192.1.1.1, part of a class C subnet, may find itself advertised as 192.1.0.0/16 in the core by an ISP that owns the 192.1.0.0 subnet of which its network is a component. Such a scheme makes it difficult for a core router to apply policies to 192.1.1.0/8 without applying them to 192.1.2.0/8 as well. The alternative—advertising 192.1.1.0/8 in addition to 192.1.0.0/16—is possible, but it undermines the route-aggregation benefits of CIDR.

The fundamental problem is one of scaling classification information. Occasionally, network administrators will want to take classification to the subnet or even the individual host level. If this degree of granularity is transmitted in routing tables, however, the amount of information in the core explodes.

Sidebar

CIDR formatting

By 1993, the Internet was facing two real problems:

- Routers were becoming increasingly overloaded in the number of routes they had to carry

- The IP address space was rapidly running out

IP addresses are simply 32-bit numbers—4,294,967,296 of them, to be precise. This amount must have seemed like a huge excess when the Internet was first conceived. Unfortunately, the way addresses are allocated is very wasteful. An IP address consists of two things: a network address and a host address. Address allocation is akin to the postal system, in which a letter recipient is identified by both the house address and the recipient's name. For example, imagine that you live on a street with several houses. A letter coming to you would be addressed to your street and house number, then to your name. A letter arriving for someone else at the same house would be labeled with the same street address, but with the other recipient's name.

IP addresses work the same way: the "street address" is the portion of the IP address called the "network address." The network address allows devices on the internetwork to locate the proper destination network. Uniquely identifying the correct destination node on the target network is done using the "host" portion of the address. Only the local router needs to know how to get to the final node. Unlike a postal address, however, an IP address makes no clear delimitation between the "street address" and the "person."

In the past, deciding where the network address ended and the host address began was done with a system called "classful" addressing. All IP addresses between 1 and 126 were considered "Class A," where the network portion was the first 8 bits and the host portion the next 24 bits. By this model, there could be up to 126 class A networks, each consisting of 16,777,216 (2^{24}) hosts. All IP addresses starting with numbers between 128 and 191 were considered "Class B," where the network and host portion were 16 bits each. That meant there could be 16,128 class B networks, each of 65,534 hosts. Networks between 192 and 223 were "Class C," where the network portion was the first 24 bits, and the host portion was 8 bits, allowing for only 254 possible hosts. Hosts above 224 were reserved for multicast addresses. Table 8–1 describes the differences between each class.

Table 8–1   Host and network components of classful IP addressing

Class	Network portion	Host portion	Address range
A	8 bits	24 bits (16,777,216 hosts)	1.*.*.* to 126.*.*.*
B	16 bits	16 bits (16,128 hosts)	127.1.*.* to 191.255.*.*
C	24 bits	8 bits (254 hosts)	192.1.1.* to 223.255.255.*
Multicast			224.* to 255.*

Consider that, under this classful IP address scheme, there was no intermediate step between a class B (65,534 hosts) and class C (256 hosts). To pursue our analogy, there were a few very, very long streets; some quite long streets; and many very short streets. No intermediate steps meant that networks were either granted a class B, and ended up wasting most of their address space, or were granted multiple class C addresses and ended up maintaining many separate class C's to support their hosts. Table 8–2 provides some examples of classful addresses.

Table 8–2   Sample classful IP addresses

Sample address	Class	Network	Host
18.72.0.100	A	18	72.0.100
132.205.7.63	B	132.205	7.63
199.84.5.1	C	199.84.5	1

As the Internet grew, it became clear that the classful system was wasting now-valuable IP address space and was filling the routing tables in core routers with many tiny class C routes. To reduce the danger of address shortages for networks and to ease the burden on routers, the class-based system was replaced with classless interdomain routing (CIDR). Rather than a strict regimen of three types of address, the division between network and host number was made variable. The routes in the network core included in their routing tables not only the address, but also the specific point at which to split the address.

For example, imagine that you ran a network with 512 hosts and, under the classful system, you had two class C addresses: 199.1.0.* and 199.1.1.*. A routing table might have expressed these as two routes, each with 24 bits of network address and 8 bits of host address. Instead, under CIDR, we can aggregate contiguous addresses. Instead of treating the two class C's as two separate networks (24 bits network, 8 bits host), you can treat them as one network of 23 bits of network and 9 bits of host, expressing it as 199.1.0/23. The CIDR address means fewer routes in the routing table and may also result in fewer wasted addresses.

CIDR has some hefty constraints, however. Blocks of network addresses must be binary contiguous—that is, they must aggregate cleanly. So it would be acceptable to have the address 199.1.0/22 if you had contiguous class C addresses from 199.1.0.* to 199.1.3.*; however, if someone else owned 199.1.3.*, you'd have to use two or three routes for your three addresses.

CIDR is useful in the core of the networks, where it allows routes to be aggregated and exchanged more efficiently. It reduces the core's ability to classify traffic based on source network (for example, to offer one subscriber preferential treatment or a different route), but IPTOS will allow coarse differentiation based on application instead.

In an IntServ-based system such as RSVP, the implicit assumption is that admission control, based on dynamically established filter specifications and associated handling characteristics, occurs at the periphery of the network. These admission controls are based on both capacity and policies about appropriate usage. To extend service differentiation across the core, we must associate RSVP service levels with tags to compensate for the lack of granularity and absence of organizational awareness in the core.

End-system classification and tagging

The end station is the ideal place for classification of traffic. Networking vendors and OS vendors are introducing classification capabilities into their stacks and drivers.[1] Because the end station has perfect visibility into the application and user that is generating the traffic, it is the ideal place to perform tagging at the network and link layers in preparation for transmission. On the other hand, because bandwidth is a scarce resource, end-node classification can't always be trusted—users may alter their classification settings to get better performance, at the expense of more important network traffic.

Schemes for authenticating classification settings from desktops are underway but have not yet hit the standards bodies. In the interim, a highly trusted environment where IT has control of desktops may be suitable for end-node classification (in a bank or trading brokerage, for example.) A school environment is probably not well suited to end-node classification, however: even if a network manager could coordinate the installation of common end-node software or hardware, students would thwart whatever controls were put in place.

Classification on the end node may be useful even if the classification information will be overwritten downstream. Imagine that a desktop is downloading a file via FTP in the background, while using an interactive whiteboard application. The file-transfer traffic, sending packets with the maximum Ethernet frame size, may interfere with the small UDP packets that the interactive application sends. You can overcome network interface bottlenecks by using a desktop classification and prioritization system, even if any packet coloring the desktop performs is ignored or overwritten later in the network path.

In addition to their sophisticated classification capabilities, end systems probably have all the tools they need to handle traffic already. The means at their disposal for packet handling include:

- the adjustment of the number packets in transit by altering session-layer parameters in the TCP stack, such as window size
- the sequencing of packets as they leave the desktop as a result of interleaving or queuing
- the marking of packets for later handling, using media and network-layer identifiers

Exotic implementations might even select from several possible routes on a LAN segment, or select from multiple VLANs on a single switch port using the latest Ethernet extensions. These kinds of specialized systems introduce substantial complexity into desktop administration—most users will be on a specific LAN or VLAN and will use the default route on their broadcast segment for all traffic.

Intermediate device classification

Switched network links to the end system push oversubscription into the core of the network. Where a shared 10-MB hub might have introduced access delay in the past, now that delay is on the uplink out of the wiring closet, or in buffer overruns on the switch.

If equipment in the wiring closet is sufficiently sophisticated, it may be able to classify on the basis of some broad settings. A sample wiring-closet default rule might be, "All traffic is best effort, with some notable exceptions for RIP, OSPF, and Peoplesoft." However, in modern wiring closets layer-2 devices typically prevail; today's bottlenecks are in the Gigabit core rather than in the switched concentrators of the network periphery.

In the core, classification should be restricted to "colored" packets (ATM QOS, IPTOS, 802.1p) and a few critical protocols that can be identified by well-known ports (such as network-management traffic.) A model of classification at the edge into a high-capacity core is the simplest approach to deploying multiservice LANs and WANs.

High granularity is vastly more complex in the core of a LAN or a public WAN, where a device must aggregate many streams of data and manage competition for scarce resources. Performing per-user classification means that too many flows must exist on the core devices; as a result, classification will generally be:

- for applications based on Assigned Numbers (port 80 for Web)

- for network-critical traffic, especially traffic going to or from the device itself rather than just "passing through" (RIP and the Simple Network Management Protocol, or SNMP)

- For network-layer tags (IPTOS)

- For link-layer information (802.1p, ATM QOS, MPLS)

- For signaling protocols that request special handling of a packet by a router (RSVP)

- For well-known servers with static addresses

LAN/WAN edge

The LAN/WAN edge consists of a pair of devices. One is owned by the enterprise, and its main goal is to transmit LAN traffic across the WAN in a sensible fashion while verifying that the company is getting the service levels for which it has contracted. The other is owned by the service provider, and its main goal is to provide error-free service within the bounds of the customer's service and to gather accounting and billing information.

Boundary devices must also maintain mappings between LAN media priority and WAN prioritization schemes. They may associate Ethernet frames with differentiated frame relay circuits, MPLS labels, ATM circuits, or specific WAN links. Finally, because of exposure to the public network, boundary devices must maintain additional security and authentication capabilities that are not needed within the LAN.

On LAN/WAN interfaces, the increased need for security and slower WAN links masks the delays that occur with high-granularity classification. As a result, classification and policing on a WAN link almost always makes sense even when the traffic has been classified elsewhere.

The high cost of WAN bandwidth means that traffic-management offerings are plentiful at the boundary between the LAN and the WAN. In addition to the traditional router, products exist to regulate between the networking device and the CSU/DSU and at the head-end box between the T1 interface and the WAN circuit.

Combination

The most effective system for most LANs will be a combination of end-station or edge-router application identification combined with a prioritization of traffic in the core of the network. The boundary devices can "help" by more tightly regulating expensive public communications, performing a policing function. Once the rules are stored in a universal central repository and published in a controlled manner, the policy system is complete.

Such a system can effectively address issues like encryption, while allowing relatively fast traffic handling using layer-2 and -3+ ASICs for cost-effective LAN infrastructure.

A system that involves multiple devices assumes some degree of standardization about the meaning of relative priorities. If an IP precedence value of 1 means high priority to the desktop, but low priority to the core, you have a serious problem.

Most QOS systems are based on the notion that handling of traffic will be better than, or at least as good as, best effort. During congestion, "opposed" priorities mean that *your* network will discard priority 5 over priority 1; they also mean that your neighbor will discard priority 1 traffic in favor of his priority-5 traffic. Opposed priorities can deliver worse-than-best-effort network service.

In the absence of standardization, you should at least ensure that your outbound packet classification is consistent with that of the network into which you are sending traffic. Inbound classification must also map consistently. Such consistency can be accomplished through properly configured filters, but access lists may introduce delays that are unacceptable on high-speed links. Nevertheless, without standards to define *how* to handle a given traffic type, checking prioritization consistency is the best way to ensure properly shared classification with your peers.

Levels of maturity in classification

Many policy systems are in fact per-device rules that must be awkwardly replicated across devices. Mature policy systems include a central repository across multiple devices via a standard protocol such as LDAP.

Similarly, devices vary in the level of classification they can perform. A simple matching of flows means comparing IP and TCP information without any statefulness, as the device does not distinguish between an established TCP session and one that is being set up. A more comprehensive classifier distinguishes between the various states of a protocol.

Some vendors' 'application' policies are actually port matching. Only devices that interact with the application, such as desktops, servers, caches, proxies, and load-balancers, can deliver true application-level classification.

Classification down the stack

We will now look in detail at the various types of information available for classification, following the OSI reference model of networking layers.

Generally, the ultimate goal of classifying traffic is to extract from its *intrinsic* characteristics (the link and network addresses, the protocol and port numbers, and the like) as much *extrinsic* information as possible. Extrinsic information consists of details such as what application generated the traffic or what user sent it.

Many network nodes run services that can convert from one type of information to another. For example, a DNS server converts from a domain name (www.mycorp.com) to an IP address (191.2.3.4). Table 8–3 lists the various network authorities and the information they can provide.

Table 8–3   Examples of network authorities and the identification services they offer

	VLAN manager	Physical topology	Asset database	DHCP	DNS	Radius server	Network server
What you know	**What you get from the server**						
Port (12.3.4.5:01)	VLAN group	Location				Dialed number/ Dialing number	
MAC address	VLAN group		Equipment owner	IP address			User login
IP address					Domain name		
Domain name (fred.acme. com)					IP address		
User/password	VLAN group		HR record			Identity	MAC, Network address

The highest level: User identification

If you have someone's IP address, you don't have the person. Many classification systems claim "user" integration or "user-based" rules. In reality, they rely on static or dynamic mapping between users and address assignment. Address-based classification may be acceptable, depending on the potential for QOS abuse in your network. We call this an *inferred user-identification system*, in contrast to the *user authentication* that occurs when user identity is verified through a password or some other authentication mechanism.

DHCP itself is designed to facilitate moves, adds, and changes to a network by automating the assignment of address, subnet mask, and server information. It works especially well in large, flat, LAN topologies with many host addresses per broadcast domain. These are typically network architectures in which routing is secondary to switching. Subnets were historically useful for subdividing broadcast domains, allowing broadcast containment and routing. Today's switched network often has more than 256 nodes per subnet, made possible through broadcast containment and increased network capacity.

The information that is stored in a DHCP server is essentially a table associating IP addresses with MAC addresses and other network resources (such as DNS servers). You may have a DHCP service in your network; to leverage this information, the network's policy components need to have access to the DHCP content in order to present information on a per-user or per-group basis. It is important to distinguish between the DHCP *content* and a DHCP *service*; the latter is a system specifically tasked with the assignment and retraction of time-limited address assignments (called leases).

For an inferred user-identification system, you must translate from lower-layer classifiers (such as MAC or IP address) to user identity. A typical sequence of lookups might be:

1. A user turns on her computer, requesting an IP address. The DHCP server now knows the MAC address of her network interface card and determines the IP address assigned to it. Alternately, login might result in the mapping of an IPX address to a login name.

2. This association is stored in a central database or directory.

3. The user logs into a network server, at which point a username and password are associated with the IP address.

4. The username and password correspond to a unique Distinguished Name (DN), such as "acroll.marketing.building2.Boston.acme.com", which points to one and only one user.

At this point, any device that sees the MAC or IP address can look it up in the central database and obtain the authenticated identity of the user.

There are other ways of associating links and users. In a dial-up environment, password negotiation occurs before the network protocols are negotiated, making reliable identification of the user far simpler. Some organizations may maintain an asset database that lists the MAC address, making it possible to immediately identify the likely user of the asset, once the MAC database is integrated with network configuration.

Such a system may be sufficient for managing performance in a network. It is certainly not strong authentication, however, as an evildoer can overcome the identification in a number of ways:

- A hacker can wait for the user to disconnect, then access the network using the same IP address but circumventing DHCP. In this case, the information in the database will still point to the first user.

- A hacker can change the MAC address to that of the user and perform a DHCP broadcast, thereby obtaining that user's IP address.

- A hacker can use someone else's machine or log on to a shared device.

More robust security systems such as X.509 make it harder to spoof name-to-address associations. On the other hand, if you have people circumventing identification to get better network performance, you probably have bigger problems than bandwidth management. Consequently, in many organizations an inferred user-identification system is sufficient.

DHCP content alone will not provide user identity. By combining DHCP with other network services and following a chain of information, however, network systems can suggest the likely identity of the source of traffic. Directory systems and improved login procedures promise to ease user-based classifications as standards mature. Directory systems are a common structure for sharing this information across multiple devices from multiple vendors, making all information about a sender available in one lookup.

Non-IP user classification

In a non-IP environment, network operating system (NOS) policy systems may have access to user information based on vendor-specific logins. Microsoft's NT Proxy Server, for example, or Novell's BorderManager, both apply user- and group-based policies to traffic by using the network login to authenticate and identify users before they are granted access.

NOS-based policy systems are useful for user classification but are generally limited to a local network. As NOS vendors embrace open systems for propagating directory and user information, the NOS information will allow user-level classification across more and more devices. Microsoft's ActiveDirectory and Novell's NDS 5.0 both offer hooks for associating a user's identity with address information, as do DHCP servers from Cisco Systems, Lucent Technologies, and Nortel Networks. UNIX users are still a problem: their identity is not readily exposed, owing to the relatively independent features of their operating systems' network services.

The real value of users is groups

A bigger question must be asked before implementing user-based classification. Does your QOS solution require user-based policies at all? Few administrators want to adjust the network on a per-user basis. The real promise of a policy is in grouping users into logical sets, so that the network can afford the group performance characteristics that are commensurate with their role in the organization.

In earlier days, this was achieved by physically locating users on common networking equipment. Today, however, increased mobility of workers and dynamic "workgroup" organizational structures make physical configuration difficult. To make matters worse, IT is burdened with constant moves, adds, and changes.

To reduce this burden, IT can integrate policy systems with directories. This allows others to make changes to the organizational structure and tells the network to take its cue from this structure. Users inherit network behavior from their place in the organizational chart. The rule about how the network should behave for someone in marketing, for example, is a function of the default corporate rules, the rules for marketing, and the rules for that individual, as shown in Figure 8–1.

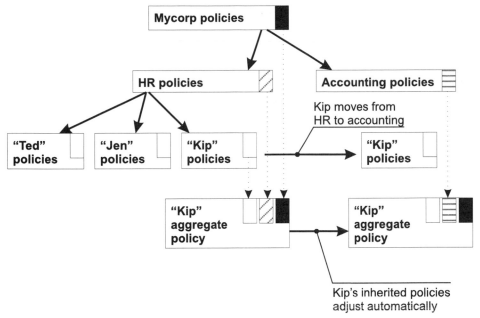

Figure 8–1   Aggregate policies in a directory tree are a function of defaults, inheritance, and individual values

If someone moves from one department to another, the network's behavior changes accordingly. In Figure 8–1, Kip's aggregate policy—the final decision on how the network should behave for him—is a function of default rules ("mycorp policies"), inherited exceptions ("manufacturing policies"), and individual policies ("Kip policies"). When someone in the company moves Kip from Manufacturing to HR, the aggregate policy changes accordingly.

This is a far more pragmatic approach than per-user policies, since the default policies will suffice for most employees and the departmental exceptions will suffice for the remainder. Occasionally, special adjustment of individual policies may also be needed.

User-based classification presents us with some challenging problems. A user may be a part of two groups and may inherit conflicting policies from each, as Figure 8–2 illustrates

This means that each hierarchy will need a priority of its own (for example, "organizational exceptions are overridden by functional exceptions"). It should be clear by now that the ability to classify users and generate useful policies from their membership in specific organization groups is a challenging and complex one. The long-term benefits of doing

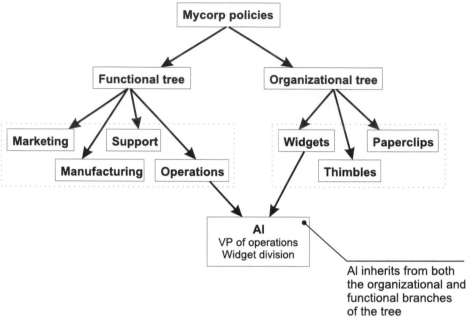

Figure 8–2   Multiple inheritance in a directory tree

so will undoubtedly lead to systems that can perform true user-based policies and that are integrated with HR and enterprise requirements planning (ERP) systems. In the short term, however, it falls to network managers to group their users logically and apply policies to those logical groupings through a variety of vendors' user interfaces that offer limited sharing of data or import capabilities.

Looking forward: Network authentication

A number of technologies on the horizon may allow traffic classification systems to move directly to user identity without referring to a series of network authorities in the ways we've seen.

IP version 6 offers some hope with authenticated addresses, but it will be years before enterprise networks can reap the benefits of planned enhancements to IP, since they will generally require significant forklift hardware updates. Similarly, some vendors have link-layer authentication in LAN environments that parallels dial-up authentication; as soon as a user connects to a switch, they transmit a username and password that is relayed to a central database. There are even some proprietary systems today that combine VLANs, short-lease DHCP clients, and login schemes to authenticate users before allowing them access to anything but a safe, "demilitarized" VLAN.

Once networks authenticate users and associate them with network addresses, user-level classification in the workgroup becomes substantially easier. User identification does not alter core routing issues, where the number of users generating traffic is too high for efficient classification. However, local routers will soon be able to implement dynamic firewalls by identifying flows and querying a directory on which a link-layer-authenticated user's addressing information has been stored, which will make the promise of user-level policies a reality.

Top-of-the-stack classification: Application

While user-based classification is important for security systems and precise controls, most companies will initially want to prioritize by application. User classification is complex, with multiple hierarchies and authentication confidence levels about which to worry. By contrast, most of the time, application-based classification is sufficient to ease the bottlenecks that are at the root of your congestion problems.

Application-based classification won't prevent the receptionist from getting high priority on a video stream and it won't let you give the CEO preferential treatment for Realaudio traffic. On the other hand, it *will* let you make some real changes to your network quickly, laying the groundwork for more granular user policies down the road.

If you know the application, you can understand both the urgency needs of the traffic it generates and the relative importance of that traffic to the organization. If the application is mission critical, it will win when the network gets congested. If the application is delay-sensitive, it may take a different (and probably more expensive) path across the WAN to ensure a sufficiently tight response time.

True application-based classification is really only possible at layer 7. TCP or UDP port numbers are *pointers* to the application, but they don't let you distinguish between, for example, Web-based access to the employee handbook and Web-based access to the order entry system. Similarly, traffic flows (an aggregate of ports and network addresses) don't give you application classification unless each IP destination service runs only one application.

Intermediate devices can make application-level classification decisions if they work at the application layer. Proxies often reside at a LAN-WAN boundary in order to economize on scarce public network addresses, so they play a critical role in controlling WAN use. Application proxies can check session content by parsing URLs, and the processor overhead from doing so is somewhat hidden by the relatively slow speed of the WAN link itself as well as optimization from a local cache.

Because proxies are generally not deployed inside the corporate LAN (i.e., they're implemented as a security mechanism for LAN-to-Internet connections), they are seldom used for prioritizing use of intranet resources. Application-layer classification is slow; at best, LAN-based proxies can tag traffic destined for a public network with the appropriate prioritization and type-of-service needed to improve performance on the public network when the WAN link supports priorities.

In the LAN, a new class of content-aware load balancing devices can offer application-level classification. The real promise of load balancers, however, is to make server response time a manageable aspect of end-to-end network QOS. Load balancers can also act on behalf of server to tag traffic and participate in bandwidth reservations.

Between flow and application: OSI leftovers

The 5-layer IP model tells us that there are one or more sessions per application. In fact, there are additional divisions between these two extremes, which were discussed in the original OSI work but left out of IP's mantra of "loose consensus and working code." For example, the presentation layer described how traffic generated by a given application was to be presented.

As network devices send traffic to an increasing array of end nodes—from text-only PDAs to digital video-capable desktops—identifying and forwarding the right information in the right presentation format is a task they will have to perform. No standard method of regulating many presentation streams per content currently exists in the TCP/IP stack.

Today's systems use discrete sessions to separate different presentations of the same information (such as the video stream and the accompanying closed captioning.) Networking devices don't classify based on presentation. Instead, they rely on multiple sessions for different formats of the same information, which is inefficient to both the development process and to network usage. As developers write to several of these end nodes, they will expect network services to offer them these capabilities automatically. Such classification capabilities are emerging from vendors like TopLayer and VIPSwitch.

Stateless classification relies on a set of addresses and port numbers to identify traffic between a client and a server, and this kind of classification can distinguish, for example, between file transfers and database queries. It cannot tell the size of the file transfer, however, so devices that do not understand the application can make decisions based only on the current traffic and traffic history, rather than on expected future behavior of a flow.

Transport-level classification: Flow

The Internet Protocols Assigned Numbers (RFC1700) defines a set of reserved values by which a device can identify what sort of protocol is contained in the payload of an IP datagram. It also defines UDP or TCP port numbers for well-known applications. When well-known application port numbers are combined with IP source and destination addresses, they form a unit known as a *flow*, which is generally the most granular piece of information available to an internetwork without some extra out-of-band signaling system to maintain additional information.

From a flow we may be able to deduce the application that generated the traffic, the source of the traffic, and its destination. Anyone who has configured an IP packet filter is familiar with the notion of flows—although, as we have seen, systems like NAT and tunneling, together with the popularity of certain ports, are making flow-based classification less useful in some environments.

The source and destination address are assumed by the classifying device to be the ultimate source and destination of the traffic. The source may in fact be an address translator, an application proxy, or a tunnel initiator. Similarly, the destination may also be an inbound proxy, a firewall, a load-balancer's virtual IP address, or a tunnel end point. In these cases the address is less useful (unless it represents all traffic from a customer or all traffic to a site), but the subnet from which the packet came may be relevant. The fact that traffic comes from a particular subnet that is not paying for a differentiated service may be reason to overwrite any prioritization information contained in the packet.

Flows are generally less useful in the core of the network. While high-speed IP circuitry is reducing the problem of classification delays and will continue to do so, access to the *relevance* of the flow—awareness of the sender's identity and privileges—does not reach the core of a public network. As we have seen in our discussion of CIDR addressing, address information is generally consolidated into blocks for efficiency. Instead of working with individual networks, a network core may work in large, contiguous address blocks. This makes flow-based classification difficult, unless a flow's QOS permissions have been requested ahead of time. The huge number of flows in a core device make this impractical as well—relegating core devices to application port numbers for classification.

The point is relevant no matter the mechanism: for proper flow-based classification, an administrative system of managing address assignment and user permissions is needed.

In many cases, multiple sessions are established by a single application. For example, earlier versions of Web browsers running HTTP 1.0 typically set up four or more concurrent sessions with the same source (the client), destination (the server), and destination TCP port (80). Only the source TCP port differs in order to distinguish each session.

Port convergence and the jumping-port problem

If all an organization's traffic migrates to a well-known, broadly available port—like Web traffic on port 80—then classification becomes harder. Rather than simply identifying port 80 as "http", we now know that it contains both mission-critical accounting data and unimportant Web browsing traffic. In fact, many organizations have punched narrow holes in their firewalls for only a few protocols (such as http). The deployment of restrictive port filters has caused many applications, such as file transfer and RealAudio, to move to the Web port in order to pass through the firewall.

To make matters worse, many applications (such as FTP or the Real Time Streaming Protocol, RTSP) use a dynamically negotiated port number. Dynamic ports make traffic classification difficult, because network devices must listen to conversations on a well-known control port in order to determine which dynamic ports are being used. Such devices are *stateful*, and they generally cost more and perform less quickly than simple packet filters. Nevertheless, stateful devices at the LAN/WAN edge make a lot of sense, as they offer better security and more precise control over who uses expensive WAN bandwidth.

Unfortunately, as many applications move to the Web for a common GUI, it is less likely that a socket number will be useful. A company may migrate its SQL-based customer database to a Web-based front-end. Unless the classification is properly configured, two clients may be reading the same content from a server, but the browser would get standard Web treatment, whereas the SQL client application would get preferential treatment.

Even if a device knows the port number for traffic, retrieving the appropriate handling of that traffic may not be worthwhile. If the packet is transactional and connectionless (that is, small, bursty, and without a setup and tear-down of the socket), then it may not be worth finding out how to classify it unless the rule is stored on the device before the packet arrives.

A number of "utility" packets on the network are unlikely to change ports, however, and can be usefully classified by devices consistently. Router updates and SNMP traffic are fairly important to the health of the network and must be given some portion of the bandwidth at all times; you can also block push news services.

Network prioritization classification: IP TOS

The solution to class-of-service packet identification exists today. It's pervasive, it's simple, and it's supported to at least some degree by every router currently deployed. So why haven't we used it? The short answer is that, while IP contains the necessary fields for end-to-end traffic classification, policies, semantics, a lack of billing, and weak discovery of COS-enabled devices have prevented its use until now.

The Internet adapts dynamically to changing conditions. Paths across the network will behave differently from one another—and differently over time. Paths will vary in terms of reliability, error rate, cost, latency, throughput, and delay variance. Often, one of these parameters will be inversely related to another, such that the lowest-cost link is also the one with the least throughput, or the least jitter-free link is the most reliable.

The Internet has also been designed to cross a wide number of administrative boundaries; for most WAN traffic, one can fairly safely assume that not every network device along the path will be aware of the sender's rights and permissions.

To allow applications and sessions to signal the network layer with their needs, the IP type of service (TOS) byte is a part of the standard IP header. Every IP packet has this stamp that indicates how the packet should be handled. IPTOS was initially defined in Request For Comments (RFC) 792 but has not been filled in consistently until recently. Routers must *support* the TOS byte to be considered standards compliant. Recently reawakened in the face of Internet congestion and the introduction of mission-critical network applications, IPTOS will allow differentiated services across shared packet networks. Because IP is the common denominator for most networks, it is the ideal place for end-to-end COS signaling.

We use the term "TOS" to refer to the entire IPTOS byte; we use the words "type of service" to refer to the specific field within the TOS byte that contains flags for traffic handling.

Some recent standards-body activities, as well as routing protocols that compute route costs based on a variety of metrics, make it feasible for networking devices to consider TOS byte values when forwarding traffic. While the existing IPTOS standards map out a general direction for class-of-service prioritization in IP, the DiffServ discussions currently underway will essentially rewrite the rule book about TOS bits in IP.

The 8 bits of the TOS field are commonly referred to as the TOS byte, illustrated in Figure 8–3. The first 3 bits indicate relative priority of the datagram, known as precedence, and the values these 3 bits can take as well as suggested traffic types are described in RFC 791. The type-of-service field consists of 4 flags for various types of services, and the final bit is unused and must be set to zero.

A packet, once classified can be handled in a number of ways. Priority is an obvious one—which packet goes first when two packets contend for the same outbound capacity. Discard eligibility is another; delay, jitter, and changes to packet tagging are other factors that may affect how a packet is handled.

As RFC 1349 points out, these precious bits in the IP header have a storied past. RFC 791 listed delay, throughput, and reliability metrics

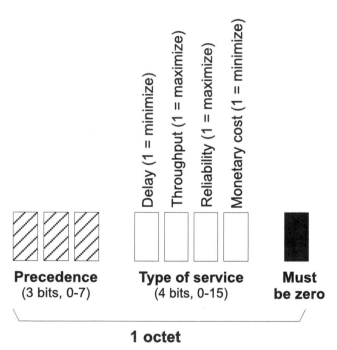

Figure 8–3   Meaning of bits in the IPTOS byte

only; RFC 1122 added the monetary-cost metric, but also included the Must Be Zero (MBZ) field as part of the TOS field. These uses will soon undergo yet another change as part of the differentiated-services effort.

Prioritization

RFC 791 defines the meaning of the eight possible precedence values, as outlined in Table 8–4:

Table 8–4   IPTOS precedence bit meanings as defined in RFC 791

Precedence (binary)	Precedence (integer)	Traffic type
111	7	Network control
110	6	Internetwork control
101	5	CRITIC/ECP
100	4	Flash override
011	3	Flash
010	2	Immediate
001	1	Priority
000	0	Routing

Early TOS byte specifications had a stated goal that a "host should never be penalized for using the TOS facility."[2] While this is an admirable intention, it cannot be sustained in widespread deployment, since a TOS setting that results in preferential handling of traffic during congestion will invariably degrade other, unpreferred traffic as a result. A more realistic statement is to say that packets that use the TOS byte shouldn't be subjected to worse handling than a similar best-effort packet in the same network circumstances.

There is no definition of how a router should behave when receiving these priorities. RFC 791 describes precedence as a "measure of importance" of the packet. The assumption has always been that precedence settings and meanings are network specific, with the definition of behavior being up to the administrator of the network. While early routers implemented for the U.S. defense department used precedence, it was many years before precedence use found its way into commercial router implementations. In response to network congestion and increased complexity, however, router vendors have included traffic-shaping and queuing systems in their devices that can use a variety of IP information (addresses, applications, and other information in the headers of datagrams).

Type of service

Precedence generally guides per-hop behavior (discards, queuing, and link transmission priority), whereas Type of Service generally guides internetwork behavior (route selection, for example).

The meaning of the type-of-service bits is somewhat confusing, since some combinations suggest mutually exclusive behavior from the network device. For example, a TOS value of 5 (0101) means, "Select a path that offers the lowest monetary cost and highest throughput." Such a connection is rare indeed!

Because of this, many people consider the TOS field to have four values, after the definitions provided in RFC 1349. These values are listed in Table 8–5.

Table 8–5   IP type of service values as defined in RFC 1349

TOS value (binary)	TOS value (integer)	Meaning	Suggested use
(per RFC 1700)			
1000	8	Minimize delay	Direct human interaction
0100	4	Maximize throughput	Data transfers with large blocks of data
0010	2	Maximize reliability	Datagram-based management functions
0001	1	Minimize monetary cost	
0000	0	Use default metric	Use default metric

This exposes one of the problems with the existing TOS byte definitions. As we have seen, IP header space is precious and rare. IPV4 is the most broadly deployed networking protocol ever, and we'd better have a good reason if we're going to alter it on the millions of desktops, hosts, routers, and switches that make up today's Internet. But here we have 4 bits, used to represent 5 values. Three bits would suffice, and we'd even have 3 values left over. The use of 4 bits seems almost frivolous in light of the "worth" of a bit in the header.

The original intent of the TOS field was to allocate these five possible values and wait for the Internet community to define other integer values; RFC 1455 is one such example, using path security as a route-selection metric as described in Table 8–6.

Table 8–6   Additional IPTOS value for secure links as defined in RFC 1455

TOS value (binary)	TOS value (integer)	Meaning
1111	15	Maximize security

The assignment of a TOS value cannot be considered a contract for a certain level of performance. For many access routers, for example, the route selected for low delay, low cost, high reliability, high throughput, and default values will be identical.

Choosing the right TOS for traffic types

How can this be used practically?

At first glance, it might seem that a TOS value should be selected for an application, and that traffic from both ends of the network link should use the same TOS value. Upon closer inspection, using different TOS values for transmission and acknowledgment may in fact make sense. Consider that fast notification to the transmitter about packet loss helps TCP to throttle itself back when congestion occurs. Consequently, a highly latency-tolerant file transfer might receive acknowledgments with the TOS field set to 8 (minimize delay) in order to notify the sender of congestion quickly. On the other hand, selection of a different TOS value for transmissions and responses can reduce TCP's ability to correctly estimate the round-trip time in a network. This kind of ambiguity in implementation guidelines has hampered deployment of practical IPTOS-based QOS systems.

The Internet Assigned Numbers listing (RFC 1700, revised frequently) contains information on a wide range of numbering schemes, including well-known ports used in flow classification and IP protocol numbers. It also offers a list of recommended TOS values for specific applications and application types, which we present in Table 8–7

Because a router may select different paths for traffic based on these metrics, a destination may be unreachable using the selected metric, but would be otherwise reachable. ICMP "host unreachable" messages can notify the sender of an unreachable host, and detection of these messages should be the responsibility of the application that generated the traffic. For example, if a low-cost path is unavailable but the destination is reachable across a high-cost path, the application may want to obtain authorization from the user before altering the TOS values it sets in the network and using the more costly path. Similarly, a videoconferencing application that relies on high-bandwidth links may be able to reach a destination via a slow dial-on-demand ISDN backup link, but this would make the application unusable. IPTOS values may imply billing or some other administrative cost, depending on how TOS values affect route selection.

When the initial TOS definitions were written, the number of network devices that could classify traffic individual flows at wire speed and prioritize them was limited. Consequently, existing IPTOS standards focus largely on the appropriate association of TOS-marked packets and routing metrics. If a sender requested that a packet be sent across a highly reliable link, for example, then the router could use a routing table that was derived from reliability metrics instead of the default cost metrics. Cost-based routing protocols like OSPF work well with TOS information.

More recently, Internet drafts by leading network vendors have redefined the TOS byte as a DiffServ field. We discuss the DiffServ use of these bits later in this chapter.

Squatter's rights on the IPTOS bits

The major challenge IPTOS faces is that best effort has been good enough for most of us so far. Nobody agrees on TOS implementations, and multiservice link layers, wire-speed classification, heavy network congestion, and the deployment of delay-sensitive applications have only recently spurred standards-body work into QOS implementation research.:

Table 8–7 Recommended IPTOS values for well-known applications

Protocol	TOS value	Meaning	Notes
Telnet	1000	Minimize delay	Includes all interactive user protocols (e.g. rlogin)
FTP control	1000	Minimize delay	
FTP Data	0100	Maximize throughput	Includes all bulk data-transfer protocols
Trivial FTP (TFTP)	1000	Minimize delay	
Simple mail transport protocol (SMTP) command phase	1000	Minimize delay	
SMTP data phase	0100	Maximize throughput	
DNS UDP query	1000	Minimize delay	
TCP query	0000	Default	
Zone transfer	0100	Maximize throughput	
Network News Transport Protocol (NNTP)	0001	Minimize monetary cost	
Internet control message protocol (ICMP) errors	0000	Default	
ICMP requests	(variable)		Test out TOS value (for example, a ping)
ICMP responses	(variable)		Test out TOS value
Any Internet gateway protocol (IGP)	0010	Maximize reliability	
External gateway protocol (EGP)	0000	Default	
SNMP	0010	Maximize reliability	
Bootstrap protocol (BOOTP)	0000	Default	

This means that IPTOS information hasn't been used to prioritize traffic in a consistent manner. When there are a few precious bytes in a well-defined place that nobody uses, vendors take advantage of the bits to deploy proprietary systems that differentiate their products. Currently these bits are used by some vendors and addressed in the IETF's multiprotocol label switching, but an industry-wide implementation is still awaiting ratification.

Cisco Systems, for example, says that network administrators must select their own settings for IP precedence and TOS bits. Cisco IOS software can map IPTOS to Weighted Fair Queuing (WFQ) algorithms or priority queuing algorithms. Cisco's Open Shortest Path First (OSPF) routing protocols can select from multiple routes based on type-of-service value, and its Weighted Fair Queuing and Netflow Switching software is also affected by TOS values.

Cisco's IP precedence implementation supports values from 0 to 7, with 7 as the highest priority and 0 as the lowest. The default is 0. In this respect, 802.1p and IP precedence seem strongly correlated. In practice, however, 802.1p's specifications of suggested mappings are more tuned to the needs of a converged voice/video/data network, whereas IP precedence is more aimed at WAN and carrier differentiated services.

Cisco routers may filter packets based on precedence (a value from 0–7) or on type-of-service level (a value from 0–15). Admission to a particular queue is based on source or destination IP address, source or destination TCP/UDP port, protocol, or TOS bits.

Cisco devices can partition network traffic into classes based on the 4 TOS bits of the IP header. Cisco offers suggested guidelines consistent with those described in RFC 1349 for IOS TOS defined values and for the metrics that should be used in route determination for a given packet when making cost-based routing decisions.

If vendor implementations of IPTOS mean that packets get handled differently by different devices, the use of IPTOS as an end-to-end QOS mechanism breaks down. Because agreement on *classification* of traffic doesn't mean agreement on *handling* of traffic, interoperability is a major issue. The IETF has handled a number of contentious interoperability issues this way: by defining a subset of the entire system and allowing implementations to "fight it out."

There are two major ways to ensure consistent handling across a network path. The first is to force each device along the path to adhere to specific per-hop behaviors and classifiers. The second is to deploy an overarching management layer that understands the intended handling and configures each device along the path according to local context. As we shall see, this second example describes an end-to-end policy system.

Who colors the IPTOS fields?

The policing function in a network is a way of guarding against theft of service or inappropriate use of network capacity. The need for policing is in many ways a function of how the network is designed, and it focuses mainly on where packet marking and re-marking takes place.

Classification of IPTOS values can occur once at the network periphery, or on a per-hop basis. Remember that per-hop does not mean per-device in today's switched cores. Instead, media-layer coloring or circuit selection may also be needed to ensure proper handling between routers. Subnet bandwidth management, which lets routers act on behalf of adjacent media links, should be an integral part of IPTOS implementation.

If the periphery of the network sets the TOS values, then every device along the path must respond to these settings in a similar fashion. If the periphery of the network is allowed to specify the appropriate level of priority, then admissibility and authentication issues must be resolved in order for the devices to "trust" the node that colored the packet enough to admit the packet. As packets traverse administrative domains, policing becomes a redundant—but necessary—element of the QOS infrastructure.

The policing function involves a trust decision and a re-marking decision; a sample trust algorithm is shown in Figure 8–4.

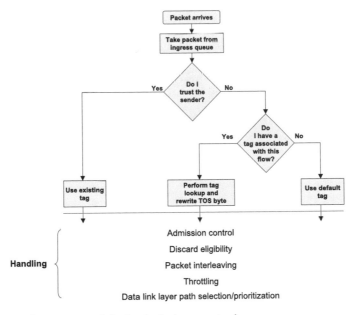

Figure 8–4   A simple trust model of admission control

Trust can also be a function of media-layer membership (in other words, certain VLANs are entitled to certain levels of service.) In some network topologies subnets will be aligned with VLANs, often through a vendor-specific or proprietary mechanism. The benefit of having subnets align with VLANs is that switches, working at layer 2, can more efficiently forward traffic than routers. By allowing switches to switch between VLANs that match subnets, broadcasts can be contained and router delays overcome—with some fast switching schemes, routing in the enterprise may be unnecessary altogether.

This is something of an anachronism. Broadcast containment and cheap layer-3 switching make VLAN-subnet association a stopgap measure for networks with slow routers and VLAN switches. Classifying traffic based on VLAN might be a useful substitute for classifying based on subnet, but this approach is unlikely to survive in the long term. Management of VLANs is generally complex, making it a shaky solution at best.

If OS vendors make authenticated DHCP or link-layer login a reality, user-VLAN association may prove useful. We would have a two-step classification: first, we would classify at the user level with the initial link-layer authentication. Then we would associate the user's traffic with that VLAN and handle subsequent traffic based on layer-2 media membership. We might put engineering on one VLAN and marketing on another. The administration of such a network today is complex, but with automatic user identification, VLANs may yet find a new life.

Should each node along the path decide on IP values for the next hop? Some might say it isn't really an appropriate use for an "internetworking" protocol and should be left to link-layer systems, such as ATM QOS, 802.1p, and prioritized Frame Relay. Perhaps more importantly, if each device looks at each packet and classifies it independently, then the value of IPTOS is questionable. If each node knew that adjacent nodes would just reevaluate and reclassify the traffic before handling it, why color the packet at all? As we have seen, asking the network core to classify traffic with the information that is available to the edge is an untenable prospect.

IPTOS values may help switches (that are unable to classify traffic) to prioritize it anyway—assuming they learn how to read the IPTOS priority fields. In today's switched LAN infrastructures, it is increasingly common for packets to traverse the network without crossing any layer-3 devices other than at the end nodes and access routers. In this case, a desktop that wants priority from a network in which both sender and receiver are on the same Ethernet segment must rely on media-layer signaling, since there are no intermediate routers to work at the IPTOS level.

The IETF standards tell us that a router must not alter precedence settings on packets it did not originate, regardless of whether it implements precedence-ordered queuing itself. Altering precedence information is not appropriate for core routers, but modifications to the TOS bits for discard eligibility, low cost, and so on are fair game. This will be altered by proposals from the differentiated services working group, since router modification of IP precedence information is vital for effective policing. Telling routers not to touch precedence is like giving QOS abusers free reign to use the highest-priority bandwidth in the network.

In link or path selections, type-of-service information is relevant. By contrast, on a hop-by-hop or switch-by-switch basis it is in the handling of the individual frame that precedence matters. Mapping IPTOS to Ethernet priority is ambiguous, because some of the 802.1p values suggest the mission criticality of traffic, while others suggest the traffic's delay sensitivity. In a later section we will revisit the issue and consider a recent proposal for using the 802.1p values to characterize an Ethernet cloud for routers.

Other uses for TOS information

Some proponents of congestion management want to set aside 2 of the 8 bits to allow routers to communicate congestion levels to one another in order to proactively throttle back traffic before congestion gets too high (rather than relying on TCP detection of congestion and subsequent transmission reduction).

There is currently no explicit congestion notification in IP. Packets must make a round trip before senders can infer congestion, and receivers are unaware of congestion issues. Explicit congestion notification—which is available in ATM and Frame Relay—may make networking stacks better able to anticipate and compensate for network bottlenecks. This would reduce the time that it takes for a sender to become aware of network delays, and it would also allow link-layer connections that can signal congestion explicitly to inform the network layer of such congestion without discarding traffic.

As a final note, on December 5, 1997, British Telecom Labs filed a patent-application disclosure indicating that it has applied for a patent relating to the support of differential IP QOS. As Internet congestion becomes an increasingly important issue, it is likely that many proprietary schemes will emerge and migrate toward "standards," and similar claims will arise from other vendors. Hopefully, such intellectual-property discussions will not interfere with the improvement of public network support for differentiated services.[3]

Differentiated Services work and the DS field

The Differentiated Services standards are an outgrowth of the Integrated Services work in the IETF.[4] DiffServ is a response to the scalability and deployment obstacles posed by end-to-end reservations across wide-area links. The long-term goal for DiffServ is to eliminate the need for RSVP reservations across the WAN, and it promises to integrate easily with Multi-Protocol Label Switching devices at the edge of the WAN core.

RSVP's scaling issues stemmed from the mechanism's need to manage stateful decisions at each hop of the network path. In order to control different traffic flows in different ways, RSVP assigns each flow a session identifier. When a packet arrives at an RSVP device, the device must figure out to which session the packet belongs and then handle it accordingly. The number of sessions grows dramatically as more and more people share the device, making it difficult and expensive to deploy in WAN cores.

DiffServ assumes that some capacity in the network has been set aside ahead of time for a particular class of traffic—in this respect, it is somewhat like a reservation. Rather than having each device determine the session to which a DiffServ packet belongs, however, DiffServ marks the IPTOS field so that intermediate nodes can classify on a packet-by-packet rather than session-by-session basis.

Most of the work in the 802.1p and IPTOS fields revolves around how to distill complex, multidimensional policy decisions into a relatively simple set of values that can be usefully deployed at high speeds by many vendors. ATM has tried to represent the set of performance attributes needed for a QOS implementation, but ATM standards lack the simplicity of IP and are replete with "slightly overlapping" parameters that can hinder the deployment of highly granular QOS in multivendor ATM environments. It is this multivendor interoperability that represents the ultimate goal for DiffServ (at the expense of some degree of control when compared with ATM).

The IETF differentiated services working group is redefining the use of the IP version 4 type-of-service information, as well as similar information in IPv6. The DiffServ group will decide on 256 possible values that the 8 IPTOS bits can contain to indicate to devices that a packet is to be handled in a special way. In fact, they won't allocate all 256 values to begin with; anywhere from 2 to 8 levels of priority will properly address most of today's networking needs for prioritization, and 8 levels maps neatly to 802.1p.

The new byte is called the DiffServ byte. By contrast with many of the complex, end-to-end systems that have emerged in recent years, Diff-Serv's preference for "simple and coarse" methods make this an appealing first step in internetwork class-of-service systems. The group is also focusing on "common understanding," which has been lacking in earlier TOS specifications.

The DiffServ charter

The DiffServ charter is spelled out in the working group's mailing list, accessible at
`http://www-nrg.ee.lbl.gov/diff-serv-arch/msg00011.html`:

> There is a clear need for relatively simple and coarse methods of providing differentiated classes of service for Internet traffic, to support various types of applications, and specific business requirements. The differentiated services approach to providing quality of service in networks employs a small, well-defined set of building blocks from which a variety of services may be built. A small bit-pattern in each packet, in the IPv4 TOS octet or the IPv6 Traffic Class octet, is used to mark a packet to receive a particular forwarding treatment, or per-hop behavior, at each network node. A common understanding about the use and interpretation of this bit-pattern is required for inter-domain use, multi-vendor interoperability, and consistent reasoning about expected service behaviors in a network. Thus, the Working Group will standardize a common layout to be used for both octets, called the 'DS byte'. A standards-track document will be produced that will define the general use of fields within the DS byte (superseding the IPv4 TOS octet definitions of RFC 1349).

> The Working Group will also assign specific per-hop behaviors to a small number of particular patterns or 'code-points' of the DS byte. The standardized code-points will only apply to per-hop behaviors already in widespread common usage within the global internet, e.g., the forwarding treatment received by best-effort traffic. In addition to the standards-track specification document, an informational framework document will be produced. The framework document will define the differentiated services architecture and a common language for differentiated services. Example uses and services will be described. Another goal of the [working group] is to experiment with other per-hop behaviors

that can be used to produce additional services. These will be documented in internet drafts. It will be decided whether these additional code-points and per-hop behaviors should be specified in experimental RFCs or should become standardized. The [working group] will also investigate the additional components necessary to support differentiated services, including such traffic conditioners as traffic shapers and packet markers that could be used at the boundaries of networks.

The [working group] may also define mechanisms such as LDAP schemata to map user service profiles into differentiated services at the network boundary. Later documents will cover these issues. The group will analyze related security threats, especially theft of service or denial of service attacks, and suggest counter-measures.

The group will not work on mechanisms for the identification of individual traffic flows within the network, or on signaling mechanisms to support the marking of packets.[5]

By contrast with complex, parameter-rich (some would say parameter-saturated) COS/QOS systems such as ATM or end-to-end negotiations like RSVP, DiffServ sacrifices granularity for simplicity—making it a prime candidate for proof-of-concept and first-pass deployments.

In the core of a large network, hundreds or thousands of traffic flows compete for processor attention. The main reason for a relatively simple set of indicators that signal different kinds of service is to reduce the administrative and computational burden of state management, authentication, and signaling that must otherwise occur to treat one kind of traffic differently from another. In the same way that a "frequent traveler" card entitles you to certain benefits such as boarding a plane early without the ticket agent having to look up your name, differentiated-services indicators are an efficiency.

IntServ systems will face serious scaling challenges in such situations with today's technology as they try to maintain state for many concurrent applications and sessions—meaning early IntServ implementation will be relegated to the enterprise.

In keeping with the Internet philosophy of simple, concise tools with far-reaching effects, DiffServ provides a basic set of values that can be assembled to produce a rich range of services. The differentiation of traffic may occur across a single link or an entire end-to-end network path. DS values may be simply a straightforward indication of relative priority, or they may indicate a class of traffic that is entitled to some special form of service

The IP Header and DiffServ codepoints

In the DiffServ model, devices at the network periphery mark the DS codepoint according to the needs of a traffic flow. DS codepoint markings can be interpreted by a service provider or mapped into an MPLS core to ensure end-to-end handling. Like IPTOS, the DS codepoint is independent of the media layer—although some degree of integration with media that support differentiated service levels will improve the granularity with which a network path can deliver QOS.

There have been two contending proposals for standards ratification before the IETF. Both take the TOS byte of the IP header and use 6 bits to signal class across devices. In one method, the first 5 bits indicate the per-hop behavior of the packet and the sixth tells the device if the packet exceeds the agreed-upon flow specification. Devices will discard traffic that exceeds its flow specification in order to slow down the sender and avoid adversely affecting other, in-profile traffic. Two bits are currently unused—but they may find a role in explicit congestion notification. The sixth "in profile" bit is analogous to an IPTOS type-of-service marking for discard eligibility.

An alternate proposal for use of the DiffServ codepoint associates all 6 available bits of the TOS byte to a specific way of handling a datagram for the hop in question (see Figure 8–5). Note that the least significant bit is leftmost; as we shall see, this provides some degree of backward compatibility with existing IP precedence implementations.

Some mandatory *values* of the DS codepoints, and their associated *per-hop behaviors* (PHBs), are outlined in standards documents. Addi-

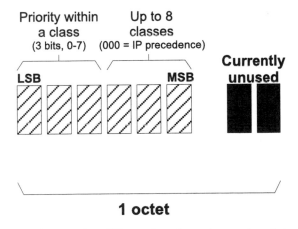

Figure 8–5   Meaning of bits in the differentiated-service codepoints

tional recommended values and PHBs will be published by the Internet community. It is the behavior, rather than the implementation, that is standardized. Traffic that is classified according to a DS bit may have a behavior enforced through queuing, throttling, discard eligibility, mapping to a given media link, and so on.

In order to overcome some of the discrepancies of earlier attempts at prioritization and differentiated-service deployment, the DiffServ working group is explicit in its requirements for DiffServ compliance. These include the assignment of a default behavior and defaults that follow the recommended defaults of the standards bodies, as well as complete configurability of codepoint-to-per-hop-behavior (PHB) assignment. Standard defaults are great news for network administrators, because they mean that devices are more likely to exhibit the same "out of the box" behavior when handling packets with the same DS codepoint information, which will ultimately make multivendor QOS a more realistic goal.

In both proposals, the DiffServ codepoint will generally work with existing IPTOS precedence information; on the other hand, it will *not* work cleanly with IPTOS type-of-service bits. In order to interoperate with networks that are not using differentiated services, "remarking" of the DiffServ codepoint to the traditional 3 precedence/4 type-of-service structure is permitted.

A flow of data marked with the default DiffServ codepoint value (known as a DF) will be transmitted in a standard, first-in-first-out manner. If a higher class of traffic arrives, it will be treated better than waiting packets with the default DiffServ codepoint markings. For example, the "expedited forwarding" marking (111000 in the 6-bit proposal, known as an EF) tells a device to put the traffic in a shorter, more frequently serviced queue. This means that expedited packets will experience lower latency, reduced jitter, and less packet loss when compared with best-effort traffic, particularly during times of congestion.

Use of the "in" bit instructs devices that a sender is exceeding some agreed-upon threshold for a flow of traffic. If congestion occurs, the device can drop excessive packets first, which will cause "greedy" transmitters to slow down transmission to within their negotiated profile. This can cause some degree of confusion—should out-of-profile enhanced forwarding traffic precede in-profile default forwarding traffic?

The 6-bit codepoint was ratified as RFC 2474. The 5-bit-plus-in model was rejected in part because of ambiguity about how to handle out-of-profile, high-priority traffic versus in-profile, low-priority traffic.

There are two approaches to specifying out-of-profile traffic. One approach is to retain the original marking and set an out-of-profile flag, as was the case in the 5-bit classifier proposal. Another approach is for the device that implements the policing primitive to "downgrade" the packet. In an uncongested network, the effect is the same—both in-profile and out-of-profile traffic enjoy the level of performance they need. When congestion occurs, the out-of-profile traffic will be dropped or delayed, either because it is out of profile or because it has been downgraded to a less privileged class. In order to avoid the potential ambiguities that have hindered earlier IPTOS standards, the IETF selected the 6-bit classifier model.

Traffic conditioning

DiffServ employs devices at network boundaries known as traffic conditioners that apply a set of rules to traffic they forward. These rules govern classification, policing, shaping, and marking and are known as "primitives." Of the four types of primitive, only classification primitives are defined, since policing, marking, and shaping functions will vary greatly from device to device. Classification primitives can be "behavior aggregate" (based on the DS byte's value only) or "multifield" (based on the DS byte and other IP header information).

DiffServ policing primitives will tell a device how to look at traffic behavior and see if it is within a given profile. Shaping primitives will tell a device how to move a traffic flow to within a given profile through the use of queues, rate controllers, and so on. Finally, marking primitives will tell a device how to set the DS information for traffic. In other words, a traffic conditioner at the edge might act upon multifield classification and marking primitives; within the network, a core device might rely on behavior aggregate classification and shaping primitives.

A DiffServ node has a default PHB which is the node's normal best-effort forwarding behavior. The recommended codepoint for this behavior is 000000, although this value may be altered by a receiving device in order to map to a non-DS domain or to characterize the traffic based on local information it has about the sender or application. Traffic that is subjected to this PHB would be forwarded as reliably and quickly as possible, as long as the output link is not used by traffic that qualified for some other overriding PHB. Traffic-handling algorithms would probably include some degree of weighted fair queuing to ensure that "best effort" applications were never completely starved of bandwidth.

Conveniently, the DS codepoint values and IPTOS values for best-effort (i.e., normal) handling of traffic are identical, providing some degree of backward compatibility. While the DS codepoint occupies the same space in the header as the IP precedence and TOS information, the DiffServ group has attempted to maintain some degree of backward compatibility.

DiffServ calls the default set of codepoints and associated per-hop behaviors the *Class selector PHB Codepoints*. In this way, DiffServ-capable devices will include the existing IP precedence behaviors—if the upper 3 bits in the 6-bit DS codepoint are all 0 (i.e., xxx000), the lower 3 bits are similar to the IP precedence values. Such backward-compatibility encourages adoption in a multivendor environment.

For a device to be DS compliant, it must allow two or more independently forwarded classes of traffic; each class is entitled to better handling than lower-numbered types (reading from left to right). In addition, because IP precedence values of 110 and 111 are commonly used in routing, the PHB for 11x000 must be preferred over the PHB for 000000.[6] The network device treats traffic that shares a common class selector codepoint as independent of other traffic; in other words, forwarding, queuing, thresholding, and discards can all be applied on a class-by-class basis. Additional PHB groups may be assigned; each of these may map to the same, or other, PHBs.

The 6 bits of the DS Codepoint allow for up to 64 possible values. These are allocated into three pools:

- a pool of 32 recommended codepoints to be defined by standards groups (xxxxx0)

- a pool of 16 recommended codepoints to used locally or experimentally (xxxx11)

- a second pool of 16 experimental codepoints (xxxx01), slated for possible use if the pool of 32 codepoints defined by standards groups ever runs out

If you're implementing a prioritization scheme using devices that offer a mixture of DS and IP Precedence, this suggests that you should stick to the xxx000 range of priorities, since they will be understood by both types of device. If you want to experiment with specific changes, work in the xxxx11 space to avoid conflict with standards down the road.

Implementing PHBs to support the DiffServ default codepoints

The DiffServ specification does not define *how* to achieve per-hop behavior. While it lists a veritable alphabet soup of potential mechanisms and tunable parameters, including priority queuing, multiple queues, weighted fair queuing, discard algorithms, weighted round robin, drop preference weighting, class-based queuing, and others, it instead defines *what* the behaviors should be, leaving it to networking implementers to select a mechanism.

Each PHB may, as an action, re-mark some portion of the traffic within one class to another (for example, if ingress traffic exceeds agreed-upon bounds) according to marking primitives. Earlier standards did not permit this in IP precedence implementations.

Does DiffServ equal policy?

For a networking device to claim it is "IPTOS compliant," it needs only to read the classification information and handle traffic accordingly. A simple access list or packet filter is enough. Determination of the *appropriate* classifier, and mechanisms for distributing the information needed to make such a determination, are the realm of policy-based networking and will be dealt with later in the text.

A router works by forwarding traffic along selected paths. The dissemination of route information is functionally separate from the forwarding of traffic; this is a conscious decision that has allowed the Internet to scale with a wide range of networking devices on it at the same time. DiffServ has been structured in much the same way: the classification and handling of individual datagrams is functionally separate from the overarching signaling needed to determine appropriate capacity and exchange information about classifier-to-handler mapping. The forwarding of traffic in a differentiated manner is relatively straightforward and is the main function of the networking device, while the processing of route tables, as well as policy and route parameters, happens in the background.

The DiffServ standards say that for a device to be DS-compliant, it must allow two or more independently forwarded classes of traffic to be handled in two different manners. So some degree of QOS is implied by DS compliance, but no integration with a comprehensive policy system can be assumed.

As with any prioritization scheme that offers preferential treatment, it is incumbent upon the devices at the periphery of a DiffServ domain to perform admission control. The DS standards are vague about this, saying only that devices must "ensure that all traffic entering the domain is marked with codepoint values appropriate to the traffic and the domain."[7] As we have seen, this is no mean feat. It requires suitable authentication and reliable identification of traffic flows in order to avoid malicious attacks or unsuitable allocation of available network capacity. These policy issues must be resolved before DiffServ systems are deployed reliably.

Layer-3 address classification

In an enterprise, the emphasis is on prioritizing certain types of *applications*—in other words, disregarding source and destination address while classifying based on port number. For service providers, the opposite is true: they have limited knowledge of what applications (i.e., port numbers) a customer considers important, but they want to offer a customer a given priority across their network based on their monthly rate.

Consequently, layer-3 source and destination information is useful for policing traffic from neighboring networks. In an ISP network, for example, the TCP or UDP port may tell devices about the delay sensitivity of traffic but not about its mission criticality to the customer. On the other hand, the source address of the packet will tell the ISP's devices whether or not that user is entitled to use premium service. For an ISP, the source address might only tell a device whether it should overwrite some TOS settings (an untrusted end node), replace them with the standard setting (not entitled to any priority), or let them remain (a trusted end node).

The use of network addresses to deliver user-based classification is possible if it is implemented as part of a dynamic policy system. In early deployments, however, user-based policies are too complex to be useful. By contrast, *device*-based policies that use network addresses may be useful. A videoconferencing machine in the company boardroom may have a static IP address. Boundary routers may have this address statically configured in their access lists or DiffServ primitives in order to allow the machine to transmit high-priority traffic that would be blocked were it to come from a user's desktop.

Layer-2 address classification: MAC information

MAC addresses are good pointers to users if an organization maintains an asset database; in this respect, they may serve as a mechanism for associating users with a given VLAN. Because MAC addresses are noncontiguous and hard to aggregate, it is unlikely that a MAC-based system will scale for traffic classification. A table of priorities associated with MAC addresses could be sent to a switch, once the software detects an Ethernet carrier and sees that MAC address on one of its ports. However, if the switch is not able to look into the network layer to discern application (i.e., port number), then it will be able to make only media-layer decisions, such as how much of a queue to allocate to a given port, or what VLAN to place that port on.

On the other hand, if the layer-2 switch is also able to route (i.e., a layer-2/layer-3 switch), then it may as well use IP address information and infer the identity and permissions of the sender through an authentication service. Consequently, while some proprietary implementations and close-domain switching systems might employ MAC-based classification, it is unlikely to scale in an internetworking environment.

Link-prioritization classification: 802.1Q/p

At the MAC layer, link-by-link handling of traffic can be performed based on the contents of the extended MAC header defined by the IEEE's 802.1p and Q extensions. The 802.1D extensions offer up to 8 priorities for traffic classification (prioritization) but no type-of-service information to indicate, for example, discard eligibility.

802.1D now includes the 802.1p and 802.1Q extensions. That is, for a device to claim true 802.1D compliance, it must also support 802.1p and 802.1Q. The IEEE has defined 802.1D as a standard 32-bit extension to the layer-2 header of Ethernet and Token Ring traffic. Twelve bits of this space are reserved for packet-based VLAN tagging; however, three bits within the 802.1Q header (defined in the 802.1p standard) are reserved for class-of-service signaling across a layer-2 link. This is illustrated in Figure 8–6.

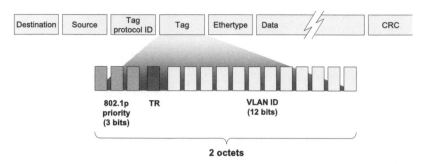

Figure 8–6   The 802.1D extended header

802.1p annex H describes the 8 possible values of these 3 bits, as listed in Table 8–8.

Table 8–8   IEEE 802.1p priority levels, examples, and characteristics

Value	Name	Examples	Characteristics
7	Network control	RIP, OSPF, BGP4	Critical to network health
6	Voice	NetMeeting audio	Latency and jitter sensitive; low bandwidth
5	Video	PictureTel, Indeo	High bandwidth; jitter sensitive
4	Controlled load	SNA transactions	Predictable response times, latency-sensitive applications
3	Excellent effort	SAP, SQL	Business-critical traffic that tolerates delays
2	Best effort	Best effort	Best effort
1	<default>	<default>	<default>
0	Background	FTP backups, Pointcast	Latency insensitive,

These classifications generally are only relevant when the device is under congestion.

Reconciling mission criticality and urgency in 802.1p values

The problem in deciding upon classification, from the perspective of a network administrator or even a switch vendor, is how to act upon these classifiers. Some decisions are relatively easy—for example, any frames with an 802.1p priority of 7 should be preserved at all cost, since they're used to regulate network activity. Other decisions aren't so simple.

If voice traffic is delay sensitive but not mission critical to my business, then I probably want to permit voice and forward it immediately when the network is not loaded. When the network becomes congested, I might slow voice traffic by randomly discarding voice packets or moving it to a low-priority queue. What should I do to the 802.1p values in this case?

It is perfectly rational for a system administrator to agree that traffic from an interactive voice application such as Microsoft's NetMeeting be tagged with an 802.1p COS of 6 (voice), and in the next breath say that voice has no business on his network and should never obstruct data traffic with a COS of 4 (controlled load). Should the traffic be flagged with a COS of 6 or 1 (background)?

Generally speaking, the traffic should not be "retagged" once it has been identified (since the 802.1p value is an indicator of what the frame contains). But it is appropriate to instruct network devices that a COS of 6 is to receive low priority and be eligible for discard before a data packet with a COS of 4. In other words, don't alter the .1p value, but change the per-switch behavior associated with the value. In this example, NetMeeting would still have a COS of 6 but would be handled with a lower priority than mission-critical data.

The 802.1p values are a good example of the criticality/delay-sensitivity dilemma. Some of the 802.1p service-level types indicate the *nature* of the traffic—for example, voice, video, network control protocols, or data—while other levels indicate relative *importance*—business critical, best effort, or background.

Fortunately, most 802.1p implementations ship with a rational set of defaults, and standards documents are emerging that detail how data link prioritization can interoperate with integrated services architectures. If you want to adjust the behavior of a layer-2 switch, make sure you understand the implications that your changes will have for the transmitting devices, the relative criticality of the applications affected, the delay sensitivity of those applications, and so on.

Three main functions: Priority, VLANs, and multicast

The 802.1p bits are designed to mark packets with information on the required handling of the traffic they contain. 802.1p also provides better support for new media types and lets bridging hardware scale beyond traditional multicast thresholds.

802.1Q was designed to provide a consistent method for tagging packets for a given virtual LAN (VLAN) across a layer-2 domain, as well as a mechanism for dynamically registering a VLAN using the Generic Attribute Registration Protocol (GARP). Media prioritization is a prerequisite for the 802.1Q VLAN work. If 802.1Q allows networks to dynamically define and assign VLAN membership, then the dynamic assignment mechanisms must take place at a reasonable pace, even when the network is congested. By creating multilevel networks with 802.1p, the VLAN management traffic can get some degree of guarantee that VLAN control packets will be delivered even when network capacity is limited.

802.1D defines not only the prioritization bit locations and suggested values, but also a dynamic multicast membership protocol (GMRP) that further optimizes network usage by allowing switches to join and leave multicast transmissions.

802.1p can be used without "turning on" the 802.1Q feature set. In this case, a null value for the 802.1Q information (termed a "null VLAN") is used, and only the 3 priority bits of the extended MAC header are used in calculating forwarding.

Impact of 802.1Q on existing equipment

You might wonder, with all of these changes, if reaping the benefits of layer-2 packet coloring means swapping out your infrastructure. As with most questions in the networking world, the answer is yes and no. New enterprise-class equipment from leading networking vendors supports 802.1D, but switches made before the middle of 1998 will not usually include 802.1D support. Most of these switches will not be software upgradable, since Ethernet handling takes place in hardware in order to deliver good speeds at acceptable costs.

The ideal model for 802.1p/Q networks is to have every device along a path support the extended header, as shown in Figure 8–7.

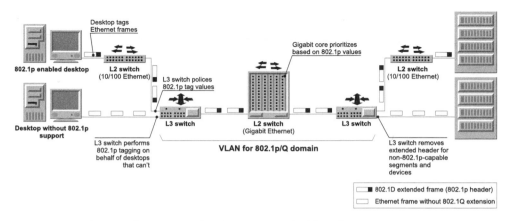

Figure 8–7   End-to-end support of 802.1D extended headers

Existing layer-3 devices—routers—generally function in software. Consequently, changing the way they handle traffic often requires only a software upgrade. IPTOS has been in existence for years, so even if a router doesn't *act* on IPTOS information, it still supports it.

By contrast, 802.1p/Q is an extension to the link-layer frame that is generally handled in hardware, because hardware-based switches give us the 10/100/1000 megabit speeds we expect and need from a LAN. A "colored" Ethernet frame with 802.1Q information is 32 bits longer than a normal Ethernet frame, which has some important consequences for legacy devices.

Very old switches that enforce the maximum Ethernet frame size will discard the 802.1Q traffic as an oversized frame (Figure 8–8). The problem of oversized frames is largely irrelevant, since any network that needs performance enough to consider 802.1p has probably replaced such devices long ago.

More modern switches that allow a frame 32 bits larger than normal to pass will forward 802.1Q-tagged packets successfully but will not be able to act upon the classification (Figure 8–9). Since the congestion of a properly designed network generally occurs in the core, where there is bandwidth oversubscription and the aggregation of traffic, this is acceptable if these switches are at the periphery of the network or if the core is otherwise designed to handle high multiservice traffic volumes.

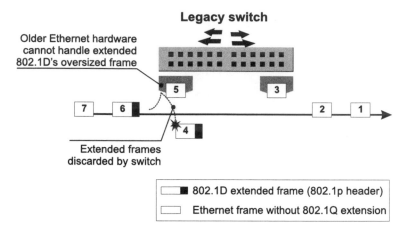

Figure 8–8   Discard of extended 802.1D frames by old switches that do not permit oversized frames

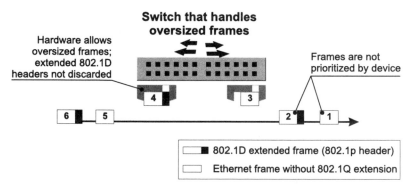

Figure 8–9   Forwarding of oversized frames without prioritization

If a router tries to read an 802.1D packet and the router does not recognize the larger frame, it will interpret the last 32 bits of the extended MAC header as the first 32 bits of the IP header and discard the packet because of the corrupt header (Figure 8–10). So intermediate layer-3 devices across an extended 802.1D link must support the extensions to the MAC layer in order for the network layer to be able to read the packets properly—including end stations (the desktop and the server, for example).

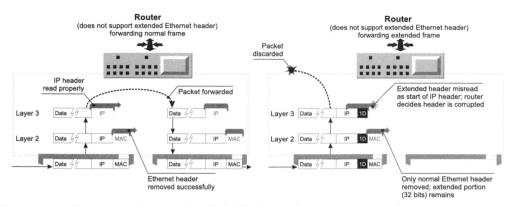

Figure 8–10   Rejection of extended 802.1D frames by a router that does not support extended 802.1D

To overcome this potential roadblock, operating system and networking vendors that tag packets with 802.1D extended headers may send a test packet (a ping) to the destination to verify that the link supports the protocol. From this, the system can infer the following:

- If the packet returns with the 802.1p and Q information intact, the link supports the protocol (although some switches may not actually prioritize frames along the way).

- If the packet comes back with the extra 32 bits in place but the contents changed, then networking components are translating between 802.1Q-enabled and non-802.1Q segments, and the packet coloring will not be end-to-end.

- If the packet does not come back, the link does not support 802.1p/Q tagging. This means either that an old switch has dropped the frame as oversized, or that a router has misinterpreted the 32-bit extensions as the first part of the IP header and discarded it as corrupt.

Based on the results of this check, the system can decide whether to tag traffic, and if so, at which network layers to perform the tagging.

A router that supports extended MAC layer information will work in the way shown in Figure 8–11.

At the same time, layer-3 devices that can perform classification and tagging can compensate for incapable end nodes, as illustrated in Figure 8–12

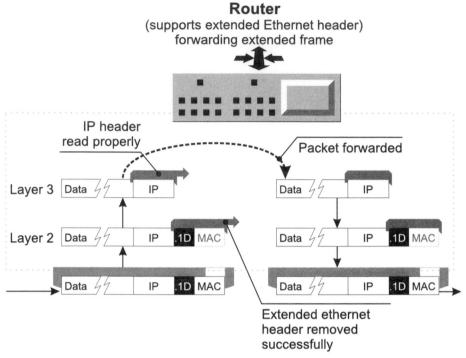

Figure 8–11   Proper treatment of extended 802.1D frame by 802.1D-aware router

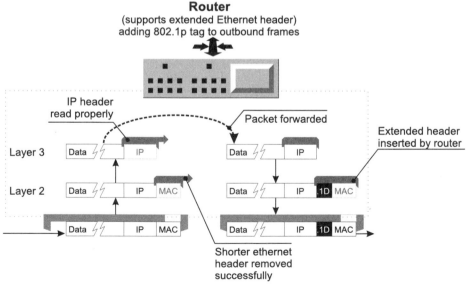

Figure 8–12   Creation of extended 802.1D header by router

There is additional complexity to such a solution. If a packet is being tagged by an intermediate, 802.1p/Q-capable switch, then it must be untagged at the far end of the link (Figure 8–13).

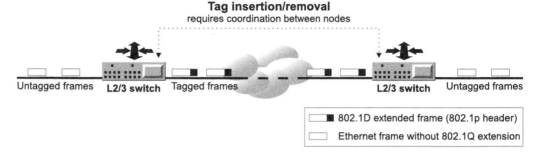

Tag insertion/removal
requires coordination between nodes

Untagged frames   **L2/3 switch**   Tagged frames   **L2/3 switch**   Untagged frames

■	802.1D extended frame (802.1p header)
	Ethernet frame without 802.1Q extension

Figure 8–13   Creation and removal of extended 802.1D frames by coordinating devices

This may involve some degree of administration, or extremely sophisticated networking equipment that understands the path across the network and can strip tags appropriately along the way. An example is a VPN-encrypted tunnel across a LAN infrastructure.

When 802.1p-capable and pre-802.1p devices communicate via a translator, an intermediate device must strip the extended 802.1D information. Because the 802.1p domain is also an 802.1Q VLAN, the act of stripping (or adding) an 802.1p/Q header can occur as a packet enters (or leaves) a VLAN. In other words, it is possible to create prioritized Ethernet segments by associating them with VLANs, while leaving other portions of the network as "best effort."

Other 802.1p/Q features

802.1Q also allows layer-2 devices to perform multicasting. While network-layer multicast is broadly deployed, layer-2 multicast offers several scaling advantages in a switched LAN environment.

When a large-volume transmission is being received by many nodes, traditional unicast (one-to-one) links mean that the traffic from the transmission is repeated many times (Figure 8–14).

Multicast reduces the redundancy by having routers split the streams of data to groups of listeners. Only one transmission stream leaves the transmitting node, and the stream is split by each layer-3 node that has more than one downstream link that wants to receive the transmission (Figure 8–15).

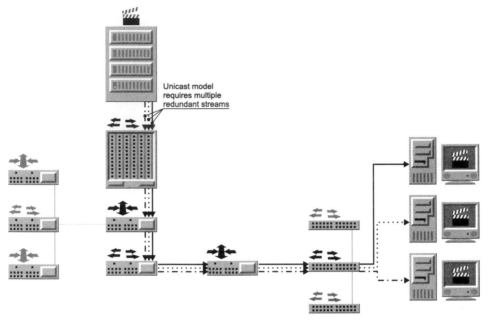

Figure 8–14 Transmission inefficiency in a unicast model when multiple listeners share some portion of the network path

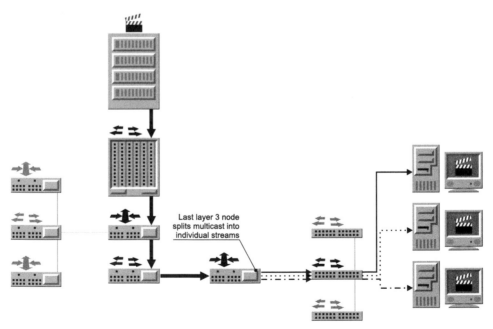

Figure 8–15 Layer-3 multicast optimizes redundant transmissions until last layer-3 node in the path

With increasingly "flat" networking architectures and large, switched backbones, L3 multicast doesn't work as well. Now that hundreds of subscribing nodes may be across a layer-2 link from the splitting router, L3 multicast can still result in many redundant transmissions across switches.

To get around this, makers of L2 switching equipment have implemented techniques such as Internet group management protocol (IGMP) snooping to "listen in" to multicast transmissions and make them more efficient. An IGMP snooping technique, however, still requires the L3 device to get involved in all the administrative work of having subscribers join or leave a multicast session (Figure 8–16).

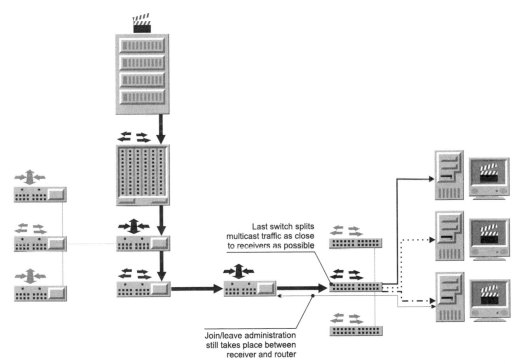

Figure 8–16   IGMP snooping optimizes redundant transmissions until last layer-2 switch, but leaves the router with the burden of administering the multicast sessions

The 802.1p/Q extensions allow GMRP, which is a true L2 multicast solution. GMRP can greatly reduce multicast overhead on switched networks and ease the burden of already taxed L3 nodes. What's more, as switching grows in the LAN, GMRP scales well for mesh topologies in which there are fewer routers (Figure 8–17).

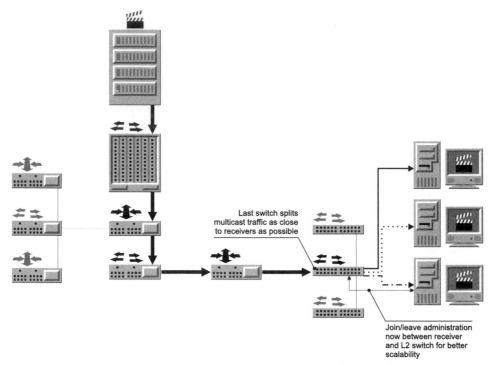

Figure 8–17   GMRP pushes both optimization of redundant traffic and administration of multicast session out to last layer-2 switch

Link prioritization classification: VLAN membership

The VLAN from which a packet arrives may tell you the group of which a sender is a member. But grouping users into VLANs does not permit overlapping group memberships, and while 802.1Q may revitalize VLANs for some specific applications, VLAN membership is generally useful for layer-2 devices like ATM switches that can map VLANs to circuits with specific handling characteristics.

With packet-based VLANs, however, an end node can mark different kinds of traffic with different VLAN tags—making it a member of multiple VLANs. The enterprise can then deploy a "video" VLAN and a "data" VLAN and provision them accordingly. Getting 802.1Q-enabled end nodes and switches may require a wholesale swap of your network infrastructure, but if you have these capabilities, then you may be able to build parallel layer-2 networks and use them to maintain traffic differentiation across switched ATM WAN links. Each node can forward voice on one 802.1Q VLAN and data on another.

A major reason for organizing users into VLANs is to speed classification by moving user-group associations to layer 2. Unfortunately, by the time user-based VLANs are properly automated and scalable, the problem may already be solved with faster layer-3 devices.

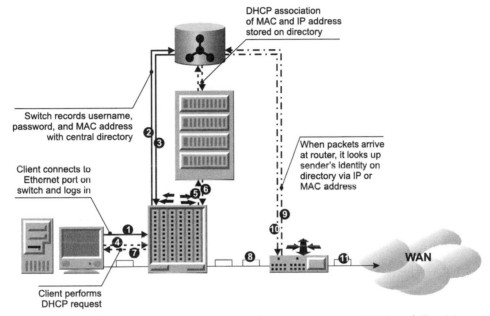

Figure 8–18 Steps in a LAN-based authentication system using MAC and IP addresses for identification

If a proper system emerges that allows link layer authentication in LAN environments the way it exists in dial-up access systems today, then the job of classifying flows is greatly simplified—and a good deal more secure. The switch can authenticate the end node (and possibly even validate source addresses to prevent the user from carrying out denial-of-service attacks without ingress filtering on the router.) A DHCP server, consulting the same central repository, can assign an appropriate IP address. A router, once again consulting the same information, can determine the sender of a packet and their associated permissions. This is illustrated in Figure 8–18. As soon as the user leaves (i.e. Ethernet carrier is lost) the switch notifies the directory in order to prevent spoofing of the port association by a new user.

In practice, a policy system such as this one may require an intermediate server to manage device statefulness.

Link prioritization classification: ATM QOS

Each virtual circuit in an ATM world has a set of parameters that describe the behavior a packet can expect as it crosses the network. If these are permanent virtual circuits, then the parameters are administratively defined when the circuit is provisioned; for switched virtual circuits, they are negotiated at the time the circuit is established.

ATM physical circuits consist of one or more virtual paths, which in turn consist of one or more virtual channels. The ATM network permits traffic based on an admission-control function; from this control, it decides to admit, renegotiate, or block access to the requested circuit. The decision is guided by the kind of service the sender is requesting from the network.

We will discuss the handling characteristics of an ATM link later on. From a classification perspective, however, the type of circuit on which a packet or frame arrives is a rich source of classification information. If we assume that the admission-control function is behaving properly and that a sender was allocated a committed-bit-rate connection, we can be fairly sure that the traffic deserves fast, low-latency handling. The fact that the traffic came from a CBR link may result in a variety of handling actions, such as:

- Writing the appropriate IPTOS and 802.1p information into the packet and frame headers as the packet enters an IP or Ethernet environment

- Forwarding the packet to a fast circuit of some other type of link, such as a Frame Relay data link connection identifier (DLCI) set aside for CBR traffic

- Moving the packet to the front of a queue on the receiving device

- Attempting to establish a reservation across an internetwork that matches the traffic parameters of the circuit using RSVP

The ATM CBR circuit and the Integrated Services Guaranteed bandwidth reservation have many similarities, which we will discuss in later chapters.

Endnotes

1. Winsock 2 offers a standard Application Programming Interface for application self-classification (i.e., the application requests some form of handling from the stack), and vendors such as 3Com Corporation offer application classification via the Control Panel, with some degree of classification distribution through log-in scripts or other methods.

2. Almquist, Type of service, RFC 1349, July 1992.

3. Alan O'Neill, BT Labs, filed in accordance with IETF rules 10.3.1-6 on December 5, 1998.

4. Nichols et al., *Definition of the Differentiated Services Field (DS Field) in the IPv4 and IPv6 Headers*, RFC 2474, December 1998.

5. Brian Carpenter, *Draft WG Charter*, Differentiated Services Working Group, February 17, 1998, at http://www-nrg.ee.lbl.gov/diff-serv-arch/msg00011.html.

6. RFC 2474.

7. RFC 2474.

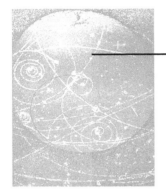

9

Complications to classification

In order for the Internet to support the diverse range of applications that it does, wily engineers have built a number of tricks into modern networks. While systems like network address translation, virtual private networks, and stateful applications might deliver compelling benefits and create entirely new uses for IP-based networks, they wreak havoc with classification.

Several network technologies interfere with user classification and proper handling, and understanding them is the key to knowing where in the network classification should occur. They include network address translation, proxy servers, tunneling, and encryption. Ironically, many of them have arisen in response to scaling issues within networking and are now themselves obstacles to extensible deployment of QOS.

Network address translation

Let's look at network address translation (NAT) in detail to understand some of the challenges it poses to QOS classification. NAT allows address reuse and improved security and is typically deployed at a boundary between an internal (private) and external (public) network, as shown in Figure 9–1.

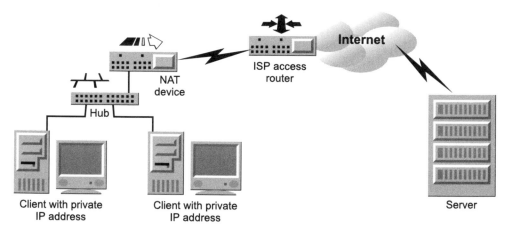

Figure 9–1   Typical location of network address translation equipment

A NAT networking device receives a packet on its internal interface. It then translates the packet's source address to another, public address (or more commonly, replaces the source address with its own external network address). It then retransmits the packet from its own link-layer interface, making it impossible for downstream devices to extract information about the originator of the traffic from the layer-2 or layer-3 addressing information therein. Upon receipt of traffic, it alters the destination address to that of the original sender and forwards it on the internal interface. As a result, user-based classification is not possible, because the source address is "invisible" (Figure 9–2).

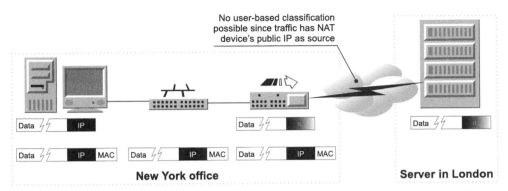

Figure 9–2   Network address translation prevents user-level granularity of classification in the WAN

To compensate for this, any devices that will use L2/L3 information to classify traffic should do so *before* the packet is translated. If the NAT device is translating packets for a videoconferencing system, it should mark the packet's TOS fields, since the source address of the videoconferencing system will be "hidden" from downstream devices. Such devices can signal their classification by tagging traffic at the media or network layer with the appropriate information. However, simply classifying and marking the traffic on the end system or in the workgroup is insufficient, unless the NAT device is prepared to use this information (Figure 9–3).

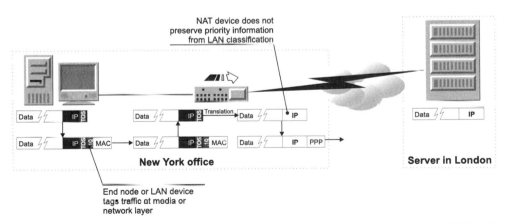

Figure 9–3   Network address translation without TOS preservation on the NAT device

A properly configured, COS-capable translating device will preserve the tags when it builds the new packet with the altered source network address (Figure 9–4).

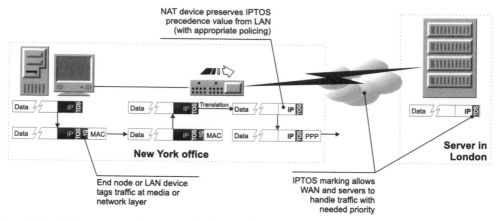

Figure 9–4   Network address translation with TOS preservation

Many NAT devices offer this kind of IPTOS preservation as an option today. In the future, NAT/WAN routers will allow policing of IPTOS or DiffServ values and preserve TOS priorities when appropriate. Ideally, the NAT device will alter the way it handles the packet according to tags in the traffic (Figure 9–5). In this way, it can use media-layer and network-layer information (as well as any other classifications that are available to it) to handle the traffic across the next hop in the network.

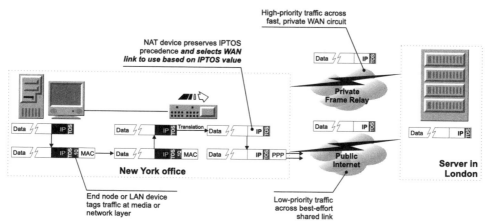

Figure 9–5   Network address translation with TOS preservation and circuit selection

Enriching classification information

TOS preservation and WAN handling differentiation will be increasingly common as devices become "QOS-savvy". The issues described above are similar for application proxies (although the proxy works at the application layer rather than the network layer) and for encryption systems (in which the network address becomes invisible). Generally speaking, any classification that intermediate devices need to know should take place before classifying information is hidden or altered, and devices should attempt to preserve or enrich (but not overwrite) classification information that they receive.

Stateful traffic

Managing stateful traffic (such as FTP sessions with negotiated data ports and a known control port) in real time is a challenge because of the processor overhead associated with sniffing data streams for port negotiations. The stateful traffic problem arises also in Enterprise Requirement Planning (ERP) systems and real-time traffic transports. Tagging of traffic will therefore play an increasingly important role in effective end-to-end classification.

Current stateful classifiers tend to work as follows:

- The control channel is processed in software by the networking device. In the case of FTP, for example, all traffic on the FTP control port is analyzed for specific messages such as "get <filename> on <port number>."

- When the software sees a negotiation for a transfer on a dynamic port, it reprograms the lower-layer forwarding plane with a transient classifier for the new port, consisting of the dynamic port numbers and the source and destination IP addresses. For example, if the software sees "get file on port 5000," it may write "prioritize from <a> to <b> on port 5000" to the forwarding plane of the device.

- Subsequent packets on the newly negotiated port are processed within the ASICs, making them faster and less software-intensive.

- When the transfer is completed or some predefined time has elapsed, the transient classifier is removed.

Sidebar

How RTSP works

RTSP is a control channel protocol for establishing and controlling streams of traffic where the sender and receiver require some degree of time synchronization. It is particularly relevant to multimedia networks, because it is used by popular clients for streamed data such as RealMovie and RealAudio. The RTSP session is independent of a particular TCP session, opting instead to use its own session-numbering scheme. It is a two-way, stateful protocol in which both client and server can initiate communications, and it is tuned to make serving content from a virtual host (i.e., a host cluster) easier.

RTSP allows the retrieval of media from a server to a client, a conference, or an existing presentation. In this way, real-time addition and presentation of third-party content from remote sites is possible during the course of a conversation. It is similar to http, making it easy to parse and troubleshoot, and it allows control of a variety of media functions including recording, editing, and capacity negotiation. Each piece of media has a related media descriptor that provides basic information about the content to be delivered.

An RTSP session begins with a client's setup request, transmitted by default on port 554, which causes the server to prepare for stream transmission and create a session state. Subsequent play, record, and pause messages cause the server to operate on the media on a separate channel from the initial RTSP session. Content developers would include a hyperlink, for example, to "rtsp://mediaserver.mydomain.com:554/files/media/movie". Connecting to this URL would instruct the RTSP-enabled client to establish a connection to mediaserver.mydomain.com on TCP port 554 and retrieve the file in /files/media called "movie" using a separate channel for streaming.

Each RTSP command can include a relative timestamp that specifies time or frame offset within the media. Once the client has finished, it issues a session teardown message. Note that the RTSP session itself may be transient; tearing down a TCP session does not terminate the RTSP session, which may effectively be reestablished from another node at a later time.

RTSP negotiates the transport port and protocol, rather than defaulting to one. Negotiating the port number means that the familiar problem of stateful classification must be considered here. RTSP uses ASCII strings of arbitrary lengths to request media transfers and negotiate port number. The nondeterministic format of the negotiation process makes it difficult for an intermediate network device to watch port 554 for setup messages, parse the negotiated port range, and set up new classifiers dynamically until a corresponding teardown message. It is hard enough already to do this for FTP, which is fairly predictable; RTSP has many more state commands than FTP. The RFC says,

"Since SETUP includes all transport initialization information, firewalls and other intermediate network devices (which need this information) are spared the more arduous task of parsing the DESCRIBE response, which has been reserved for media initialization."

However, the example setup message looks fairly complex and contains data deep in the packet, beginning with a client request:

```
SETUP rtsp://example.com/foo/bar/bar.rm RTSP/1.0

  CSeq: 302

  Transport: RTP/AVP;unicast;client_port=4588-4589
```

This is followed by a subsequent server acknowledgment:

```
RTSP/1.0 200 OK

CSeq: 302

Date: 23 Jan 1997 15:35:06 GMT

Session: 47112344

Transport: RTP/AVP;
  unicast;client_port=4588-4589;server_port=6256-6257
```

An intermediate security device may be willing to parse this kind of message; security is more important than performance, and the initial setup must happen only once. For a networking device trying to optimize flows, it may be too much to parse this efficiently. The RFC refers to several different port ranges, so it does not seem that any default port is suggested. Given the flexibility that RTSP intends, the port ranges are negotiable to allow multiple concurrent data streams; nevertheless, easier flow classification of a default range would be an admirable addition to such a system.

RTSP clients such as Real Networks' RealPlayer offer a number of options for advanced users. One of these is the selection or definition of specific port ranges (UDP port 7070 is the default in the RealPlayer client), so a basic step might be to mark all UDP traffic on port 7070 as jitter sensitive. If a default range of ports (for example 7070 to 7099) were specified in the player, then classification might be easy, but it is unrealistic to expect all users to configure this information manually in a large organization.

RealPlayer users can also choose UDP or TCP, using only port 80 for all traffic, and automatically trying to use multicast for live content. UDP connections can resort to TCP after some level of timeout to guard against heavy discards.

RTSP control channels allow the client and server to exchange information about the level of service that the network is currently offering and the establishment of cache parameters. It also offers a facility for the client to ping the server on the RTSP port. Both of these features are useful to monitoring and application adaptation.

VPN traffic

A Virtual Private Network (VPN) consists of a tunnel around a control channel and one or more data channels. All user traffic—from multiple senders, and often generated by multiple applications—travels within the tunnel. The only devices that can effectively control how the tunnel is handled are the end points, because they are the only ones to see the various application flows as distinct streams of data.

In practice, the VPN tunnel entry point should identify high-priority traffic and tag the *carrier* protocol—generally some form of generic routing encapsulation (GRE) within IP—with the corresponding header, using IPTOS and IP precedence as was the case for NAT (Figure 9–6). The tunnel exit point will use this information to prioritize traffic handling and can translate it to the appropriate media-layer identifier on the destination network.

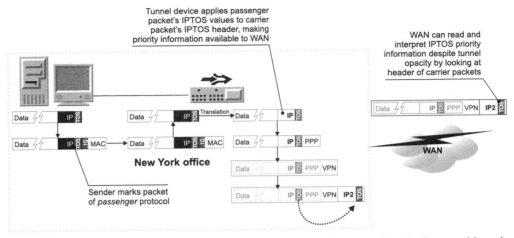

Figure 9–6   VPN end-points apply "passenger" IPTOS values to "carrier" tunnel header

This has the effect of making priority information available to the intermediate WAN links, as well as preserving the original IPTOS of the packet, once it is decapsulated at the far end of the tunnel. Depending on the TOS settings and interpretations of the intermediate service provider, the IPTOS settings on the carrier IP packet may be different from those on the client IP packet in order to extract the same behavior from both networks within the constraints of a service agreement.

Conditional statements

In many cases, a classifier is a simple match between a look-up and a packet. But as policy systems become increasingly sophisticated, conditional rules will emerge. A simple match will be replaced by familiar operators such as "contains," "does not contain," or "is in." Boolean operators that allow multilevel analysis of packets are needed to properly identify layer-3 precedence and write the correct information into the adjacent media layers. As we begin to build rules with Boolean operators and multiple-directory hierarchies, complexity will increase exponentially.

Furthermore, sophisticated policies will use relative notions such as "more than" or "before" that require advanced interpretation and translation into specific parameters.

Extrinsic conditions

Outside conditions are also important if conditional classifiers are to contain meaning. For example, a condition such as "limit exceeded" to show that a user has transmitted more than its fair share of traffic enables more precise comparisons.

Time and geography

As soon as we introduce time-based conditions, we need to take into account geographic differences. A properly designed policy system will set up conditions according to some base time such as GMT, and each device will consider its local time when implementing the policy. Even this may be flawed: for a connection that crosses many time zones, devices must choose whether to use the sender or receiver's local time zone. The sender's time is probably a more accurate one to use in evaluating policies and is easier to rely upon, since policing occurs at the entry point to the network. For full-duplex connections like TCP, however, the server will generate the majority of the traffic and may dictate the appropriate time zone to use. Weekly or monthly policies are less likely to cause problems, but if you plan to set up time-based conditions, careful consideration of things like time zones and mobile users is important.

Time-based policies are simpler to implement in a geographically contained area such as a LAN campus. They are also relatively straightforward at a specific access point (such as a dial-up access concentrator), although even this is dangerous—traveling workers may experience poor performance or have their access to the network blocked because of the time at headquarters.

Time-based policies are more relevant for repeated events (such as nightly backups). Careful selection of the timing of these kinds of events is important and should be based on the organization's geographic distribution. For example, a company with offices in London, England and Boston, USA, may want to perform backups between 11 PM and 2 AM, Eastern Standard Time. A company with offices on the US East and West coasts may choose 2 AM to 5 AM Eastern Standard Time instead.

One other consideration about time is that of local load. Imagine that a company has two Internet servers that can fulfill a query—one in London and one in New York. It is 10 PM in New York (and 3 AM in London.) A New Yorker may be better serviced by the London server if the amount of traffic in New York makes the server's response time outweigh the additional network delay of a round trip to London.

Congestion conditions

In addition to time, a device may consider absolute level of congestion (an average of the queue size or percentage of queue used over some time) as well as relative levels assigned to a class of traffic or particular port or application. Running counters for these kinds of metrics can be processor intensive, so the availability of this information will depend on the vendor implementation and level of granularity available in the management system.

Be aware that some queuing mechanisms (random early discard (RED), for example) take into account congestion levels and queue depths automatically by virtue of the way they work. In other words, your network may be reacting to congestion levels without your having explicitly configured anything. Typically, however, a queue has a level at which it begins random discard, a discard ramp-up rate, and a saturation point. Lowering the level at which discards begin to occur allows you to notify transmitters of pending congestion, but it may also have the consequence of reducing overall network performance and increasing the number of retransmissions in the network. We'll look at RED in coming chapters.

Organizational conditions

A final set of conditions that is common in emerging policy systems is that of group membership. As we have seen, the mechanisms by which sender identity can be determined are complex at best; once identity is established, however, traffic handling may be modified by group membership or job function. For example, all personnel who manage the network may be members of an admin group; for them, telnet traffic is considered "network critical," whereas it is considered "best effort" for all other employees. The members of the admin group may come from throughout the organization, so their membership in the admin group may have to override the aggregate policies generated for them within an organizational hierarchy.

RSVP and ATM admission-control systems will offer some degree of policy-based decision-making, and COPS may introduce admission control for DiffServ-based QOS. In current implementations, ATM admission controls are based on VLAN membership; for RSVP and DiffServ, the policy controls reside on a policy server using a protocol such as COPS to maintain reservation states.

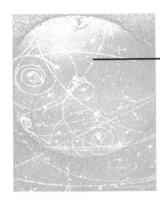

Traffic handling within a device

Once traffic has been identified, a device can handle it in a number of ways in order to satisfy QOS policy objectives. These include queuing, discarding, rate control, throttling, and bandwidth reservation. Associating the right handler with a given traffic type is critical to successful QOS deployment.

Once a packet has been classified by a device, it can be handled in many of ways. Internal to a particular network device, a number of mathematical mechanisms can be employed that have the effect of prioritizing, throttling, or smoothing traffic levels. The device may also make decisions "outside the box" by selecting alternate routes, forwarding interfaces, or tunnels or by marking packets for downstream handling.

In this section we'll look at the various ways that traffic can be handled within a device. There is considerable overlap between "in-device" and "downstream" handling, however, since actions that are taken locally, such as packet marking, may result in different handling only by adjacent network nodes.

Common ground

A network can offer some fixed set of services when it is completely unloaded. These fixed services represent the ideal quality of service (IQOS) that the network can offer—whether it is Ethernet, ATM, Frame Relay, or cans and string. To get better quality of service than this, you must choose another path across the network or replace the networking equipment. There's no way around this.

Service levels start to drop off when there is contention for network resources. As we've seen, it is economically unsound to over-engineer your network to the point where everybody gets the IQOS. Some purists may argue that in an all-constant-bit-rate, streamed environment, it makes sense to engineer bandwidth to exactly the level needed. While this is technically accurate for CBR traffic, it assumes no change to the network capacity, usage, or architecture and in our opinion is still unwise—primarily because of network growth and the burstiness of data applications.

Service levels generally decline in three stages.

- Stage one is where queues begin to fill some of the time, due to the bursty nature of traffic. Some degree of queue depth is a normal consequence of properly planning your capacity. The average time that a piece of data waits in queues as it crosses the network will increase gradually as burstiness and utilization go up, but individual packets, frames, or cells may still make it across the network at the IQOS some of the time. Nevertheless, we see jitter (as a result of the level of burstiness, which drives queue delay variance) and increased latency (as a result of the buffering needed to deliver a smooth stream of information to the applications at either end).

- Stage two is where things get messy. The queues aren't full yet, but the networking devices are beginning to anticipate queue overflow. In other words, they've looked at the sustained rate of traffic into and out of the queues and determined that if the transmitters don't slow down, buffers will be full and no further traffic will enter the network. Saturated queues are particularly bad for TCP, because transmitters will all enter "slow start" mode, cease transmission, and then ramp up relatively quickly until they get a repeated acknowledgment (ACK) from the receiver, from which they infer loss or delay. When many TCP transmitters enter slow start together, the result can be wild fluctuations between congestion and network silence. With no feedback, TCP senders assume the worst.

In order to inform the transmitters that congestion is imminent, different networks employ different mechanisms. Recall that some network links (leased lines or X.25 circuits, for example,) don't have problems like this. Once these layer-2 pipes are full, it's incumbent on the devices at either end to deal with the problem. TCP, ATM, and Frame Relay are some examples of networks that can offer "bursting" capacity and so have to deal with oversubscription.

- **TCP uses packet loss, delay, and repeated acknowledgment** to infer congestion. So a routed network discards packets randomly (using RED) to force TCP to take notice. Another method, known as an *ICMP source quench*, is seldom used and is considered relatively ineffective.

- **ATM uses a Connection Admission Control** to regulate the admission of traffic into the network, so it can consider the state of the network before granting admission. ATM relies on a Cell Loss Priority (CLP) control to indicate which cells should be discarded first. Since ATM has more control over what comes into a network, it doesn't need to passively "anticipate" congestion.

- **Frame Relay uses Discard Eligibility** (DE). But neither CLP nor DE protocols is used much at stage two; instead, Frame Relay employs Forward and Backward Explicit Congestion Notification (FECN and BECN) to tell the end switches in the Frame Relay link that the core is becoming congested.

- When the network becomes completely saturated, it drops packets. In stage three, all packets arriving at a device are discarded. If there is some metric—for example, an IPTOS bit, a CLP of 1 on a cell, or a set DE bit in a frame—then this tells the router or switch what traffic should be discarded first. Discard eligibility is generally driven by the mission criticality of an application, the relative usefulness of delayed traffic, and whether the traffic is within the agreed-upon traffic profile for the application. Greedy, useless, or unimportant traffic is dropped first.

What distinguishes stage two from stage three is the motivation for discarding traffic. In stage two, packets are dropped before buffers fill in order to avoid congestion. In stage three, packets are dropped because buffers are full.

With all of these discards, queues, throttles, and admission-control systems, things can get pretty confusing. It's important to remember that they are all mechanisms for moving networks toward IQOS for those applications that need it, and keeping the network away from stage three.

Queues, buckets, and admission control

Unless you're either incredibly rich or you've misconfigured your network, your network devices will always have to make decisions about how to receive more traffic than they can transmit. Oversubscription is the way networks deal with the inherent burstiness of packet-based communications without costing a fortune. Oversubscription also occurs regularly because of outages and failures, which must be considered in any effective network architecture.

Oversubscription means temporary delays, and when traffic is delayed, it's held in a queue. We have already seen that QOS and policy are rife with analogies, but in this case the analogy is no stretch of the imagination. It's easy to think of packet queues as if they were lineups at a bank or a ticket counter.

Until recently, popular network wisdom held that sophisticated queuing was not suitable in the core of high-volume networks. Complex queue processing required the involvement of the software layer in the router, introducing unacceptable delays. With the emergence of cheap, wire-speed queuing mechanisms implemented in hardware, traffic-shaping mechanisms such as queues and buckets are seeing new popularity for their relative simplicity.

We'll look at various methods of handling traffic, including:

- Queues, which are simply holding areas for network traffic. Just as a bank may see periods of heavy use and periods of idleness, so a networking device will experience varying degrees of congestion. In both cases, a simple, first-come-first-served (or FIFO, for first-in-first-out) queue holds surplus volume (of customers or packets) so that some degree of order is maintained. Different queue lengths mean different delays.

- Specialized queues that allow different packets to be treated differently. Some are good at equitably assigning traffic so that high-volume flows don't starve out smaller flows (WFQ); others lump traffic into classes and then assign each class some portion of available bandwidth—using class-based queuing (CBQ). These systems are analogous to an airline that breaks large groups into smaller parties so regular travelers can get through and offers a separate lineup for first-class passengers—as long as there are first-class passengers waiting.

- Traffic shapers, such as leaky buckets and token buckets, that can smooth out the flow of traffic into the core of the network to shield it from burstiness.

- Discard algorithms that can tell congestion-aware transmitters that they are sending too much traffic for the current capacity of the network. Some queuing algorithms intentionally discard traffic to throttle back transmissions, but this is a two-step method—discarding the packet results in timeouts on the client, and timeouts result in reduced packets in transit. In some implementations an intermediate device alters the TCP signaling information directly in order to throttle clients directly. While limited to TCP traffic, this is a useful tool that can provide precise control over network traffic across a specific point.

We'll also discuss bandwidth reservation, although this is arguably out-of-the-box handling among adjacent devices.

Queuing systems and prioritization

Information on relative priority can suggest three major courses of action. These are the selection of later prioritization through packet marking, queue behavior, and congestion control or discard eligibility. Most of the methods that devices employ for enforcing traffic policies result from one or more of these systems.

Queues "push back" by delaying TCP acknowledgments and smoothing the delays that packets experience. Queues increase the round-trip time of a packet and require memory on the networking device; for some multimedia applications, a deep queue may result in the slow delivery of "stale" information that should instead have been dropped. By contrast, discarding packets pushes back against *transmitters* in a way that reduces queue depths and is relatively cheap to implement on a networking device but doesn't necessarily work with non-TCP traffic.

Sidebar

How deep are your buffers?

A queue is a waiting area for network traffic. Too small a queue, and packets will be discarded—resulting in a high number of retransmissions. Too "deep" a queue, and packets will wait around for transmission for too long while depriving their transmitting nodes of the information they need to throttle themselves back. So how deep should your buffers be? The answer, as with many networking problems, is that it depends.

• For hubs and some switches, you don't need buffering. Hubs don't use RAM, they just forward electrical signals without decoding the contents in some higher-up-the-stack kind of way. Cut-through switches also don't use any RAM. Congestion is not avoided at the link layer, it's avoided at the network layer (3).

• Router-to-router connectivity needs RAM. If you're assuming TCP/IP traffic that is elastic, you can stipulate that the amount of memory you require to buffer streams of TCP traffic is equal to the maximum number of concurrent TCP streams you will ever have, multiplied by the maximum TCP window size. This is the deepest buffer you'll need.

• The application mix in your network will dictate queue depth. Delay-sensitive traffic needs shorter buffers (and consequently, less RAM), while mission-critical "elastic" traffic that can tolerate delays will benefit from deeper buffers.

The problem with queues is that they "soften" the signaling that protocols rely on to understand congestion.

Devices first buffer incoming traffic (to smooth out bursts of data without interrupting transmission) and then assign traffic to a specific transmitting queue for forwarding. Deciding on queue membership involves assigning a packet (or in some cases, a session or frame) to a specific queue according to the classification systems we've seen. An algorithm is then used to decide the order and quantity in which queues should be emptied onto outbound links.

FIFO queuing

The simplest form of queue is first in, first out. FIFO is cheap and easy to implement, and it doesn't require the device to look at anything other than the order of entry to decide which packet to handle next. On the other hand, during periods of congestion FIFO queues exhibit interesting behavior. First, they queue all traffic indiscriminately, introducing latency equivalent to the size of the queue divided by the transmission rate. Then, when the queue is full, they discard all traffic. Discarding all traffic results in lost packets and transmission delays. Consequently, in a congested network a simple FIFO queue can magnify the effect of congestion and cause sizable variances in the performance of the network. **A bank queue with a single teller is FIFO.** FIFO queues are used for holding traffic, but to actually enforce different PHB's we need a differential queuing mechanism.

Priority queuing

Perhaps the simplest mechanism for deciding which packet to forward next is the strict priority queue (Figure 10–1). Rudimentary class-of-service behavior can be achieved through a simple priority mechanism. Instead of weighting traffic equitably, we can identify high-priority traffic during periods of congestion and forward them.

The concept of prioritizing some kinds of traffic by moving them out of the queue and onto the wire first is a good one; it simply needs refinement. **An airline ticket counter where all first class passengers are handled before any coach passengers is analogous to a simply prioritized queue.**

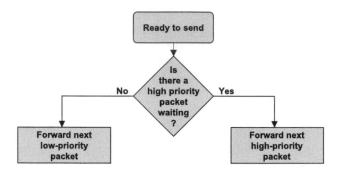

Figure 10–1 The simplest mechanism for forwarding: strict priority

This kind of forwarding is simple and efficient, but it can starve the low-priority queue, preventing low-priority applications from receiving the information they need to characterize the network's congestion and back off. While this seems like an excellent system for deciding how an arbitrary number of traffic types are handled, its impact on congestion signaling is an important weakness. Prioritized queues delay low-priority traffic indefinitely—more so than a FIFO queue in many cases. Because lower-priority traffic suffers all the jitter of higher-priority traffic, even medium-priority applications will often function less well in this queuing model than they would in a best-effort network. In our analogy, some coach passengers might miss their plane entirely because first-class passengers with later flights occupy all the ticketing agents.

We'll look at a more complex (and realistic) version of this diagram once we've learned more about different queuing mechanisms.

Round-robin

In an environment where some bandwidth-hungry application dominates the traffic mix, a FIFO queue can starve less "noisy" applications. The first step to a "sophisticated" queue is to make FIFO fair. A fair queue is one that distributes outbound bandwidth among traffic flows equitably.

One of the simplest systems for scheduling is a round-robin forwarding method. Round-robin iterates through multiple queues of packets and transmits equal amounts from each source, regardless of how full each source may be. If the iteration is weighted, the device selects an "unfair" amount of traffic from a particular source. The weighting between traffic classes (flows, applications, TOS or precedence bits, and the like) is used to decide on a ratio at which packets in each queue are forwarded.

Round-robin is the simplest starvation-avoidance method. Rather than forwarding traffic blindly, a round-robin system selects from waiting packets according to some classification. **A fast-food restaurant lineup with one teller and multiple queues (while somewhat annoying to consider) is analogous to a round-robin system.**

Weighted Fair Queuing

Round-robin forwarding is a selection method. If queues are used to hold traffic, then admission to queues is determined algorithmically. In weighted fair queuing (WFQ), some form of weighting is assigned to each traffic flow. Weighting is done according to a predefined ratio based on classification. The ratio ensures that high-volume traffic (such as a file backup) won't consume all available resources and block other applications, while at the same time giving applications with special needs (such as videoconferencing) the service they require.

WFQ algorithms smooth traffic based on a detailed analysis of the packet's contents. Different implementations of WFQ are available from many vendors. Cisco systems, for example, offers access queuing and distributed queuing. **The flow controllers on a highway's access ramps are analogous to weighted fair queuing.** As cars arrive at the highway, they are admitted at specific rates—but carpool traffic is subject to different ratios than those to which regular drivers are subject.

Custom queuing

As a predecessor to class-based queuing, custom queues are a series of access lists that allow an administrator to set relative priorities based on weights and packet matches. The forwarding engine on a network device removes some number of bytes (ideally some small multiple of the MTU for traffic in that queue) in a round-robin manner; by adjusting the number of bytes, you can assign relative weights to traffic. But because of the complexity of this model, custom queuing has generally given way to class-based queuing: coarseness wins over complication.

Class-based Queuing

CBQ is a refined form of queue priority. Instead of assigning absolute priorities (A before B, B before C), a CBQ system groups traffic into classes, then assigns a ratio or metric to each class. By moving a traffic flow from one class to another, you can easily alter the way in which that device handles the traffic; similarly, by adjusting the weighting, you can adjust how that class performs relative to others. CBQ offers the benefits of traffic equity and prioritization without bandwidth starvation.

If there's unused bandwidth, it's available to applications—which makes CBQ more useful than a simple throttle on traffic. **An airline ticket counter where first-class passengers have more check-in counter space than coach passengers is class based.** In our analogy, first-class counter personnel service coach class travelers when there are no people waiting in the first-class queue. This is an important element of CBQ.

Problems with queues

Since we're talking about airlines, one other analogy springs to mind. When an airplane is loading passengers, the attendant typically announces boarding by rows. Some passengers have a priority to board. Priority may be handed out by boarding groups when you arrive at the gate, somewhat like local policing or in-box classification. Alternately, priority may be selected by a travel agent when the ticket is printed, based on the seat assignment, somewhat like end-station tagging and packet marking.

If your fellow passengers are well behaved and you're in the first boarding group, you'll board first. Often, passengers in the last boarding group are milling around the boarding ramp, and they delay even the priority passengers. This is analogous to the intermingling of misbehaved and well-behaved applications. You may configure your network to throttle back low-priority TCP traffic through selective discard, weighted fair queuing, and the like; the TCP stacks will back off in the face of congestion accordingly. UDP traffic generated by "network-aware" applications will probably also reduce its load by dynamically increasing compression, reducing frame rate, and so on. Unfortunately, despite your careful design, badly behaved UDP traffic will continue to send, regardless of congestion signaling, and may impact the overall health of the network by filling up queues. This is known as head-of-line blocking.

What can you do about this? You can regulate this traffic into a rate-controlled bucket. You can also seek out the culprits and tell them to stop using the application. There is also a special discard algorithm called Flow

RED (FRED) that will relieve some of the congestion, which we'll look at in a moment.

Often the miscreants are home-grown applications designed by desktop engineers who opted for UDP's low overhead over TCP's reliability, because the traffic they wanted to generate became "stale" extremely quickly and discards were acceptable. Policy begins with good network architecture, and in today's IP services network, this means properly designed applications. Application designers are not network experts, and often they will resort to the simplest or easiest-to-design communications protocol over one that behaves properly in a multiservice network.

The impact of queue depth

We've looked at the way in which packets populate queues, and the algorithms with which packets are chosen for forwarding. Another element of queue management that's important to understand is queue depth and its effect on latency. The relative queue depth of each class that's assigned to a queue can be adjusted. Robust data applications that can withstand delays and jitter can benefit to some extent from a deep queue—they will retransmit less traffic, and their packets will remain valid and useful to the application even after a significant delay. Also, long queue delays will allow their TCP algorithms to adjust to the increased delay gracefully.

By contrast, latency- or jitter-sensitive interactive applications may want a shallow queue alongside a high relative priority. A shallow queue will mean early discards, which is appropriate for stale packets in a voice session, once the acceptable latency threshold has elapsed.

Devices may offer one or more queuing types, and their exact behavior can be complex. Some key points to consider when deciding on a queuing solution are the following:

- Prioritization features are especially useful if they group traffic into discrete classes for ease of configuration.

- Bandwidth equity is important to ensure that greedy applications don't monopolize the network. Starvation avoidance is vital—some amount of low-priority traffic must get through to let the low-priority applications know they need to back off.

- Queue-depth adjustment is useful if you're running applications with varied degrees of latency or jitter sensitivity, or applications in which traffic becomes useless after a certain elapsed time.

Discarding traffic

Now that we've seen some of the methods by which traffic is moved to or from a queue, we need to look at how excess traffic is discarded, once the queue overflows or congestion is predicted. Under normal conditions, bursts of traffic arrive in the queue and are selected for forwarding based on one of the systems we've seen—but the average available transmission capacity exceeds the speed with which the queue fills. During periods of sustained congestion, however, the queue fills faster than the queue-emptying algorithm can free up space, and discards must occur.

Note that queue saturation isn't the only reason for discards to take place. Low-latency traffic may become "stale," and proactive discards may occur in anticipation of growing queue depths.

Simple discard

To understand the importance of discard in modern networks, it is vital to realize that the TCP model assumes a "dumb" network core. By "dumb" we mean that the network offers minimal functionality other than forwarding. It does not attempt to guarantee delivery or shape traffic proactively. TCP's "smart" end nodes rely on discards to detect congestion; they diagnose the health of the network through a relatively limited set of symptoms.

Things have changed, however, and the network is now "smart" (meaning service-rich) in many ways. Modern IP networks are shifting from single-service media offering simple packet forwarding to rich, configurable transports that include, among other things, multicast pruning, packet filtering, and differentiated services.

TCP's low opinion of the network's services means that if today's networks are to communicate with a TCP stack that thinks they're "dumb," they can signal only through a very limited number of symptoms, such as packet loss or round-trip delay. Discarding selectively is the most important tool at their disposal. Dropping packets signals senders to slow down; dropping many packets from a specific session forces a sender into slow-start mode. Queuing traffic in a buffer increases the round-trip time of a packet, thereby delaying the subsequent transmission.

The most basic system for discarding traffic from a queue is to refuse entry to any new packets when the queue is full. Refusing new packets has the effect of causing all transmitting applications that apply some form of rate control—including those that already have packets in the queue itself—to back off and return to a slow start. There is no discrimination in queue admission, and low-priority applications are blocked alongside high-priority ones. Unfortunately, by the time the queues are full it may be too late for transmitters to slow down. As a result, discards that are made simply because of saturation are not really traffic "shaping."

RED

IP networks use round-trip time and discard levels to understand the congestion in the network and know when to back off. Random early discard (RED) and weighted random early discard (WRED) algorithms watch the amount of buffer space available and start discarding packets early on to signal transmitters that the network is congested (Figure 10–2). RED implementations are *proactive* (in other words, they anticipate the fact that the buffers will overflow and randomly drop packets to slow things gradually), which makes them far better than a simple discard. The RED mechanism is elegant in its simplicity. RED will automatically "single out" greedy applications, because packets from traffic that consumes more of a queue are more likely to be discarded by the random selection process.

If queues in a bank hold customers in order to shield tellers from varying levels of customer traffic throughout a day, then RED is rather like kicking a customer out every now and then for no apparent reason. Unlike you and I, however, the "customer" will not change banks when this happens. Being kicked out of the bank is simply a sign that the bank is busy, and to the TCP "customer" it is simply a message that customers should visit the bank less often.

The "goal" of a RED algorithm is to keep the average queue depth within a certain threshold. The threshold is an administratively configured level that balances the needs of real-time, inelastic, CBR traffic (short queues and low latency) and the needs of self-regulating, elastic traffic (guaranteed delivery and low discard rates). By discarding from the front of the queue, RED can reduce the amount of time it takes the sender to notice congestion by the length of time it takes to clear the queue. RED also aims to avoid filling up buffers that do not add to throughput but only contribute to delay.

RED queues sacrifice a few packets early on instead of throwing away large numbers of packets later. A full buffer means that *all* traffic will be discarded, which will reduce the network's ability to signal and result in heavily fluctuating application performance. It is essential to factor the behavior of TCP into queue and prioritization decisions. If moving a type of traffic into the low-priority queue on a vendor's device means that *all*

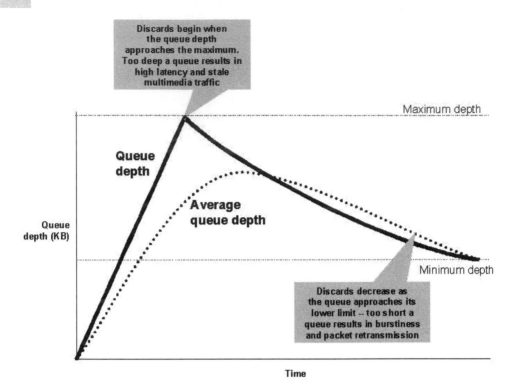

Figure 10–2 Queue depth with a RED algorithm

traffic of that type will be blocked when there is any other kind of traffic to send, then you will cut off that application's ability to detect congestion in the network early on and adjust itself accordingly. The moral? Don't put applications into "starved" queues unless they can handle bandwidth starvation robustly.

If the device uses some intelligence in selecting which traffic to discard first, then it is running a weighted random early discard (WRED). It is effectively singling out traffic types or end nodes and throttling them back at different rates. Weighting is more computationally intensive, but with the appearance of discretely classified traffic, WRED queuing systems are feasible even in the core of the network. A WRED scheme based on IPTOS or 802.1p schemes is a powerful tool for shaping core traffic.

WRED assumes some kind of explicit agreement about the capacity of a link. When you configure WRED weightings, you are provisioning how fast a given class will slow down compared to other classes across a device. Once you define a level of service for a given application or class, traffic falls into two categories within that class: traffic within the agreed-upon profile, and traffic that exceeds the profile. Both are subject to some degree of loss in a connectionless network. WRED ensures that out-of-profile traffic is dropped far more aggressively during times of congestion than in-profile traffic, however. Aggressive discard of out-of-profile traffic offers characteristics of "bursting" when excess capacity is available, and it lets administrators engineer the network into a differential best-effort system.

Advanced forms of RED, such as Flow RED, look at more information on queue behavior. FRED, for example, tracks per-flow queue depth and discards packets from deeper flows first in an effort to reduce the amount of nonadaptive traffic in a device. The rationale is that nonadaptive traffic flows will consume a disproportionate amount of buffer space when congestion occurs, since well-behaved senders will back off in the face of discards. FRED tells senders to slow down, and those that don't (as demonstrated by queues that don't get smaller) are assumed to be inelastic and treated accordingly.

Maximum-delay discard

As we have seen, for some applications traffic becomes useless after a given delay. In voice applications, delayed packets are simply static on the line; for video, they're jumpy frames. In a converged network, therefore, a maximum acceptable delay for a class of traffic is a useful indicator that allows graceful backoff for robust applications and quick signaling of congestion to interactive traffic.

Many UDP applications carrying time-sensitive data would sooner have their packets dropped than delivered so late as to make them unusable. The rationale is simple: discarding late traffic now might let traffic arrive on time later. Putting UDP traffic into a shorter queue effectively regulates the maximum delay that a packet will experience in a queue before it is dropped. Class-based admission into queues is a more sophisticated way of doing this; the traffic type's maximum delay is compared to the current queue length, and the traffic is dropped if it would be discarded by the receiver anyway. Maximum-delay discard can be summarized by the notion that "by the time it gets there, it'll be useless."

Front-of-queue discard

As we have seen, the sending TCP stack backs off when the receiver does not acknowledge a packet in a sequence. If congestion occurs, then the receiver will continue to receive TCP transmissions that are already in the queue—delaying congestion notification. One alternative is to discard traffic from the *front* of the queue, which results in a faster notification of the transmitter due to more immediate packet loss.

Front-of-queue discard can be implemented in conjunction with other queuing algorithms; a device can randomly discard traffic from the front of the queue instead of the back in order to improve TCP performance.

Our model for traffic handling has packets arriving at a device, moving into a queue, waiting to be selected based on some criteria, and being discarded during times of saturation. The remaining piece of the prioritization puzzle consists of traffic shaping, using buckets.

Leaky-bucket algorithms

The classic leaky-bucket analogy, as the name implies, is that of a bucket being filled at an irregular rate. The volume of water in the bucket may change constantly, but the resulting stream from a hole in the bottom of the bucket is smooth and constant. WAN cores tend to exhibit relatively unbursty traffic patterns due to aggregation.

This is achieved using a "leaky bucket" algorithm. The network device receives traffic at bursty rates but forwards the traffic at a constant rate. It is therefore an "antiburst" mechanism and a useful tool in reducing the variance in data rates from a device. Leaky buckets can be used to throttle traffic into a network so that it conforms to a predetermined portion of a link. Because they prevent bursting, however, they are somewhat inefficient—they do not make good use of excess capacity.

Imagine that you are a customer at a delicatessen. The deli is set up such that it will serve one customer every 30 seconds, and three salespeople are waiting to take your order (in other words, it takes at most a minute and a half to process an order). During busy periods this works quite well—customers can queue up, and the salespeople have 90 seconds to serve the customer.

But wouldn't you be annoyed if you were made to wait 90 seconds for your salesperson to complete an order while two other salespeople stood idle? Clearly, in the real world, you'd like to be served by any available excess capacity. Simple leaky buckets have this problem.

Each bucket releases only a limited number of packets. The queue also regulates the traffic "into the bucket" so that inbound traffic exceeding the drainage rate of the bucket over time (i.e., leading to saturation) is discarded.

What about the flow from the bucket onto the network? If the device is able to smooth the introduction of traffic into the network, it can make work easier for downstream devices and help prevent transmission fluctuations. Smoothing flow at the edge of the network makes the core load more consistent and reduces the need to overprovision the core in order to accommodate burstiness without saturating access queues.

Leaky buckets are especially useful for service providers who want to allow a user to transmit some subset of the actual network capacity into the network based on how much the user pays. A leaky bucket that restricts admission into an ATM cloud can offer finely tuned subsets of a high-volume circuit, for example. Without leaky-bucket throttling of traffic, the customer can order relatively coarse chunks of bandwidth (56 Kbps, T1, T3, etc.). Instead, with a bucket in place the ISP can open the bucket's "hole" in fine increments based on month-to-month need and plan their backbone expansion accordingly.

Token Buckets

A close cousin of the leaky bucket, the token-bucket system is able to deal with burstiness. It offers the same ability to regulate traffic up to some known limit, but does so by making "tokens" available to inbound traffic based on the capacity of the outbound link. Tokens are handed out according to traffic-shaping rules, so that specific classes of traffic get a certain portion of available tokens. The tokens represent space on the link that is being controlled, and each arriving packet "takes a token" from the bucket, which it uses to gain access to the outbound link.

A token bucket is a leaky bucket that incorporates feedback about the state of the network into queuing decisions—less bandwidth means fewer available tokens. By contrast with a leaky bucket, however, an application can use an excess of tokens if no other applications are around to claim them. A bursty application can use all the tokens it wants, provided that the link is uncontested; in times of congestion, tokens are distributed equitably. Returning to our deli analogy, imagine that an attendant hands out tokens as you arrive at the store. You can take three tokens and have all three staff work on your order if there's nobody else in the store.

By comparison with the overly simplified, strict priority queuing mechanism we saw earlier, we can now envision a more complex and pragmatic algorithm that would divide traffic among four possible handlers, as shown in Figure 10–3.

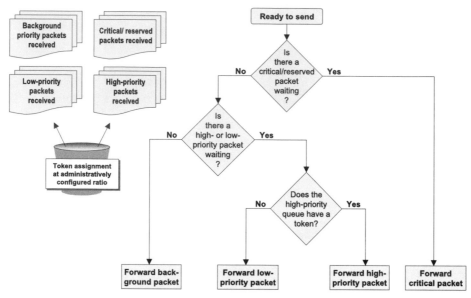

Figure 10–3   A complex forwarding mechanism

In this scheme, critical (or reserved) traffic is always forwarded immediately. Careful admission control is required here to ensure that the total of this traffic will not saturate the network; classes of traffic to admit include network monitoring, management, and control traffic, as well as router updates. In addition, any capacity that has been guaranteed (such as a properly allocated RSVP flow) must be placed into this queue in order to meet service agreements established when the reservation was set up.

Background traffic—traffic that can sustain an indefinite delay—can be transmitted only when spare network capacity exists. Moving robust-application traffic into background queues is a useful way to squeeze all available capacity from the network. The real trick, however, comes in the implementation of high- and low-queue behavior. Traffic from each queue is transmitted according to an administratively defined ratio, rather than as an absolute. Low-priority applications that may suffer when starved can be placed in the low-priority queue and will still receive some portion of the available bandwidth. They are restricted to a lower percentage of network capacity remaining after reservations when compared to high-priority traffic.

In-profile and out-of-profile

If a sender has agreed to restrict transmissions to some specific level, then receivers have a "traffic profile" to which they expect the sender to adhere. Traffic that is within this profile is subject to the agreed-upon service for which the sender has negotiated. On the other hand, devices treat out-of-profile traffic is treated differently.

If additional capacity is available, the nodes along the network path may want to treat out-of-profile traffic as best effort. Should congestion occur, however, the devices will want to mark out-of-profile for discard in order to throttle senders back into their profile. In Frame Relay, this may mean setting the discard-eligibility information in each frame; for TCP, it will mean discarding out-of-profile packets. One QOS algorithm that works with in-profile and out-of-profile traffic is Committed Access Rate (CAR).

Committed Access Rate

CAR is the name for a combination of prioritization and discarding that attempts to deliver an assured service. CAR will treat all traffic of a certain class well if it falls within agreed-upon levels. CAR may also set priority bits or forward to a high-priority queue. For out-of-profile traffic of the given class, CAR will either mark it as eligible for discard or discard it outright, depending on device configuration and the congestion of the egress interface.

Because CAR treats in-profile and out-of-profile traffic differently, one might be tempted to send out-of-profile multimedia over an alternate, slower network path. This would be wrong. It is better to discard traffic in this case. TCP performance will degrade substantially if traffic takes alternate routes through the network. Recall that TCP tries to determine the capacity and latency of the network—in-profile packets and out-of-profile packets would travel in different ways, which would confuse TCP. By selecting alternate paths for a flow, you will give the sender ambiguous information about response time and cause fluctuating TCP behavior. On the other hand, discarding traffic will inform the sender that the flow specification is being exceeded.

CAR is really a combination of token buckets and weighted fair queuing, with administratively configured specifications for various flows.

Rate controllers

TCP traffic regulates itself by looking at specific metrics such as packet loss and round-trip time. Consequently, we can "trick" TCP into acting a certain way by playing with these parameters. RED is a perfect example of using artificial discards to cause TCP to back off. Discarding is slightly inefficient, since packets are lost in the course of signaling through packet loss.

A class of device known as a TCP flow controller or rate shaper acts as an intermediary between a TCP sender and receiver. By artificially delaying the receiver's responses (adjusting the TCP window size and delaying ACKs when congestion is imminent) it can give the sender's stack false information about round-trip time and, therefore, modify the amount of bandwidth the TCP application consumes. In effect, these devices alter a TCP sender's perception of the available bandwidth in the network without wastefully dropping otherwise useful traffic.

TCP rate control regulates transmission well, but it works only for TCP-based applications. A TCP rate controller does nothing to regulate the introduction of UDP traffic into the network—which includes most real-time traffic. As a proactive congestion-avoidance tool for much of today's network traffic, TCP rate shaping is very useful. When combined with other handling systems described here, it can be a part of an excellent QOS system. Such a system might look like this:

- Separate queues for TCP and UDP traffic, with token buckets for each.
- TCP rate control on the TCP queue, possibly with weighted RED and front-of-queue discard if the TCP rate control does not elicit a fast enough reduction in TCP traffic during congestion.
- Class-based queuing of UDP traffic, with a short queue, on the assumption that some traffic needs priority and that the useful lifespan of a multimedia UDP datagram is relatively short (i.e., highly delayed packets should be discarded rather than sent late).
- Flow RED for controlling nonadaptive UDP traffic

Queuing, discards, buckets, and rate controls allow IP to offer some of the control characteristics that ATM sought to deliver at the data-link layer, without the complexity that ATM engenders. By using a simple set of handlers and traffic shapers, IP QOS mechanisms can produce a surprisingly rich range of behaviors.

Bandwidth reservation

So far, the handling techniques we've looked at have functioned within a device. In the next chapter we'll cover handling methods that work between devices, but first we'll look at a "hybrid" approach: bandwidth reservation. Reservation takes place across a network path and involves many devices. Once the reservation is negotiated, however, each device needs to apply a set of per-hop behaviors that handle traffic in the agreed-upon manner. Bandwidth reservation is therefore both interdevice and intradevice.

The Integrated Services philosophy holds that some portion of bandwidth must be precisely guaranteed. To understand why we might need to set aside bandwidth—reserve it—rather than simply prioritize it, let's review the difference between a constant-bit-rate data stream and a packetized, high-priority data stream.

We've already seen many ways in which traffic can be delayed as it crosses a network—from outbound queuing on point-to-point circuits, to transit time across links, to intermediate device queues. Because of the techniques that senders and receivers employ when smoothing transmission of packet-based data, we're hard pressed to deliver interactive voice even on a fast LAN.

Recall that the lowest delay we can expect from today's voice-over-IP systems is 125 milliseconds (25 milliseconds for G.729 compression and 100 milliseconds for jitter buffering). Since 200 milliseconds is the most delay that we'll tolerate, the IntServ position is that conversational voice traffic has to have a guarantee, because the network must offer the ideal QOS to this traffic. In other words, for delay-sensitive traffic, the network must behave as if it were overprovisioned and uncongested.

Guarantees allow the optimization of jitter-smoothing buffers on the receiver. Through the reservation's flow specification, receiving buffers learn the latency and the latency variance on the link. They can therefore tell the application whether there is sufficient capacity to establish a useful call. It will be possible for a heavily loaded network to become "busy" when no reservation capacity is available if the receivers cannot find a suitably fast flow reservation. This has the same effects as a telephone switch becoming busy today, when all circuits are occupied.

There are several ways to reserve bandwidth. One is to have each device set aside a portion of the next hop's capacity for a type of traffic, either through administrative parameters or by associating a particular class of service with a portion of the available bandwidth. Setting aside a portion of the link is an effective system, since the attached device has complete control over the ingress pipe of the hop.

- For a point-to-point link, this means simply restricting the amount of traffic into the link using flow buckets, access lists, or some kind of rate shaping.

- For a subnet "cloud" such as Ethernet, media-level reservation may come from a subnet bandwidth manager.

- For a circuit switched infrastructure such as ATM, reservation will come from the negotiation of a set of QOS parameters that characterize the link.

- For a circuit switched public network like Frame Relay, the reservation should come from a portion of the bandwidth that is "below" the CIR of the link. Reserving below the CIR will mean tagging excess traffic that is "pushed over" the CIR level by the reserved traffic as discard eligible, but the ability to do so will depend on the networking devices.

Another way to set aside network bandwidth is to use an internetwork reservation scheme (currently RSVP). Doing so implies some degree of common real-time control (a policy) for consistent admission and permission decisions. Consequently, RSVP will initially be deployed at the edge of the network within a single administrative domain, with signaling to some form of reserved switching fabric or class-of-service mapping (MPLS, IP precedence, DS code point) in the core. True end-to-end reservation will require that the edge of the administrative domain has the ability to set up committed links across the WAN link on demand. In other words, the edge devices must link the local RSVP flow into the public core's capacity.

The economics of reservation—congestion insurance or pay-as-you go?

If you subscribe to a higher-quality network service, you're reserving a portion of the capacity that is less likely to be impacted by congestion. The ultimate expression of reserved capacity is a leased line. When the network is unloaded, you'll get the same capacity as everyone else; when the network is full, you'll be in a queue that is less affected by random early discards, for example. You're paying a premium for the ability to survive congestion—congestion insurance.

On the other hand, if the network is congested and you want to get a high-priority application through, you might opt to send tagged traffic and pay a per-packet or per-minute fee at the end of the month. You're paying as you go, based on traffic you generate—congestion cure.

Subscription is easier to price and administer than pay-as-you-go. Subscription happens in human time—you subscribe monthly, and your traffic is administratively configured on the router. By contrast, pay-as-you-go demands instant billing and policing, and dynamic admission control on traffic. In a subscription system, you're less aware of the benefits than in a curative system. It's rather like buying medical insurance or relying on socialized medicine versus paying for medical treatment: you pay for insurance whether you need it or not. In a pay-as-you-go system, hospital admissions may require a credit check and the establishment of billing mechanisms.

Additional economic factors are at work here. Service providers are unlikely to degrade their "best effort" offering just so that premium customers can feel better about themselves. Curative systems can cause a "run on bandwidth"; congestion occurs, which causes everyone to upgrade their transmission class, congesting the high-priority capacity. It will be wise for service providers to upgrade their backbone capacity when they roll out differentiated services, just to ensure that customers don't feel cheated. Complex market-economy paradigms have been extensively researched. These mechanisms may one day pit our network devices against one another as bidders in excess-capacity auctions.

Negotiated versus mapped

When end stations negotiate for reserved bandwidth across a link, each device in the path of the attempted reservation tests the request for *admissibility* (the requestor is entitled to the bandwidth) and *capacity* (the bandwidth is available). By contrast, explicitly tagged traffic is mapped to the appropriate queue when it arrives at a device. Within a queue, multiple traffic types may compete with one another for forwarding precedence.

The IETF's "Integrated Services over Specific Link Layers" (ISSLL) is chartered to define the mappings between the advanced features of various link-layer technologies (such as the association of 802.1p and ATM, or of RSVP and ATM QOS).

Some link types (such as ATM) offer guaranteed delivery and are suitable for mapping RSVP-guaranteed load flows. ATM networks are characterized by an admission control to ensure that additional reservations do not violate existing contracts. Other link types (such as 802.1p) offer prioritization, or better-than-best effort. These link types do not have admission controls of their own and must rely on network-layer admission control (such as a trusted tagging end node, or a router with a policing function) to avoid priority abuse. Nevertheless, prioritized media can help achieve far more control than best-effort media, even if the resulting "guarantees" may in fact vary somewhat.

Static

Static allocation of bandwidth is performed by a network administrator. Static allocation is generally configured in one of two ways:

- Packet interleaving states a ratio of forwarding for several classes of traffic. For example, 3Com's NETBuilder II routers can, by default, classify traffic into 3 classes (high, medium, or low.) The forwarding ratios for these classes is defined as "HHMHMHLH", which results in 5 high-priority packets, 2 medium-priority packets, and 1 low-priority packet leaving the device at a reasonably regular interval.

- Static bandwidth reservation assigns some portion of the available network link capacity to traffic that matches a given filter. The reservation can be absolute (i.e., no traffic can use the space on the link), but it is more generally dynamic (i.e., if any traffic that matches the filter arrives, it is allocated up to the reserved link capacity). Excess capacity can either be discarded or forwarded as best-effort.

Neither of these methods takes into account changing circumstances, and both must be reconfigured by humans. In this respect, they are *provisioned* QOS rather than QOS policy systems.

Dynamic (admission control)

Before we delve into the intricacies of bandwidth reservation, it's important to understand the goals of reservation from a broad perspective. Traditional routing protocols rely on *link-state* or *link-metric* information to decide what path traffic should take across a network. The level of service a traditional link can offer is fixed: you can't get a T1 to behave like a T3. Some network service providers offer "burstable T1." Upon closer examination, you will find that this is a link with a maximum throughput of greater than 1.544 Mbps—in some cases, even an Ethernet circuit—with software support for bursting and throttling.

With the advent of "burstable" links like Frame Relay or ATM as well as the introduction of shared media and routed WAN clouds for delay-sensitive traffic, you may be able to grab an extra portion of the available bandwidth. Suddenly, knowing the state of links isn't enough. Router protocols take a long time (in computer terms) to converge on a stable network model, and bursting means taking advantage of excess capacity within an extremely short span of time. Because bursting implies some degree of admission control, discard, and queuing, the network now needs to know the state of the nodes themselves. For this reason, in ATM, the path-selection mechanism (PNNI) gathers information not only on link state but also on the state of the devices and their capacity.

Any kind of bandwidth regulation in a burstable network requires link-state and node-capacity information. While ATM and Frame Relay handle most of this within the network itself, the TCP/IP protocol suite has traditionally handled such issues at the end nodes. TCP's coarse, network-has-no-services model has allowed rapid deployment of an incredible number of end nodes. On the other hand, this coarse approach has given us the Internet at the expense of rich network services in the infrastructure that might otherwise ease scaling and permit a broader range of application development. RSVP is changing this.

RSVP

The addition of complex reservation services to otherwise simple networks is a hotly contested issue in Internet standards bodies. The Internet has grown largely because of its relative simplicity and the ability of a few simple actions (such as discard) to have far-reaching implications (such as bandwidth throttling). Making the core of the network "smart" means that the simplicity disappears. On the other hand, the Internet as we know it today (and most intranets) simply cannot offer bandwidth guarantees, and this creates an obstacle to next-generation networking.

The Resource Reservation Protocol (RSVP) allows network nodes to request a guarantee from the network that a flow will receive some specific kind of treatment, provided that it remains within profile. These requests are evaluated on a hop-by-hop basis by all layer-3 devices along the chosen path. Each device must determine whether it has the capacity to reserve a portion of bandwidth (the "admission control"), as well as whether the requesting node is entitled to the bandwidth (the "policy control"). RSVP classifies traffic based on IP addresses, IP protocol, and UDP or TCP port.

Engineering groups are working to extend user-based policies and subnet reservations to the system. RSVP is an admission-control system suitable for use within an administrative domain, but it has limitations in terms of cross-domain policy and scalability, since performing suitable policy controls on traffic flows from many sources doesn't scale well.

RSVP attempts to offer a "guaranteed" and a "controlled load" service to the network.

- The guaranteed service is for real-time applications that are unable to handle delay—it tries to deliver a predictable, constant stream of network capacity that is as close as possible to the end-to-end network delay. The sender and receiver tell the network how much traffic they will send, and they provide a measure of how much "slack" there is between the proposed end-to-end delay and the desired delay of the application. Guaranteed loads consist of a predefined flow specification and corresponding set of per-hop behaviors in the form of a contract between the receiver and the device. The contract states that a given flow will be handled in a certain way.

- The controlled-load service is a better-than-best-effort service; it tries to deliver end-to-end network capacity that is as close as possible to the condition of an unloaded network, but still best effort. The sender tells the network what the traffic it will send will look like, and the network strives to ensure that all traffic within this description is handled as well as possible. Controlled-load contracts agree that a flow will be handled within a certain range, but variance is anticipated.

Let's look at the establishment of a dynamic reservation in detail.

The reservation begins when the sender generates a *path* message. This is a special packet sent through the network to document the reservation's route from end-to-end. The packet contains a filter that uniquely identifies the intended flow, as well as a description of the kind of transmission parameters the sender expects the flow to have. In this way, each node in the path learns how to identify the traffic flow as well as the volume, latencies, and tolerances of the flow.

The path message makes its way along the routed path, gathering information at each router as RSVP nodes append their particular per-hop behavior to the message, as illustrated in Figure 10–4. At any given point, the packet contains the IP addresses of the previous hop, as well as information on the capacity and approximate delay that each node will introduce. This information is called a *flowspec*.

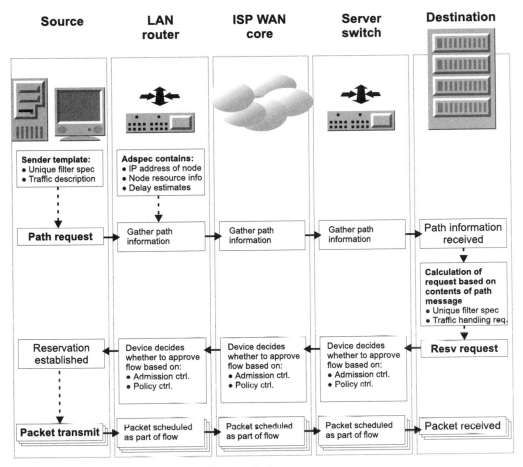

Figure 10–4 Traffic flow for an RSVP negotiation

For all service types, each RSVP node must provide information on the adjacent egress links across which the intended flow will travel (such as MTU, packet size, and framing overhead related to the media type). The node must also signal available bandwidth and minimum latency. In addition, the "break bits" used to detect non-IntServ devices must be correctly set. For guaranteed load, the node must also specify constant- and rate-proportional-delay bounds from the responding node to the next node in the path, and the transmit and receive resources needed to deliver per-hop behavior identical to the minimum latency (i.e., how much of a queue or a link would need to be set aside). For controlled load, the node must just specify transmit and receive resources.

By the time the path message makes its way to the destination, the receiver has a complete picture of the route across the network, as well as the relative services and capabilities the network can offer. By comparing the path's capabilities with the sender's traffic description, the receiver can formulate an appropriate request for services (called a reservation message).

The reservation message contains the same unique classifier to identify the intended flow for which the reservation is being established, as well as a flow specification that describes the kind of reservation wanted. The reservation can be either a controlled load or a guaranteed service. As the reservation request makes its way back to the original sender, each intermediate device subjects it to two tests. An admission control checks to see if bandwidth is available, and a policy control checks to see if the user is entitled to make the reservation.

A few key points should be made about this relatively simple treatment of RSVP:

- The reservation occurs in a two-step process (path, then reservation) for a number of reasons. Key among these is the ability to reserve on a multicast stream. The multicast subscriber client would first subscribe to the multicast transmission, then reserve bandwidth by sending a path message up the tree along a single possible route. The path message *determines* the path even as it gathers information on the intermediate devices. In this way, the receiver reserves bandwidth up the tree. If the multicast sender made the reservation to each subscriber, it wouldn't be able to reserve bandwidth for an individual user easily and, consequently, wouldn't scale well.

- Reservations are "soft" in RSVP, unlike the committed contracts that exist until link termination in ATM. The receiver sends periodic updates to maintain the reservation. These updates are needed to maintain a reservation in a connectionless environment like IP, where the route may change periodically.

- When a device receives a path message, it can tell from the enclosed information whether or not the message crossed a non-RSVP-enabled device. If this is the case, then any information after the non-IP device cannot be relied upon by the receiver. RSVP messages can therefore probe a network for QOS capabilities—something that is missing IPTOS, 802.1p, and DiffServ.

RSVP reservations can apply to three types of classifier, or filter:

- a fixed-filter style, which explicitly specifies a sender and a unique reservation

- a shared-explicit style, which explicitly specifies a sender but shares the reservation with other senders

- a wildcard-filter style, which allows a group of senders to share a reservation

Sharing reservations improves scalability by aggregating flows.

In the early stages of deployment, most networking devices will make the decisions about reservation themselves. In the case of admission control, the device is aware of the demands for its capacity and can make a reasonably informed decision. In the case of the policy control, however, a consistent set of rules from a central authority is needed to ensure that the network behaves in accordance with the business goals of the organization.

The first release of RSVP standards did not take into account policy controls. However, the authors of the standard included a placeholder for bandwidth reservation based on user admissibility, and in early 1998 two IETF drafts were introduced that extend RSVP to include policy-based decisions and user authentication.

Policy and reservations

The RSVP router and a central decision point work together to decide whether a reservation should be granted. The device that is going to reserve bandwidth is called the Policy Enforcement Point, and the server that evaluates the request for bandwidth is called the Policy Decision Point. The conversation occurs using a protocol called the Common Open Policy Service (COPS). We'll go into the mechanics of COPS negotiations later. Let's look first at the characteristics that an enforcing RSVP-capable router must have in order to deliver guaranteed service and controlled-load reservations.

A basic router forwards traffic based on arrival—it is a FIFO system. Some routers can implement static reservation through predefined packet filters, but these do not take into account currently assigned bandwidth (Figure 10–5).

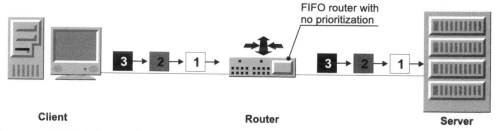

Figure 10–5   FIFO forwarding of traffic with no prioritization

In such a device, the order of packets does not change as they move through the router. Any static handling algorithms are provisioned in human time rather than established on a session-by-session basis.

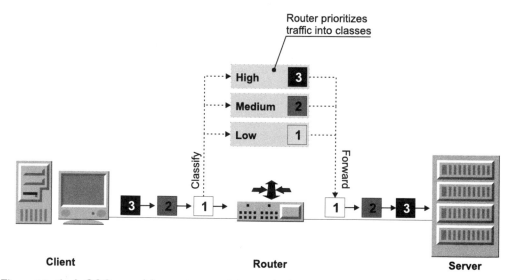

Figure 10–6   A COS-capable router applying prioritization decisions to traffic

Compare this to a COS-capable router that can make classifications and forward to one of several outbound queues (Figure 10–6). The packets are then ordered according to priority. These criteria are relatively simple and can be configured administratively in the form of access lists. Nevertheless, there is no regard for the characteristics of a given reservation, and so the system is still best effort. Policy systems that order packets without regard for the specific needs of each flow reservation may not be able to deliver the predictable handling that a guaranteed service aims to offer.

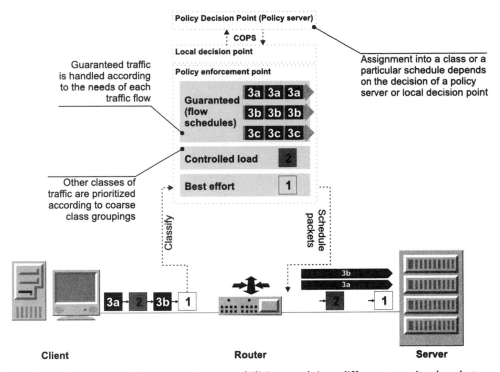

Figure 10–7   A router with reservation capabilities applying different service levels to traffic

To implement true guaranteed service, a router needs to control admission to reserved capacity that is set aside specifically for this purpose (Figure 10–7). The router then allocates this reserved bandwidth through a packet scheduler, allocating the remaining bandwidth through the aforementioned priority system. In this way, reserved traffic enjoys guaranteed, deterministic behavior, while all other traffic gets differentiated (but not guaranteed) network performance.

Overcoming scaling issues through aggregation

One way to overcome the problem of many flows in a network core is to aggregate reservations. RSVP can be used to identify flows with special needs going into an edge router, but across a busy WAN core the edge router would use a single reservation to another edge router and would aggregate flows with the same set of needs. Instead of multiple flows needing similar PHBs, the WAN will see only one flow, whose aggregate bandwidth is the sum of the flows being aggregated by the edge.

This approach reduces the amount of state information that the network core must maintain. It is unclear, however, whether the granularity of RSVP is needed for these aggregate reservations rather than relatively coarse signaling methods such as IPTOS, DiffServ, or MPLS.

Putting it all together

A complete system within a networking device (Figure 10–8) includes many of the classification and handling capabilities we've just seen. These include:

- classifying the traffic at various levels
- inserting traffic into class-based queues
- discarding stale time-sensitive traffic
- setting discard eligibility
- performing proactive discard or flow control
- applying a committed access-rate constraint
- supporting dynamic bandwidth allocation

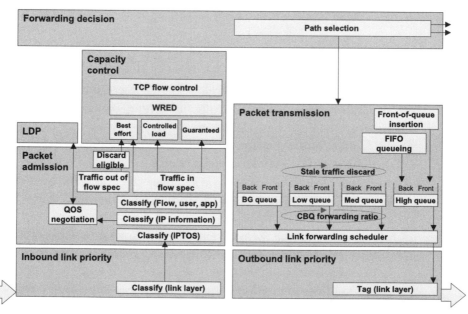

Figure 10–8 A combination of QOS technologies working as a system

In addition to these internal mechanisms for handling traffic, each device can affect treatment on subsequent devices through a number of mechanisms:

- selecting an appropriate path
- forwarding to the outbound link with appropriate link-layer priority information

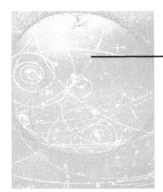

Traffic handling by path selection

In addition to handling traffic differently within a device, the network can effect interdevice handling using alternate routes, explicit packet marking, and even the dynamic creation of premium-service circuits. By combining interdevice handling with mechanisms such as queues and discards, the entire network works toward a set of QOS goals.

There are three main ways in which a device can change the way traffic is handled beyond the device itself:

- It can mark the traffic at the link layer so that intermediate media will handle it in a certain way, or mark it at the network layer to pass explicit messages to adjacent routers.

- It can forward the flow to an interface that it knows offers certain handling characteristics. This may be a provisioned ATM permanent virtual circuit or a Frame Relay circuit, a previously established VPN tunnel, or a point-to-point link. This is often known as "next-hop" forwarding.

- It can dynamically establish a link to a destination with a set of handling parameters. ATM switched virtual circuits, RSVP reservations, an on-demand VPN tunnel, or a multiprotocol label-switching connection are examples of this.

Marking the traffic: Ethernet prioritization

Link-layer infrastructure can now offer some degree of differentiation. For example, a combination of differential queuing, admission control, and signaling allows a modern Ethernet network to offer better-than-best-effort services. In addition, because it recognizes "less-than-best-effort" systems, it can be used to signal discard eligibility for traffic flows that exceed their predefined parameters.

In circuit-based media such as ATM, RSVP nodes can map flows directly to circuits or to "classes" of circuit. This kind of mapping is not so straightforward in a shared Ethernet LAN, because the switches cannot associate fine-grained RSVP per-flow reservations with coarse 802.1p classes. There are two main ways to leverage Ethernet class-of-service facilities. A simple mapping of network-layer type-of-service information is relatively straightforward and works well between DiffServ values and media priorities. A subnet bandwidth manager allows routers to characterize and regulate intermediate media layers.

Mapping to 802.1p values

A proposal within the IETF[1] would map classes of traffic into "aggregated flows" based on the notion that 802.1p priorities can offer some degree-of-service and latency bound. In this model, when a packet arrives at the edge of an Ethernet cloud, it is tagged with the appropriate 802.1p priority level by the admitting router. The proposal simplifies the ambiguity of 802.1p values by describing the approximate latency bound that an Ethernet cloud will introduce to those values listed in Table 11–1.

Table 11–1   Proposed mappings of IntServ to 802.1p priority values

802.1p value	Service bound
7	Network control
6	Delay sensitive, 10-ms bound
5	Delay sensitive, 100-ms bound
4	Delay sensitive, no bound
3	Reserved
2	Reserved
1	Reserved, "less than" best effort
0	Default, assumed to be best effort

The advantage of this simple classification is that it allows an RSVP path/reservation sequence to characterize the delay that the Ethernet segment will introduce into the network. If a router adds 20 milliseconds' delay to the connection and it will tag an 802.1p value of 5 onto Ethernet frames on the adjacent segment, it can add a 120-millisecond PHB to the RSVP path specification.

This system assumes some degree of admission control (for example, token buckets or queues that limit the amount of delay-sensitive or network-control traffic that enters the cloud). The proposal does not suggest mechanisms for achieving these levels of service. In the simplest possible multilevel switch (i.e., 2 queues), all delay-sensitive traffic will travel via the high-priority queue, at the expense of best-effort traffic. The "less than best effort" can be used to mark traffic that has exceeded its flow-spec; it can be compared to the discard-eligibility bit in Frame Relay. The LAN will forward it, but not at the expense of even best-effort traffic.

For an IntServ controlled-load service, the calculation of these parameters does not have to be precise; it is assumed that the system is somewhat self-regulating and will adjust itself gracefully. For a guaranteed load, calculation must be more precise, owing to the application's inability to adjust itself readily (as is the case in a constant-bit-rate voice application).

This initiative allows today's smarter LANs to become active partici-pants in the networking process. With proper use of the "less than best effort" bit, the LAN effectively offers a discard system and multiple queues *within* the network.

How a Subnet Bandwidth Manager works

LANs are priority based and coarsely classified. Because they operate at layer 2, they cannot participate directly in an RSVP negotiation. The Inter-net community's response to this weakness is to make the aggregate band-width of a subnet an active participant in integrated-services negotiation. To this end, a subnet bandwidth manager (SBM) characterizes LAN behav-ior and makes that information available to the path of layer-3 devices. SBMs offer admission control to an Ethernet cloud. Admission control at the edge of the LAN, combined with rate control on the end nodes and link-layer priority systems such as 802.1p, may be able to offer something akin to the IntServ controlled load and guaranteed traffic handling.

An RSVP-capable router or layer-3 switch "controls" the LAN seg-ment. It is responsible for characterizing the per-hop behaviors across the subnet, and it performs admission control for the segment. When the router initializes, it tries to decide if it is responsible for that particular subnet. Either it becomes the designated subnet bandwidth manager (DSBM) or it determines which device *is* the current DSBM.

On each segment there is only one DSBM. Instead of sending an RSVP message on to the next hop in the routed path, any RSVP-capable node on a bandwidth-managed subnet forwards the message to the DSBM. The DSBM adds the appropriate information to the pathspec or reservation on behalf of the subnet, and it forwards the message on to the next hop. In other words, a DSBM inserts itself into the routed path as a representative of the subnet for which it is a manager. In this way, the DSBM is able to regulate access to the subnet *provided that all devices include it in admission-control decisions*. If one attached router does not include the DSBM in its decisions, the system breaks down.

In order to support this "side-stepping" along the path, extensions to the RSVP protocol have been proposed that will maintain the next hop in the path (along with the MAC address of the next hop, in case the switch is unable to resolve the MAC address itself) when the message is passed to the DSBM. In addition, a traffic-class indicator (an 802.1p priority value) will be added to the path and reservation messages in order to allow the routers adjacent to the layer-2 cloud to tag the packet correctly.

Microsoft's SBM implementation uses RSVP path messages from the client to determine if the network can support QOS. If a successful RSVP exchange cannot be completed with the destination, the SBM will revert to sending all traffic from a node as untagged at all layers—circumventing a COS implementation in IPTOS or 802.1p that could otherwise differentiate service. This approach is taken because no other standard method (such as 802.1p, for example) offers explicit signaling and end-to-end QOS checking. Some vendor implementations employ pings with the desired 802.1p or IPTOS values in the packet and evaluate the response to determine the availability of QOS services. For now, however, Microsoft relies only on RSVP when it characterizes a network's QOS capabilities.

Network and media priorities working together

When today's routers forward traffic across an interface, they make the assumption that the traffic across that interface is serial. In other words, they assume that when they send two packets out the same physical interface, destined for a topologically adjacent router, the packets will arrive in the order in which they were sent.

Within a router, packets are received, queued, subjected to routing and forwarding metrics, and sequenced for transmission to the next hop in their path. The reception may involve flow smoothing or traffic shaping; the transmission may be according to absolute or relative priorities, depending on the classification. The underlying assumption is that shifting of packet order must take place within the router, because the wires between routers are first in, first out.

With the traditional model of media layers, the link between two network nodes (i.e., IP routers) was strictly FIFO. A packet transmitted first across Ethernet would arrive first (Figure 11–1).

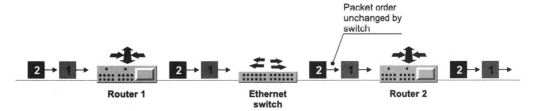

Figure 11–1 Routers treating a traditional Ethernet network as a FIFO link

It is useful to think of a multiservice LAN as an "Ethernet cloud." In much the same way as a WAN cloud is a set of indeterminate forwarding services with only the periphery visible to the access routers, so a modern switched Ethernet infrastructure is a set of queues, buffers, and links that the router cannot assume will behave as point-to-point circuits. Some vendors may also refer to this as a "link-layer bubble"; the use of a "cloud" to refer to network layers and a "bubble" to refer to link layers is not universally accepted and may be a result of vendor politics rather than industry terminology.

TCP/IP is well suited to the sequencing problems that can occur in out-of-order delivery, so nothing has to change if the media layer alters packet sequence—TCP will correct the alteration at the receiver. But if today's media layer can often be relied upon to offer even two "media queues," then instead of forwarding traffic into a queue on the router itself, the router can forward traffic into the media with different media tags (for example, by setting the 802.1p priority information in the 802.1D header) *and use the media as a queue.*

In this case, a high-priority packet may leave the first router after a low-priority packet and arrive at the second router beforehand (Figure 11–2).

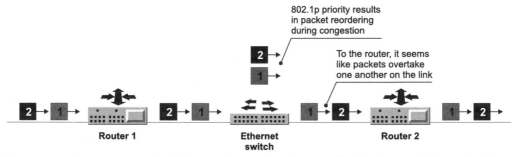

Figure 11–2   Routers may find that packet order changes if priority-capable media lie between them

This is an important notion that may substantially alter the design of internetworking devices where the media can be relied upon to be multiservice. Such a design would reduce the cost and complexity of the routing devices but would only work when the media's capabilities were known. Simple layer-3 class-of-service tagging does not fully leverage recent innovations in media switching, both on the WAN and in the LAN. Nevertheless, it is likely that integrated router/switch systems such as this will emerge from networking vendors, once protocols become more broadly implemented.

Marking the traffic: Leveraging your ISP

IPTOS already offers the facilities needed to signal differentiated services. Enterprise networks are waiting for ISPs to offer differentiation of their traffic on demand in order for IPTOS to be useful at the enterprise/provider boundary.

Until recently, ISP regulation of available bandwidth has been the networking equivalent of duct tape. Some providers use periodic pings and calculate the average ping time to determine whether a customer is generating a greater sustained load than the agreed-upon amount. Other systems include traditional traffic counters, which sample traffic every 5 minutes and average the amount to determine the fractional line usage. When customers exceed this rate, they move to the next fraction of the available link charge. Similar methods are applied to higher-rate connections such as dual T1 links with load sharing, tiered T3, or direct OC-3.

Carriers like MCI, US West, and AT&T offer differentiated frame relay services. UUNET is promoting differentiated VPN services. The deployment of IPTOS capabilities in routers makes this sort of "premium Internet" service available to most carriers and ISPs. However, it will be a long time before the political and administrative issues involved in billing for differentiated services on and end-to-end connection are resolved.

At the same time, new gear in the carrier backbones is making service providers more daring in their claims. MCI is guaranteeing less than 95 ms across its Internet backbone, for example, hoping that extranet partners will sign on with the same carrier to ensure fast throughput. US West's prioritized frame relay service guarantees 50 ms nationwide. Some vendors even offer credits if delays exceed advertised amounts. These guarantees are relatively safe for ISPs to offer: most large North American carrier backbones have a delay of no more than 70 ms.

One of the simplest ways to improve performance among the various remote locations of a distributed organization is to use a common service provider for IP services. By doing so, you will traverse only one autonomous system and will avoid notoriously congested peering points on the Internet. Because the carrier will now have complete control over all latency between your corporate nodes, you'll get less finger pointing and a more reliable agreement about levels of service. UUNET offers service-level agreements and publishes its latency statistics for trans-US and transatlantic links, guaranteeing transmission times across the UUNET backbone (Figure 11–3).[2]

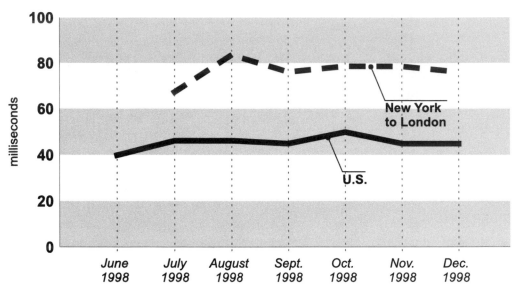

Figure 11–3 Round-trip latency on UUNET's backbone, averaged at 15-minute intervals over a month.

Within an autonomous system, many ISPs optimize performance with route-then-switch systems that try to move high-latency routed sessions towards faster switched sessions. They do this by routing the first packet and using this information to determine if both nodes are reachable across a switched network. If so, then a switched link is established between the two nodes. and further communication can occur more quickly.

Router metrics in the enterprise WAN

Router metrics are used to determine which path to use to transmit data. Metrics can be applied that select paths based on reliability, throughput, or cost. Configuring devices to route based on latency or jitter is one way of telling devices along the routed path to select for a lower-latency link. Typically, this is achieved by using a cost proportional to the reciprocal of link bandwidth ($1/_{\text{link bandwidth}}$).

A cost-based routing protocol such as OSPF uses different cost metrics based on the type of packet it is forwarding. In this way, packets that are tagged as "low cost" with IPTOS can be routed according to a different set of metrics from packets tagged as "low latency." QOS-based routing is currently being researched by the IETF.[3]

Forwarding to a permanent circuit

Boundary devices that join two media types must apply prioritization information from one media to the other. In the absence of information on the inbound media layer, the device may attempt to classify the flow for tagging using source address or application port. It may also consult higher-layer information such as IPTOS to help make a decision about priority for the next interface.

Boundary devices are not necessarily routers. Rate-shaping and queuing products may sit next to a router on the last LAN link, such as those from Packeteer and Structured Internetworks that manage TCP negotiations or those from Ukiah, Checkpoint, and NetGuard that manage queues. Finally, the WAN access device itself may allow the provider to regulate traffic on the customer premise through a number of mechanisms.

Properly mapping LAN traffic to the appropriate WAN interfaces has compelling cost motivations. Mapping videoconferencing packets to a best-effort link will result in poor performance, lower adoption of the service by employees, and reduced productivity. Mapping background file backups to a deterministic, isochronous link will blow your budget in no time.

When mapping network-layer or LAN-media-layer metrics to WAN circuits, the major challenge is that of passing useful information between the TCP/IP network layers and the link interfaces. With the proliferation of IPTOS implementations, many vendors now support the ability to set the Frame Relay discard eligibility bit in transmitted frames according to congestion or type-of-service discard bits. Doing so allows them to burst transmissions above their committed information rate while protecting traffic that is more important. Perhaps more importantly, the WAN discards have the same effect as a RED algorithm, gradually slowing the transmitting nodes before heavy congestion occurs. To some extent, then, WAN circuits can already "talk" to the sender's TCP stack.

By using parallel links, a device with limited traffic-shaping capabilities can still allow a high-priority packet to "overtake" a lower-priority one by using parallel links between routers at points of congestion (Figure 11–4). A next-hop filtering system redirects some portion of the network traffic across a specific link. Next-hop filtering is generally only useful on an access router with multiple WAN interfaces. For control over path selection within a routed network, using router protocol cost metrics is a far cleaner and more scalable mechanism.

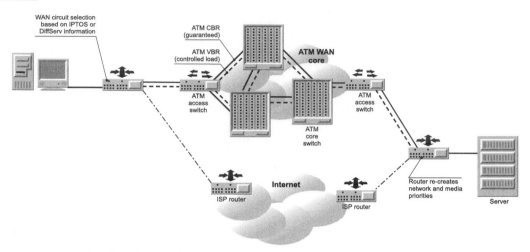

Figure 11–4 Circuit selection based on traffic needs

Alternately, multiple Frame Relay DLCIs between a customer premise equipment (CPE) router and an ISP's access router can be assigned different CBR values to create access to a multiservice network. If different virtual circuits can be given different forwarding characteristics, a single physical interface can be given multiple logical paths to a destination.

Differentiated PPP

In a slow point-to-point link, a large datagram can make the connection unavailable to other packets for a considerable amount of time. A 1500-byte packet, sent across a 28,800-Kbps modem link, fully occupies the link for approximately 400 milliseconds.[4] Since most voice applications are unacceptable to humans when their round-trip latency exceeds 200 milliseconds, this is clearly a barrier to real-time interactive multimedia over low-speed links, even for applications in which the quantity of traffic is substantially smaller than the link's capacity (such as voice). A worst-case estimate for two nodes communicating across an internetwork terminated by a pair of 28,800-Kbps modems might be as high as 1.5 seconds. As we've seen, VoIP applications use between 44 and 200 bytes per packet to avoid this kind of delay.

Recent Internet drafts propose a method of fragmenting large datagrams destined for a slow link in such a way that small, high-priority packets can be transmitted in between the fragments of large-packet, low-priority traffic. Simply fragmenting traffic and reordering the introduction of datagrams doesn't work well because of the way a multilink connection maintains a single sequence for traffic across parallel links and uses this to reassemble traffic at the other end. The proposals would use spare bits in multilink PPP headers to maintain multiple concurrent connections across one (or more) aggregated point-to-point connections. When the link is first established [using the Link Control Protocol (LCP)] several independent sequence number sets are defined. The two nodes on either side of the link maintain multiple concurrent sequences—four concurrent sequences with a 12-bit multilink header, and 16 concurrent sequences with a 24-bit multilink header.

This addressing scheme provides from 4 to 16 classes of service to which a device can map one or more traffic classes, allowing small, high-priority traffic to bypass slower, best-effort traffic without "breaking" the multilink sequencing and reassembly system. In other words, you can FTP traffic while talking on the IP phone over a dialup link.

While this proposal is only a draft at the time of writing, it is an interesting indicator that engineers and technicians are starting to address the real issues of application requirements and the adjustment of common IP stack implementations to better support them.

Frame Relay multilevel DLCIs

By using multiple, parallel PVCs between networking devices, routers at each end of a Frame Relay link can create differentiated WAN services. Because the routers have control over admission to the various circuits, they can treat each as a class-based queue. One router admits its traffic to the circuit, and the other applies algorithms for removal. It is also easy to modify the capacity assigned to a given class by administratively adjusting the circuit capacity and CIR for a given link. Provisioned WAN circuits are the simplest means of implementing WAN QOS, but the resulting redundant mesh topology can become an administrative nightmare.

Note that TCP traffic that exceeds a committed rate should either be sent down the *same* circuit as high-priority traffic within this range or discarded outright—not transmitted down a lower-priority link. Using different paths for a single flow makes it difficult for TCP to properly evaluate the round-trip time it needs for smooth transmission. Instead, either discard the packet on admission or forward it along the link associated with the traffic class and set TOS information to indicate discard eligibility if the next hop's upstream link is congested. Discards will allow the client's TCP implementation to better estimate round-trip time

(RTT) variance and more accurately characterize the capacity of the link.

Eventually, routers will dynamically request virtual WAN circuits with distinct traffic-handling properties and a common physical infrastructure. One of the most promising ways of simplifying the dynamic creation of switched circuits across a large network is multiprotocol label switching.

Dynamic circuit creation

Dynamically establishing and tearing down expensive connections is perilous. Provisioning errors can have a huge impact on service availability, and the proper billing and auditing technologies are in their infancy. Nevertheless, on-demand bandwidth and QOS is a goal to which most global carriers aspire. Originally, this was to have been delivered with ATM switched virtual circuits. Multiprotocol label switching is a promising alternative to the scaling and administration issues that characterize ATM.

ATM QOS and switched virtual circuits

You can map COS or RSVP to ATM virtual-circuit services or associate them with simulated queues. Understanding the various service classes that ATM can offer is the key to properly associating other QOS mechanisms with ATM. Mapping occurs in the ATM-attached router or on a LAN switch with an ATM uplink. ATM can offer provisioned, permanent virtual circuits as well as dynamic, switched virtual circuits. SVCs have not been broadly deployed for a variety of reasons, which means that most ATM networks look like a mesh of point-to-point links with tightly regulated forwarding capabilities.

ATM QOS was initially conceived for the WAN. It offers an extremely precise manipulation of bandwidth in which each virtual circuit has specific behaviors and bandwidth specifications. ATM defines several QOS types, or bit rates, that guarantee certain levels of service to traffic on the circuit.

ATM QOS is cell-based. In practical network deployment, packet-based end stations and wiring closets transmit frames of traffic, sometimes with associated class-of-service tags at multiple layers, and usage varies widely. As such, regulated, cell-based QOS must be married with packet-based COS effectively. All cells that make up a given frame or packet should be treated in the same way.

Mapping IPTOS values to ATM QOS services is the simplest mean of preserving QOS within ATM. The issue of marrying LAN and WAN traffic needs is then pushed into the device that assigns the IPTOS information. Furthermore, the complexity of multiple virtual circuits can introduce configuration overhead and unnecessary support issues. In a PVC-based ATM network, routers simply forward traffic to one of several parallel PVCs according to classification. As the mesh network grows, the redundancy of parallel links present scaling problems.

Sidebar

ATM versus Gigabit Ethernet

ATM and Gigabit Ethernet are the predominant backbone technologies of the late 1990s. Both deliver performance between 500 Mbps and 1 Gbps. We compare their relative features in Table 11–2.

Table 11–2   Comparison of Gigabit Ethernet and ATM

	GE	ATM
Physical media	Fiber (generally)	Fiber (generally)
Size of transmission unit	Up to 9018 bytes	53 bytes
Collision detection	N/A (switched implementations)	N/A
Admission control	None	Inherent
Integration with 10/100 LANs	Automatic	Needs special servers
QOS (traffic mixing with true guarantees)	None (class of service only)	Sophisticated (CBR, VBR, ABR, UBR)
Speed	1 GBPS	622 Mbps

GE's most compelling advantage is simplicity. ATM's granularity of control is unquestionable; it is the ease with which administrators familiar with Ethernet can grasp GE that gives the latter a real edge.

Establishing ATM circuits

ATM offers various classes of service for a virtual circuit. For a PVC, they are configured by the administrator at the time the circuit is setup. For SVCs, they are configured during circuit setup by the network.

When an ATM circuit is established in real time, the network performs connection admission control to regulate the establishment of a circuit. A connection is established when there is sufficient capacity to deliver the requested service category with the specified parameters—a model very similar to the RSVP admission-control process.

During the course of the session, the ATM devices use a cell-loss priority indicator to determine whether or not a given cell can be discarded. Cells are marked as suitable for discard when the ATM usage parameter control detects that traffic is in violation of a negotiated set of traffic parameters—similar to the assured-service model in which traffic outside a negotiated flow specification is marked as discard eligible in the IPTOS byte. The ATM devices schedule the transmission of cells in order to meet the agreed-upon service contracts; they do so through the maintenance of reservations, the denial of reservations that would oversubscribe or impact existing services, the use of leaky-bucket traffic shaping, the discarding of errored frames (when a cell is discarded), and the transmission of flow-control messages for ABR services.

ATM parameters

The admission process is based on the negotiation of various ATM parameters. These parameters describe the traffic that the sender will introduce into the network, as well as the quality of the ATM link. Relevant ATM parameters and metrics are listed in Table 11–3.

Table 11–3   ATM parameters

Parameter name	Meaning	Relevant to	Indicates
Administrative Weight (topology metric)	Weighting set by an administrator to indicate a preference for a certain circuit	All	
Available Cell Rate (topology attribute)	Measurement of actual available capacity (as opposed to maximum capacity)	CBR, rt-VBR, nrt-VBR	Should roughly match the sustainable cell rate to ensure no discards or bottlenecks
Cell Delay Variation (CDV) (topology metric)	Measurement of the change in delay that a circuit will offer	Real-time (CBR and rt-VBR) services	Cumulative delay across links; jitter
Cell Delay Variation Tolerance (traffic parameter)	How much jitter a sender can tolerate	CBR, rt-VBR, nrt-VBR	Worst level of CDV appropriate for a link
Cell Loss Ratio (topology metric)	Ratio of lost cells to successfully transmitted cells	CBR, rt-VBR, nrt-VBR	Cumulative cell loss across links
Cell Rate Margin (topology attribute)	How much "extra" capacity there is between the available rate of a link and the rate at which a sender will introduce cells	Optional for VBR; not applicable to CBR, ABR, and UBR	A measure of the "margin of safety" for a link.

Table 11–3   ATM parameters

Parameter name	Meaning	Relevant to	Indicates
Maximum Burst Size (traffic parameter)	The largest number of contiguous cells that a sender will transmit on a circuit	All	How much the sender will monopolize a circuit; more specifically, it tells the network how long a set of cells at the peak cell rate will last
Maximum Cell Rate (topology attribute)	The maximum forwarding rate of connections in a service category	ABR, UBR; optional for CBR, rt-VBR and nrt-VBR	Capacity of a single link in a network
Minimum Cell Rate (traffic parameter)	The lowest rate at which cells can be transmitted along a circuit to be useful to the application		How low a level of throughput the sender can tolerate
Maximum Cell Transfer Delay (topology metric)	Worst-case measurement of the end-to-end delay across the ATM cloud		When a sender knows the maxCTD and CDV, it can characterize the end-to-end latency and jitter and negotiate the appropriate application parameters for the traffic (such as receiver buffer depth)

Table 11–3   ATM parameters

Parameter name	Meaning	Relevant to	Indicates
Peak Cell Rate (PCR) (traffic parameter)	The maximum rate at which cells will be forwarded by the network		In a constant-bit-rate connection, the PCR is the rate at which the sender will *always* introduce traffic into the network; as a result, the network knows how frequently it must schedule the transmission of a cell in order to meet this rate and maintain an acceptable level of jitter
Sustainable Cell Rate (SCR) (traffic parameter)	The typical rate of transmission by a sender		The average amount of traffic forwarded over time should equal the SCR; excess traffic may result in cells (and the frames of which they are a part) being discarded
Variance Factor (topology attribute)	Indicator of variance in cell rates over a link	Optional for VBR; not applicable to CBR, ABR, and UBR	

Other measurements, ratios, and parameters are defined within ATM. The high degree of control and granularity that they afford is offset by the complexity of their implementations.

Generally, topology attributes and topology metrics (which describe the state of the network) are matched to traffic parameters (which describe the traffic a sender will introduce into the network). Depending on the kind of ATM service being requested, different attributes and metrics are matched to different parameters in order to determine whether a circuit should be established or whether traffic should be admitted to a circuit. The matching of metrics to circuit types is similar to the RSVP reservation message (which contains a flow specification) being compared to the router's capacity information by the RSVP admission-control process.

ATM service categories

The Traffic Management v4.0 specification from the ATM Forum defines five possible traffic-handling classes (Constant Bit Rate, Real-time Variable Bit Rate, Non-real-time Variable Bit Rate, Available Bit Rate, and Unspecified Bit Rate.) Each service offers some set of behaviors to devices that use it, and each is suited for specific application types.

- Constant Bit Rate (CBR) services are designed to deliver traffic in which transmitter and receiver need a constant amount of bandwidth and a predictable response time—such as video or voice. In practical terms, CBR circuits are used to emulate dedicated links. A CBR connection can be described using the Peak Cell Rate, since the application will constantly transmit at this rate without appreciably bursting above it or falling below it. CBR circuits carry delay-sensitive, inelastic traffic.

- Real-time Variable Bit Rate (rt-VBR) services are suited for bursty applications that require time synchronization between sender and receiver. Unlike CBR, a VBR circuit expects that traffic will burst *up to* a peak cell rate but will generally transmit at a sustained cell rate and may burst for some maximum burst size. rt-VBR traffic may be delayed (unlike CBR). However, any cells delayed beyond the specified maximum delay (Cell Transfer Delay) are considered to be "stale" because of time-synchronization requirements. They are no longer useful to the application—and may consequently be dropped if congestion occurs. rt-VBR circuits carry delay-sensitive, conversational, elastic traffic.

- Non-real-time Variable Bit Rate (nrt-VBR) services offer the same characteristics as rt-VBR but assume that there is no need for time synchronization between sender and receiver. nrt-VBR is suited for transactional applications in which the guaranteed delivery of data is more important than timely delivery—such as two-phase commit purchasing or online transaction systems. Discard as a consequence of delay makes less sense to nrt-VBR traffic than to rt-VBR traffic. nrt-VBR circuits carry delay-sensitive, streaming, elastic traffic or informationally delay-sensitive traffic.

- Available Bit Rate (ABR) services are similar to nrt-VBR but are tailored to adaptive protocols like TCP that will adjust themselves to changes in available bandwidth. ABR circuits use special signaling mechanisms to manage transmission rates, and ABR traffic defers to CBR and VBR traffic. Just as TCP probes to use the maximum capacity of the network, so an ABR service tries to deliver throughput up to the peak cell rate that was negotiated for the service. ABR can be considered better-than-best effort.

- Unspecified Bit Rate (UBR) services are true best-effort circuits that do not attempt to manage congestion. These circuits are the bottom-feeders of the ATM world, beholden to all other circuits and relying on excess capacity for transmission. UBR simulates the "dumb," service-poor network that TCP assumes.

ABR differs from UBR in having mechanisms that can signal congestion explicitly to the devices on the edge of the ATM circuits. By contrast, users of a UBR link must rely on implicit notification in the form of packet loss or router delay. A TCP session over a UBR circuit will learn of congestion through packet discards, whereas a TCP session over ABR may "learn" of congestion through the ATM adaption layer on the IP devices at the edge of the ATM circuit (which might queue the traffic rather than dropping it).

Each of these service categories works within a set of QOS bounds. Dynamic negotiation of service characteristics on a per-circuit basis doesn't scale well, unfortunately, since it requires the establishment of one circuit for each traffic type in the network, creating a considerable burden for administrators and management systems. Consequently, the implementation of dynamic QOS circuits in ATM is years behind the standards that promise it.

An alternate way to preserve COS information across an ATM network is to ensure that LAN emulation software maps 802.1p information into administratively provisioned ATM QOS. Network designers must establish ABR, CBR, VBR, and UBR circuits and then decide how to map 802.1p COS tags and IPTOS precedence bits into each, which is still relatively complex.

When the ATM forum developed the LAN emulation user-network interface (LUNI) version 2.0 specification, they began to discuss support for 802.1p across an emulated LAN. 802.1p support was not, however, released as part of the specification. A recent proposal from 3Com corporation has been submitted to the IEEE and the ATM forum for simulating multiple LAN queues on an ATM ABR circuit.

As congestion appears and disappears in ATM, devices gradually adjust the amount of traffic a switch will allow. ATM is full of adjustment "knobs," and network administrators can even tweak the *rate* at which the forwarding rate increases or decreases.

Queue simulation is achieved by adjusting maximum and minimum cell rates according to link capacity, then setting different decrease and increase factors based on the COS types. Effectively, the system transmits different rate-control information for different kinds of traffic during congestion, approximating the TCP rate-control mechanisms discussed earlier.

When there is no network congestion, traffic can flow freely—there is no need to regulate capacity. Recall that this does *not* address latency or jitter, however. Once congestion occurs on the network, the ATM devices throttle back low-priority traffic more quickly than high-priority traffic.

During times of congestion (which are the only times that matter from the network's perspective) higher-priority traffic gets a higher percentage of the line rate. For example, when the network is 50 percent congested, low-priority traffic might get approximately 10 percent of the actual line rate while high-priority traffic would still get approximately 90 percent.

The proposal simulates a multilevel packet network across a single ATM ABR circuit. In this way, it is possible to provision a single ATM circuit (rather than mapping a series of complex, parallel, ATM CBR/VBR circuits) across a WAN connection or a backbone. The ATM link can then be used to multiplex voice, video, and data traffic.

Practically speaking, you may want a provisioned CBR link for isochronous traffic and ABR circuits with queue simulation for the remaining traffic. This will allow your ATM mesh to deliver reservations and priorities across a WAN or backbone with a minimum of fuss.

Why isn't ATM the perfect solution?

Link-layer protocols are not end-to-end. If we all had ATM to the desktop, we'd have rich QOS everywhere. But we don't. IP offers an end-to-end networking layer atop which application developers can write their applications. IP is therefore a more enticing prospect to the busy developer than writing versions of software to support Ethernet, ATM, Frame Relay, and so on.

A consequence of this is that innovation is happening at layer 3. The focus these days is on moving lower layers into silicon, making them as cheap and fast as possible. Historically, the lack of application integration with enhanced link-layer services (such as virtual LANs) has delayed their rapid adoption long enough for wily engineers to find a way to do the same thing in IP. With the development of acceptable controlled-load and guaranteed-load technologies—and a relative increase in network capacity from new signaling systems and faster switches—ATM's benefits for granular QOS are less evident.

In addition, an ATM network lets people design suboptimal internetworks that appear to function properly. This statement is somewhat contentious, so we present some concrete examples. The ability to set up dynamically switched links at layer 2, and then dynamically determined routed paths at layer 3, means that the IP topology and the ATM topology may have difficulty converging. Dynamic link layers fight the IP devices' ability to converge on a stable topology, which can reduce the effectiveness of the network. Network engineers must use ATM SVCs *extremely* judiciously as on-demand high-performance alternatives for carefully selected routed flows that need low-delay alternatives. Establishing effective route metrics for a link-state protocol at the internetworking layer requires a good deal of study by the administrator. The temptation is to set the values arbitrarily without a proper understanding on the effect the change will have on TCP behavior or routing flaps.

ATM and IntServ

ATM tries to offer quality-of-service controls at the link layer. IntServ tries to offer them at the network layer. As a result, merging the two into a useful whole is complex and can cause problems if not properly configured. Implementations fight over which layer performs what function.

The simplest way to integrate the two is to use ATM as a set of fast point-to-point links with a range of provisioning options. Administratively configured PVCs between routers behave like other point-to-point links, and the network handles QOS based on RSVP negotiations. Unfortunately, this simple approach ignores some of the powerful capabilities that ATM can offer for multiplexing traffic economically while delivering rich differentiation.

The ATM UBR and ABR services closely approximate a best-effort network; RSVP controlled-load services are similar to nrt-VBR; and RSVP guaranteed services are a direct parallel to ATM CBR or even rt-VBR. In addition, link-layer congestion signaling using cell-loss indicators signals ATM-attached routers to perform admission control, queuing, and selective discard at the edges of the ATM cloud, just as RSVP routers perform admission controls based on capacity.

ATM CBR is inefficient for applications in which traffic levels vary even slightly, since it must deliver the peak cell rate regardless of throughput. Most data applications involve some degree of compression or optimization because of their packet heritage and the fact that they've been moved to IP's best-effort model in recent years. Consequently, CBR is generally used for "non-data" systems such as raw video streams. Certainly, if an application developer knew that CBR was an option, application design would be far simpler. The huge lure of the Internet means that almost all of us build some level of adaptivity into our applications, making them VBR rather than CBR.

RSVP guaranteed service can be deployed atop ATM rt-VBR by mapping the information from the RSVP flow specification to the ATM traffic parameters described above. For a more detailed discussion of associations between ATM and IntServ, we offer three relevant IETF Internet Drafts:

- "A framework for Integrated Services and RSVP over ATM," E. Crawley et al., draft-ietf-issll-atm-framework-00.txt, July 1997

- "Issues for Integrated Services and RSVP over ATM," E. Crawley et al., draft-ietf-issll-isatm-issues-00.txt, July 1997

- "Interoperation of Controlled-Load and Guaranteed services with ATM," M. Garrett et al., draft-ietf-issll-atm-mapping-02.txt, July 1997

Multiprotocol Label Switching

Explicitly defining circuits each time a connection is needed carries a great of overhead. On the other hand, once a circuit is in place, traffic can travel across it quickly, because the intermediate devices don't need to make complex forwarding decisions the way they do when routing. A hybrid approach is to switch according to a tag that is inserted ahead of IP information. The most promising standard for so-called "labeled" switching is MPLS. MPLS works by placing variable-length headers in front of IP datagrams; the headers help the MPLS switches to forward the datagram at switch speeds without needing full IP awareness. Consequently, MPLS speeds networking by overcoming the complexity of route selection.

MPLS inserts a fixed-length label ahead of the IP address (Figure 11–5); it functions as a label for the selected route. While this is much like a link-layer protocol that defines the virtual circuit through switches, the header is generated based on IP route information (like a network protocol). It may therefore be useful to think of MPLS as "layer 2.5."

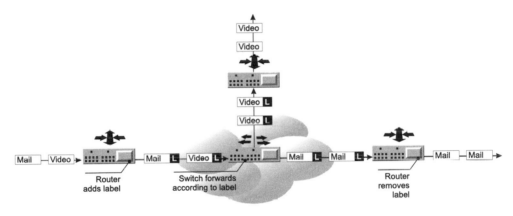

Figure 11–5   MPLS label insertion and removal by edge routers

In a traditional routing decision, a packet is forwarded along the most specific path to the destination by each router in the path. For example, if two routes exist for a destination network, but under CIDR formatting one is advertised as /20 and one is advertised as /16, then the /20 route is the "longest match" for the destination network. Performing these path selections uses up precious cycles in an internetwork core.

The fundamental goal of any kind of QOS-based circuit assignment by a router is to try and select the appropriate transport (and possibly the right routed path) for a particular traffic type. Rather than relying on the parameters that your service provider is willing to share with you, however, you can transmit IP datagrams into a multiprotocol label switching

(MPLS) core and have the service provider map IPTOS information into appropriate circuits.

MPLS is not tied to IP, although it has promise in terms of scaling the Internet. An MPLS edge node inserts and removes MPLS labels from packets entering or leaving the MPLS cloud; in an ATM network, the MPLS label can map to the ATM virtual path and virtual circuit fields.

The MPLS label is a 32-bit number that contains the label itself, a class-of-service field, time-to-live information, and a "bottom-of-stack" bit. Cisco Systems' proprietary Tag Switching, which has been submitted as part of the MPLS standardization effort, matches IP precedence information from the IPTOS byte with the MPLS class-of-service information. The initial MPLS framework documents mandate that MPLS must interoperate with RSVP, and the availability of class-of-service information as well as the focus on speed make MPLS an excellent candidate for deploying future QOS services over fast IP clouds.

Because MPLS access devices must map between the IP destination and the appropriate MPLS tags, they are able to request different services for various flows at the point of entry into the MPLS cloud. These flows can themselves be aggregated to reduce the number of distinct flows. For example, all video server traffic can be aggregated to use the WAN more efficiently. In a label-switched environment, different labels may lead to the same exit point in the network domain via different paths. This means that, unlike most practical IP deployment, the edge device can select many paths to the same destination in order to meet some kind of handling objective or service contract.

In the long term, MPLS edge devices may be able to select different paths through the network based on traffic classification. With the IPv6 flow label (a 24-bit label that functions similarly to MPLS) in the plans for the next version of the Internet, label switching seems like a promising method of speeding up networks, reducing complexity, and squeezing additional capabilities out of a fast WAN core.

Making ISP QOS a reality

At least one Internet RFC (2430) tackles the issues of service-provider-based policy through a combination of RSVP on the edge of the network and MPLS flows in the core. The proposal is entitled "Provider Architecture for Differentiated Services and Traffic Engineering" (PASTE).

PASTE works by entering both forwarding and reservation information in the MPLS header. The Label Switching Routers (LSRs) around the

MPLS core define a Label Switched Path (LSP) that is associated with a given reservation based on RSVP negotiation. PASTE describes three traffic classes (best effort, priority, and network control), but the specific number of classes is not defined in the proposal. Once a set of flows is associated with a traffic class, it is transmitted across the LSP and forms what we call a traffic trunk. Each LSP may have multiple trunks, and each trunk may have its own traffic class. PASTE shows promise because it does not pose the per-flow state scaling issues of traditional RSVP implementations. Trunks can be combined dynamically ("spliced") if they contain the same class of traffic between two LSRs. In addition, the best-effort traffic class simply uses the normally computed path across the network.

PASTE employs RSVP in a different manner from that originally conceived by the IntServ group. While RSVP was originally designed to establish reservations for flows across a destination-based routed path, in this model RSVP is used to install a state for the collection of flows that shares a common path and pool of resources. Furthermore, RSVP now requests forwarding in addition to traditional resources such as delay and capacity, and the state is not associated with the chosen route. In other words, RSVP has been co-opted by PASTE to allow a pair of routers—as well as a sender and receiver—to negotiate LSPs with different QOS characteristics. PASTE defines new RSVP objects, including the Explicit Route Object (ERO), to this end.

It is the approach to interdomain service-level agreements that makes this proposal important to the Internet community. A consistent technical architecture will allow service providers to cross-bill and engineer traffic in order to offer more competitive services to different market segments. PASTE requires classification at the edge routers using the three COS bits of the MPLS header and the three precedence bits in the IPTOS byte. PASTE is a pay-as-you-go model, which means that policing may be less critical, since there is no need to restrict high-priority packets. On the other hand, network-control traffic must be policed to prevent denial-of-service attacks, and the ability to inject priority packets into the network must be limited to sources within the agreed-upon address spaces.

Trunks that span two or more service providers are defined administratively through bilateral forwarding agreements that will describe financial compensation, classes of service, handling characteristics, upper bounds on third-party sourced traffic, and capacities that each will offer the shared trunk. These are similar to peering agreements between ISPs today, creating what the RFC calls an interprovider SLA. Traffic is shaped to conform to this agreement using some of the enforcement methods we've seen earlier.

Quick and dirty

If you absolutely have to get it there on time, you can; but you'll pay for it. There is a new class of service providers (such as BusinessNet, Digital Island Abovenet, and InterNAP) that offer premium bandwidth at premium prices, paralleling the public Internet with peering and load balancing. By combining high-speed switched backbones and load-balancing technologies, these companies can offer "one hop away" networking for high-performance intranet or public sites.

Endnotes

1. Mick Seaman et al., *Integrated service mappings on IEEE 802 Networks*, Internet draft, August 1998.

2. UUNET latency figures are available at `http://www.uunet.com/lang.en/customers/sla/stat.html`. UUNET's latency statistics are derived from NTP collections at 15-minute intervals, averaged monthly.

3. See RFC 2386 and others.

4. Carsten Bormann, The Multi-class extension to multi-link PPP, Internet draft, August 1998.

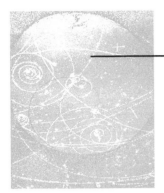

12

Server-side delay

Network delay is complex and can be tuned in a number of ways. It is important not to overlook server-side delay, however. In many cases, the delay the server introduces will be greater than the network round trip. Furthermore, forwarding a server error message at expensive speeds seems questionable at best. Server-side delay can be mitigated through load balancing, caching, and other network services that form what we call the IP Front-End Processor.

We've seen a number of handling methods that shape traffic across a network. Controlling server-side delay and the response times of a service involves yet another set of handling methods, including caching, session load balancing, and service load balancing.

A considerable portion of the total delay when accessing dynamic sites or online databases is generated on the server and its back-end databases. Tuning your network to provide multilevel differentiated services won't fix a slow server or poorly distributed database.

So far, our discussion of network policy has centered on the regulation of network capacity. However, as lower layers of the stack become standardized, administrators are beginning to view their network as a system for delivering *services*—specific applications or resources that the network can fulfill. These include processing services (such as compression, stream aggregation, multicast distribution, and so on) as well as directing traffic to a service that can fulfill it.

If this all sounds somewhat theoretical, it is perhaps because the concept of a "service" resides between the network and the application. Load balancing, proxy caching, subscription management, application presentation formatting, encryption, geographic redirection, availability guarantees, and so on are all examples of services a network can deliver. Since they're services, they vary in quality—which makes them at least peripherally relevant to our discussion.

Session load balancing

Session-level load balancing arose primarily as a mechanism for introducing fault tolerance and failover capabilities into server farms. As Internet services become increasingly mission critical, we need mechanisms for ensuring their availability. The TCP paradigm—a unique connection between a single server and a single client—does not lend itself to such guarantees automatically.

Load balancers solve this problem. Load-balancing devices may be traditional switches with higher-layer content inspection and redirection features, or they may be dedicated network appliances. They may have a single LAN connection through which all traffic travels to both the router and the server farm, or they may have dedicated ports for each server.

The systems offer a common external virtual IP address (VIP) to which clients connect. They select from among available candidates that can fulfill a client's request, then connect to the most appropriate server.

In a simple availability system, the load balancer might select a server using a simple round-robin algorithm. More sophisticated models of server selection include a weighted round-robin (which allows a manager to administratively weight servers based on their relative performance) as well as a least-connection approach.

Load balancers are not necessarily fast, since they frequently connect to a WAN across a T1 or other relatively slow link. At first glance, it might seem that the slow connection would be the bottleneck, since modern servers are perfectly capable of saturating the 1.5 Mbps of a T1. On closer inspection, it is often the back-end processing activities—encryption, page creation, and database queries—that reduce server performance and require that the load be shared.

Advanced load balancers offer content awareness and response-time-based balancing. Content awareness allows the load balancer to selectively direct queries to servers or caches that are better able to service them by looking at the requesting URL or other application-layer information.

Response-time load balancing is based on the notion that the truest indicator of server health is the speed with which it responds to queries. A response-time metric automatically adjusts server load: for example, if an administrator begins a local download of a file on one server independent of the service being balanced, that server's performance will drop and response time will change. Administratively configured weights cannot take this into account; consequently, response-time-based systems are easier to configure and more accurate than administrative response-time metrics. Vendors like IPivot offer such features as part of their load-balancing algorithms.

Load balancers have an important role to play in QOS establishment. One of the real criticisms of network QOS is that it disregards the server response times and delays inherent in providing content. A load balancer can act as a "service advocate" to the network—for example, a load balancer can set aside a portion of server capacity for high-priority users.

Load balancers offer some degree of geographic distribution; some of the most advanced systems can balance disparate content across multiple sites and forward visitors to an offsite server for their query to improve response time or enable disaster recovery.

Gigabit Ethernet and server farms

In a next-generation network, servers are grouped into server farms. Whereas traditional networks make the assumption that the majority of traffic stays in the workgroup, with the emergence of intranet and extranet systems this is no longer the case. Server farms will generally be clustered near a high-performance backbone. Depending on the server load and application needs, servers may use a Gigabit Ethernet network interface directly into the backbone.

Since almost all of the delay in a LAN-attached server's response stems from server load, script parsing, and back-end database queries, the emphasis for a LAN server farm is distribution or reduction of the processing overhead within the farm. For WANs, server and network response times are both critical; nevertheless, a well-optimized network will not fix a broken server.

One of the major causes of server load is network protocol processing. In 10- and 100-Mbps Ethernet, the maximum frame size is 1,518 bytes. But large file transfers across these links can generate a surprising amount of processor load—transferring even a 100-MB file over 100BaseT will create a sustained load of 8,000 packets per second for 8 seconds. This kind of load can consume a significant amount of the server's capacity, and in many configurations servers have multiple adapters attached—further compounding the processing overhead and introducing routing decisions into the equation. Server-load overhead is multiplied by the use of faster links like ATM or Gigabit Ethernet.

Recall that Gigabit Ethernet can support a "jumbo frame" of up to 9,018 bytes. This means that roughly 6.25 times the information can be transmitted per packet, substantially reducing the amount of network processing overhead that increases server response time.

In a LAN server farm, a high-speed switch that lets fulfillment servers and back-end "second-tier" servers such as databases or backup systems interoperate using jumbo frames can reduce back-end processing delays. The same servers can respond to client requests with traditional frame sizes, and load is distributed across the fulfillment servers by a load balancer (Figure 12–1).

It is important to consider the back-end services as part of a server farm. Many modern Web servers must process scripts and make queries to databases before returning pages, so the round-trip delay of a server can be considerable—enough to thwart any carefully architected QOS configurations on the LAN or WAN connection.

A number of other server-farm technologies can speed network performance. Secure socket (SSL) coprocessing hardware can greatly increase

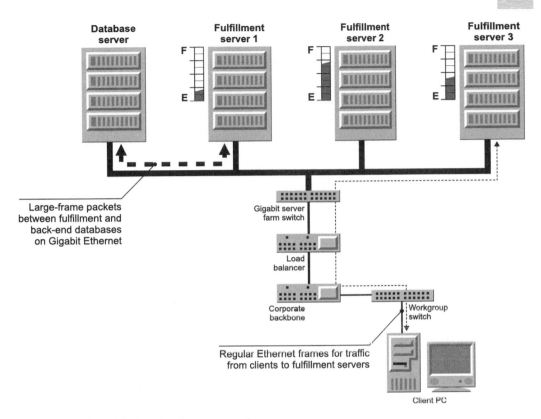

Figure 12–1 Load balancing in a server farm

the number of secure connections that a server can maintain by offloading key generation and encryption functions from the main processor. Caches near the servers can respond quickly with static content, keeping servers free for processing of dynamic pages or transactions.

Finally, load balancers that are aware of the content that is being returned to a user can tag it with the right QOS values. For example, a stream of multimedia might be prioritized differently if the server farm were aware of the content of the packets. Similarly, knowing content means not wasting priority. In a lower-layer QOS environment, a load balancer might mark a Web page as high priority even when it contained only a 404 error because the page was unavailable. A content-aware system could override the default packet-marking policies with content-based policies to make better use of bandwidth.

Service load balancing

Session-level load balancing occurs within a server farm. Before a client reaches a fulfillment point for a service, however, it needs to obtain the address of the service from a DNS server. This presents another opportunity to balance load and improve performance.

Simple DNS load balancing performs a round-robin algorithm across a set of two or more possible fulfillment points for a requested service. The problem with basic DNS round-robin is that it does not take into account site availability or server load and to some extent is hindered by caching of hostname and address associations on DNS clients. Sophisticated DNS load balancers check with fulfillment points—either by testing servers directly themselves or by talking to remote agents at each site—before returning a DNS address to a browser.

Because these DNS servers can return addresses selectively, they make geographic load balancing possible. By selecting from a number of possible servers one that is logically near the client, performance can be improved.

Choosing which of several sites is closest to a browser is a complex task. Once the first TCP session is established to a site, the load balancer knows the client's IP address. Consequently, it can monitor round-trip time and check response time by pinging the client. But even if there are no firewalls between the client and the server that would prevent pinging, it is simply too late at this stage to select a fulfillment site—the client has already selected a destination.

Before the TCP session is established, however, the client must perform a DNS lookup for the IP address of the fulfillment site. If the DNS server that responds to the lookup has some control of the various fulfillment sites, it can tell each of them to check their proximity to the client's DNS (which it knows because it received the query). Cisco Systems has proprietary interfaces to its routers that allow them to carry out diagnostic commands such as ping, so routers at each fulfillment point may be able to test network distances.

Such a model assumes that the client's DNS server is relatively near the client. The response time from the various fulfillment sites to the DNS client must be considered in terms of server load and capacity as well, but such a system does allow the fulfillment of a client request from the closest of several possible sites. It may be suitable for streaming or real-time interactive gaming sites on a WAN.

In addition to selecting the "most local" server farm during the DNS query, router protocols can be used (Figure 12–2).

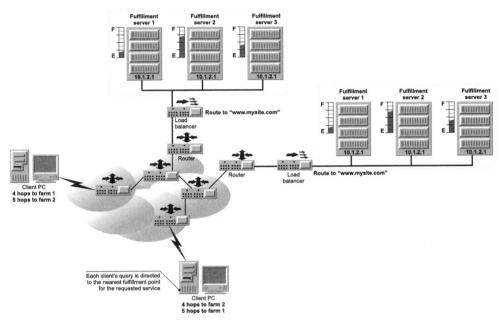

Figure 12–2   Selection of closest fulfillment point within an autonomous system

One method of "most local" site selection is through simple route selection based on the least number of hops within an autonomous system. If each load balancer advertises a route to the same virtual service, the routers will automatically select the most cost-effective route (generally in terms of hop count.) Route-based load balancing is a useful system when the sites are logically distant, but there is no guarantee that the *closest* site will also be the *fastest* site. In addition, such a system requires that the various fulfillment points be within the same autonomous system. In practice, multiple fulfillment points will often be collocated with alternate service providers so that your Web site is immune to problems with a particular provider's backbone.

DNS load balancers can look at a number of metrics in order to determine which server to use. In addition to simple availability or network proximity, they can rely on weighted round-robin, number of connections, and response time.

Caching

Web traffic was nearly two thirds of all Internet traffic in late 1997,[1] and it continues to grow. Multimedia clients are integrated into the latest versions of browsers. Consequently, core bandwidth is scarce, while faster local loops place greater and greater demands on access providers to deliver content quickly. Faced with this explosion of traffic, many service providers and enterprises are turning to caches to bring copies of content onsite.

Caching requires a good deal more coordination between the networking professional and the server content professional than many of the other systems discussed so far. The main motivation for deploying a cache solution is to save on WAN costs, but caches also improve response time, enable the scaling of networks, and offer "hooks" for application-level monitoring. Caches are available in three flavors: proxy caches, which require the browser to solicit information from them; transparent caches, which rely on a router to redirect certain ports to them for fulfillment; and in-line caches, which replace a network cable and parse traffic as it passes by to see if they have a locally cached copy.

Types of cache

- In browser-based caching the client PC keeps a copy of static content. The browser can send a simple "get if changed" message and use the current copy, reducing bandwidth consumption and improving performance. Browser-based caching still requires a copy of a given Web object to be downloaded on each desktop, even if everyone is retrieving the same object.

- Campus-level caching can be achieved with a proxy. Clients retrieve their information from a server on the LAN that performs retrieval and maintains a cache. Proxies allows excellent monitoring of network usage, improving efficiency and performance for everyone at a location, once one person has visited a site. However, traditional proxies require the reconfiguration of every browser and can constitute a single point of failure. Proxies also interfere with site-usage tracking, since a successful cache "hit" may not be seen by the real site. Furthermore, proxy-based caches can impact performance when heavily loaded, because they work at the application layer and they must maintain huge numbers of TCP sessions between clients and servers.

- Campus-level caching can be performed through redirection. Using this method, a router on the campus forwards all traffic from a certain port—such as http—to a cache for fulfillment. Redirection reduces the burden on the network administrator in terms of reconfiguring desktops, but it can still offer single points of failure if the cache becomes unavailable. Integration of routers with caches helps to overcome this.

- Cache clusters improve the availability of proxies and redirected caches, but require load-balancing hardware either on the network interfaces or as discrete network appliances to deliver high levels of availability.

- The WAN access point is a critical location for caching. Increasing numbers of ISPs are caching content for their subscribers locally, which improves the customers' perceived response times and reduces the amount of costly WAN traffic they generate. ISPs send requests to their access caches through redirection on their routers based on port number, eliminating the need to configure browsers. Savvy ISPs recognize that they are in the business of selling access, rather than connections, and will transition from WAN capacity to service availability by mingling caches with their traditional circuits.

- In-line caches combine the functions of load balancing, redirection, and failover. As the name implies, these systems sit on a network link and watch for traffic they can fulfill from their cache, intercepting queries if appropriate. This interception model allows them to be daisy-chained serially for multiple tiers of caching.

- Some caches offer content-provider notification by sending a hit (in the form of a "get if changed" message) on behalf of the client. The response will notify the cache if content has changed. Consequently, at most a single "stale" hit will be delivered, and the client will not waiting around for confirmation from the content server that the information is current. When combined with other caching algorithms and information, an in-line cache with provider notification is a useful way of improving local response times for browsers.

Caching data locally can almost entirely avoid network delay and is faster than asking a busy server to transmit a file. By some estimates, 60 percent of Web information is redundant[2] (i.e., someone at the local node has already pulled it down when a hit occurs). This is especially true for graphics; when a site's text changes, the bandwidth-intensive graphic files are less likely to change.

For a distributed organization, the benefits of caching and mirroring should not be overlooked. If you have information that is updated infrequently, replicate it to remote locations proactively. If the information changes often, then implement a caching system, through either proxy or redirection. By storing information near the user, expensive WAN bandwidth is conserved and server-side delay in receiving the file is reduced. Choose your cache carefully to ensure transparent operation and high cache hit rates.

A normal Web query is illustrated in Figure 12–3.

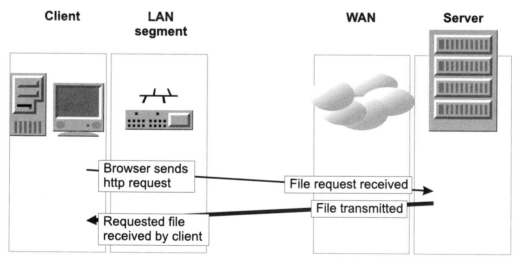

Figure 12–3   Traffic flow of a normal Web query

If a file is stored locally, the cache still needs to verify if the cached content is valid by querying the server, although it does not have to retrieve the entire file. It does this through a "get-if-modified" query instead of a simple get (Figure 12–4).

While the second visit to a page does not require that the client retrieve the already cached object, it nevertheless involves an extra trip across the network to confirm that the cached copy is the most recent. This saves bandwidth but does not reduce latency.

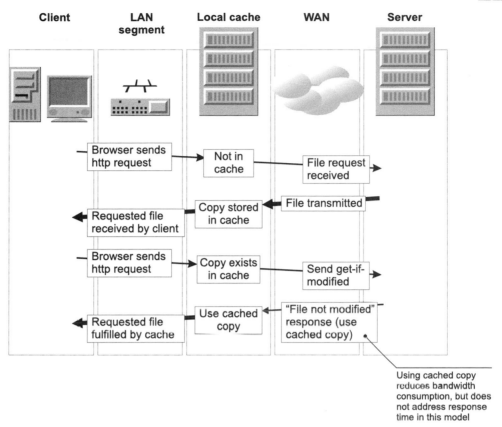

Client **LAN segment** **Local cache** **WAN** **Server**

Figure 12–4 Traffic flow in a cache without time-to-live (TTL) values

Objects on a server can have a time-to-live (TTL) value associated with them that tells the cache when it next needs to check the validity of a file (Figure 12–5). Because TTL is not commonly used by harried Web designers, however, browsers and cache servers implement their own controls. Some browsers can be configured to check for a new file all the time, once per session, once per use of the application, or only when refreshed. The same is true of caching devices.

This delay in retrieval that occurs on cache checking is mainly important when a human operator is subjected to the delay, so it is of particular concern for Web sites where operators are waiting for information. Next-generation caches proactively retrieve cache information (based on complex algorithms of time to live, hit rate, and so on), so that a recent copy of an object is available before the browser requests it (Figure 12–6).

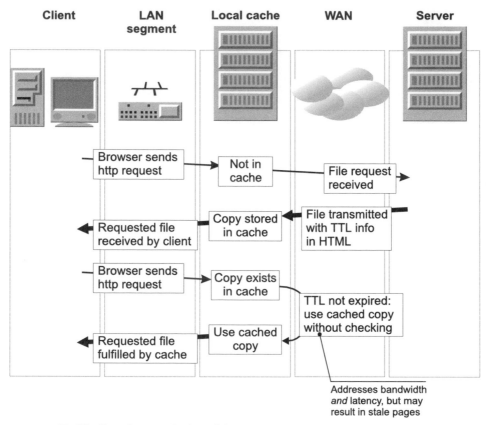

Figure 12–5   Traffic flow in a typical caching system

Proactive caching systems can gather pages for which they anticipate a demand in order to optimize bandwidth usage. Proactive caches employ pre-fetch algorithms and are often application aware, making them able, for example, to surf a site and follow hyperlinks. Caches can also exchange information among themselves via a number of standard protocols such as Cache Array Routing Protocol (CARP) and the Internet Cache Protocol (ICP), as well as proprietary ones like Cisco Systems' Web Cache Control Protocol (WCCP).

ICP was developed by a cache research project called Harvest to coordinate content among multiple cache servers. It works by having each cache talk to the others in order to see whether a copy of an object is stored locally. Consequently, ICP generates additional network traffic and does not scale well as the size of the cache grows. Microsoft Corporation has proposed CARP as a way of coordinating cache content with less

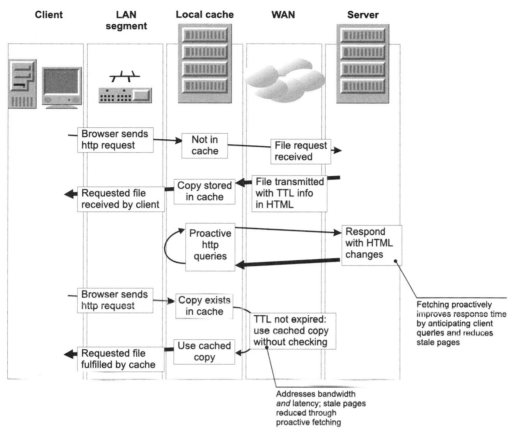

Figure 12–6   Traffic flow of a proactive cache with HTTP 1.1 get-if-modified queries

impact on the network. CARP takes a different approach to finding content, relying on algorithms that associate a URL with a particular server in a cache array. Since all browsers requesting information from the cache use the same algorithm to obtain an object, the cache is populated in a structured manner. Adding extra servers to the array makes the array adapt to the new mappings transparently.

Recent developments in caching that rely on persistent queries to constantly update the cache can allow local servers to cache changing information (Figure 12–7), reducing WAN traffic and speeding response times.

If a cache is able to register itself with a data source and receive push-based content changes, it becomes possible to schedule cache population. As caching systems mature and protocols for distributing and registering data appear in standards bodies, the role of the cache in moving "relatively recent" information around in cost-effective ways as background traffic will be increasingly important.

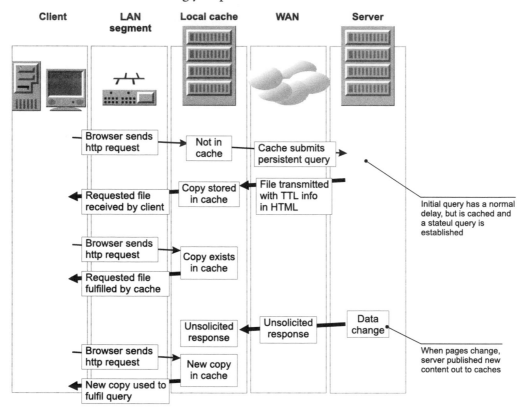

Figure 12–7 Traffic flow in a proactive caching system

The location of a cache in the network will dictate the makeup of its content and its relative hit rate. Caches near clients will contain content relevant to the clients (for example, an enterprise cache will typically contain graphics from competitors' sites and industry information pages). Caches in the core of the WAN contain the most popular, most frequently accessed information that crosses a particular peering point. Reverse proxy caches near the servers contain copies of static content from the servers for which they are caching data.

When designing a server farm, consider the impact of load balancing and caching on availability and response times. An effectively balanced server farm will incorporate mechanisms for reducing network latency, optimizing processor usage across servers, and guaranteeing some degree of performance for classes of users. Consistent integration of server performance characteristics with network QOS measures is an important component of a complete QOS system and is only now being addressed by networking devices, server vendors, and management tools.

There are some alternatives to this kind of system. They include server mirroring (replicating the entire server at a local site on a regular basis)—a good approach for static content, or for dynamic content if the server's scripts are also copied. For a highly dynamic site, mirroring may simply move the delay to the databases or back-end servers used to generate the dynamic pages, instead of alleviating server delay.

Co-processing

In many cases, the service may be processor-bound. Performing compute-intensive tasks such as encryption or key generation will substantially reduce the number of connections per second that a server can sustain—often by a factor of ten or more.

One approach to scaling a service and reducing the end-system response time is to employ some form of hardware assistance. Security co-processors come in a PC card form factor, as an attached "dongle" that offloads processing, or as an in-line network appliance that translates from secure to plaintext traffic.

The IP front-end processor

Additional "virtual services" will become broadly available as networking systems migrate up the stack. Instead of requesting a specific device by address, these systems allow a subscriber to request a service and have it fulfilled by any system that is capable of doing so. They also allow application developers to rely on the network, rather than the platform operating system, for some of the critical services needed to deploy an application.

With the explosive growth in "application-over-IP" products of recent years, major networking vendors are moving away from the "price-per-port" or "speeds and feeds" mentality toward an "IP services" mentality. Such a move means the tighter bundling of user identity, network management, virtual service, replicated directory, policy decision making, and dynamic configuration systems into a "programmable network." The network will be in charge of managing access to virtual services and eventually even to the *service topology* and *content topology* that make it able to match clients with the information they seek.

We call this set of features an IP front-end processor, or IPFEP. The IPFEP is a set of services that are offered at the edges of the network, before the clients and servers. IPFEPs perform load balancing, encryption, network address translation, proxying, caching, session management, page assembly and content presentation, and a number of other services that lie below the application but above the network.

For IT, this means that strategic product selection will be based on a complete IP service suite, rather than just a set of devices and features. As new IP services become broadly accepted, they will become integrated first as reseller agreements, then as OEM agreements, and finally as acquisitions integrated into the network devices themselves.

A summary of handling techniques

In summary, we present a taxonomy of traffic-handling mechanisms (Figure 12–8) that can be used to modify per-hop behavior of traffic.

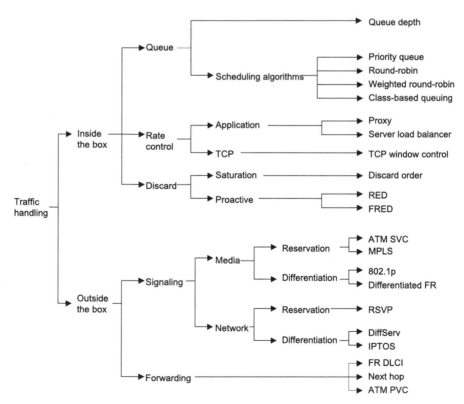

Figure 12–8   A taxonomy of traffic-enforcement mechanisms

Every network device will be different in terms of the specific classification and handling capabilities that it offers, as well as the parameters it uses for each mechanism. With this kind of complexity in every device, detailed metrics for performance monitoring and systemwide management applications such as policy servers are the only way to keep the network running smoothly. Centralization of large amounts of information is offered through directories, and dynamic provisioning is achieved through the use of network policy.

Endnotes

1. K. Thompson, G. J. Miller, and R. Wilder, *IEEE Network*, Nov./Dec. 1997.

2. Inktomi corporation estimates that 60 percent of the traffic on the backbone of one ISP it works with is redundant.

Directory infrastructures

Policy information must be stored in a manner that supports heterogeneous networking environments. It must also be available quickly so that devices can make split-second decisions; at the same time, it must be replicated throughout the network to ensure high availability. Directories, fronted by protocols such as LDAP, offer such features. With industry initiatives afoot to standardize their content, directory systems offer the optimal system for storing the data needed to manage bandwidth.

We've looked at the needs of applications, how to identify them, and how to handle them. Clearly, with the frightening number of options available to a network manager, what really matters is *orchestration*. In order to manage all of these functions in a consistent manner, we need a central repository for information as well as a set of protocols for distributing the information in a clean, efficient manner.

A **directory** is a database that is optimized for reading information as a series of attributes and values. A printed phone directory, for example, is designed to provide basic attributes (name, address, and telephone number) that are easy to retrieve because they are indexed. Telephone directories are harder to modify than simple databases, because they represent a consolidated view of data from many sources and are often not themselves the primary source of data.

A directory service provides a *unique namespace*, whether you run it on a single computer or distribute it across a network over many servers. A query will always return the same information. The Domain Name Service is an example of this unique namespace; it allows a query for a properly formatted Web URL to return one or more network addresses, regardless of which DNS server you ask in the same namespace. A properly configured directory should also offer a common management interface for all servers, services, applications, and devices.

Computers that serve directory information are optimized for rapid responses to queries, at the expense of slow additions or modifications to their content. Network directories don't manage change well—other systems need to be put in place to handle rapidly changing information such as dynamic data on network performance, link congestion, or available bandwidth.

Many directory services run on the same platforms as traditional databases. They are often relatively limited in database functions, such as server-side query handling, content management, replication, and rollback of transactions. Directories by themselves also don't provide support services required for reliable operation. User access control and authentication, backup, and similar functions are all delivered by external applications on the server platform. Systems operate *on* the directory content.

The availability of consistent, pervasive information about users and devices is an important change in networking that makes it possible to automate and personalize network services. User-based directories have been around in mail and server systems for years, but only recently have they been applied to networks as a whole.

Directory deployment today

Directories exist throughout companies today. Some are obvious, as in the example of last-name telephone directories. Others are hidden, such as those used by network operating systems' user account information. As networking equipment grows in configuration complexity and service diversity, one important role for directories is that of tracking the various network resources—devices, users, address space, and the like—in a centralized fashion. One of the critical resources that a network offers is bandwidth; consequently, no discussion of bandwidth management is complete without a look at directories. While directories are useful for a variety of problems in information storage and data structure, the discussion here is admittedly networking-centric.

Today's networking directories include Internet domain name and address servers (such as DNS, DHCP, LDAP, and Radius) as well as vendor-specific server directories from companies like Novell, Microsoft, Netscape, Sun, and Banyan. Many equipment vendors also rely on directories as part of their network management systems.

The main value of directories is common information, but multiple parallel directories undermine this value. The information contained in the directories is seldom consolidated and often redundant. Inconsistent naming conventions, and multiple attributes with similar content, mean that an employee's last name can be stored in many different ways throughout the company's databases. A Radius server, a security system, an asset database, and a Human Resources database may all contain information on the same person—but the information is seldom consistent and often hard to interrelate. We've already seen some of these inconsistencies at work when we looked at associating user identity, MAC address, and IP address.

Sidebar

Relative installed base of directory systems

The grandfather of directories is X.500, a robust, structured, and extensively documented directory system. Despite its heavy investment in development, for data networks X.500 remains a distant second to commercial, enterprise-based directory applications. Enterprise directory users outnumber X.500 users by nearly 100 to 1. The relative installed base of leading directory solutions is listed in Table 13–1.

Table 13–1   Installed base of various directory platforms

Directory platform	Number of clients in 1996
X.500 users	1 million
Lotus cc:Mail	8 million
Novell NetWare 3.x	35 million
Novell NetWare 4.x	15 million
Lotus Notes	3.3 million
Microsoft Mail (exchange as primary server)	6 million[1]

Until consistency and sharing of this information is achieved, the usefulness of directories is limited. If an employee is deleted in the human-resources database because she leaves the company, this does not automatically result in her removal from the security system or the network server. The lack of coordination between directories presents so many potential loopholes that companies have resorted to manual checks and balances, reducing the systems' effectiveness.

Directory nirvana will occur when an organization has a single, pervasive directory for everything it does. On the one hand, this is a great way to structure and organize business; on the other hand, it's "modeling the universe" and an onerous, if not impossible, task to undertake. But the costs of *not* integrating this data in today's business environment can be disastrous, exposing the company to spiraling operational costs and ineffective security.

Basic components of a directory service

Directories are useful because of their pervasiveness. A directory's associated protocols standardize the structure of its information as well as the methods that may be applied to the directory. Such standards allow a variety of client systems—from telephone switches to corporate administrators to e-mail services—to get the information they need from a common namespace reliably. The protocols generally cover some or all of the following:

- Rules for how to read from and write to the directory service from a client.

- Rules for identifying valid users (authentication) and the actions they can take (authorization).

- Rules for how to perform operations (such as searches) that execute on the directory.

- A structured, consistent naming system that allows the retrieval of specific information regardless of the source of the query or the element of the directory that is queried.

- The replication system by which information is distributed among the directory servers, as well as the synchronization methods that the system uses to maintain consistency.

- A common structure or schema for the content of the directory itself. The schema includes the format of information (binary data, text, date, etc.) and the dimensions of the information (sequencing, length, and so on).

Information in a directory is arranged in a hierarchy "tree" that makes organizational sense—for example, by geographic location or role. The directory stores associated information for each node in the tree, and different nodes are members of different classes. For example, a company's directory might be structured according to building, and building 2 might contain both "users" and "printers" as Figure 13–1 shows.

A node in the schema is identified by moving along the tree from the root, using values for each branch in the tree. The directory client can therefore retrieve information from a unique node. In this way, the directory hierarchy is similar to a file system on a computer—a file may be uniquely identified as

```
/maindir/personal_documents/engineering/Fred_smith/address.txt
```

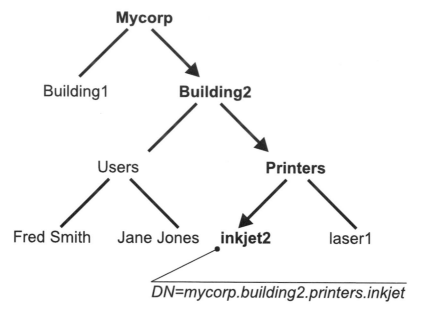

Figure 13–1 How names are constructed in a directory hierarchy

No other node can have this identification. In X.500, this is known as a Distinguished Name (DN), made by identifying the branches in the Directory Information Tree (DIT).

Just as a file may be uniquely identified, it may contain standard information. Assume that the above example pointed to Fred Smith's address. We could, with a computer's file directory tree, look up any engineering employee's address by querying for `maindir/personal_documents/engineering/<employee_name>/address.txt`.

We'd still have to agree on the content of the `address.txt` file—not only is the structure of the nodes essential, but the information *within* each node must be known by the clients.

A directory behaves in a similar manner. At the end of every DN is a set of attribute-value pairs. Both the client and the server know the structure of these pairs, and this makes the retrieval of the information consistent across multiple clients and servers. In a directory, a client in the previous example might refer to `"acmecorp/employees/engineering/fred smith"` and obtain a set of attributes (street, city, country, telephone number, and so on) as well as their corresponding values.

Now imagine a different DIT path to a printer. The attribute/value pairs that would be stored in `"acmecorp/devices/building2/print-`

ers/printer7" would be substantially different from those for Fred Smith. They might include the serial number, make, model, and address of the device. Because of this, printers and employees are two different *object classes*. The directory client and directory server share a common structure for information pertaining to each class—that is, they share the same schema. Most directories—from computer file systems to telephone directories—conform to these principles.

One standards-based directory is X.500, a heavyweight of the directory world. X.500 is used for a number of mission-critical applications such as telephony, but its ponderous software and hardware requirements make it difficult to implement economically in enterprise networks.

The X.500 directory standard

X.500 was initially defined in 1988, and was revised in 1993, by the International Standards Organization (ISO). It describes the steps for communications between a server and a client, as well as the schema, or structure, of that information. X.500 was specifically designed to address the problems of making a very large body of information available across a large number of servers while maintaining consistency.

In addition to the object-class schema and the hierarchy discussed above, X.500 outlines the various functional components of a directory. X.500 is a complex system of distributed agents, each of which maintains a fragment of the entire directory and knows how to respond to its peer agents in order to retrieve additional information. X.500 also defines client agent functionality, mirroring agents, and request-forwarding agents. While a complete discussion of X.500 is beyond the scope of this book, it is important to understand the fundamental parts of a "heavyweight" directory in order to see what we sacrifice when we adopt a lightweight directory protocol such as LDAP.

X.500 proved too heavy for implementation in most networks. The lack of available software and the high demands of the server system, combined with reliance on the OSI stack, limited the adoption of the standard. Instead, X.500 has become something of a reference standard for directories, much as OSI provided a reference model for discussions about IP, IPX, and the like.

Common data structures

With a protocol for accessing information in directories, one can build a single application easily. A company can, for example, build an HR directory using the LDAP definitions that exist. They will have to define their own schema, and store a representation of the various object classes in a well-known location to allow discovery, but they can succeed nevertheless. Once we try to reconcile two or more divergent applications on a single directory, we need a way of extending the schema without adding redundancy.

The most relevant function of a directory within the scope of this text is that of network management. Specifically, a directory can act as a common repository for device and user information that allows scarce bandwidth or precious low-latency connections to be allocated to the users and applications that are allowed them. In other words, a directory is the repository of content with which a policy-based network enforces rules.

Multivendor interoperability is not possible unless networking vendors agree on a common structure for the information. Since the industry cannot know today what information it will need years from now, the schema must leave room for expansion and extension. Extensible schemas consist of a generic structure of information, with a minimum of required attribute-value pairs. They leave out the many optional parameters that vendors may want to include in the directory. Over time, the mandatory elements may be modified to encompass more common optional parameters.

A directory moves the configuration and setup information from the device itself onto a central location. By divorcing configuration from hardware, directory-enabled networks make hardware easier to swap out. The configuration also becomes much easier to manipulate—we can process it without translation via SNMP or command lines, we can replicate it, we can back it up, and so on.

For example, if I want to make a change to a router with a traditional device-based configuration, I can run a configuration utility that issues a number of commands to the device via a telnet link or SNMP commands. I might also connect to the device with a Web browser and use its management interface. With a directory, I would instead modify the directory's *representation* of the device. It is far simpler to program the directory, because I'm changing logical objects rather than talking to the device itself. When it comes time to publish my changes to the device, the configuration system replicates the settings from the logical object (stored in the directory) out to the real device. If I want to apply the logical object to other devices, it is trivial to do so. Similarly, if the router fails and I need to swap it out, I can publish the configuration to the new device easily.

Policy is a dynamic, rapid form of automated provisioning. Directories allow provisioning to happen quickly enough that devices can work on a session-by-session basis, handling reservations such as RSVP requests without introducing large delays.

Deciding to agree: The DEN ad-hoc working group

The Directory Enabled Networks initiative (DEN) is an industry working group chartered to propose a structure for a common network directory. Under the auspices of the Desktop Management Task Force (DMTF), DEN has created a structured schema for data that vendors can use and extend to permit some degree of informational interoperability among them.

DEN contains a good deal of fundamental device information used for basic configuration, and the DMTF began by modeling networking components to facilitate management and asset inventories. In recent years it has shifted focus to more dynamic attributes of a network. DEN defines provisioning and policy management, as well as information on security, traffic prioritization, and permitted applications. Consequently, the DMTF will begin to encompass policy information and user information in its standards.

DEN defines a high-level schema and implementation-specific schemata that models common networking components such as routers, switches, and their subcomponents (interfaces, ports, and addresses). Initial prestandard DEN implementations began to appear in vendor equipment in early 1998, although the standardization process is an ongoing effort under the DMTF.

DEN was assembled from a number of existing standards and vendor implementations, including those from the DMTF's Common Information Model (CIM), X.500, Microsoft, and other vendors. Some vendors are now using DEN and CIM interchangeably, and this is a reflection of the degree of integration that DEN has undergone within the DMTF.

LDAP

DEN leverages a lightweight cousin of X.500 called LDAP. LDAP releases the client from many of the burdens of a complete directory service, at the expense of a measure of robustness and some esoteric features not needed in networking environments.

LDAP has been under development since 1993. It is defined in a number of Internet Engineering Task Force standards, including RFCs 1487, 1777, and 2251. Originally intended as a simpler front end for X.500, LDAP has become the basis for a number of directories built atop lightweight databases. While X.500 was built on the work surrounding the OSI stack, LDAP is a lean, efficient IP directory. Specifically,

- LDAP is IP based, using TCP for session management.

- LDAP attribute-value pairs are simple strings.

- LDAP has less support for security.

- LDAP supports Internet-style distinguished names.

- LDAP does not define the functioning of the back-end directory or replication.

- LDAP clients are a part of many popular browsers already, and NOS vendors have announced their support for LDAP interfaces to the proprietary data structures of their servers.

LDAP's focus is on access to information, rather than on the replication of that information throughout a directory service. As such, it has been criticized for its lack of scalability. However, there is no reason that an LDAP front end can't be put on top of a robust X.500 directory— indeed, most X.500 implementations support LDAP interfaces. Front-ending an X.500 directory with LDAP combines the reliability of X.500 and the simplicity of LDAP for those companies that need a mission-critical directory service with lightweight end systems.

Version 3 of the LDAP specification adds features that address some of the weaknesses of earlier revisions of the protocol:

- Referral, by which a server that cannot respond to a request can return a pointer to another server. Referral allows the directory system to adjust to changing conditions, as well as being able to return pointers to non-LDAP information sources such as agents on networking devices.

- Discovery, by which a client can retrieve the schema of a directory service by looking in a standard branch containing the information structure of the directory's contents.

- International-character-set support.

- Improved security, using the same secure-sockets technique (SSL) employed by Web browsers and better authentication systems.

- Extensibility of the schema to support new operations on the directory.

Nevertheless, LDAP is an access protocol—not a complete solution. Alone, an LDAP directory does not offer global naming conventions, a discovery protocol, or a schema. Many LDAP implementations rely on DNS for service location and use an X.500-style naming system as well as a DNS-style name structure.

LDAP implementations often include the Lightweight Internet Person Schema, a standard building block by which LDAP clients can query a user directory according to a well-known set of information structures. As a result, messaging and user directories are beginning to offer standardized LDAP interfaces both as clients and servers.

DEN is intended to be a similar standard for network information. DEN's schema consists of a set of hierarchies and corresponding object classes that can create logical representations of many devices. The DEN schema also offers *inheritance*. Inheritance means that a generic "switch," as defined by DEN, has a subset of typical values. Each vendor-specific definition can override or add to the list of value-attribute pairs described in the schema, making multivendor interoperability possible while still supporting vendor-specific or proprietary features in the system.

Putting directories to work

Creating and enforcing policies in a network means moving common information around the organization consistently. Initial deployments of centralized information systems and management tools will be vendor specific, like Cisco's Assured Network Services, 3Com's Transcend Policy Server, or Nortel Networks' Optivity Policy Services. As management vendors like HP and Computer Associates begin to introduce policy tools, directory-policy systems will eventually encompass multivendor implementations, much as HP OpenView uses a number of standard MIBs to communicate to many different networking devices.

Directory systems already offer many benefits for simple configuration management and provisioning storage. They also work as common ground for multiple policy servers. In this respect, directories deliver a single, central point for administering policy and user information—especially when tied to DNS, DHCP, and authentication servers. They also replicate timely copies of information throughout an organization readily—something with which networking equipment vendors don't have a great deal of experience. We'll look at policy systems more in the next chapter.

Directories are stores of information. They must be augmented with a set of services that understand the information they contain and the relationships within that information. These services need to know how to make changes to that information in order to produce useful changes in the network that the information models. Network-management systems that use directories will have to offer this set of services in order to allow network managers to maintain the logical model of the network.

For directory systems to be successful, they require a common access protocol (LDAP v3 seems to be the currently favored implementation), a common schema (the Directory Enabled Networks forum and the Desktop Management Task Force are working on this), and replication systems. The means of replication among directories is the missing piece that has led some engineers to declare LDAP unready for real deployment. Replication is a function of the underlying protocol for interserver communications. Also lacking from early LDAP implementations are a robust information model, clearly structured relationships between pieces of information, and transaction and rollback capabilities.[2]

These problems will soon be overcome. Many proprietary implementations have resolved them in a fairly lightweight manner that works for enterprises: Novell's NDS, or Banyan's VINES/Streettalk. With the release of NT 5.0, Microsoft also hopes to have a scalable replication system as well. The IETF is also taking steps to remedy LDAP's weaknesses.

The time to investigate a directory system is now. Be ready for vendor implementations that include directory-based configuration, and prepare for policy systems for QOS deployment. A pervasive, reliable directory service is a cornerstone of a next-generation, multiservice network.

Endnotes

1. From a white paper by Zoomit corporation, a metadirectory vendor, available at `http://www.zoomit.com/directories/am_whitepaperpaper4.htm` "there are only around one million X.500 users worldwide, commercial LAN products such as cc:Mail are used by almost 100 million users, including some 35 million NetWare 3.x users, 15 million NetWare 4.x users, eight million cc:Mail users, 3.3 million Notes users, and more than six million Microsoft Mail users.

2. In June, 1998, a number of vendors (IBM, Packeteer, Telstra, and Intel) submitted a schema to the DEN mailing list for service-level administration of differentiated services and integrated services in networks. The schema describes one way of administering QOS—both IntServ and DiffServ models—through an LDAP directory.

Policy systems

A policy system unites the classification, handling, and information-storage systems we've looked at. Policies are high-level rules about how a network should behave. A policy system bridges the gap between these rules and the device configurations that make them happen. Policy systems have grown from bulk provisioning and authentication models, and they include standards such as COPS today. A policy system must publish configurations dynamically and proactively, often across administrative boundaries.

Now we're ready to look at the big picture of network policy. A **policy system** manages a set of rules that are circulated to the various components of a network so that they can classify, police, and enforce a set of behaviors for applications, users and groups.

Armed with this new knowledge, let's review the diagram of a generic policy system (Figure 14–1). Information storage comes from the directory; enforcement is achieved through device classification and handling techniques. What remains is the decision-making functions within the policy server and the interfaces to the clients and information sources.

Policy-based networking is a shift in the way that networks are managed and network resources are allocated. Instead of emphasizing devices and interfaces, a policy-management system focuses on users and applications. It does this by hiding the user-to-device mapping from the network administrator and relying on a set of "network authorities" to provide dynamic associations between the users of the network and the traffic they generate.

Policies for networks can govern everything from security and configuration to service levels and monitoring thresholds. Policy systems communicate with networking devices, either in response to network events or by proactively pushing out rules and information to the network. The IETF has added a working group for policy-based networking standards development. In a sharp change from earlier IETF work, the policy group will not focus on protocol development but will instead work on common data structures that can tell devices how to handle traffic based on specific conditions.[1]

Policy protocols

In order for network devices to function according to the policy "master plan" of the network, information on how to handle traffic must reach the components of the network. To do this, a number of policy protocols have been developed.

Statefulness

There are many ways to transmit configuration to a network device. The most recent iteration of such protocols is different because it is *stateful*; it has shifted from a traditional client-server to a manager-agent system in which the manager can respond to agent queries but can also transmit changes to the agent in an unsolicited manner.

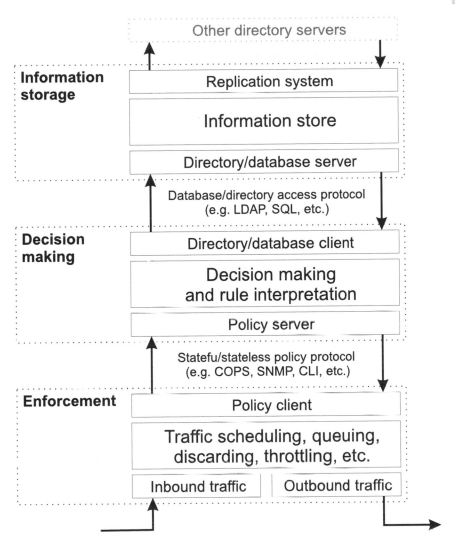

Figure 14–1   A generic policy system revisited

A stateful protocol is one in which the "server" (the manager) keeps track of the "client" (the agent). If the manager detects a change that means the agent's configuration or information is no longer accurate, the manager pushes out current information to replace the old information stored on the agent. To better understand this, let's look at an example.

In a traditional client-server model for authentication, a dialup user connects to an access concentrator and authenticates. At that point, the access concentrator retrieves the username and password, verifies them against a password authority, and allows the user to connect to the network. If the user's rights to the system are changed *during* the session, the access concentrator does not disconnect the user. The authority is not keeping track of which users are currently connected and whether their permissions have changed. Even if the authority *were* watching rights and permissions, the protocol itself does not offer a mechanism for notifying the client in an unsolicited manner (Figure 14–2).

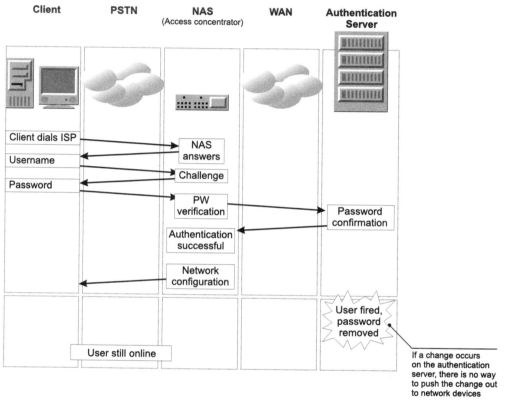

Figure 14–2   Traffic flow in a stateless authentication model (Radius)

By contrast, in a manager-agent model, the password authority would inform the access concentrator when a permission changed because it would have such means (Figure 14–3).

Statefulness is more than just an academic issue. It is the nature of internetworking that resources will become available and resources will become scarce. As the network's capacity changes, management systems will need to modify the settings of network devices and the permissions and reservations that have already been granted in order to adjust. A stateless protocol is not suited to the delivery of unsolicited changes in configuration that characterize a policy-based network.

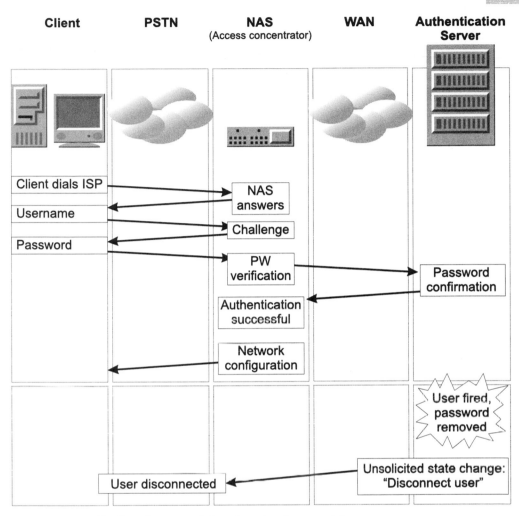

Figure 14–3   Traffic flow in a stateful authentication model

Radius

The Remote Access Dial Up User Services (Radius) is used to pass sets of attribute-value pairs between a client and a server. It is stateless and is broadly deployed for authenticating dialup users as well as for controlling access to network-management consoles. In response to a successful authentication attempt, the Radius server will return a number of standard and vendor-specific attributes to the client. These attributes may be simple parameters for use in the establishment of a network protocol (such as the IP address to assign to the remote device) or they may contain complex information for virtual private-network tunnel establishment. Radius also offers accounting functionality for logging caller activity.

In a dialup environment, the low speed of the link has discouraged the deployment of applications that require QOS features. Those applications that *are* latency or jitter sensitive generally include a good deal of buffering and robustness at the application layer in order to overcome the unreliability of the Internet across a dial up connection.

With the deployment of higher-speed local-loop technologies like ADSL and cable modems, as well as the increased penetration of ISDN, work is underway to offer priority at the link layer. Take, for example, an access environment in which many modem users share a T1 connection between the network access server (NAS) and the Internet. With this the connection might have offered an acceptable level of bandwidth oversubscription at 14,400 Kbps, it is four times as congested under peak load with a set of 56-Kbps modems connecting in. If the ISP is not ready to upgrade the T1 connection, it may be able to offer differentiated services in which premium customers are less likely to have their packets discarded by the NAS when congestion occurs.

This sort of differentiated-service model would require coordination between the Radius server (a vendor-specific attribute for discard eligibility), and the access concentrator (discarding user traffic based on the value of the attribute). This mechanism would throttle back lower-priority customers during congestion. The access concentrator could also mark the IP precedence or DS codepoint information as needed to request priority handling within the network.

If this differentiated service were created with stateless protocols, changes to a customers' service would not take effect until the next time they connected to the network and triggered a service negotiation. With a stateful protocol, changes to a customer's level of service would be effected immediately.

Diameter

Diameter is a successor to Radius (as its name suggests). It was originally called "Enhanced Radius" but was changed to avoid confusion.

Despite its popularity, Radius lacks some important features of policy decision-makers in a network. Extensibility and statefulness are the two biggest differences between the traditional client-server model of Radius and the manager-agent approach that Diameter takes.

Radius has a limited range of standard and vendor-specific attributes. The shortage of command space has led to divergent implementations, and Radius server platforms often maintain a look up table of IP-address and access-concentrator vendors so they can sort out the various Radius query formats across multiple vendors in a multivendor point of presence.

In order to ensure backward compatibility, Radius and Diameter can run side by side on a system, with Radius listening on port 1812 and Diameter on port 1645. Both daemons use a common data set to ensure consistent behavior regardless of the protocol used.

Diameter does not describe implementations, although it is targeted at the same problems that Radius addresses (authentication, authorization, and accounting systems). In practice, the attribute-value pairs that are passed from client to server can define any number of parameters—the specification suggests RSVP admission, dial up access management, and voice-over-IP user session management.

A Diameter implementation would create a number of policy like capabilities that simply extended Radius fundamentals. For example, packet filter definitions used for authorization might be extended to support service-level features like packet interleaving or next-hop routing over differentiated circuits.

COPS

The Common Open Policy Service (COPS) Protocol is used by networking devices to determine the validity of a request for reserved bandwidth by a component of the network. It is a stateful mechanism by which a device can register itself to a server and then maintain the state of multiple policy objects on both the client and the server. If the manager or agent gets "out of sync" or if the state of the object needs to be changed, either party can notify the other of the change.

At the time of this writing, COPS systems are in early deployment but are generally restricted to relatively small spheres of influence, such as RSVP signaling within a campus network. At the borders between a COPS-managed network and other administrative domains there is generally a conversion from RSVP services (guaranteed load, controlled load, and best-effort) into suitable IPTOS, MPLS, parallel-circuit, or ATM service categories.

The network as an operating system

We'll look at COPS in more detail in a moment. But it may be useful at this juncture to consider the fundamental shifts that have moved networks from a simple, configuration-based model to one in which stateful protocols and device-initiated classification are important.

Consider an operating system. In an event-based, object-oriented OS, a number of self-contained components are gathered together as an application with an overarching set of instructions that unifies their behavior for a specific purpose. A calculator application, for example, contains buttons for the numbers from 0 to 9. Each button is an object—it can have a state (up or down) and it has effects (when it is clicked and released, it passes a message to the application to let it know that its number was selected). To do so, each button *registers* itself with the application to which it must send messages, and it maintains its state. At any given time, the application can check the state of the button; the button can also notify the application of a change.

Complex, graphical operating systems have moved to this model for a number of reasons. The model allows rapid application development and component reusability; it also allows some functions to be managed by the component (button up and down, event handling) and some broader functions to be managed by the application (processing operators, refreshing displays.) To be more specific, a component has things it can do (called *methods*) and properties or values (such as the button's state, its size, or its contents). These functions may be local to the component, or they may be more globally available.

To those familiar with object-oriented systems, this may seem like a review. But it is vital to recognize that the same challenges that moved applications toward an object-oriented model—the need to deploy quickly, reduce complexity, create reusability, improve ease-of-use and troubleshooting, and so on—are motivating the designers of networks. The way in which components of an application are registered with the application is a direct parallel to the way in which networking devices use COPS to register themselves with a network management and policy system.

Imagine our calculator application without an object model. The application would have to constantly check each button to see if the mouse were clicked over it. Constant checking would reduce performance. If the mouse *were* in fact over the button, it would have to redraw the button as down—first checking its *current* state to verify that the button wasn't down. Redrawing would add statefulness and complexity to the code. Instead, in an object-based model the application needs to worry only about a specific event and can be far simpler.

Policy without statefulness

A worst-case scenario for policy is that the networking devices are completely passive. In this case, a policy system must constantly poll each device to see if a change has occurred. Constant polling is prohibitive because of the high volumes of excess traffic that are generated, and provisioning changes so quickly that it is nearly impossible to poll a device quickly enough to determine the appropriate policy.

Consequently, a stateless policy system looks somewhat like this: The device sends SNMP traps to a server, and the server then acts upon them. Upon receiving a trap, the server connects to the device, retrieves its configuration, parses it to determine the appropriate changes, and rewrites the configuration to the device. Reading the entire configuration and writing it all back to the device ensures that the changes the policy server is about to make won't break an existing change.

Sadly, this complex sequence is the model we have today. COPS gives us a more streamlined manner of replicating state between two elements in a network. But there is another, perhaps more fundamental, reason why stateful protocols are essential.

In the earlier part of this century, learning by rote was the norm. Students could list off the lengths of the world's longest rivers, the heights of the tallest mountains, and the capitals of all the countries. Rote learning is far less important today; instead of imparting raw knowledge, education focuses on teaching how to *get* knowledge. We learn the Dewey decimal system and the World Wide Web. We might argue that this is a human response to the increasing amount of information and relative specialization—in late twentieth-century society, there's no such thing as "general" knowledge any more, and no one person can know everything.

The same is true of a distributed network. If a company has thousands of users, then implementing rules for all users on all devices is prohibitive. Even with a reasonable set of application defaults and a few exceptions, the need to provide security and billing on an individual basis means that no single networking device can maintain all of the information about a network of any real size economically. To do so would generate an impractical amount of real-time updates between devices.

Instead, devices solicit the information they need when they need it. They classify a user's traffic, and if they don't know how to deal with it, they look it up.

If an employee works in Florida, it is reasonable to put the policies and classifications for that employee on the router in Florida—in other words, to teach the Florida portion of the network about the facts that are relevant to it—in an administrative manner. But in today's distributed, telecommuting, remote-office, nomadic worker world, it is increasingly likely that the employee will be in New York tomorrow and in London next week. The employee may also call in from home, connect across the Internet, or even let a colleague use his machine. As multiservice networks are deployed, it will no longer be reasonable to teach devices the facts; we will instead have to teach them *how to get* the facts.

This has already happened in the access world. Dial up systems must deal with mobile, untrusted users—and they have systems such as Radius in place to cope with the problem. The addition of stateless clients and stateful manager-agent protocols allows an object-oriented approach to network deployment, providing devices with the tools they need to actively solicit what they need to know in an economical manner.

These are the high-level reasons for deploying stateful protocols and policy systems. The notion of the true network operating system (as opposed to the misnomer of the NOS, or server operating system) is finally emerging. Object-oriented, stateful protocols between dynamic devices and information authorities will allow rapid, cost-effective application deployment. The transition to object-oriented, stateful networks will be a significant shift in the coming years, and their adoption by enterprises will face significant hurdles, both conceptually and in terms of altered network design. Protocols such as COPS are the *lingua franca* of QOS networks.

Where COPS came from

COPS originally was tightly associated with the Resource Reservation Protocol (RSVP).

The manner in which the device determines if it should allow the reservation is both internal ("Do I have enough bandwidth to set some aside?") and external ("Is this requestor allowed to reserve this bandwidth?"). The mechanism that a device uses to look up external information is COPS. Because all the devices in a path register the state of the traffic flow with a COPS server, the server has the ability to see the end-to-end impact of a flow. By contrast, each router in the path can see only its per-hop behavior for the particular flow.

At its simplest, COPS is a simple protocol for obtaining policy information. Because of its roots in the RSVP field, COPS is initially well defined only for RSVP requests—but the protocol extends easily to support other types of policy queries such as authentication. A number of vendors are working on COS, QOS, VLAN, addressing, and packet-filter definitions. COPS is therefore a likely candidate for common transfer of policy-related information throughout a network.

COPS defines a policy decision point (PDP, often referred to as a "policy server") and a policy enforcement point (PEP, often referred to simply as an "enforcer"). The PEP and the PDP communicate across a TCP connection, and the communication is stateful. The PDP maintains the state of the PEPs that have requested policy information, and it can push unsolicited updates to them if the policy information changes.

In order to speed things up, each PEP can make a local decision about admission, much as our calculator button could handle certain functions locally. The Local Decision Point (LDP) must ultimately inform the PDP of its decision, and the PEP must defer to changes imposed upon it by the PDP. Having both local and remote decision points improves scalability of the system and provides a mechanism for temporary local handling of policy when a link to the central authority is down.

Sidebar

How COPS works

The PEP queries the PDP on TCP port 3288 to begin a manager-agent session for policy. The PEP can be configured with the IP address of the corresponding PDP, or it can rely on other mechanisms such as the Service Location Protocol (SLP) to obtain the address automatically.

Usually a COPS transaction is one of the following:

• The PEP queries the PDP about the specific client objects for which it is seeking information; the PDP returns the appropriate information. The client type is a part of each COPS message, allowing different PEP/PDP pairs to communicate different kinds of policy using the same basic system.

• The PDP revokes or updates a previously assigned policy when conditions change.

• The remote device's LDP sends messages to the PDP informing it of policy assignments it has made, which may in turn be overridden by the PDP.

• The PEP informs the PDP that a given resource usage has ended.

These communications are broken into ten specific COPS messages. Each is a combination of the COPS header, the client object identifier, and the message type:

• A request (from a PEP to a PDP) asks the PDP to begin tracking the state of a PEP. The request assigns a "handle" which is used to identify subsequent requests.

• A response (from a PDP to a PEP) acknowledges the assignment of the state handle and the policy decision (the initial decision the PDP has made). If an error has occurred, the error notification is returned instead.

• An unsolicited response (from a PDP to a PEP) is a change to a previously passed response—for example, terminating a flow that had been previously permitted. The state handle is used to tell the PEP which state the PDP is talking about.

• A report-state (from a PEP to a PDP) message updates the PDP with the current status of a state that has already been installed with a request. Report-state messages are used to provide accounting information at regular intervals.

• A delete-state request (from a PEP to a PDP) releases a previously installed state. In order for the PDP to maintain resource information correctly, it is vital that the flows (and corresponding resources such as bandwidth) be freed up once they are no longer needed.

• A synchronize-state request (from the PDP to the PEP) asks a PEP to retransmit state information (either for a specific state handle or for all states). Synchronization is used to ensure that states on the PDP and PEP are consistent.

• The remaining messages (client open, client close, client accept, and keep-alives) are used by the PEP and PDP to identify new PEPs and assign time intervals for keep-alive messages, identify the client objects at PEP can support, and verify that a PEP or PDP is still active.

An example of COPS in a unicast RSVP negotiation

This is fairly complex, so let's look at a concrete example. Figure 14–4 summarizes a complete COPS-based establishment of a bandwidth reservation across an Internet path.

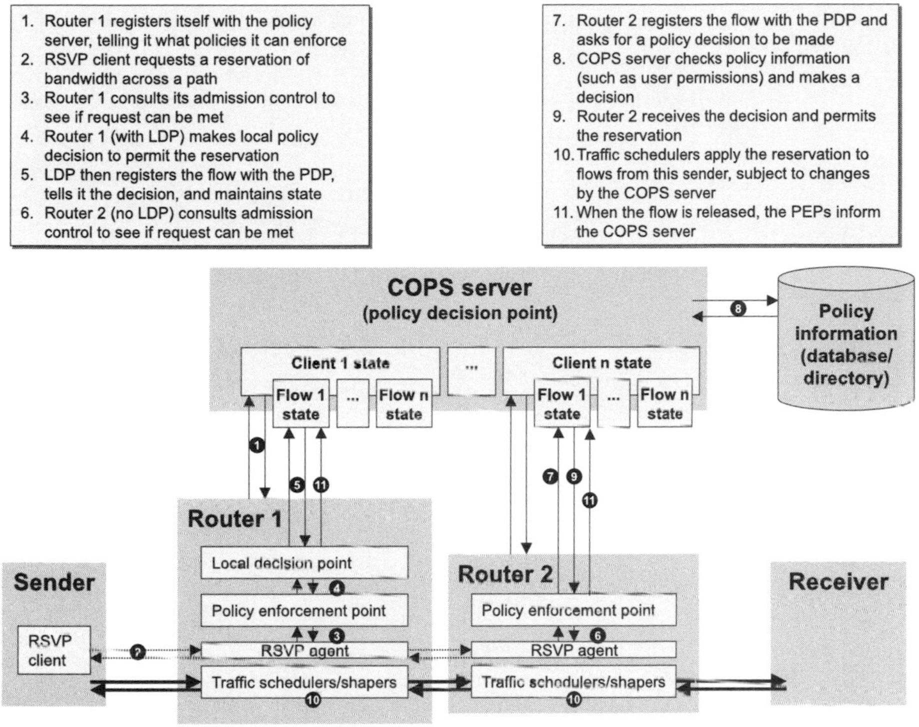

1. Router 1 registers itself with the policy server, telling it what policies it can enforce
2. RSVP client requests a reservation of bandwidth across a path
3. Router 1 consults its admission control to see if request can be met
4. Router 1 (with LDP) makes local policy decision to permit the reservation
5. LDP then registers the flow with the PDP, tells it the decision, and maintains state
6. Router 2 (no LDP) consults admission control to see if request can be met
7. Router 2 registers the flow with the PDP and asks for a policy decision to be made
8. COPS server checks policy information (such as user permissions) and makes a decision
9. Router 2 receives the decision and permits the reservation
10. Traffic schedulers apply the reservation to flows from this sender, subject to changes by the COPS server
11. When the flow is released, the PEPs inform the COPS server
COPS server
(policy decision point)
Policy information (database/ directory)
Client 1 state
Client n state
Flow 1 state
Flow n state
Router 1
Local decision point
Policy enforcement point
RSVP agent
Traffic schedulers/shapers
Router 2
Sender
RSVP client
Receiver

Figure 14–4 Step-by-step analysis of COPS transactions in an RSVP negotiation

This is an excellent point at which to put together all the pieces we have seen so far. A general model of QOS traffic management has these components:

- Traffic is transmitted across the network. It is subject to some kind of differential handling to facilitate either application delay sensitivity or mission criticality according to organizational goals. This happens in several ways.
  - Explicit reservation on a flow-by-flow basis (RSVP, ATM QOS parameters)
  - Implicit differentiation, based on packet marking in the link or network layer (IPTOS, 802.1p)

— Administratively configured preferential treatment (access lists in a router)

• Each network device receives the packet and must decide how to handle it. The decision may take place locally (packet-handling algorithms); it may be a decision from some network authority (Radius servers, COPS servers, and so on); or it may be a preconfigured rule set by a network administrator (static association of flows with handlers). For dynamically provisioned systems such as ATM SVCs or RSVP, some form of admission control is applied to regulate access to reserved capacity.

• The devices forward packets from the traffic flow according to the per-hop behaviors that are defined. Forwarding is achieved through queuing, shaping with buckets, throttling, selective discarding, and so on.

• Devices remove the policy from the policy server when the flow disappears or the state of the permissions changes.

COPS is designed in such a way that network components can vary in their decision-making ability. Various routed domains come under the policy control of a given PDP, and each may have an LDP to speed decision-making (while deferring to the PDP). Some devices may even have their own PDP functions (consulting the same information set as stand-alone PDPs).

The COPS protocol is a straightforward, extensible method of registering objects and maintaining state synchronization between a manager and an agent. It offers information on how to create new client objects to support additional policy protocols, and already there are proposals for supporting differentiated service assignment via COPS.

COPS challenges and issues

COPS is a promising protocol for stateful policy communications. It faces challenges of complexity, scaling, and protocol overhead.

The Internet is an environment in which the judicious application of simple mechanisms to complex problems allows great scalability. Components in an internet coexist with relatively little interaction unless they are involved in the transmission of data together. By contrast, a COPS server will need to maintain the state of a wide range of users, applications, links, and device capacities. It will have to manage revocation and allocation, and do so in a timely manner without adding a prohibitive level of network overhead. Similar systems for state management in voice telephony have taken years to develop and deploy, and COPS servers have a great deal of work ahead of them before they can claim the level of reliability that the voice network does today.

COPS also depends on TCP and a standard protocol for IP security (IPSEC) for secure communications. By contrast, Radius and its successor, Diameter, are UDP-based. One reason for this is the high overhead of TCP signaling for occasional bursts of short messages. Radius and Diameter contain session-identification information in the protocols themselves rather than in the underlying session layer. TCP also generates keep-alive traffic to ensure constant availability, which can add network overhead. Consequently, TCP may present COPS with scaling issues when many concurrent policy conversations are underway.

Publishing

Many of the mechanisms we've seen so far for distributing policy involve explicit look ups by the enforcing device. In a high-speed network, it is not practical to perform look ups for every new flow—especially in the core. Consequently, administrators must publish the static associations between a relatively small number of classifiers (802.1p, IPTOS, DiffServ, etc.) and the per-hop behaviors that should be applied to such traffic.

Sending out changes is typically performed through a series of SNMP set commands by an operator, a management console, or a script. All of these present problems in terms of state management, complexity, possibility for operator errors, and bandwidth consumed by the transmissions. New communications models exist that can optimize this process.

- Push systems consist of devices that are listening for unsolicited updates. A push system is good when the devices must each get individual configurations but are unable to parse the portion of the message that is relevant to them from the whole message. User- or group-specific information, as well as information that is associated with topology, is suitable for push systems. The pushing server determines the relevant messages for each listening device

- Multicast updates are a bandwidth-efficient method of distributing a global set of configurations. The sender transmits all configurations on a well-known multicast address to which the receivers have subscribed. Multicast is good for broadly applicable settings—such as the association of a few classifiers with per-hop behavior parameters. It can also be used for sending device-specific information, if the information is marked in such a way that devices to which it does not apply can discard it.

Multivendor interoperability

Having a COPS server in place doesn't give you magic interoperability, of course. COPS object classes are likely to be vendor specific for some time. There are three basic ways in which multiple vendors in a policy system can interoperate:

- "Stealth" policy, in which one vendor's policy server manages another vendor's device through SNMP, command-line, and Web interfaces. This kind of adaptation layer between COPS and older management protocols allows the policy server to manage virtually any device, but it requires considerably more development within the policy server to handle the scripts and translation layers for each device.

- Directory interoperability, in which multiple vendor-specific policy servers coexist in a network, each talking to that vendor's equipment and each using the same decision-making criteria and information set in an attempt to offer similar per-hop behaviors to the traffic in the network.

- COPS interoperability, in which all vendors support a set of COPS client types and can all talk to one server. While this is clearly the intent of the COPS protocol and standards body work, it is unlikely that any one vendor will expose all of its features to a standard protocol. To do so would be to sacrifice any competitive advantages afforded by a certain implementation or feature set. Instead, much as a device is managed by a set of standard MIBs and a set of vendor-specific MIBs, so a COPS server will manage the common policy types but will not offer full support for all the features of a particular device (such as specialized parameters for per-hop behavior).

Policy across administrative domains

The deployment of pervasive management systems will be as much a political struggle as a technical one. A pragmatic analysis of network policy must include the boundaries between the enterprise, one or more service providers, the remote user or customer, and the extranet business partner. For example, the service provider's IPTOS settings may not be the same as those of the company. At the very least, the ISP will overwrite signaling from the enterprise as part of its policing function.

Circuit selection

ISPs are currently offering differentiated services via separate circuits rather than via packets. Circuit-based differentiation lags the technological transition from circuit-based networks to modern packet- and cell-based systems. For example, some service providers offer special "SNA Frame Relay" services with low-latency links at a price premium. By configuring the WAN interfaces on the router to perform next-hop routing to the SNA link for tn3270, tn5250, and DLSw traffic, this can be used to offer rudimentary differentiated services over the WAN.

Reservation

ISP services that cross multiple domains—such as IP-based networks for VPN tunnels—are a problem that ISPs haven't yet resolved among themselves. Equitable billing among multiple intermediaries is difficult to manage. In an international telephone call, the establishment of each circuit carries with it a corresponding accounting event, so that each carrier is compensated appropriately. Telephone billing occurs only once for the duration of the circuit. Similar systems on a per-packet basis would introduce unacceptable delays and a good deal of additional network traffic. Done on a per-flow basis, they would require an enormous amount of state information on each router.

The flow-scaling problem is an operational one: publishing user information doesn't scale beyond an administrative domain. Current authentication systems such as Radius have proxy capabilities, in which the initially queried authentication server can parse the name (such as "fred@acme.com") and relay it by proxy to a Radius server at acme.com for verification. Once again, this is a setup-based system. In the WAN and high-speed LAN core, per-user classification across administrative boundaries remains too difficult to implement practically. In addition, Radius is generally limited to dialup environments, although it is enjoying increased deployment in network-management authentication systems.

Simple mapping

Assuming that adjacent administrative domains offer some degree of classification, a simple perspective is to assign common mappings between layer-2 and layer-3 protocols—for example, 802.1p to IPTOS, IPTOS to ATM ABR, ATM ABR to differentiated Frame Relay circuits, and so on. But this approach suffers from two major political obstacles. Mappings are not currently standardized, and owners of the costly links (the ISPs and those managing WAN circuits) are loath to allow others to specify service levels without some degree of authentication and accounting back-billing in place.

Perhaps more importantly, simple mappings may rob upper-layer protocols of useful information unless they are applied judiciously. It makes perfect sense, for example, to map IPTOS information that indicates traffic is suitable for discard during congestion to Frame Relay DE bits. But it may make less sense to assign 802.1p frames tagged as "network critical" to ATM committed-bit-rate circuits—the traffic is important, but it doesn't need the sender/receiver synchronization of, say, a videoconference.

Within the enterprise, it will be far easier to divide the network's policies by applications first, since this will cause less disagreement than choosing which department gets better performance. Once you've done so, be prepared for a debate in the boardroom about the relative importance of manufacturing systems, sales tracking, and financial applications. The answer, of course, is that they're all vital—and network capacity should accommodate them all.

In a large network, it may also make sense to split the types of policy up by function. A capacity manager would be in charge of service-level policies, QOS, and RSVP. A security manager would be in charge of authentication and authorization systems. A billing and usage manager would run the accounting and monitoring systems. An asset manager would be in charge of configuration systems. Splitting up roles is an effective way to share the burden of policy across multiple operators; clearly defining responsibility for types of network policy will avoid ambiguity and confusion later on.

Once the policy infrastructure is in place, the tools to adjust the network may even be handed over to the application managers (with suitable restrictions in place). Think that you'll never "give the reins" of the network to department managers? Remember that in a few short years office administrators may be setting up videoconferencing circuits the way they plan a conference call today. Policy-based networking elevates many of the complex, lower-layer, topological issues to a level at which application managers can understand them. Similarly, broad understanding of the Web-based interface makes configuration easier. Instead of being presented with routes and addresses, administrators see users and traffic types. Working in these terms is an excellent way to engage application and server managers in the strategic growth of the network.

Becoming an internal ISP

A final approach to mitigating the political side of policy deployment is to adopt an "internal ISP" approach to bandwidth. Set a clear demarcation within the network, and make sure everyone understands a simple, consistent set of classifiers (such as IPTOS or 802.1p) that you will respect. Then set billing rates for premium traffic, and present each user group with a bill at the end of the month. The bill may be informative, or it may actually be related to your funding. Either way, it provides excellent motivation for the proper deployment of policy-enabled applications.

Policy information- and rule-management systems

Policy systems promise a shared information source that can break down administrative barriers. By using a common directory schema and directory system, neighboring administrative domains can perform "policy peering." This involves sharing a subset of information (such as users and their permissions) to allow some degree of policing by the ISP or adjacent provider.

In practice, the DEN schema is similar to the ATM QOS specifications: both are designed by a committee intent on building consensus and being inclusionary rather than by a group trying to pick the simplest, best way. What will probably emerge will be a subset of DEN's proposals that are sufficient to perform rudimentary policy exchanges. Like ATM and the OSI model before it, DEN has done an excellent job of educating people about the ideal world and the issues involved in the problem. What DEN needs is interoperability bake-offs and reference implementations.

Publishing policies

Policy servers will eventually communicate with devices using stateful management systems and protocols like COPS. They may even work from a common library of application knowledge and offer relatively automated functionality, eliminating the need for policy configuration.

Today, however, most vendors are shipping traditional bulk provisioning and talking about COPS tomorrow.

The problem with this is that until standard management information attributes (MIBs) for QOS management are broadly adopted, any management system must develop a custom set of MIB libraries and command-line-interface (CLI) scripts for each piece of networking equipment. With the recent acquisitions and mergers of the networking industry, interfaces and command sets differ not only from vendor to vendor, but also from product to product.

Early policy systems resemble nothing so much as the scripted provisioning and roll back tools that network service providers use to provision their frame relay circuits. Unfortunately, in the absence of proactive device agents that request policies, the roundabout systems that rely on traps or sniffing introduce bottlenecks and delay into establishment of PHBs, making it impossible for devices to respond in real time to network events.

Most currently deployed network devices don't have the intelligence to recognize QOS events in the network. For example, a router can shape traffic easily with queues and access lists, but it won't proactively alter its handling of traffic based on what happens in the network. We therefore need to generate the event through some other means on behalf of these devices. This can happen through human intervention, a smart sniffer, or a trap manager. All of these methods publish policies out into the enforcers as needed.

Manual provisioning and GUI insulation

The most basic way to configure policy using existing devices is to manually define a set of access lists on the device, and rely on these filters to modify the handling of packets. Many security systems and firewalls are configured this way, even though such configuration is a complex exercise. To hide the complexity, front ends that can establish priorities in an intuitive GUI and translate them to the otherwise error-prone commands that a device needs are now emerging from many vendors. These consoles generally emphasize single-device configuration and do not operate dynamically, but administrative configuration of devices is the first line of defense for congestion or oversubscription.

Sniff-and-configure policy distribution

A second approach is to monitor traffic on a specific segment that is either costly or subject to congestion, and then reprogram the enforcing device with new rules for a traffic type when that traffic crosses the segment. The "sniff-and-configure" model (Figure 14–5) assumes that the enforcing device is unable to properly classify traffic itself. While this happens in real time, it requires additional hardware and is more complex to manage than a proper QOS system would be.

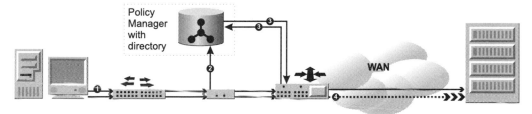

Figure 14–5   Sniff-and-configure policy publication

1. The client sends traffic, which is initially treated as best-effort
2. The sniffer observes the traffic and triggers an action by the policy manager
3. The manager signals the device using a CLI, SNMP, or an http interface and reconfigures its per-hop behavior for the traffic in question
4. Subsequent packets are now handled differently

Trap-and-configure policy distribution

A third method of triggering policy distribution relies on traps from the networking device, which trigger modifications to that device's configuration. Trap-based configuration modifications are common in a VLAN environment, where they move a user's port onto a VLAN once a MAC address is detected. Trap-trigger models can also be used to set QOS parameters like 802.1p when a new device is detected.

Trap-and-configure systems (Figure 14–6) can be more efficient than sniff-then-configure models, but they will block communications while the trap is being processed and the device is being reconfigured. Often, the newly attached device must wait until the trap from the switch is pro-

Figure 14–6 Trap-and-configure policy publication

cessed and the switch is reconfigured, whereas in a sniff-then-configure model the client has at least a best-effort connection while awaiting router reconfiguration.

1. The switch detects an Ethernet carrier from the client

2. The switch sends a trap or notification to the policy manager

3. The policy manager interprets the information in the trap and, based on the switch model and capabilities, uses a particular management protocol to reconfigure the way the switch handles the client's traffic.

4. The traffic is then forwarded in some altered manner

Multicast publication

In some systems, a central device publishes out configurations on a well-known multicast address. All devices listen to this address, and when they see settings that apply to them, they configure themselves accordingly. The multicast messages must be "addressed" to each device, and while the system is economical in terms of traffic usage through the use of multi-cast, it is not well suited for rapid, device-specific alterations to traffic handling in a large network.

None of these methods is perfect, but all are available now. In select-ing an interim solution, it is important to consider how it will migrate to a complete, stateful, directory-enabled system in the future.

Endnotes

1. Sandra Glitten, "IETF to work on policy-based networking," *Network World Fusion*, August 25, 1998.

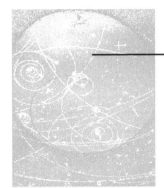

Monitoring service levels in a network

Once a network is QOS enabled, we need to understand how it is behaving. Multiple classes of traffic make this a challenge. Simple capacity across a link might once have sufficed, but we now need to consider that link in terms of the queues, priorities, and reservations it is currently maintaining. Trusty tools like traceroute and ping must be used in new ways to truly understand network health.

With all of these mechanisms for classifying and shaping network traffic, we're still somewhat at a loss as to how to understand the performance of the network. A multiservice network increases management complexity in many ways. Instead of a single, best-effort plane, you are faced with several best-effort planes (where service on each plane is to some degree better than on the planes "beneath" it). In addition, you have some number of reserved-bandwidth streams to manage, each of which is being negotiated and established dynamically.

A traditional network-management approach might be to characterize each of the planes with the usual metrics of aggregate queue depth, percentage congestion, and latency and then to let users drill down into individual devices. By the same token, aggregate reserved bandwidth across a device might in turn drill into a particular user's reservations.

Deploying sophisticated probes with per-segment monitoring, the best trending and visualization tools, and the most advanced expert systems still won't tell you much about user experience. As the network strives to provide consistent access to a set of services, the focus of management will be on characterizing the behavior of those services and tuning them. In addition to the traditional device management that monitors server, router, and switch health, we need to worry about application behavior.

This is nothing new. As we have seen, early computer networks offered deterministic controls, and applications were centralized on mainframes. The network operator had complete control over the "user experience" when the application and the network were so tightly integrated. As we return toward the deterministic, mission-critical networks, we need to return to this way of managing things.

Network management is still used for configuration of devices. Similarly, provisioning and rollback systems are used to deploy services administratively. With the arrival of policy systems, however, we need simulation tools and the ability to run commands remotely within device shells in order to effectively troubleshoot multilevel networks.

Service-level agreements

A service-level agreement (SLA) was historically a measure of network availability put in place to describe the relationship between a customer and an ISP. When WAN links were circuits, throughput and delay were "givens" and the only variable was availability. While most SLAs today deal with availability and time-to-repair metrics, they are increasingly being extended to include latency, throughput, CIR, burst levels, sustained average traffic level, and jitter information.

Most SLA systems rely on averages of multiple pings. To be meaningful, these must be monitored over a reasonable period of several weeks. Monitoring also helps to identify cyclical trends in availability on a daily or weekly basis.

In a Web-based survey of the networking industry, International Network Services found that the number of organizations using end-to-end response-time statistics to measure their application performance will have more than doubled between December 1998 and June 1999.[1] SLA information can be gathered through sniffing, client agents, client simulation, and active monitoring. Each method has advantages and disadvantages in terms of its intrusiveness in the network, the reproducibility of its tests, and the way in which it mimics user experience.

Stand-alone application sniffing

Modern sniffers can look at traffic on a network segment and analyze response times with an understanding of the application needs. The benefit of these devices is that they are nonintrusive; while they may not have access to the level of information that the client and server do, they work without any change to the end nodes. Once sniffers are integrated with directory systems that can translate the bits they see into users and groups, they will become far easier to understand.

In a switched networks sniffers must be placed near the client or server in order to generate useful information. Populating a switched infrastructure with probes is an expensive prospect, but with broad RMON2 information on networking devices, management systems will soon be able to parse a large amount of application data without additional hardware. It may be difficult to justify the independent instrumentation of a network when the capabilities are already in place on the devices. Furthermore, remote monitoring (RMON and RMON-2) probes generate a great deal of network traffic, which makes them inappropriate for heavily congested networks.

Client agents

Software agents (such as INS' VitalSigns) probe the client stack to provide useful data. Agents see more deeply into the application needs and client environment (such as what applications are running concurrently). This can be important—a sniffer may see slow SAP traffic and nothing else on a segment, but a client agent might reveal other, less important traffic going elsewhere in the network. In addition, these clients have a great deal of visibility into the desktop environment—reporting true username rather than a DNS lookup of the IP address, for example. Because they sit on the end node, they can be remotely triggered by an operator to perform simple monitoring and diagnostic functions from ping and traceroute to complete packet captures.

Client agents are not without their drawbacks. Software must be installed on the desktop, and it may introduce instability or processing delay of its own. Some of these agents attempt to take corrective action (such as adjusting TCP and IP parameters) that might skew results if it were not disabled. Furthermore, because each agent's results depend on the network activities of the user on whose machine the agent is installed, it is difficult to infer general network behavior unless many clients are instrumented.

Client simulation

If you can't instrument a desktop effectively, the next best thing is to pretend to be a client. Client simulators query applications at regular intervals and are able to carefully measure server response and network characteristics. The major drawback here is that the simulation may not be typical of actual usage. For example, if clients use a Web page that is dynamically generated, but the simulator uses a static page, then the simulator's results may not be reflective of the actual user experience. What's more, these simulators introduce delay by creating more traffic—so administrators must carefully balance the need for granular information with the acceptable level of monitoring load.

Some independent organizations offer reporting services that can qualify the performance of critical applications like Web sites by retrieving pages at regular intervals. Keynote Systems, for example, averages the response time from a site and reports it to site managers (Figure 15–1). Keynote publishes a weekly index of 40 important sites and calculates the average time to retrieve a home page of these sites between 6 AM and noon Pacific time. It also offers reports of best and worst performance by U.S. metropolitan area.[2]

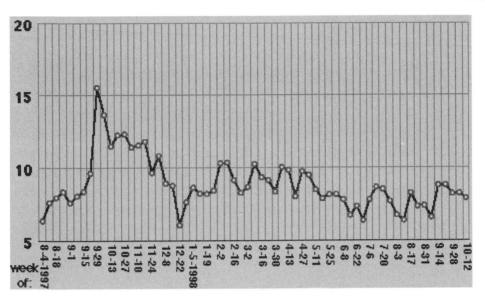

Figure 15–1   Sample of Keynote Business 40, showing average page retrieval time for popular Web sites in North America. *Source:* Keynote Systems, Inc.

Active monitoring and server agents

A network device or virtual resource allocator, such as a load balancer, has access to all the traffic characteristics for a given virtual service. A load balancer in front of a server farm knows exactly how much of the delay is from the server and how much from the network. Actively monitoring traffic by using networking devices can incur a delay—for some high-capacity routers, the "debug" mode needed to enable this kind of granularity introduces unacceptable processor overhead. On the other hand, active monitoring allows you to look at application behavior from a virtual service, rather than a server, perspective.

Active monitors can be a part of server applications (and to the extent that network managers have input into application purchasing decisions, this should be a critical requirement for purchases going forward). They can also function as agents that reside on the server and monitor specific server processes, watching for load and health metrics in addition to maintaining counters and running averages for applications.

In many cases, server- or balancer-side monitoring gives you a better view of the virtual service the network is offering, although it lacks the granularity and remote-control capabilities of a client agent. Server-side agents are easier to deploy and license than client agents, and they can make useful decisions about network performance by analyzing information such as TCP round-trip times. Many of the devices at the edge-of-service location in the network are well instrumented anyway (for example, load balancers use many complex metrics to find the most available server), so the overhead of reporting this information is minimal.

There is a discontinuity between application-level monitoring systems and traditional device-configuration systems. In making the transition from a service perspective to a device perspective, service-level monitoring tools such as those described above are the best hope so far and can be considered essential for a production multi-service network.

Metrics

There are a number of parameters we can use to characterize the health of a service. Traffic classification for queue handling, queue depth, and discard eligibility can be performed according to a number of traffic metrics. One of the most useful sets of metrics for understanding traffic handling comes to us from the ATM world.

The development of ATM gives us an interesting look at philosophies of design. In stark contrast to the "loose consensus and working code" approach of the IETF, the ATM forum sought to design the ultimate network by committee. Design by committee has its advantages and disadvantages: as a result of the Forum's work, we have a rich model for understanding quality of service without much practical experience.

While many of ATM's rich metrics and parameters are useful for characterizing a network—any network—they are seldom implemented. In many environments the LAN core is ATM based simply because, at the time, ATM was the only way to get 155 Mbps. With Gigabit Ethernet this is no longer the case. On the WAN, ATM was the next logical step in the progression from X.25 and Frame Relay—offering multiplexing with a good deal more promising control than its predecessors.

The fundamental characteristics of a service are latency, jitter, reliability, burst capacity, and traffic volume. If you know these parameters for a service, you're well on your way to understanding the health of the network. Table 15–1 presents a loose association of these parameters for several network-connection protocols.

Table 15-1   Associations between TCP, Frame Relay, ATM, and IntServ serv
parameters

Parameter	TCP	Frame Relay	ATM	IntServ
Latency	Round-trip time		Cell Transfer Delay	Adspec information
Jitter	Standard deviation of round-trip time		Cell Delay Variation	Adspec information
Suitability for discard	TOS bits	Discard Eligible	Cell Loss Priority	Best-effort handling
Bursting	Current window size	Exceeding CIR	Peak Cell Rate	Flowspec
Error rate	Number of ACKs received for last good segment		Cell Error Ratio	

Latency

Simple round-trip latency is a function of a server's ability to respond. When considering true latency, however, we need to view the network from a service perspective.

We can test responses across a network in three main ways. A simple ping is a measure of the round-trip network latency and the server's ability to respond to the ping. A TCP probe (which involves setting up a TCP session and timing the response) measures a specific *server process*. Finally, an application probe (which involves a complete application-level interaction such as Web page retrieval) tells you the true behavior of the service.

A server with a heavily loaded Web daemon may still respond to pings reasonably quickly, depending on how the server's various server processes are prioritized. Similarly, a server with a responsive Web daemon may have a large Web page that is poorly structured—something that an application probe would reveal. Imagine, for example, that the page consisted of many graphics and a complex page design. Until the HTML code for laying out the page is received by the browser, the graphics cannot be displayed. Even if all of the graphics in the page are cached locally, the service's real response time is a function of the delay in retrieving a single HTML file.

Jitter

Jitter is a reflection of the inconsistency of delay. High levels of jitter tend to indicate fluctuating queue depths, which are a symptom of poorly shaped traffic at congestion points. Leaky-bucket and token-bucket algorithms on concentrating routers may ease jitter in the network core.

On the other hand, an unusually low level of jitter for a particular class of traffic in the network may mean that lower classes of traffic are unfairly penalized when this class is still receiving the IQOS across the network. In this case, packet-interleaving ratios and weightings between traffic classes probably need adjustment.

Signaling and delivery attributes that characterize traffic

Different protocols use different methods for signaling congestion. QOS monitoring systems will count and document the levels of congestion, priority, and discard signaling of various LAN, WAN, and network protocols in order to summarize the health of the network.

Frame relay relies on FECN and BECN bits to signal to the sender and receiver that congestion is occurring in the network core. Assuming a proper switch configuration at the interface to the Frame Relay cloud, the switch will then exercise discarding based on discard eligibility or some other rule to avoid core congestion. So FECN, BECN, data rate, and CIR, as well as discarded packets and DE bits, are all metrics that can be used to characterize a Frame Relay circuit. For a Frame Relay network, management tools should track congestion notifications, response time, error rates, and packet loss.

Reservation-based systems such as RSVP rely on admission control and PEP/PDP negotiations to maintain a central understanding of capacity as well as a list of currently active flow reservations. For an IntServ-style network with central management, the COPS server is the most QOS-informed device, and it will offer the best understanding of network health through its vendor-specific (and eventually, standards-based) management interfaces.

TCP uses discarding and a worsening response time to detect congestion; it responds by reducing the number of packets that are currently in transmission between the sender and receiver. Packets in transit (window size) and current data rate, as well as some form of averaged packet loss and the current trend in round-trip delay (increasing or decreasing), are all metrics that can characterize a TCP session. At the IP layer, traffic can be characterized by its distribution in terms of precedence or type-of-service information from the TOS byte. For an internetwork, management tools should record sender and receiver information as well as round-trip times and throughput, because the monitoring characteristics of the intermediate network links is unknown.

ATM has a complex traffic contract that includes a number of metrics. These vary, depending on the ATM service—an ATM committed-bit-rate circuit, for example, *will* deliver all traffic up to the peak cell rate; by contrast, an ATM unspecified bit rate will discard packets without warning and rely on higher-layer protocols to manage flow control. Available Bit Rate circuits offer feedback mechanisms to notify senders of congestion, and ATM has a cell-loss indicator to signal discard-eligible cells. Note that when an ATM cell is discarded, the datagram of which it was a part may as well be discarded. A typical IP datagram will consist of one or more cells. For maximum effectiveness in relieving congestion, when a frames-in-cells transmission of IP discards a cell, it should also discard other cells in the now-errored frame. Doing this, however, requires an ATM adaption layer that has awareness of the start and end of the frame. For an ATM network, management systems will query devices through SNMP MIBs on each device to take advantage of the rich instrumentation of the switches.

802.1p networks can generally be characterized by querying the subnet bandwidth manager or by looking at the queue levels and RMON statistics for a point in the network. If we adopt the belief that "altruistic" traffic (i.e., less than best effort, 802.1p value of 1) will occur only when a networking device overwrites the end node's requested class (i.e., nobody will *request* less than best effort but devices may use it to indicate excess transmission), then an 802.1p value of 1 is similar to a discard eligible bit. Such a configuration is reasonable; a router can tag all excess traffic from a sender that exceeds the flow specification with an 802.1p value of 1 and rely on the subnet to discard it if any other traffic will be impacted. So the percentage of traffic on a subnet that has an 802.1p value of 1 may be a measure of how much traffic has been introduced into the subnet in excess of expected flows, CIRs, and so on. For an 802.1p subnet, management tools can query the devices directly or communicate with the DSBM for the subnet to determine the health of the segment.

Monitoring the condition of the network with traditional tools

The traditional way of monitoring the network is to measure utilization. There are several problems with such an approach: It doesn't yield useful information in a classful network; it doesn't emphasize round-trip performance; and it doesn't work at the service or application level.

There are several ways to get around these problems. Next-generation networks rely on service-level agreements that result from ping, traceroute, TCP and application probes, test reservations, and 802.1p test packets.

Utilization

A common and useful tool for capacity planning and the measurement of network health is that of **utilization**. Utilization varies by link type. Collision-based systems such as Ethernet require a sustained congestion level that is substantially lower than their maximum theoretical throughput in order to reduce media access delay and handle burstiness, but in full-duplex switched infrastructures this is less of an issue.

Multilevel networks bring additional variables into traditional utilization metrics. Each of the metrics at which we've looked must be considered in terms of various traffic types, services, or multiple queues. To further complicate matters, admission of a high-priority flow impacts not only other flows in the same class of service, but also those flows below it in lower-priority classes. The impact of congestion at one level of the network must be considered for those applications running at lower levels as well.

Ping and QOS

RFC 1700 indicates that ICMP echo request messages can be configured with any IPTOS settings needed (but doesn't cover precedence) and that an ICMP response should use the same IPTOS values as the received packet. The Windows 95 shell supports TOS values in its ping command, and most servers will respond to a TOS ping with the correct TOS values. So a ping can be used to characterize network type-of-service handling, as long as a policing function doesn't overwrite or ignore the TOS values.

For example, if a router were configured to treat a ping as a network-control message and alter its TOS setting, then a ping might get excellent response time when in fact the traffic class in question was experiencing congestion.

TCP probes are a simple mechanism for checking on the response time of a service. Repeated, incomplete TCP setup messages may be misinterpreted by some firewalls, however, as denial-of-service attempts or hostile traffic, so they should be used judiciously.

"Application ping" systems such as the synthetic clients described above are the best supplement to a ping in a multiservice network. Creating loopback or server-side ping functions on application servers is another way to verify that the return response time and transmit response time match. Some of the client agent and network simulation tools, as well as more traditional network-management applications, can generate scheduled logins and trials through scripting. Many come with predefined scripts for common Internet protocols like SMTP, POP3, HTTP, and FTP.

The difference in response time between a TCP probe and an application probe may be a rough indicator of server application delay.

Traceroute and QOS

One method of preferential handling can be to route different classes of traffic across different network paths. As route selection becomes increasingly based on dynamic link states such as performance or load, paths across the network may be subject to change.

The difficulty here is signaling the network that a traceroute packet is to be treated as a certain class of application. If we could create a traceroute that established IPTOS precedence and type-of-service settings, as well as link-layer priorities like 802.1p, then administrators could trace the path a packet would take with certain classifications. Because of the way that traceroute works, however, this would require a fairly substantial overhaul of the network infrastructure. Also, traceroute doesn't reveal switch-circuit paths in increasingly switched backbones.

RSVP and 802.1p tests

Attempting to establish an RSVP flow reservation through the transmission of a path message and the reception of a corresponding resv message will let you learn about the RSVP features of the intermediate network. Similar end-to-end discovery facilities do not exist for IPTOS, DiffServ, or 802.1p. On the other hand, pinging the adjacent router with various 802.1p settings will tell you whether the adjacent device preserves 802.1p settings within the segment.

The lack of discovery protocols in class-of-service systems is a very real challenge to their rapid deployment in networks.

Key Performance Indicators for policy networks

Some critical metrics are nevertheless useful. Network-level metrics allow you to set thresholds in network-management systems that can monitor RMON, RMON2, or SNMP-advertised information.

- Sustained full queues on a device are important to watch. More granular information (such as queue depth for a number of class-based queues on a device) can ensure that you don't get paged when streaming MP3's are filling up best-effort links, but that you are instantly aware of SAP delays. Queue metrics become far more useful when information on applications, services, and user groups (in directories, for example) is linked to network-management platforms.

- Breakdown of traffic across key nodes can show you the makeup of traffic, replacing the traditional best-effort trend line.

- Once a COPS server is in place, it will keep track of bandwidth reservations and the latency and jitter guarantees that the admission controllers on routers are currently offering. Reservation and guarantee information gives you an excellent idea of the kind of network performance that RSVP-authorized applications can expect from the network.

Endnotes

1. From an INS press release dated Monday, December 7, 1998. The results of this and other surveys by INS are available at www.ins.com/surveys.

2. Keynote Systems can be reached at www.keynote.com. The Business 40 Internet Performance Index, as well as the geographic distribution of Internet performance, are available at www.keynote.com/measures.business/business40.html.

PART 4

We have seen motivations for deploying QOS. We've looked at classifying and enforcement methods. We've reviewed techniques for maintaining and distributing consistent QOS rules. In the fourth part of this book we'll look at design and operational issues that move from a traditional network to a QOS-managed infrastructure. We divide this into three sections:

- A high-level look at the shape of bandwidth-managed networks

- Approaches to practical bandwidth management

- Real-world case studies of QOS deployment

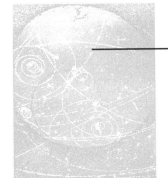

16

The shape of bandwidth-managed networks

Modern networks can be thought of as a series of concentric rings with switching at the core and edge (for performance) and routing in the middle (for scalability). Classification is granular at the periphery, and coarse at the core. Such a network is substantially different from the traditional architecture of best-effort networks in terms of the classification, differentiation, and configuration that must be a part of the system. IT managers must configure the network to manage bandwidth in real time, but they have important roles to play at both the tactical and strategic levels in running such a network.

Traditional networking: L2 on the edge, L3 at the core

The old school of networking puts Ethernet on the edge of the network, with routing in the core and a high-speed, dense mesh of interconnects (Figure 16–1). In this model, scaling consists of adding Ethernet ports to the periphery, buying faster routers, and expanding the WAN capacity by buying fatter pipes. Network designers couldn't rely on any rich services from the WAN core or on anything other than raw capacity in the campus backbone.

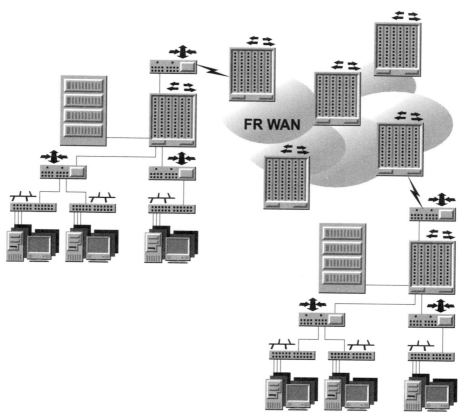

Figure 16–1 Topology of a traditional network

This is a tried-and-true model for networks. It overlooks some new technologies that can introduce efficiencies, but it works. With some software reconfiguration of end nodes, access routers, and core routers, it can be optimized for those parts of the network over which you have control. IT managers have at their disposal classification and IPTOS marking at the edge, with IPTOS-based route selection and IP precedence-based queuing and discards. By using these techniques, network designers can offer a differentiated-services network in which some classes of traffic will get better service *relative* to others. On the other hand, this model doesn't leverage emerging technologies that can scale performance by orders of magnitude in coming years.

On the WAN, carrier deployment of systems such as Multi-Protocol Label Switching (MPLS) and other differentiated core protocols will expose the benefits of their switched WAN cores to subscribers via well-understood "common denominator" IP mechanisms like TOS.

Next-generation networks: L2 at the core and edge

A newer model of networks takes into account some important innovations in processor and protocol technology. It is typically drawn as a set of concentric circles—LAN switching on the edge, routing in the access layer, and WAN switching in the core (Figure 16–2).

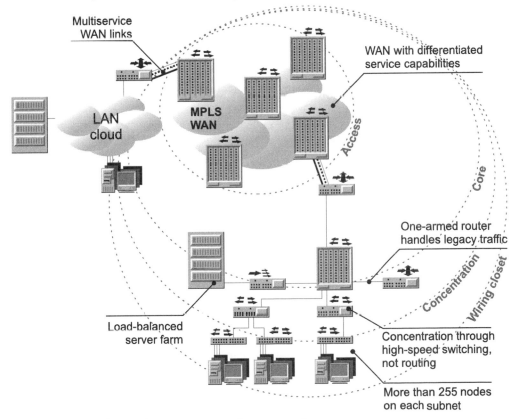

Figure 16–2 Topology of a next-generation network

The LAN switching layer offers a dedicated pipe to each desktop, overcoming the media-access delays characteristic of shared hubs. The price of LAN switches has dropped so significantly that it is almost irresponsible to install anything less than switched 10-Mbps ports at this point. The LAN periphery concentrates traffic—offering buffering and congestion-management capabilities along the way—into a high-speed backbone of Gigabit Ethernet or ATM that can differentiate traffic.

As IETF engineers turn their considerable talents to the problems of network policy, the ability of ATM to deliver quality of service at the link layer will be eclipsed by the end-to-end nature and pervasive deployment of IP. ATM won't vanish; it will instead become a common option for administratively provisioned WAN data links.

The routing layer delivers scalability and control. Routing scales because it uses connectionless packet forwarding that eliminates the need for a full-mesh topology, since not every attached node needs to be aware of every other node. While switches have a great deal of capacity, switching is not well suited (with the possible exception of ATM's PNNI or of MPLS) to aggregating traffic and using route-exchange methods to maintain route state. The control arises because of a router's generally increased vision into the datagram and its ability to exercise a wide range of controls and handlers.

In the WAN core, most of the underlying infrastructure is switched. But these switched connections are traditionally presented to subscribers as fixed pipes, even though they may in fact be administratively configured Permanent Virtual Circuits. Increasingly, ISPs are exposing the switching infrastructure and allowing enterprises a greater degree of control over it. As enterprise routers learn to take advantage of more complex switched WAN cores and ISPs deploy systems that offer greater control, the WAN core will become dynamically switched, both in terms of QOS properties and destination selection. This will allow enterprise equipment to reserve (and pay for) premium services on a minute-by-minute basis, as well as to set up CBR links on demand. Whether this functionality is offered as true ATM SVCs, or as an MPLS cloud, remains to be seen.

In a switched LAN that delivers routing via layer-3 switches, legacy protocols such as DECnet are often overlooked, because the focus of the application-specific integrated circuit (ASIC) implementation is primarily on IP. One way to solve this is to implement a protocol-based virtual LAN. The layer-3 switches recognize the traffic as something they cannot route, and they forward it to a legacy router on a dedicated VLAN for that protocol. The router routes the traffic to an appropriate destination on another VLAN. In this manner, the router is "one-armed"; it has only one physical link to the network but is routing legacy protocols between VLANs. These one-armed configurations are also appearing in IPFEP devices like caches and load balancers.

Clearly, the router's role has changed in next-generation networks. In addition to its primary functions of scalability and control, it plays a vital role in translating between link-layer prioritization systems. By associating WAN and LAN link types or priorities judiciously, the edge router preserves and polices prioritization information as well as using it to influence the way the router itself handles the packet.

A managed internetwork must be pervasive. Because of the organizational and administrative boundaries that exist in an internetwork, this will generally mean either deferring to the lowest common denominator in a network path or restricting the number of administrative groups involved in a path as much as possible.

By deferring to the lowest common denominator, we mean that if an ISP doesn't offer some sort of differentiated service, you may have to set parallel WAN circuits and implement differentiation on the attached routers or switches. The alternative approach of restricting administrative groups means, for example, sharing a common ISP among your extranet partners in order to take advantage of their cross-backbone latency guarantees and service-level agreements.

Either of these is a pragmatic method of delivering some portion of the benefits of QOS today. Within your network, you can rely on desktop software, access router classification, and properly configured queuing and discarding to ensure smooth handling of latency-sensitive traffic.

Building mission criticality and delay sensitivity into configurations

Now that we've seen the mechanisms for classifying and handling traffic, let's consider how a network might be configured to implement policies that recognize the specific needs of traffic types. Figure 16–3 illustrates such an algorithm.

Note that Figure 16–3 does not describe the actual operation of a particular networking device. A number of other factors such as queue depth, delay, and token availability on egress links must be considered.

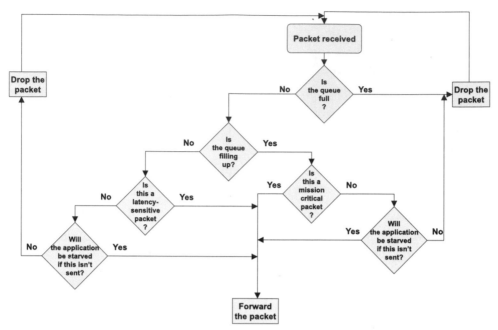

Figure 16–3 Sample mechanism for implementing importance and urgency in networking devices

Real-time, tactical, and strategic

Networks are managed through a combination of real-time or near real-time measures, operational measures, and strategic planning.

- Real-time measures are the instantaneous steps the network takes to regulate itself; only the networking equipment can respond quickly enough to effectively guarantee rapid handling of changing conditions without affecting users of the network. Real-time changes are session by session.

- Operational measures are the steps that network operators can take in human-time to anticipate and correct network problems. Operational measures occur on a device-by-device basis.

- Strategic measures are the long-term steps that go into capacity planning, analysis of trends, and design of the network architecture. Strategic changes occur on a service-by-service basis.

Real-time measures

Properly configured network devices take suitable actions to ensure that congestion is avoided and packet delivery occurs in a time span that is useful for the application. Congestion avoidance and delivery guarantees are achieved through classification and the resulting path selection and per-hop behavior. If devices are unable to behave in this manner, then they should notify the administrators of the network quickly. They should also take steps to see that the notification, diagnosing, and subsequent correction of the problem don't suffer the same problem. Devices may be unable to meet congestion or delivery goals due to misbehaving applications, poor configuration, malicious theft of service, or heavy oversubscription.

Traffic shaping

The real-time actions the network can take to maintain a steady state for a subset of applications, and to optimize performance for another set, generally revolve around predictive modeling of metrics like rate of queue-depth change and round-trip time. Such metrics measure the rate at which packets are injected into the device compared to the rate at which they leave the device. If the analysis shows that the queue depth is growing, proactive congestion avoidance through selective discard (or possibly through the establishment of additional on-demand capacity, such as adding multilink circuits) is required.

Automated provisioning

Two kinds of "automatic" QOS behavior can be built into a managed-bandwidth network. The first kind automatically considers the state of the network within the device. The second relies on an "intelligent" third-party analysis of network events and a corresponding automatic reconfiguration of the network.

Certain parameters act as automatic rules that allow networking devices to act in real time and avoid congestion. An excellent example is the discard levels in a RED system. Figure 16–4 illustrates some of these trade-offs. By setting parameters for the threshold at which packets are discarded and the aggressiveness with which they are discarded, you are effectively setting up rules for the device to follow when congestion occurs without needing to communicate to a central authority.

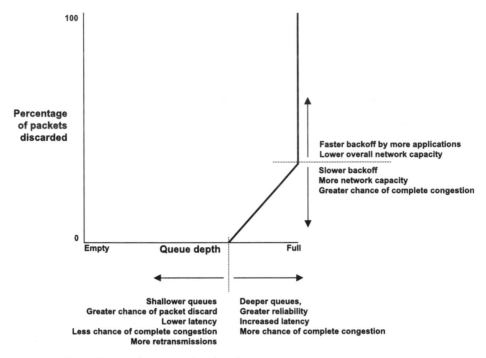

Figure 16–4 The effects of queue-depth adjustment

Intelligent systems that can analyze groups of alarms or network events and change the network configuration may be able to help with real-time management of the network. On the other hand, even if management systems are able to gather the data and interpret the appropriate course of action (no mean feat in itself), then the scope of action that they can take is somewhat limited in today's network model. The limitation occurs because most policy-enabled devices today are administratively provisioned. The administrator has selected a set of parameters that make sense for a general business model. Once network devices start to *request* capacity, admission, and policy information from a network authority, then expert systems will be much better equipped to feed network devices the information they need to modify the network's behavior without human involvement.

Imagine, for example, that a router is experiencing congestion. The router sends the management system series of alarms and events about discard rates. An automated system might see these as a sign of impending failure, and it would therefore set new values for queue depth, discard rate, and so via TFTP, SNMP sets, or some command-line-based script.

The notification and reconfiguration traffic would be susceptible to the same delays that are causing the problem, making this exactly the *least* appropriate time to be changing router configurations. By contrast, if the router were making admission-control decisions with the help of a COPS server, the expert system might tell the server to reduce the maximum guaranteed flow on new connections by some percentage to gradually reduce the level of guaranteed-load traffic across the device. This second model is far more equitable and scalable than the first.

Consequently, most "out-of-box" rule systems lack the appropriate tools to effect networkwide dynamic adjustment in real time. Proper parameters, proactively provisioned, are what matter most in a QOS network.

Networking vendors are loath to implement true automation—the days of the self-managing network are far off. The reluctance has to do with the individuality of each network environment as well as the liability associated with an automatic decision having the wrong effect. Instead, real-time errors or faults are reported up to operators so that they can make an administrative change and overcome the real-time problem.

Operational measures

Operational measures are the steps a human can take to respond to changing conditions in a network. For a differentiated-services network, this will mean monitoring key thresholds and making administrative changes to the network, such as restarting devices, modifying connections, or investigating downed links.

Gathering and analyzing trends at regular intervals is at the core of operating a multiservice network. It is important, for example, to trend the relative class-based makeup of traffic on the network in order to see if a certain class is growing. If voice traffic is increasing steadily day after day, in- and out-of-profile levels or admission criteria must be changed.

The availability of directory-based network information systems is essential in order to make operational management of a QOS network possible. The shift from link- and network-layer management to the notion of "IP services" means that more of the operator's time will be spent verifying and diagnosing round-trip, latency, and jitter information and less time in front of a telnet client.

Strategic measures

Policy systems won't fix a bad network. Many of the technologies we've covered so far allow you to deploy a network infrastructure that can offer new services, which in turn permits the deployment of new applications. The underlying assumption is that the network is properly architected and that capacity planning involves both the network operators and the application developers.

Most service roll-outs happen in two phases: application development and operational deployment. The two-phase approach invariably leads to a great deal of finger pointing between developers and operators when the application is completed and begins testing. One of the most fundamental strategic steps a company can take is to implement a proper evaluation, testing, and impact-assessment program for the installation of new applications and services.

It is useful to think of the application and network combining to create a service that must be tested, nurtured, and managed cohesively. A service is a combination of application functionality and network distribution. Services are strategic, as they contribute to organizational effectiveness and competitive advantage. Consequently, strategic QOS planning involves trend analysis, capacity planning, network architecture, network-aware application development, and the deployment of a policy infrastructure to manage the service in real time.

Baselines and trends

As differentiated networks emerge, bar graphs and pie charts will become complex and meaningless unless they are related back to the end-user experience and the critical business applications. So a proper baselining strategy built around gathering the *right* information—application round-trip and availability, for example—is far more important than the volume of data collected. Similarly, in order to manage a service the network monitoring systems must work with the service by extracting relevant context from directories so they can work at the user and application levels.

Baselining before the deployment of a new service allows you to evaluate the success of the deployment and understand the actual impact of the application on your network. Baselining gives you the information you need to understand the effect of future installations. A number of application-simulation and service-level monitoring tools exist to permit this kind of analysis.

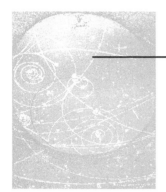

Practical bandwidth management

We've looked at a wide range of technologies and protocols in the course of learning about QOS. In this chapter we present some fundamental guidelines that will assist you in designing and implementing multiservice networks. We also attempt to compare many of the mechanisms we've seen, so that service levels can be consistently mapped at intersections of different network infrastructures.

We'll now look at practical guidelines for managing bandwidth in a network. We begin with some general guidelines for network configurations and selection of bandwidth-management systems; then we examine some typical network configurations from a service-level perspective.

Policy and QOS are complex at best. We've collected some basic observations about how you can begin to deploy a practical subset of QOS and evolve in the coming years to a truly multiservice network.

Where to begin?

You should start by protecting existing applications from the coming storm, especially business-critical systems like SAP and SNA access (tn3270/tn5250, DLSw). This can be done by configuring some kind of assured service for these traffic types at critical network junctures; by prioritizing critical traffic; and by limiting the maximum amount of traffic introduced by bursty applications using a leaky-bucket or token-bucket admission scheme. Where possible, if your hardware permits it, use desktop or end-node tagging to aid in high-priority traffic identification. It will be easiest to justify spending when WAN costs are controlled, so deploy QOS devices at the boundary between the enterprise and the WAN.

Ready for real time?

Per-flow signaling is complex and not ready for deployment until proper, robust policy decision points are available. Building an RSVP network based only on admission controls (without policy controls) makes them subject to abuse and exerts no "back pressure" upon requesters to justify the premium bandwidth they request. To avoid this, networks should initially rely on packet tagging or coloring at layer 2 for link-layer LAN domains (802.1p) and at layer 3 for internetwork signaling (IPTOS). On the WAN, use multiple circuits if needed but consider Internet-based VPN tunnels for background traffic, with rate shaping and queuing at the edge.

Setting up consistent, device-by-device, class-of-service configurations enables the network as a whole to deliver a relatively coarse set of end-to-end COS capabilities tailored to specific application types. Without policy, RSVP is viable only in small-to-medium access networks in which administrators have a great deal of control over desktops.

You should pick a simple subset of protocols and tools to build a real network, then test the changes using appropriate metrics. While the technologies for providing differentiated services are updated almost daily and make it hard to pick a solution today, even a small change will produce significant effects. Imagine, for example, that the Internet offered two classes of traffic—best effort and high priority—and best effort packets cost half of what high priority cost. This alone would create a complete shift in the feature sets of most networking vendors' products.

Scalable QOS networks implement admission control and granularity on the periphery—either through edge router policing of packet tagging or through bandwidth reservation. They also perform a simple mapping to a known network capacity in the core (using 802.1p or ATM) and the WAN (through agreed-upon IPTOS settings with your ISP or administratively configured ATM permanent virtual circuits with different QOS types).

Deployment roadmap

What steps does a QOS roll-out involve? Let's walk through the various stages in corporate deployment of QOS.

The first step is to baseline traffic. By monitoring the LAN/WAN edge and recording traffic levels over a period of several weeks, the network manager has a good idea of the point from which they are starting. This will serve as justification for expenditures, as well as a tool for comparing the relative impact of various technologies.

The company begins by installing rate-shaping devices at the edge of the enterprise network. These offer point-product QOS; each device must be manually configured with specific flow ranges and applications, but once configured they can apply queues and adjust TCP window sizes to restrict traffic into the costly WAN. At this point, the devices can be used to baseline WAN traffic and understand the major flows within the network. By using the devices' management interfaces, the network manager can identify traffic in terms of key destinations and traffic volumes.

A cache adjacent to the access router can also be used to improve response time and further reduce WAN spending. Caches offer insight into user behavior and popular WAN destinations since they see all traffic from some applications such as http. The caches will generally be inline or redirected; for inline caches, the adjacent router will implement failover systems to ensure that a cache failure does not interrupt services.

As a part of the policy infrastructure, the company migrates its DNS/ DHCP solution to a DEN-compliant LDAP directory. The user and address information contained in the directory form the basis for a range of policy services and make configuration across multiple devices simpler and more consistent.

From a strategic perspective, the company decides to divide network traffic into four granular classes. These include network-critical traffic (such as RIP and OSPF); delay-sensitive traffic (such as videoconferencing and voice-over-IP), best-effort traffic, and discard-eligible traffic. Queues and buffers will have to be configured in such a way that best-effort traffic isn't starved, since it will include mission-critical network applications. Note also that the company does not distinguish between conversational multimedia and streamed multimedia at this stage.

The company baselines traffic once again, to see the impact that WAN QOS and caching have had on traffic patterns. Once this information has been understood, they are ready to deploy some degree of consistent QOS throughout the organization.

The company enables a committed access rate algorithm in their network. Based on the classes that were defined earlier, they program all concentration routers to set IPTOS bits based on the traffic application. In some specific cases (such as streamed training multimedia applications on port 80) they use the source address of the multimedia server to establish the tag. Desktops that are able to set 802.1p and IPTOS values based on port number are similarly configured.

Now that traffic is being tagged according to its application type, the firm must configure appropriate enforcement. An algorithm consisting of class-based queues ensures proper prioritization of delay-sensitive traffic without background application starvation; network critical traffic has absolute priority, and background traffic is delayed indefinitely. Multimedia traffic that is out-of-profile is discarded rather than set to "background," since the long wait in the queue would adversely affect the multimedia applications and needlessly congest the routers.

The company performs yet another baselining, this time comparing LAN and WAN traffic. Since packets are already tagged, they can use IPTOS and 802.1p values to better classify at the LAN/WAN edge.

It is now time for the big push to policy. The company deploys a policy server that can read from the same LDAP directory used by the DNS and DHCP servers. The policy server knows of all enforcing devices, and maintains a list of servers, applications, and priorities. Since the routers do not yet support a dynamic policy protocol, the policy server publishes new configurations out to the routers via SNMP messages when an operator makes a change to the relative priorities and applications.

A new code release is available from the routers, supporting both COPS and RSVP. The policy server can now respond to router queries using a stateful policy protocol, and it no longer needs to use SNMP to publish information out to the network.

The company realizes that the popularity of voice-over-IP is degrading performance. Consequently, they need to explicitly reserve a portion of bandwidth for each conversational session so that it does not compete with streamed multimedia for available capacity. They do this by turning on RSVP in the routers, and modifying the directory information to include a list of users who are authorized to use voice-over-IP connections. They then send out e-mail to all authorized users instructing them to turn on the RSVP option in their IP telephony applications.

Now, when an IP phone wants to connect across the network, it sends an RSVP path message to the destination. The path message describes the phone connection being requested—a 16-Kbps constant-bit-rate session. The receiver returns a reservation message, and each router performs a COPS policy query to confirm that the user is allowed to place the call. The COPS server compares the requesting IP address to the username stored in the central directory; if it approves the call, it creates a call-start event in its accounting log. When the call terminates and the reservation expires, the COPS server records the end of the call.

Baselining, once reservations are in place, lets the company better understand the effect of the reservations. In addition, the company has deployed response-time probes that compare ping, TCP, and application response rates from a variety of locations in the networks and make the information available via a Web console.

The reservation of telephony circuits over IP is working well, so the firm creates a Web-based application that allows managers to authorize voice-over-IP use for their employees. The application modifies the information in the directory on a per-user basis, and billing records are used to justify expansion or share billing costs with each department.

A final step for the firm is to link the boundary devices to the central directory. These access routers and traffic shapers perform policing of LAN traffic to ensure that it meets the classifications and permitted profiles before it travels across the WAN. At this point, the network manager can effect a central change to the relative priorities within the network, and have them propagate out to all devices automatically.

Don't work below user groups or services

As we have seen, networks now deliver virtual services to users. New tools for managing your network should emphasize users and services, not addresses and interfaces. As addressing schemes shift to accommodate layer 3 switching capabilities, it will no longer be cost-effective to work below this level. If you work to add application-based signaling to vendor requirements, you will eliminate much of the complexity of network configuration for policy and application classification.

Deploy the infrastructure that will allow you to abstract management of the network's business services from the actual network—such as DNS/DHCP, asset tracking, LDAP directories, and public key infrastructures. A simple system for populating asset and address databases is to deploy a Web page that asks users to enter their name, employee ID, and other corroborating data and logs this, along with the source IP address of the connection. If such a site is set up on each broadcast domain, then MAC address can also be logged—an increasingly plausible scenario in today's wide broadcast domains.

Initially, user-based management will be found wanting. To compensate for lack of security measures in differentiated-service request mechanisms, set thresholds to detect abusive users who have hacked their priority stacks. As you move toward user-based management, the next step will be a node focus. This is less granular than a user focus, but it works for most of the company. User focus happens on the access WAN and VPN tunnel today; in the LAN, asset tracking of the MAC address is probably sufficient. Managing by IP address or subnet, as well as by VLAN, may be appropriate if your VLAN or DHCP services support easy mapping between user identity and network or link layer addressing.

Building a differentiated-services strategy

Start by deciding on the business goals. What problems is your network trying to solve? How well are they solved today? What could be improved? How will the improvement benefit the company's bottom line compared to, say, a similar expenditure on marketing, sales, or product design? With networks as a fundamental component of business, the expansion of network services will come under the same scrutiny as traditional business expansion.

Knowing what could be improved, develop a list of ways in which improvement could be made. Are you losing money with parallel networks? Negotiating a cheaper WAN connection or multiplexing across a common circuit may be more economical than deploying differentiated services and migrating everyone to one wire. Do you want to deploy "universal workstations" to cut the cost of moves, adds, and changes? You'll need to know how much the current deployment of a phone, a data link, and a videoconferencing room costs first.

Once you know what you're trying to deliver and have a list of possible ways in which that can be achieved, evaluate the various products that can satisfy each of these ways. Consider them in terms of completeness, self-sufficiency, standards compliance, cost, simplicity, and performance.

If there are common features that these deployments will need—such as a centralized directory—then begin to research and deploy these technologies in parallel with traditional product selection. Make sure that the criteria you establish for vendors includes interoperability with the common features you've identified. Furthermore, get your internal development teams to write to these same common features. Your role is to force some convergence of your own, so you should pick a set of technologies and evangelize them internally, as well as making them a requirement of external bids.

Since these common technologies will become the rallying points for your internal and external deployments, base them on known, tested systems. Don't expect internal development teams or external suppliers to commit to delivery of products that work with prestandard protocols or unreleased software.

Picking a philosophy

A design philosophy for next-generation real-time networks is vital. If network designers keep selecting new technologies as they become available rather than adopting a pervasive system for traffic handling, they are likely to deploy conflicting or incompatible systems, and they will increase the chance of inconsistent behavior.

Decide whether you are a service or a department. If you run your network as an independent service provider, then justify expansions and deployments with billing and accounting systems. If you are a department, then set objectives for the network and meet them; if you can't meet them, make a case for expansion. The decision between a service and a department will guide much of your thinking about network configuration, payment, and motivations for expansion.

Accept bandwidth management as inevitable

Your company no longer views its network as optional. Certain expectations of availability and functionality have been set, and as new traffic types compete with business-critical information, the financial, HR, and call-center applications that make the company work will need defensive measures to ensure that they get the capacity they require. Just as *having* a network is essential today, having a service platform for delivering differentiated-connectivity services tomorrow will be vital.

Putting it together: Multiple mapping systems

The fundamental mechanism for this end-to-end COS is consistent mapping—mapping classifiers to handlers, mapping classes to queues, and mapping traffic identifiers to one another to preserve signaling. To that end, Table 17–1 lists the various mechanisms available for prioritizing traffic from various network and internetwork layers. We have tried to map them as closely as possible, but differences abound: for example, there is no notion in IP precedence of anything below "best effort," but 802.1p-tagged traffic with a value of 1 is actually of *lower* priority than untagged, best-effort traffic. Nevertheless, this is a useful comparison of some of the associations that one can draw from the various standards we've discussed.

As standards emerge for mapping across these systems, we will have better information on the impact of various network and link layer systems on one another. In the meantime, point-product solutions to fix problem areas coupled with the deployment of IP services such as load balancing are a great way to begin to address QOS. At the same time, formulate internal policies about network usage and try to understand the needs and characteristics of load in your network, and shift from an "address and port" philosophy to a "groups and services" philosophy. This last, fundamental shift in networking is a reflection of the vital role networks play in modern life—and this shift will be the only way we can manage them effectively going forward.

Table 17–1 Loose comparison of priority systems and service classes across networking protocols

802.1p value	802.1p Category	802.1p IntServ mapping	ATM Traffic Class	IPTOS precedence value	RSVP/IntServ flow type	Ipv6 value (loose match)	Also known as	Examples	Characteristics
7	Network control	Network control	Constant bit rate	Network control / Internetwork control	Guaranteed	Internet control (routing, SNMP)	Assured service	RIP, OSPF, BGP4, SNMP	Critical to network health
6	Voice	Delay sensitive, 10-ms delay bound	Real-time variable bit rate	CRITIC/ECP	Guaranteed	Interactive traffic (Telnet, rlogin)	Premium service	NetMeeting audio, VoIP, CBR video	Latency and jitter sensitive; low bandwidth; no self-regulation
5	Video	Delay sensitive, 100-ms delay bound	Non-real-time variable bit rate	Flash override	Controlled load		Rate controlled	Picture-Tel, Indeo	High bandwidth; jitter sensitive; self-regulating
4	Controlled load	Delay sensitive	Available bit rate	Flash	Controlled load	Attended bulk transfer (FTP)	Rate controlled	SNA transactions	Predictable response times, latency-sensitive applications
3	Excellent effort	Reserved	Unspecified bit rate	Immediate/Priority	Best effort		Assured service	SAP, SQL to critical business application	Business-critical traffic that tolerates delays

Table 17–1   Loose comparison of priority systems and service classes across networking protocols

802.1p value	802.1p Category	802.1p IntServ mapping	ATM Traffic Class	IPTOS precedence value	RSVP/ IntServ flow type	Ipv6 value (loose match)	Also known as	Examples	Characteristics
2/0	Best effort	Default	Unspecified bit rate	Routing	Best effort	Unattended data/ Uncharacterized	Best effort	Web browser traffic	Able to survive latency, but operated by humans
1	Background	Reserved, less than best effort	Unspecified bit rate	Routing	Best effort	Filler traffic (NNTP)	<default >	<default>	<default>

Case studies

Let's use what we've learned. The following case studies describe specific network situations and the way in which the network administrators deployed QOS in each case. They vary from the complex to the simple, and from tiny to international.

New technology, or stable networking?

When deciding to purchase new technology for a major upgrade, how far ahead of current standards should an IT manager look? There is, of course, no simple answer to this question, but consider the example of buying a computer. A buyer's dilemma is whether to purchase the latest, fastest machine available, or to opt for a "current" system that's sufficient, but less testosterone-ridden than its cutting-edge counterpart. Inexperienced buyers often try to buy a computer that will last for "at least five years." Their rationale is that buying a high-end computer will save the cost of frequent upgrades. On the surface, this seems like a perfectly reasonable philosophy: Pay a little extra now, and save in the long run.

As experienced buyers will tell you, the latest and greatest programs that computer users want to use usually require a machine that's considered "recent" to "current" at the time of software release. According to Moore's Law, computer power doubles every 18 months or so, so no PC purchased five years ago will ever be considered "current," no matter how powerful it was at the original time of purchase.

What's more, the latest and greatest systems always carry an "early adopter tax"—a price premium that manufacturers charge to the portion of the market for whom the value of cutting-edge hardware outweighs cost substantially. The latest and greatest systems often cost more than double what a good "current" system costs, so not only is today's cutting-edge equipment not going to be considered "modern" in five years, it also comes at a premium.

A veteran computer buyer often will stay with mainstream equipment, buying expensive components (such as monitors) only when they don't become obsolete easily. This means more frequent upgrades, but assuming that computers and operating systems are increasingly plug-and-play, the benefits of such an approach often outweigh the work involved in upgrading. If every two and a half years a person buys the latest, greatest PC available, he will spend about $3,000. Upgrading systems on an ongoing basis will cost from $600 to $800 a year instead.

What does all this have to do with networking? Consider that the problem with networking equipment is the same as the PC problem: new equipment is always better, but fresh-off-the-press gadgets will land a hefty price tag, and may not be what you really need anyway. If you really need the functionality of a cutting-edge QOS-enabled router, you may have to suffer the early-adopter tax, uncertain standards support, and immature feature set. On the other hand, if you're just trying to build a network with a decent level of performance, there are always less sophisticated ways of solving the problem.

Some of the technology and standards discussed in this book aren't ready for "production" yet, so the following case studies will demonstrate the difference between what's practical today, and what will be practical in the coming years. By then, today's "bleeding edge" systems may seem mundane and commonplace.

Case study: A distributed retail organization

Introduction

Large retail outlets have had networked point-of-sale systems for a long time. The volume of transactions and variety of products sold mean that a centralized database of transactions and inventories is necessary. As companies look to broaden their franchise and extend the reach of the head office into the branches, the department stores form a distributed intranet with special needs.

The situation

As a result of acquisitions and expansions, this regional department-store chain has roughly 50 outlets. The stores are linked to headquarters via frame relay circuits. There are three main kinds of traffic on the network.

- The point-of-sale traffic is transactional, meaning delivery guarantees are essential. Because the performance of this traffic has a direct impact on the speed with which customers can be processed, it must be handled relatively quickly. The legacy system—which was not adaptive—has been replaced by an IP-based system which is better able to cope with some level of delay.

- The intranet traffic is traditional store and forward e-mail or messaging traffic, used by store managers. At night, the bulk of traffic is backups and price-list updates. Backups and pricing information can withstand substantial delays but are important for the functioning of the organization.

- Pricing and inventory-requirements planning systems track sales and orders on an ongoing basis and are critical to the company's operations. The system is TCP based, and traffic is rate adaptive and somewhat tolerant of delays.

In addition, the company would like to hold monthly employee "town hall" meetings via videoconferencing. The video application consists of a multicast stream from the head office to each store, and unicast audio streams from the stores to the central site. The video stream is bursty and consumes a considerable amount of bandwidth; the audio streams are relatively compact but jitter sensitive.

In the past, the retail organization consisted of point-of-sale networks in each department store, connected to a central financial server via dedicated X.25 circuits. Each store was on a corporate network, which handled data and batch updates from financial systems. Special events such as videoconferencing were handled offsite by a separate private network. With just-in-time inventories and the convergence of voice, video, and data networks, the company wants to aggregate traffic on a backbone.

Migration to a policy-based network

The retail network has shifted from a store-and-forward model of past years to a real-time network that can converge data, point-of-sale transactions, and even voice traffic. The retail intranet carries financial information, operating procedures, and sales data.

The system administrator wants to ensure that the cash registers always have priority over the inventory application's stock queries, and that stock queries have priority over bulk data transfers such as network faxes and e-mail. Making customers wait in line because of a large e-mail from an innocent user is simply bad business. However, if traffic classified as "cash registers" peaks beyond a threshold of 50 percent of all traffic, the system operator must get an automated SNMP trap so the company can investigate the cause of congestion.

From a WAN perspective, the company relies on leased lines and privately owned networking equipment. This gives it a great deal of control over device configuration. The frame relay circuits are delivered across a public frame relay network, but within an administratively provisioned PVC the company has full control. The company has standardized on a single router platform at the edge of the WAN, which makes policy configuration more straightforward to deploy by hand. Routers were selected based on their ability to classify traffic and deliver a sophisticated set of relative priorities for various applications. The single-vendor approach makes vendor incompatibilities because of lack of standardization and indeterminate traffic levels less of an issue.

The company's network topology is shown in Figure 18–1.

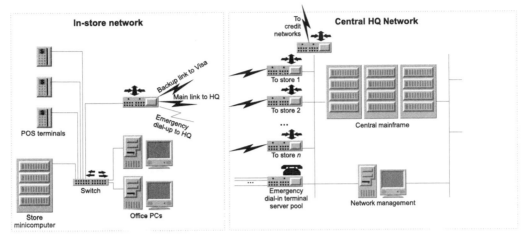

Figure 18–1 The distributed retail company's network topology

The in-store network combines intranet, point-of-sale, and require-ments-planning traffic on a single LAN. Office computers, a local mini-computer, and POS terminals all have access to the LAN traffic via a switch that ensures confidential POS transactions are not visible to other users. LAN bandwidth is abundant, and the company has a mixture of 10BaseT and Fast Ethernet network cards in its computers. All traffic bottlenecks will occur in the WAN, and egress routers are configured accordingly.

Each router's traffic will normally flow over a T1 carrying a Frame Relay PVC. If the main frame relay link should go down for any reason, the router will bring up a dialup link to the company's headquarters. Should the link with the central office fail, a direct connection to credit-card authorization services will be established, and all other WAN traf-fic will be blocked until connectivity returns to the frame relay circuit.

The routers are configured to recognize POS traffic and tag it using IPTOS precedence values. This will help the adjacent router at corpo-rate headquarters to prioritize traffic in the more congested central LAN. POS traffic is marked with a precedence of 2 (immediate); inven-tory traffic with a precedence of 1 (priority), and all other traffic with a precedence of 0 (routing). If the routers need to send route information to one another, they can use precedence to ensure that network-control messages get through; SNMP traffic is also treated with the highest priority in order to allow operators in the company's headquarters to manage the remote stores.

Routers enforce absolute priority for network-management traffic. POS traffic has a profile of up to half the WAN circuit's capacity, and any POS data within profile is forwarded before inventory or background traffic. On a busy day, POS traffic never exceeds 20 percent of the WAN capacity, so this is a healthy margin of error that still prevents faulty POS equipment from blocking all other transmissions. Out-of-profile POS traffic, inventory traffic, and best-effort traffic are interleaved according to a weighted round-robin algorithm.

The corporate headquarters has a reasonably simple pair of LANs. One LAN services local clients, and the other is set aside for traffic between the remote offices and the central mainframe. The company could have used a single LAN for all traffic with 802.1p-based prioritization, but they decided to simply connect the central server to both LAN segments in order to insulate mission-critical retail activities from network usage in the corporate office.

Looking forward

In the future, voice traffic may even be integrated into the data network. This would be accomplished via RSVP-enabled clients and routers. Most long-distance calls from each store go to the company's headquarters, so when IP bandwidth is available, the company may be able to reduce long-distance spending. Voice requires a constant low-jitter stream to make the connection useful, but this queue should be given low priority: Voice should never compete with stock transfers or POS traffic and should instead be handled through the traditional PBX and voice circuits during congestion.

Before this solution can be deployed, however, the company needs a reliable RSVP implementation and IP-aware PBXs that can redirect long-distance calls over IP when possible. Today, companies successfully routing voice traffic over their networks typically have bandwidth to burn and aren't hampered by lack of traffic-management equipment.

Once on-demand circuits from ISPs are available, the company will use these to hold its videoconferencing meetings, paying as it goes. The infrequency of the meetings and the availability of offsite suppliers for the events make migrating videoconferencing to their network less critical.

Case study: An academic campus

Introduction

The Internet began as a research project. Academic networks are populated by students, teachers, and researchers, but the network is both a means to an end and an end in itself—a research platform for information technologies. Because of this, an academic network must have appropriate security mechanisms in place to protect sensitive information. It must also offer logical separation of research traffic from other traffic.

As information technologies become a part of the curriculum for all academic disciplines, teachers want to include online content in their classes. Universities are also deploying "Ethernet to the pillow" in many residences to satisfy student demands for network access.

Universities are proving grounds for network administrators. Most companies have fairly well defined, steady flows of traffic that can be readily mapped and occasionally planned for. By contrast, a university is traffic nightmare, aggravated by students' uncanny ability to always consume any and all available bandwidth.

Despite this chaos, university traffic falls into two basic classes: local traffic between groups of clients and groups of servers physically near one another, and WAN traffic in the form of mail and network traffic. For example, research labs will often have a cluster of equivalent servers, serving many client workstations, usually on the same floor of the building. Users of those workstations will generate most of their traffic between their client workstations and the lab servers, but they will also have connect to mail and file servers elsewhere in the campus.

Today's student is armed with a computer and a modem, and for many schools remote study programs are a profitable innovation. As a result, there is a significant amount of remote-access traffic either through dialup connections or across the Internet link.

The situation

This university has 20 buildings distributed around a large campus. The demands on the network are considerable—everything from experimental student traffic to academic and personal information is available. Each building has a router connected to a fiber distributed data interface (FDDI) ring, with concentration switching in the wiring closets. Specialized networks for graphic arts, computer science, and physics are also connected behind firewalls, and these are based on GE, with ATM in the physics facility. There is some legacy DECnet traffic, as well as SNA from an old AS/400, that runs across certain portions of the network. The majority of traffic consists of IP over Ethernet.

A 10BaseT Ethernet connection is available in each dormitory room. To support users who do not have computers, all student mail and files are stored on shared network drives accessible from terminals in the various campus computer lab. Students with their own machines run mail clients that map to the remote mail store when connected. A network administrator accesses each student's computer at the beginning of the semester to set up the appropriate drive mappings and permissions. While the school offers standard Ethernet packages, it does not have control over student hardware.

The organization must divide traffic both by groups of users and by locations.

The campus has three major classes of user. Students make up most of the users, and they are entitled to basic best-effort bandwidth unless they get special approval from their department head for a different class of network service. Teachers are entitled to better-than-best-effort, since many of them use their network accounts for in-class demonstrations or to prepare course materials. Finally, administrators run mission-critical business applications to manage finances and payroll.

Dormitories, for example, are areas in which network managers have no control over use of the network. Research traffic can generate large volumes of time-sensitive data, so it is segmented by research project using VLANs. In-class demonstrations must respond reasonably quickly in order to allow teachers to use them effectively. QOS policies must therefore take into account location.

Given the level of "curiosity" and the relatively limited control that administrators have over the traffic on the network, admission control is needed close to the end station to restrict the impact that a misbehaving student can have on the network. For similar reasons, authentication services are key in the network.

The university is experiencing a great deal of congestion, and it needs to prepare itself for the coming semester with a strategy that will guarantee important traffic gets through. Unfortunately, its resources are somewhat scarce, so the administrators are looking for creative ways of restricting bandwidth that are both secure and cheap.

Migration to a policy-based network

After baselining traffic usage, the university's network administrator determines that student traffic from the dormitories and research traffic that "spills over" into the backbone are the causes of much of the congestion. Consequently, the first targets for policy are to restrict less important traffic and insulate research traffic from the rest of the network.

The administrator deploys a cache server and configures the routers that handle dormitory traffic to transparently redirect all queries to the cache. This will immediately reduce WAN usage by the dormitories by some 40 percent. In addition, the cache gives her the ability to monitor network usage in order to document any that violates the school's proper-use policy. More importantly, however, it gives her an easy way to identify dormitory traffic, so that precious WAN bandwidth can be rationed for the cache, and other sources of Web queries can be handled equitably.

The administrator also takes advantage of the summer lull in traffic to reconfigure the student network with 10BaseT switches culled from elsewhere in the network. Because most of the other labs are upgraded to Fast Ethernet, this makes it absolutely impossible for dormitory ports to consume more than 10 percent of available bandwidth—no matter how wily the student hacker. The dormitory student network may become heavily oversubscribed, however, and this "brute force" approach to traffic management will not separate the students who are doing real work from those playing games.

The accompanying topology diagram (Figure 18–2) illustrates a section of the network that is shared by a classroom and an undergraduate computer lab.

Students using the student lab share a LAN segment and a server cluster with the classroom. The network administrator wants the classroom to have nonexclusive priority over router capacity, server processing, and the Internet link.

The network administrator cannot rely on student desktops to tag traffic in an equitable manner here, so classification will have to happen on the shared router. She classifies traffic into three groups, and assigns

Classic contention spots in a shared network environment

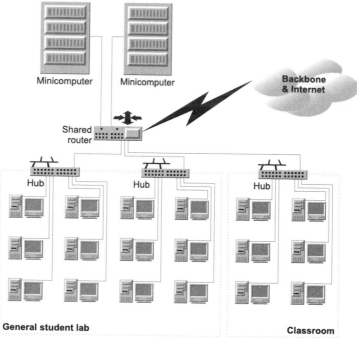

Figure 18–2 University network topology

flows that fall within each class according to source and destination as described in Table 18–1.

Table 18–1   Traffic priority based on source and destination address

	From student lab	From classroom
To internet	Low	Medium
To servers	Medium	High

The router weights traffic from each of these queues in a ratio of four high-priority packets, two medium-priority packets, and one low-priority packet. Packets are interleaved by the router according to the source and destination address ranges; the router also checks to ensure that all source addresses are coming from the right source LAN to prevent a student from manually entering an address of a classroom machine and getting better priority.

There are many other ways of classifying traffic among groups in this manner, including VLANs, application-aware switches, and so on. Because of the university's spending constraints, however, a solution that worked with existing software-based routers proved best.

Looking forward

The simple router-based system has some limitations that the administrator may want to correct, once she can afford to do so. The classification is based on groups of users, and it assumes that each machine has a correct address that was configured statically or assigned by a DHCP server on each LAN. Consequently, no user can have higher priority than any other, and no application-based classification is performed.

Lab administrators using the general student lab are assigned the same priority as other users, regardless of who they are or what protocols they are running. Once link-layer authentication allows users to log in, a lab technician could identify himself to the switch and receive better performance based on his identity.

A home-grown approach to this would be to create a Web site within the student LAN to which a technician could connect and "turn on" high-priority handling for a given terminal from a Web page. The server would then connect to the router and issue the appropriate SNMP commands to override the default classification with the higher priority according to a table of terminals and IP addresses.

Case study: A centralized financial institution

Introduction

At the other end of the spectrum from a university is a single-office financial institution. These organizations have rigid control over network equipment, and they pay top dollar for gear that will shave hundredths of a second off a transaction.

Online transactions are revolutionizing the financial-services market. With freely available, relatively recent stock information now on line, customers' expectations of information access have increased. The broker's role is often as that of a transaction facilitator, and companies are judged by their online presence. At the same time, round-the-clock financial coverage means that access to market data by the investment company itself must be instantaneous.

Referring back to our earlier example of a trading floor, imagine a network in which the delay of a packet can cost thousands of dollars. The *application* may not be delay-sensitive, but the information certainly is. Most of us wouldn't want to be the IT manager, once it was discovered that a large e-mail created bottlenecks with expensive consequences.

In the past, networks like this had some very stringent policy limitations. Trading applications either ran over an entirely separate network, or users were required to shut down all other applications and let only direct-trading software use the LAN during business hours. If policy technology can be trusted enough to reserve portions of the network for trading traffic at certain times of the day, there are compelling cost and productivity benefits to be had by moving to a single, multiservice network.

The situation

This investment and trading firm works from a single location. It wants to perform videoconferencing with its key clients and with companies for briefings, and it needs instant response to stock-trading traffic. Client information is streamed to an offsite backup site for failure protection, and trade executions need real-time response from traders. The company also has a stock-trading application that must not fail.

Financial transactions are time critical, but not because the protocols themselves do not adapt to latency; rather, it is the potential loss from late information that matters. On the other hand, video traffic is delay sensitive, but less important than the transfer of funds. The way in which the LAN is deployed must be a reflection of these relative importances.

The network administrator has one key advantage: desktop control. Tight restrictions over desktop software and hardware have allowed him to standardize on network cards that can mark 802.1p precedence information. Deep pockets also mean that he can upgrade the 200 or so Ethernet ports to 802.1p-compliant switches and deploy a GE core connected directly to the minicomputer on which the company runs its applications.

The company also has a routed connection to the trading floor, which carries only trading information. The connection to the router is redundant in case of failure.

Migration to policy-based networking

In this model, there are two types of information: business-critical trading information, and everything else. Trading information takes precedence, possibly to the exclusion of everything else. Any reserved capacity in this network comes from a lower-priority portion of the network.

The company's network topology is shown in Figure 18–3.

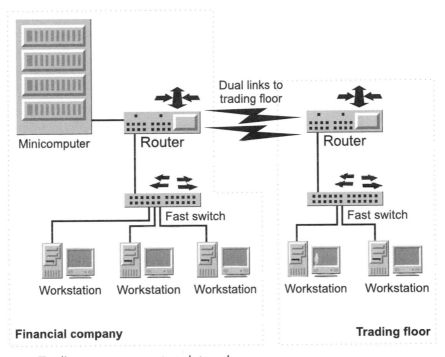

Figure 18–3   Trading-company network topology

The administrator defines a set of TCP port-number and 802.1p value mappings within the login scripts that each computer uses to initialize. Since the relative importance of applications is unlikely to change dynamically, this model is sufficient to propagate policies out to each node.

The LAN switches offer two hardware queues. All traffic from the trading application is sent to the high-priority queue, which has absolute priority; all other traffic is deferred to the low-priority queue. Delay-sensitive applications do not need bandwidth reservation because of the heavy overprovisioning within the network—each desktop has a switched Fast Ethernet connection into a gigabit core.

Tagging and prioritizing on the desktop not only classifies traffic within a layer-2 infrastructure, it also helps by prioritizing packets on the desktop itself. With QOS-aware protocol stacks and vendor-specific media-layer controls (such as those in Winsock 2.0) it's possible to have multiple queues even in the operating system. In case there's heavy network traffic, high-priority packets may back up within the buffers of the operating system itself. With QOS in the client, the mission critical-data can be sent out first, ahead of less important data like e-mail or FTP.

The goal of all this overprovisioning is to deliver delay-sensitive information as quickly as possible. Consequently, we give trading traffic absolute priority. The administrator needs to implement checks and balances on this traffic, however, so he enables RMON2 traffic monitoring on the switches to keep track of usage. He also runs a service-level monitoring tool to test application response time throughout the day and prepare for problems in capacity or performance.

In order to support videoconferencing, the administrator has deployed a firewall with traffic-shaping capabilities. The firewall is needed in order to ensure good security for the network, and Internet connections are available only from certain ports in order to offer complete security for trading systems. The traffic shaper has a set of standalone rules defined on a Web-based interface, and while the system may not scale, it is sufficient for the needs of the company.

Looking forward

Once the company integrates electronic trading from its Web site, it will implement load-balancing to share the processor-intensive generation of encrypted, dynamic HTML across multiple machines. It will further reduce the load on these systems with hardware-assisted SSL encryption and key generation. These machines will tag trading traffic with the same 802.1p priorities that traders' desktops use, ensuring prompt response.

The administrator may want to consider multiple high-priority queues on the router if certain traders handle large-volume accounts. Their million-dollar deals may need to get to the floor faster than a few smaller trades.

Case study: A 2-coast consulting firm

Introduction

Consulting and contract work is a growing trend, driven by the twin engines of work-at-home self-employment and just-in-time labor markets. Today's consultant is the mercenary of the corporate world—a gun-for-hire recruited for special knowledge in a short-term relationship with a customer. As consulting firms strive to survive in these transitory interactions, their information systems must be able to connect and disconnect readily with customers while holding together their admittedly loose corporate structure.

Fortunately, the ubiquity of IP and the broad range of applications that can run atop it make nomadic work a practical reality.

The situation

This consulting company provides strategic business services from two main offices, one on the East Coast and one on the West Coast. The company spends a great deal of money on long-distance calls between the two offices, but its data network is not currently suited for real-time traffic, because most of its applications are elastic and handle delay well. Data traffic consists mainly of messaging and periodic replication of shared documents between local servers at both locations. The exception is videoconferencing and associated digital whiteboard applications, which the company is increasingly using in its dealings with customers and analysts.

The company's staff often work from customer locations, and confidential communications are essential. The remote workers' communications systems (such as virtual private networks or dialup remote access) must be fault tolerant. For traffic at customer sites, the firm's only option is the Internet. No other public technology can be reasonably expected at a customer's site, and on-site consulting contracts generally last for less than six months, which makes temporary installation of networking equipment uneconomical.

Because the consultants often rely on the networks of their customers for network access, security systems and firewalls will be a critical component of the network. This means that many of the directory and access-control systems pertinent to a security system will be available to policy systems, making true admission controls possible earlier in the company's network future.

Migration to policy-based networking: Three areas

The firm has three main issues to address. These include secure, ubiquitous remote access at a reasonable pace; consolidation of WAN voice and data traffic; and on-demand constant-bit-rate traffic to customer sites.

Remote access and QOS policy

Remote users cannot request performance from their customers' networks. In addition to being an administrative headache for customer IT managers, it would be politically unsavory in terms of customer relations. Consequently, the consulting firm's IT managers can make changes only within the corporate network and by adjusting server performance.

The company has implemented VPN tunnel terminators that receive both Virtual Leased Line (VLL) and access VPN connections. The access VPN tunnels run between desktop clients running Microsoft's Dial-up Networking version 1.2 or higher, which offers the point-to-point tunneling protocol (PPTP) for tunneling between the client and the VPN access terminator.

PPTP simulates a PPP connection within a tunnel; consequently, the remote user has a public IP address assigned by the customer's IT personnel, and a VPN address assigned by the tunnel terminator. The virtual or "passenger" address is chosen from a pool of addresses allocated to the tunnel terminator, allowing the consulting firm's IT personnel to classify remote-user traffic by the packet's source address.

When traffic arrives at the tunnel terminator, it is tagged with 802.1p and IPTOS values that give it a higher priority than that of onsite user traffic. Similarly, the server load balancers are configured to treat packets from the VPN terminator's address range with a higher priority. While the Internet portion of the packet's round-trip may be beyond the control of the remote user, the packet's LAN transit and server response time are optimized for remote users to encourage maximum productivity while onsite.

Figure 18–4 shows remote access to the firm's East Coast headquarters.

Because the company uses a tunnel system that begins at the remote client, it has outsourced its dialup access services to a global ISP with local dialup ports throughout North America. The QOS system functions in the same way for connections provided by the ISP. The company's WAN links are consequently on the same backbone as the dialup POPs, resulting in fewer transits across autonomous systems in the public network. For emergencies the firm has several dialup ports connected to a 1-800 number for immediate access, and all traveling consultants are equipped

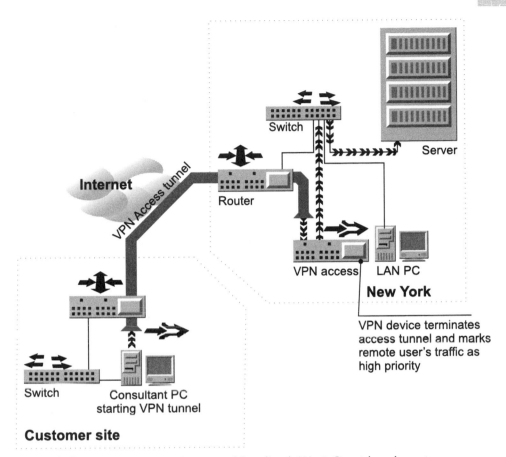

Figure 18–4   Remote access to the consulting firm's West Coast headquarters

with devices that allow analog modem connections to work over a customer's digital PBX.

When all else fails, the company has deployed a Web-based front end, relying on its being secured via SSL. The secure Web application allows remote employees to access mail and other basic messaging services, as well as to fax documents on demand, without sending information across customer devices such as SMTP servers.

The company also experiences spontaneous bulk file transfers. On closer inspection, IT has discovered that this is a result of laptop resynchronization: remote consultants replicate the contents of their hard drives with LAN-based servers when they return to the office. This can often involve the transfer of hundreds of megabytes of data between a notebook and a file server, and a reasonably fast notebook (Pentium 266 MMX with a 10/100

Ethernet card) can easily introduce 650,000 bytes per second into a network. Routers and layer-3 switches in the company's LAN are therefore configured with token buckets to ensure that no one workstation within the consultants' address pool is able to monopolize the LAN.

WAN and voice consolidation

The company has a dedicated Frame Relay circuit between the two offices, which costs a substantial amount of money because of the distance involved. A main driver of QOS implementation is to reduce the cost and improve the performance of this link. The firm is using three main innovations to achieve these cost savings: Virtual Leased Lines, mirrored caching, and an IP-enabled PBX. These are not specifically QOS technologies, but they all require integration with the company's QOS strategies and can all help to achieve acceptable levels of performance for the business.

VLLs are terminated on the Internet access router, and a portion of the router's WAN capacity is dedicated to this traffic. The VLL "looks like" a leased line between the company's two offices, delivering secure communications across the Internet. Instead of using costly Frame Relay circuits for the company's delay-tolerant traffic, routers direct this traffic across the VLL and save a substantial amount of money. Both offices are connected to the same ISP. The ISP offers service-level guarantees across its North American backbone, and the firm monitors response time with a simple tool in order to ensure that these guarantees are met.

The routers perform VLL classification by source address (since replication is a substantial portion of the traffic) and by TCP port. Traffic that is considered "delay sensitive" is forwarded to the Frame Relay links, whose capacity has been reduced.

The company has implemented redirected caches at each router. When combined with the mirroring of company information between the two offices, this redirection improves response time and reduces congestion of the router's Internet link—making the VLL perform better. Using redirection rather than proxy makes the caches impossible to circumvent and lowers the administrative complexity of deploying the cache; on the other hand, the routers must run software that detects cache failure to ensure availability of common services.

Both the VLL and the caching pave the way for an IP telephone switch. The VLL offloads traffic from the Frame Relay circuit, and the caches make the VLL perform better by reducing competing Internet traffic and lowering the VLL traffic itself so that VLL response time is acceptable.

The IP phone switch selects from either an external phone line or an internal circuit based on the number that the user has dialed; internal calls are routed over IP and across the Frame Relay circuit if bandwidth is available. Bandwidth availability is verified using an RSVP mechanism, but only admission controls are implemented, and the routers will only accept RSVP messages from the PBXs to prevent abuse. The PBX uses a G.729 codec, which requires approximately 10 Kbps of sustained bandwidth, so the impact of voice streams on the network is relatively small.

In addition to savings when making internal calls, special exchange codes are established so that users can place a local call from the office on the opposite coast. Employees dial an 8 to connect to the PBX on the East Coast and a 7 to connect to the PBX on the West Coast. They are then presented with a second dial tone and can place a local call from the remote PBX using off-net calling.

With these three developments, the company has improved application and Internet response time, reduced the amount of Frame Relay capacity it needs, and lowered the cost of long-distance calling. It may also be able to reduce the number of outbound phone circuits needed at each office.

CBR to customers

The third—and perhaps most challenging—problem the company faces is that of deploying delay-sensitive videoconferencing and whiteboarding applications to its customers. While voice can be transmitted relatively economically over the WAN, the video system is both bandwidth intensive and dynamic (i.e., intended for audiences at a range of locations).

One approach is to have WAN links to multiple, global service providers and establish video connections over the ISP that the customer uses; another is to rely on on-demand digital links such as bonded ISDN circuits for the connection. Unfortunately, the company's IT staff rejected both of these as too expensive and hard to administer.

As a result, the current solution is to settle for lower-quality video with substantial buffering across their ISP, and to use offsite facilities offered by a videoconferencing service that has conference facilities in major cities. In other words, the company feels that no reliable, economical service exists that can offer both performance guarantees and destination independence. The firm's IT personnel continue to monitor service offerings for an acceptable solution to this problem.

Figure 18–5 shows the integration of PBX, data, and VPN between the two offices.

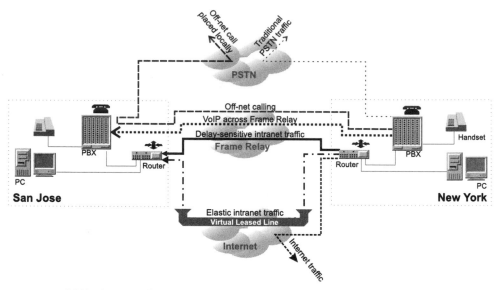

Figure 18–5   PBX, data, and VPN integration between both offices

Looking forward

The main problem the company needs to solve is that of economical, dynamic constant-bit-rate traffic. Once MPLS-based differentiated services are available, the firm will allow routers to send traffic over the MPLS network if they come from videoconferencing terminals or authorized users' desktops. Packets destined for the MPLS link will be tagged with a DiffServ codepoint value that requests fast handling (below 100 ms) for every datagram. The deployment of such a WAN will require integration between the consulting firm's ISP and the customer's ISP, with the appropriate billing mechanisms, so IT managers aren't anticipating a reliable system for the short-term future.

The company may also deploy reservation systems such as RSVP to allow critical applications to reserve a portion of the Frame Relay link instead of passage across the virtual leased line. Such a reservation requires policing because of the additional cost of the WAN circuit, but it will allow desktop applications that need guaranteed throughput such as collaborative application sharing to respond quickly between offices.

Because of the move to VLLs, the firm can easily add a new office with relatively little overhead and without waiting for the installation of permanent virtual circuits at the new location. In addition, the deployment of an IP PBX means that if the ISP's backbone is fast enough, voice calls can travel across it to further reduce the need for the dedicated WAN circuit.

Case study: A distributed manufacturing company

Introduction

A distributed company can often benefit the most from bandwidth management. Instead of buying "more than you'll ever need" and paying accordingly, a pay-as-you-use model is more cost effective and easier to track. Two of the biggest drivers for QOS technology are the high price and lack of determinism that today's WANs offer.

The situation

This company produces mechanical components at four plants that are reasonably far apart. It runs a common manufacturing and process-management package, but the sales force is not currently integrated into the information the company uses. An Enterprise Requirements Planning system is needed to coordinate component availability and manufacturing processes across the company's various factories and design centers.

Since the company sells to business buyers, it wants to make order placement and tracking available on line. It will continue to use traditional telephone systems for voice and fax but may consider outsourcing long-distance faxing to a fax service from the company's ISP to save long-distance charges.

There are three main types of traffic on the network: SQL-like client-server traffic for ERP, time-insensitive data like e-mail, and high-throughput data such as file sharing. Manufacturing networks such as process control are deployed through an entirely different network that relies on radically different signaling methods, and they are consequently not candidates for convergence at this time.

The ERP application that the company runs uses a control channel, which is well known, and one or more negotiated data channels. It is a two-phase system in which clients interact with servers, and servers interact with back-end platforms. This means that classification of traffic is harder than usual, requiring stateful application awareness and traffic marking.

The company's motivations for deploying QOS are to protect the mission-critical ERP traffic from an increasing amount of "background" IP traffic and to pave the way for the adoption of converged voice and data.

Migration to a policy-based network

The company classifies traffic by mission criticality, as delay-sensitive applications are not yet strategic to its business. It has established a committed-access-rate algorithm on its routers and has deployed a high-capacity Gigabit Ethernet core. The routers perform admission control and policing based on application type, and ERP servers are configured to tag traffic by marking IPTOS fields in order to make classification of stateful traffic at high speeds easier for the core routers.

The high-speed backbone connects directly to high-volume enterprise servers. A group of Fast Ethernet switches with GE uplinks concentrate traffic into the core, and departmental servers attach to these switches. 10/100 Ethernet switches in the workgroups connect client machines and workgroup servers, and the three-tier model ensures that GE traffic will not overwhelm a 10-MBps port.

To reduce the impact of high-volume file sharing, the company's routers implement token buckets and flow RED that favor well-behaved, in-profile traffic flows. As the firm's online business grows, it will be increasingly important to restrict flows in order to ensure proper response time to online customers.

Table 18–2 summarizes the relative importance—and resulting priority—of the traffic on the network. In order to avoid starvation, application types are weighted with a value that routers use to calculate the ratio of forwarded traffic.

Table 18–2   Weighting by application type in the network

Business application	Weighting/ priority	Maximum link percentage	Examples
Network control	Absolute	10	RIP, OSPF
ERP	10	80	SQL, PeopleSoft
File transfers	5	30	FTP, Windows SMB
Timely business traffic	3	40	Mail (SMTP, POP3, IMAP), Printing
Other internal traffic	2	40	Intranet http
Internet traffic	1	20	Pointcast, Internet http

Note that the effort here isn't to guarantee a particular jitter level per application, or even a certain bit rate through the network, but to guarantee that any one data application does not monopolize capacity or cause a more important kind of traffic to fall below acceptable performance thresholds. This could have been achieved by physically separating the traffic through different LAN and WAN links or virtual circuits, or by overprovisioning the WAN. Cost is once again the main impetus for QOS deployment, because it is cheaper to police a lower-speed line than to purchase higher-speed lines. The company's network topology is shown in Figure 18–6.

Looking forward

Because the company has no mission-critical jitter-sensitive applications, a bulk data carrier like the Internet would suffice for bandwidth between the various manufacturing plants. Data can be privatized via simple, secure tunneling mechanisms like L2TP or IPSEC, delivering the logical equivalent of a leased-line mesh network without the associated high costs.

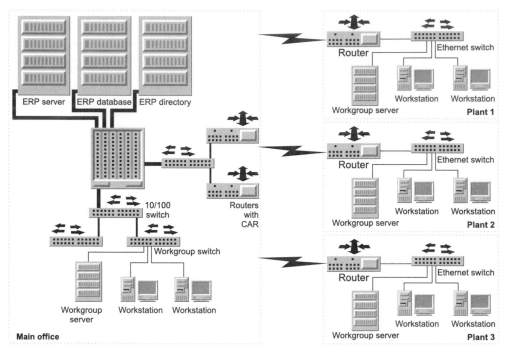

Figure 18–6   Manufacturing company's network topology

Case study: A small business

Introduction

Small businesses might seem like the least likely candidates for QOS systems. While this is generally true—a shared 10-MB hub is more than enough bandwidth for a handful of LAN users—the business as a whole has some special needs in terms of fast network access and ensuring that communication systems continue to function correctly. The limited bandwidth a small company has at its disposal can be rendered more useful in several ways.

The situation

This small legal firm has six employees—four lawyers, a receptionist, and a contracts administrator. A bookkeeper visits the company for a day each month to perform accounting services. The company has a server that acts as a mail gateway, print server, and file-sharing server. The firm currently relies on a dial-on-demand connection to the local ISP, using a small access router with an integrated modem that performs network-address translation. When the router is not connected to the ISP, it will accept a single dialup connection for remote access.

The company wants to put its Web server on line but cannot afford the nailed-up link required to locate the server on its premises. The firm is increasingly reliant on Internet technologies for connections to the outside world. Customers want contracts by e-mail, in a variety of formats. Similarly, research and case libraries are available on line via secure connections.

Migration to a policy-based network

The company has ordered a dial-on-demand ISDN router. The router offers two analog telephone lines, and one of these is connected to the small voice PBX the firm uses to handle calls. This gives them additional speed when needed, and an extra outside line for phone calls.

The 64- or 128-Kbps WAN is very easy to saturate. By deploying QOS controls at the access router, the company can obtain better performance for interactive applications such as querying legal databases and browsing. In this way, the company can regulate WAN bandwidth usage among the internal users and applications. The firm cannot, however, signal QOS into their service provider until some kind of differentiated service is available from the ISP.

Should the firm want to engage in interactive Internet applications like voice-over IP, it is critical that the constant flow of small packets from the voice application are not delayed by large datagrams from FTP traffic. Configuring a small MTU on the device is one approach to this, but it will negatively impact the performance of maximum-datagram traffic because of a higher header-to-payload ratio. Consequently, the router employs a prioritization scheme that interleaves voice and data across the link. Figure 18–7 shows this small business network.

Note that many of these functions will be configured by a networking consultant, since the firm does not have a dedicated IT manager. If the ISP's personnel deploy the customer-premise equipment, they will be less motivated to optimize the router's performance, because the ISP's main goals are to reduce support costs through standardization and to achieve the lowest usage of the WAN backbone while maintaining customer satisfaction.

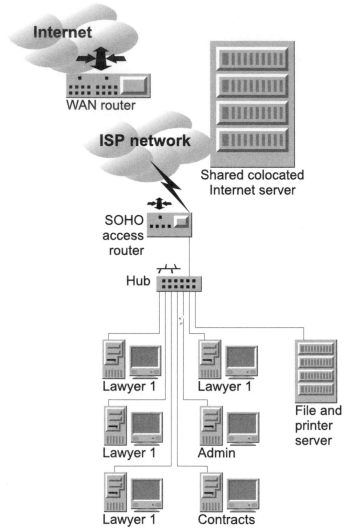

Figure 18–7   A small business network

Looking forward

Many of the technologies that can help a small business deploy QOS are only now becoming available. They include faster local loops, differentiated point-to-point connections, turnkey caching, simple collocation, and differentiated Internet services.

The company may consider replacing its ISDN circuit with a different local-loop connection such as ADSL or a cable modem. In many cases, affordable local loop is only available to home users. In addition, most of these devices will support only 1 or 2 MAC addresses, limiting the usefulness of a turnkey solution. However, if the company can obtain a high-speed local-loop connection and configure its server to act as a network-address translator, it may be able to share the faster connection across many users.

Differentiated PPP offers a way of more efficiently interleaving delay-sensitive and large-packet applications. If class-of-service parameters for the ISDN-based PPP connection are deployed by the ISP, then the law firm can use these to optimize performance of delay-sensitive applications.

With a server already in place at the law office, it makes sense to enable proxy-based caching in order to improve network response times and reduce the amount of redundant traffic on the network. Each of the four lawyers will probably have similar content that they browse, so the hit rate on the cache will be fairly high. As the server takes an active role in internetworking, however, it is important to ensure that confidential information such as client records is properly protected through the router's firewall.

The law firm will collocate its Web presence with the ISP, relying on turnkey server publishing tools to make changes to the site without requiring a great deal of server knowledge.

If the provider starts to offer a "gold" class of service, the law firm can request better performance as an administrative change, since it will simply pay a larger amount each month for a premium service. On the other hand, if the provider offers a "bill by byte" service that understands IPTOS or DiffServ code points, then the company can tag critical traffic (such as legal searches) and pay accordingly.

PART 5

The final part of this text offers some conclusions about QOS and bandwidth management. We also present a review of TCP and its specific functions for QOS systems as a review.

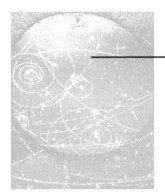

Conclusions

QOS networks have important consequences for enterprise IT managers, designers of networked applications, service designers, and network operators. As QOS technologies appear in operating-system APIs and business applications, they will become a part of network management in general. IP networks will deploy a simple set of QOS identifiers—in keeping with the flexible designs of the original Internet—that will deliver rich application variety and make IP networks even more a part of our lives than they are today.

We've covered a broad array of networking technologies in this discussion, in part because the issue of QOS touches nearly every aspect of a network. A considerable amount of research is available on the subject that goes into far more detail. We shall end with some practical observations about the consequences of QOS for managers, designers, operators, and developers of networks.

Consequences for IT managers

Everyone's dissatisfied with networking performance. Fortunately, with a differentiated network you have the tools to call the complainers' bluff. If people in a department want better network performance, they can have it—for a price. The ability to differentiate services internally allows you to better administer the network and reach pricing that reflects the actual cost of deploying and maintaining it.

The National Laboratory for Applied Network Research[1] offers some basic suggestions:

- Use multicast to aggregate high-volume multimedia traffic and reduce the amount of redundant traffic on the network, freeing up capacity for intolerant or latency-sensitive traffic.

- Since 90 percent of Internet traffic is TCP and roughly 60 percent of this is Web, use the most recent versions of http whenever possible. By using a single session to retrieve multiple objects from a site, http 1.1 dramatically reduces the amount of TCP session overhead and allows a client to characterize the network over a longer period, rather than ramping up a new session over time for each component of the page.

- Deploy caching, having some form of content-provider notification in place to ensure that online providers aren't deprived of user information when a cache fulfills the request on behalf of the content server.

- Keep your eye on information-discovery and replication tools that can sort and index information stored in a distributed manner. By understanding the distribution of content, a load balancer can better associate a client's request with the best source of information for that client.

- Adopt a pricing mechanism that allows differentiated services and associates a cost to the user with these services. Whether you will be billing internal users or simply justifying next year's budget, pricing for differentiated services is essential. By better aligning the actual cost of bandwidth with the performance characteristics delivered, an equitable pricing model for differentiated public and private networks can be attained.

• For high granularity of control, use ATM. Centralized decision making, traffic management, and QOS come built into this system; their price is the "cell tax" that ATM imposes. On the other hand, for compliance with familiar monitoring and measurement systems, use GE. Be sure that the core switches offer at least two queues and decent queuing algorithms to appropriately handle and signal congestion.

• RSVP makes sense between the application and the network edge, but it must be mapped to a simpler WAN circuit such as MPLS, ATM, or differentiated PPP in order to make it feasible across a shared core.

• Routers running IP are able to tolerate breakages in connectivity by finding alternate routing paths and using cost metrics. In a switched infrastructure, multihoming critical switch junctures in the core is essential, since they handle faults less well. Look for standards-based multihoming to allow vendor interoperability.

• Experiment with an application-level monitoring system, and find out if client agents are right for you. Monitoring virtual services, rather than network metrics, will be the way in which multi-service networks are managed.

Business-class network traffic will become a reality. No longer will your mission-critical data compete with Pointcast or multi-player gaming. With this higher-priced, preferential treatment, delay-sensitive technologies that are too fragile to build your business on today will become a reality. The deployment of VPN tunneling, voice-over ISP (public voice-over-IP services), and even legacy traffic over the Internet will be practical.

Today, the precursors of such applications are already on the market. Latency-insensitive voice (i.e., faxing services) and hybrid VPN/ dial-on-demand configurations are appropriate for modern enterprises, as in one way or another they mitigate the weaknesses of best-effort WANs. As Internet services improve, it will be relatively simple to migrate toward a differentiated services public network, once such a hybrid system is in place.

The trick here is to balance on the edge of the wave of real-time networking technologies. Deploy aggressively, and you spend too much time managing or you buy into proprietary schemes; wait too long, and you'll find your network outdated and your company unable to compete.

The differentiated services you will offer will probably consist of a premium service for controlled-load traffic (voice and video with a constant, defined rate and little adaptability); an assured service for guaranteeing some degree of network capacity to adaptive traffic within a predefined specification; and best-effort traffic. In addition, you may want a mechanism for keeping network management and monitoring traffic completely separate from the rest of the network to ensure manageability.

Perhaps the most fundamental, and important, consequence for network managers is that of the virtual service. Networks no longer offer networking—they offer access to virtual services. IP and MAC addresses are transient attributes of the most fundamental building block in a service-based network: the user. Similarly, hosts and routes are ways to fulfill a network service. IPFEPs offer the network functions that enable services through content control, streaming, load balancing, replication, and delivery optimization.

Thinking in terms of users and services—rather than in terms of addresses and interfaces—will be vital if we are to keep track of our networks. With the growing complexity that differentiated or guaranteed services introduce into communications infrastructures, systems that represent users and services will insulate network operations from the underlying devices. The future of a network lies in the services it can offer and in the enabling technologies that allow it to offer those services in an equitable, efficient manner.

Consequences for designers of network services

There are as many ways to price services as there are salespeople to sell them. Most differentiated-bandwidth systems, however, fall into one of three pricings: congestion insurance, congestion cure, and capacity-on-demand. In general, these focus on raw bandwidth or preferential treatment. Neither the customers nor the network-management applications are mature enough today to negotiate other quality attributes (such as jitter or discard rates) across administrative domains. Each can be priced using a flat-rate pricing for in-profile traffic and either decreased reliability (drop eligibility) or additional charges for out-of-profile traffic.

Congestion insurance

The congestion-insurance approach to pricing gives some traffic preferential treatment during congestion. During times of no congestion, all traffic is treated equally. An "insured" user's traffic would be less subject to discards during congestion; it might enjoy a better forwarding ratio in a priority queue or preferential insertion into a queue.

Congestion insurance is easy to bill for, but hard to get people to pay for until it's too late. Insurance pricing systems must rely on the negative impact of congestion on the user's traffic. They represent a nice, predictable pricing system for service providers, and it's relatively easy to build a business case for them. What is seldom considered is the impact on the remaining, uninsured users—during congestion, their performance will degrade from its current level. Critics of an insurance approach point out that for public networks, congestion is nearly always present—some estimates show only 50 Kbps per user in the core of the Internet.[2] Certainty of congestion means that an insurance scheme will be popular—everyone will buy it, resulting in no improvement. Congestion insurance is rather like selling medical insurance to people who know they'll get sick. If so, then congestion insurance is simply a repricing of best-effort traffic.

Congestion cure

A pay-as-you-go pricing model would allow users to tag certain kinds of traffic as preferred. The service provider would then count this traffic and bill accordingly. The complexity and processing needed to administer such billing are considerable by comparison with the relatively static system of congestion insurance. The ability to "cure" congestion will result in a bidding situation in which customers will pay what they can afford and will get an appropriate level of performance. The problem with a congestion cure is that the price of a given quality of service cannot be determined ahead of time. Effectively, users are buying at a "market price" without knowing what they're getting (to be more precise, they're paying a known price, but not getting a deterministic system).

Of course, with the ability to reserve bandwidth comes the ability to price it. Once the offering is known (a contract of latency, jitter, packet loss, and capacity for a period of time), the price can be established. Practically speaking, setting up this kind of contract during the real-time operation of a network requires a great deal of computational and management infrastructure. So while a congestion "cure" will be better at finding the true value of QOS to customers through a market economy, it will be easier for service providers to implement bandwidth insurance today. Customers understand the notion of best-effort and premium service—they see it in everything from airline travel to gasoline—and the billing mechanisms are in place already.

What must occur at the same time, in order not to degrade best-effort traffic, is an increase in capacity so that customers measuring their new, improved performance will notice a change for the better. Some less scrupulous service providers will undoubtedly use service differentiation as a means to reduce the capacity they offer for their base-level pricing; nevertheless, the deployment of differentiated services should coincide with network expansion to minimize the impact on best-effort users.

Capacity on demand

Once a true capacity-on-demand system is in place, billing is relatively simple. If an ISP can offer a virtual circuit—either simulated using an RSVP guaranteed load or established as a switched virtual circuit—then the circuit setup and tear-down phases provide the appropriate mechanisms for billing. The main concern at this point becomes one of appropriate use and security.

How the system would work

A model for on-demand networking might have the admitting device querying a network management host for billing information based on information it receives in an RSVP request. It is probably a good deal easier to bill "as you go" when a reservation occurs than by looking at the priority bits on a flow and translating the flow's source to a user's permissions. If you don't want to use RSVP, then the system will have to allow users to request a one-time change in the policing function of the admitting router. For example, if an ISP's network access servers have a default behavior of setting all TOS and precedence bits to zeroes, then dial-in "premium" users would have a vendor-specific attribute that alters the priority information for these users.

Dynamic modification of these values will require a stateful authorization protocol (such as Diameter or COPS) in the place of Radius, in order to alter permissions for users in midsession (for example, when their credit runs out). It will also require a network architecture that consists of a concentration layer, a policing or admission-control layer, and a forwarding core. Systems for differentiated pricing are gradually being put in place that will let service providers deploy first congestion avoidance, then real-time purchase of premium traffic capacity, and finally dynamic bandwidth reservation.

Consequences for those who run networks

Get ready for dissatisfaction of the masses. Class distinctions on the Internet mean the poor will get poorer service, and cheap ISPs may find themselves unable to maintain their already squeezed margins as users drop them for properly installed service providers. Faster local loops will exacerbate the congestion, and the deployment of POP caches to compensate will further aggravate users with stale pages and cache-configuration issues.

In the coming years, you won't be running a data network any more: you'll be delivering connectivity. At first blush this may seem somewhat of a platitude, but it's got real meaning. You will transition from network provider to connectivity provider; your job will be to deliver appropriate access to a set of virtual services so that requests from clients can be fulfilled. This means a greater involvement in the selection and implementation of clients for those services—you will be asked to participate in the testing of new telephone handsets, or in the validation of a groupware application's network characteristics. It also means that you will have to deploy unconventional systems for providing virtual services—from distributed inline caches to global load-balancers to server clusters.

Most QOS models assume that the network knows a certain flow is to be handled preferentially. When you visit a site, if you're a paying customer, your traffic moves no more quickly than anyone else's. The *bulk* of traffic is from the server, so that can be tagged with the appropriate packet information to ensure speedy delivery, but a complete solution will require customer server systems that provide better performance or availability to specific sessions. It's the site managers, not the users, who will pay to roll out the red carpet. In the RSVP model, this means that the path message (from the client) indicates the source of payment, but the reservation message (from the server) is what actually *gets* the reservation itself.

With the improved performance of networks and the increased sophistication of multilevel caching or replication, you may want to consider the benefits of outsourcing an application to the network provider rather than deploying it yourself. These so-called "packaged applications" include help desk, backup, or connectivity. Packaged applications can be a compelling alternative to big-ticket custom applications, and they offer the ability to share data across a trusted community of interest. Today, outsourcing a private network in the form of a VPN seems cutting edge; tomorrow, outsourcing the application or virtual service may be commonplace.

Consequences for application developers

Application developers create the systems that generate traffic, and the availability of a differentiated-services network can be seen as a set of function calls that make programming certain types of network application easier. In spite of warnings to the contrary, application developers will want high priority from the network so that their programs appear to be working well. High priority may cover up poor architecture in the short term, at the expense of network congestion down the road.

Priority-aware applications

"Policy-aware" or "directory-enabled" versions of enterprise applications will use class-of-service and reservation capabilities to reserve network capacity. This is promising for QOS; after all, who is more qualified to know the application's needs than the application itself? However, until devices support standards-based service differentiators like DiffServ, RSVP, and 802.1p, these implementations may be proprietary or vendor specific, limiting their usefulness. When developing applications that will use policy systems, remember that network managers will want to know the following:

- Are differentiated services invoked prudently to enable otherwise impossible uses of the network, or are they used to allow poorly architected systems to work in a shared environment? If the latter is true, you'll soon wind up with a "best effort" situation in the reserved capacity of your network.

- How open are the protocols? How many hardware vendors does this application work with?

- Are diagnostic systems available? Reliable diagnosis of a multiservice network is hard without proper tools at the application layer. Application-level loopback capability is one of the few true measurements of quality of service, and it requires support from the application vendor.

- Now that the application is a "network-aware" citizen, how well will it integrate with management systems? Will it send some form of notification or trap when service thresholds are exceeded? Will it obtain permissions from a directory before reserving bandwidth?

If the application is using policy-based networking to support some latency-sensitive applications, or if it is a critical business application looking to shield itself from reduced reliability during times of heavy network congestion, then it is probably suitable for deployment with special QOS handling.

Nevertheless, a pragmatic view might be that applications *requiring* policy-enabled networks simply aren't deployed. Robustness is the price of entry for networked software on today's Internet. One might argue that policy-enabled networks, while allowing applications to perform better, won't actually pave the way for entirely new classes of application.

Priority-aware operating systems

In addition to applications that can request preferential treatment, operating systems are exposing the networking hooks needed to set QOS. Eventually, this will extend to the link layer and expand to include the DiffServ codepoint. Already some vendors of networking hardware offer agents that allow you to associate applications with specific 802.1p and IPTOS values—but it is left to the administrator to ensure the network supports these values.

As operating systems expose these interfaces in a cleaner manner—using application programming interfaces—more and more developers will make their products QOS aware. Once this happens, network managers will need to police priority requests to ensure that all nodes are signaling only classes of service that are appropriate to them.

Adopting standard protocols

A QOS capable network is no place for a messy implementation. If you are developing an application that is not getting flow control "for free" from the TCP/IP suite, for whatever reason, then you need to properly architect flow control and congestion detection into the application itself.

Whereas streaming multimedia was once available according to a number of proprietary protocols, there are now attempts to standardize mechanisms for controlling the delivery of real-time data.[3] Such systems will support TCP, multicast UDP, and UDP, and present a generalized interface for deploying real-time custom applications.

The adoption of networking standards for application-level control of multimedia means that networking devices can better support the application. By converging on a standard set of ports for signaling and traffic, it becomes easier to establish class-based queues for such traffic and put the proper guarantees or regulations in place. For example, the Real Time Streaming Protocol is a standard for remotely controlling the playback and recording of streamed multimedia. Using it rather than creating your own protocol will mean that your application will work with network devices that can parse the control channel and detect multimedia streams as a result.

Sloppy integration of applications with the network can have increasingly disastrous effects in a multiservice network. For example, because a router may select different paths for traffic based on these metrics, a destination that would otherwise be reachable may be unreachable using the selected metric. There are ICMP "host unreachable" messages that notify the sender of this; typically, detection of these messages should be the responsibility of the application that generated the traffic. If a low-cost path is unavailable but the destination is reachable across a high-cost path, the application may want to obtain authorization from the user before altering the TOS values it sets in the network. Similarly, a videoconferencing application that relies on high-bandwidth links may be able to reach a destination via dial-on-demand ISDN backup, but this would make the application unusable. Multiservice networks require more user involvement in QOS billing and accounting systems.

A multiservice network can also mean that jitter from high-priority applications affects lower-priority classes. If a lower-class packet is delayed while higher-class traffic passes, then even if the lower-class application generates relatively constant traffic levels, packet arrival will vary greatly from the perspective of the receiver. An application that functioned correctly in a best-effort network may behave erratically in a multiservice one.

Directory APIs

Directory systems are the perfect place for applications to encounter networks. They are information rich and relatively easy to process through a number of publicly available libraries. Using a directory, an application can publish information which will allow a network to make decisions about traffic. The application will also be able to discover network characteristics from the directory schema. Writing to a standard schema (on which DEN is working) will ensure that the application works with many networking vendors' equipment. A number of APIs in Java (using the Java Naming and Directory Interface, or JNDI) and client software from Netscape, Sun, Novell, Critical Angle and Microsoft are available.

A final word

The Internet, and corporate intranets, have ushered in an era of fantastic invention. Current uses for today's best-effort networks are pushing these incredibly robust protocols to their breaking points, but each time we think we've broken them, someone discovers a new way to use what we've got.

Differentiated-service networks will pave the way for a new wave of applications and systems. However, it is vital that such systems be simple and scalable. The designers of the original Internet protocols couldn't possibly foresee today's World Wide Web, but they architected for the possibility with a few simple, powerful rules.

Pascal said that the best of all possible worlds is the one in which the fewest causes give the greatest number of possible outcomes. This sentiment is echoed in the rule of parsimony, or simplicity. The Internet is clearly such a world; to effectively broaden its scope and useful impact on human life must mean that we implement the fewest, simplest extensions to it that will deliver the broadest, most far-reaching consequences.

Endnotes

1. National Science Federation Cooperative Agreement No. ANI-9807479 and the National Library for Applied Network Research. A wide range of information on advanced networking issues, primarily focused on wide-area networks and IP, can be found at http://moat.nlanr.net.

2. http://www.netcraft.co.uk/survey/reports/current/graphs.html, as quoted by InfoLibra.

3. Schulzrinne et. al, *Real Time Streaming Protocol (RTSP)*, April 1998, RFC 2326.

Appendices

An overview of TCP

"TCP is the predominant protocol on public and private internets today. Entire books have been written on TCP (*Internetworking With TCP/IP, Volume I,* by Douglas E. Comer) and a complete description of the protocol is beyond the scope of this text. If we are to regulate traffic on networks, however, we will need to take advantage of certain characteristics of the TCP protocol stack. A quick review is therefore presented here, with an emphasis on traffic-regulation characteristics."

IP is a connectionless protocol that makes no effort to correct transmission errors. Data that flows directly over IP can be damaged, lost, duplicated, and delivered out of sequence at any time. Applications that require reliable data delivery use TCP. It is a connection-oriented, full-duplex protocol with sender flow management that simulates a reliable connection across a connectionless, unreliable network by establishing virtual connections.

TCP setup

Several steps must take place between sender and receiver before traffic can be delivered. A TCP session between two network nodes consists of a series of setup messages to establish the link, followed by the transmission of network traffic and acknowledgments in either direction, simultaneously if desired.

A TCP connection is established by the exchange of a series of three packets, known as a three-way handshake:

- A client (e.g., a Web browser) sends an "open TCP connection request" (commonly referred to as a SYN packet) to the server.

- The server, if it is able to open a socket on that given port, sends back an acknowledgment packet and asks to open the return channel. The return packet is called the "SYN-ACK" because it is acknowledging the original request and asking for the reverse channel.

- The client acknowledges the "SYN-ACK," and the connection is open for full-duplex data transfer.

TCP is employed for file transfers or other long sessions that use the maximum possible packet size; it is also used for short, interactive applications like telnet or http. Long-session TCP traffic accounts for the majority of public IP traffic volume; short-session TCP traffic accounts for the majority of public IP traffic flows.

Guaranteed delivery

TCP guarantees that the stream of data leaving the sender will be reassembled intact at the receiver end, provided the network doesn't completely break in-between. It maintains first-in-first-out ordering through a sequence number that the sender and receiver use to break up and reassemble information in a first-in, first-out manner. It ensures delivery through a system of delivery acknowledgments. TCP also serves other functions, such as retransmission of lost information and adjusting the rate at which it introduces traffic into the network.

By performing acknowledgment at the TCP layer, the network and link layers are not burdened by the need to guarantee delivery, which makes them simpler and more scalable. TCP makes some basic assumptions that the network will generally deliver traffic and that the sequence of data will generally be the same at the receiver and the transmitter. A simple form of TCP might work according to Figure A–1.

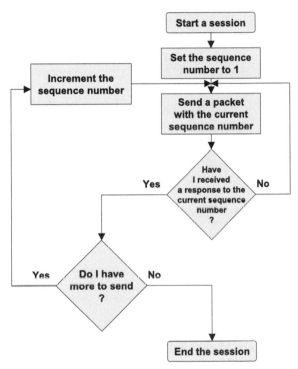

Figure A–1   An overly simple algorithm for guaranteed delivery

At first glance this is a sensible system. The transmitter sends a packet and waits for acknowledgment before sending another. Unfortunately, this simple model has several shortcomings.

• A host that is no longer responding can cause an indefinite delay; there's no notion of "timing out" and assuming a loss has occurred.

• The model assumes an instantaneous transmission and response to get maximum performance from a network. If a sender transmits a single datagram (for example, a 1,500-byte packet across a 28,800-bps dialup link), the datagram will take 400 milliseconds to clear the link. If the total round-trip time between the sender and receiver is 800 milliseconds, then there could be four packets in transit, but the above model would only send one.

• The model does not allow the sender and receiver to adapt to changes in the capacity of the network. For a best-effort network, optimal usage of the network by clients is essential to attain maximum efficiency.

• There is no "efficient retransmission" in which a sender can resend only lost information. If a receiver gets packets 1, 3, and 4, there's no way of just resending packet 2.

As a result, TCP is considerably more complex than the simple algorithm described above.

TCP does not acknowledge packets by packet numbers. Instead, it acknowledges data successfully received in sequence by the byte position. For example, when a receiver has correctly received all data up to 2048 bytes in the stream, it will send a packet back with the ACK bit set, and an acknowledgment number set to 2049. The acknowledgment tells the sender that the next segment the receiver expects to get begins with byte 2049. TCP will never send back a negative ACK, or a message indicating that "the last packet didn't make it." Instead, the receiver tells the sender, "I have received up to position 2048, but if there's more data, I don't have it yet."

When a TCP client notices that a segment has gone missing, it won't tell the sender that a piece of the transmission has been lost; rather, it will buffer new packets as they arrive and keep telling the sender that it has currently received up to the byte position of the lost segment (for example, x-1). The sender will eventually realize what has occurred and will resend the segment at position x. This is illustrated in figure Figure A–2.

Because the connectionless medium over which TCP runs is inherently unreliable and unpredictable, the real trick to TCP is in knowing how long to wait before declaring a packet missing, and when to resend it. If the sender waits for too short a time, it will resend packets that may have been just a little late—resulting in frequent unnecessary retransmissions and wasted network capacity. If the sender waits too long to resend a packet, the TCP connection will be slow because receivers buffer a con-

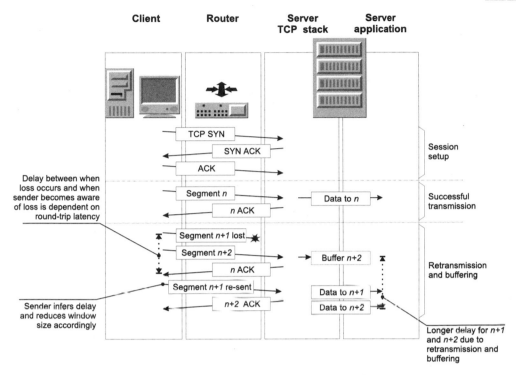

Figure A–2   Flow of data and acknowledgments in a TCP session

siderable amount of traffic while awaiting a missing segment and delay delivery of the TCP stream.

The original TCP specification (RFC 793) suggested waiting for twice the round trip time before re-sending. This approach did not really account for the level of jitter in a network—in a perfectly predictable network, acknowledgment should arrive at exactly one round-trip time after the segment was sent; in a very jittery network, this may be worse. Modern protocol stacks vary this delay between 1 and 2, depending on their measured characteristics of the line. For example, if the line has a high variance in delay (as shown by a high standard deviation of RTT), then it will wait closer to twice the measured RTT. If the line has a low variance in delay, it will retransmit closer to the RTT.

In TCP, data delivered out of sequence to the receiver will be buffered until the entire sequence is available for correct reassembly. Buffering can lead to considerable delays in cases where a discarded portion of the stream would have been acceptable to the application in return for faster delivery of later data.

Rate adaption

TCP is designed to be adaptive. A TCP sender constantly adjusts itself based on the current level of network performance. The receiver tells the sender how much data it's allowed to send without receiving an ACK (Figure A–3). The results of network congestion are increased round-trip delays and lost packets, which are signs that the sender is introducing too much data into the network.

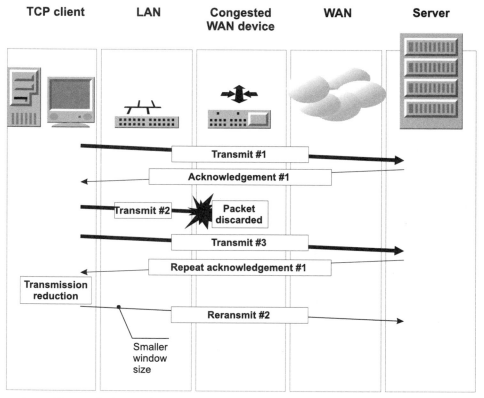

Figure A–3   Transmission reduction in TCP

The flow-control mechanism is useful if the receiver decides it can't handle data too quickly. Imagine, for example, another kind of network appliance—a networked coffee pot.[1] If a mainframe opens a TCP connection across the Internet to our perturbed percolator and the coffee pot has only an 8K buffer without the CPU power to process heavy data loads, the pot may begin by advertising an 8K window. As data arrives that the appliance doesn't have time to process, it reduces the window size as necessary to throttle the mainframe's transmission rate and prevent it from sending more data than the receiver has buffers. Such sender throttling may become increasingly important with the emergence of networked electronic equipment and personal digital assistants.

Flow control enables congestion avoidance. Without some system for avoiding network traffic jams, an oversubscribed router will begin to drop packets when its buffers become full. Dropping packets will cause the sender to resend traffic—which can cause even more congestion. In the past, many networks and internetwork peering points have ground to a halt from these congestion storms.

To correct this, when a TCP sender determines that a packet didn't make it through the network, it lowers the amount of information it has in transmission (called its window size), typically by half. This slows the rate at which the sender introduces packets into the network.

If the sender detects excessive loss, it enters a "slow start" phase (Figure A–4). Slow start is designed to prevent the original bottleneck from recurring right away, thus causing a cycle of bottleneck to empty link. Upon entering slow start, clients cease transmission and begin transmitting a single packet and waiting for acknowledgment. They double the number of packets they insert into the network until they experience discards with acknowledgment, and they continue to "probe" gradually for additional available bandwidth.

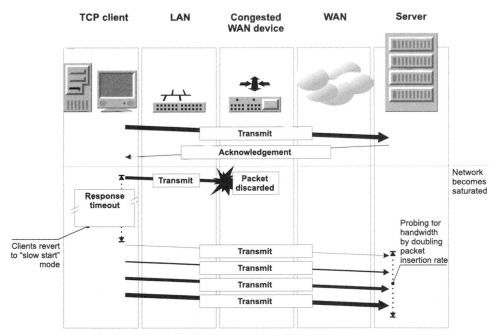

Figure A–4   Packet loss and slow start in TCP

The slow-start algorithm applies not just to errored connections but specifically to the start of *any* connection. The idea is to probe a network connection before you saturate it with traffic.

Probing for additional capacity

During normal operation, when a packet is sent successfully through the network, the client enlarges the window size by increasing the amount of traffic in transit by the size of one TCP segment in an attempt to gain maximum usage of the network. The TCP sender will send as much information as it thinks the network can handle. In order to avoid overloading the network right away, TCP begins with an assumption that the network can handle very little information. When a sender first starts transmitting, it increases bandwidth fairly aggressively: each time it receives a successful acknowledgment of traffic from the receiver, it increases the number of datagrams in transit exponentially.

If the sender receives an out-of sequence acknowledgment, it assumes that traffic was delayed significantly or lost. TCP sessions show some specific characteristics in terms of capacity over time (Figure A–5).

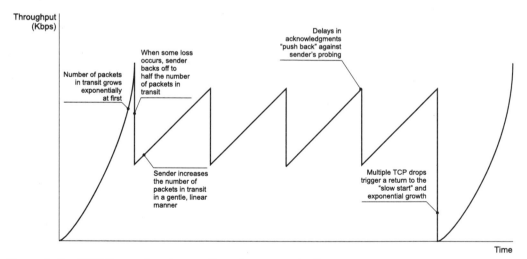

Figure A–5   TCP throughput over time (exaggerated)

Dropping a single packet is a useful way to reduce the amount of traffic that a sender introduces into the network. We can also observe that, even with a completely uncongested link, TCP will not allow a sender to use all available capacity all of the time.

If many senders enter a "slow-start" phase at the same time, the network may experience wildly fluctuating periods of congestion and available bandwidth, as clients everywhere gradually back off, then ramp up, in a cyclical fashion. One advantage of random-discard algorithms is that they avoid this kind of sender synchronization by causing different senders to ramp up at different rates.

Networks can assume that TCP clients will be adaptive—that is, a TCP implementation will respond to congestion and probe for available capacity; networks assume that UDP traffic is not adaptive. These characteristics have far-reaching and vital implications for TCP traffic shaping, since client behavior can be tuned by what happens to TCP segments in the network. TCP-based applications are typically described as controlled-load, rate-adaptive, and elastic.

When is UDP better than TCP?

In contrast to the adaptive, error-correcting nature of TCP, UDP makes no effort to guarantee delivery and does not adapt to network congestion. It sacrifices these in return for no setup overhead, no acknowledgment traffic, and no sequencing. Any guarantees of delivery or rate adaption must come from the application itself. This may be a benefit to voice applications: a voice telephony system may find that delayed packets are useless—getting most of the information, on time, is more important than getting all of the information, with delays.

Because of this, highly latency-sensitive traffic such as interactive voice and video, as well as one-way high-volume traffic like streamed multimedia, sometimes run over UDP. UDP-based voice applications are self-regulating; they use UDP to get less overhead than TCP, but in the process they lose rate control. This means they must implement rate controls at the application layer.

A TCP sender retransmits a segment when the acknowledgment for it is not received for a delay somewhere between one and two times the round-trip time of the network. If a receiver gets segments 1, 2, and 4, but does not receive segment 3, then it will buffer segment 4 until the retransmission of segment 3 arrives. TCP may transmit prematurely—for example, segment 3 may have been slightly delayed and the acknowledgment may have been on its way. In TCP, premature retransmissions cause congestion, but overdue retransmissions result in inefficient use of the network link. Because of the way out-of-sequence traffic is buffered,

TCP-based applications don't have control over when data is obsolete. By contrast, in our example a UDP-based system would allow the application to continue with segment 4 and beyond rather than waiting for segment 3 to arrive successfully. In UDP, the application developer must do more work, but the application can discard late traffic and avoid filling the receiver's queue with stale data.

TCP is nevertheless the dominant protocol on public networks today. In a sample of Internet OC-3 traffic, over 90 percent of all Internet traffic was TCP based, and in the fall of 1998, 70 percent of all Internet traffic was Web traffic. While an equal number of TCP flows were established from client to server and from server to client, the number of bytes transmitted from server to client was roughly 10 times that of the traffic from client to server. So approximately 63 percent of all Internet flows on the sampled link were TCP running on port 80 from server to client. The dominant source of UDP traffic was domain-name service information, which consumes a relatively small number of bytes per flow when compared with Web traffic.[2]

TCP is an excellent example of elegant engineering at work, and its resiliency has contributed in no small part to the broad adoption of IP as a global networking platform. TCP was originally designed for WAN internetworking, and its robustness may even be considered excessive on modern LANs and North American carrier systems. Some degree of delivery guarantee is needed, and TCP's sliding-window controls may prove increasingly important, even as its guarantees of error-free delivery become less so.

Endnotes

1. L. Masinter, *Hyper Text Coffee Pot Control Protocol (HTCPCP/1.0)*, April 1998, RFC 2324. Specifically, April 1.

2. National Science Federation Cooperative Agreement No. ANI-9807479, an analysis of Internet OC-3 trunk traffic.

Glossary

Term	Meaning
ABR	Available Bit Rate, an ATM service for rate-controlled applications
ACK	In TCP, an acknowledgment that a receiver has received TCP segments up to a specific byte position
ADSL	Asymmetric Digital Subscriber Loop, a local-loop technology that sends more traffic downstream than upstream, hence, asymmetrically
Adspec	RSVP add specification, an RSVP message that an intermediate router attaches to a *path* message to indicate the per-hop behavior it can offer a reservation
affordances	Cues or hints about how a thing should be used
ASIC	Application-specific integrated circuit; custom-build circuits that perform a specific set of operations at extremely high speeds
Baselining	Measuring capacity at an initial level in order to evaluate the effectiveness of a change
BECN	Backwards Error Correction Notification, a flag in a Frame Relay frame to notify the transmitting switch that congestion is occurring
BOOTP	Bootstrap protocol
bps	Bits per second
BRI	Basic Rate Interface
Burstable	The ability to introduce more than the agreed-upon level of traffic into a network for brief periods of time
Burstiness	A network in which traffic levels vary widely over time
CARP	Cache Array Routing Protocol
CBQ	Class-based queueing
CBR	Committed Bit Rate
CDV	Cell Delay Variation, a measurement of the change in delay that an ATM circuit will offer

Term	Meaning
CIDR	Classless Inter-domain routing
CIM	Common Information Model
CIR	Committed Information Rate
CLI	Command Line Interface
CLP	Cell Loss Priority
codec	Compression/decompression
colocation	Locating a portion of a network service at a remote location, such as within an IP point-of-presence
COS	Class of service, dividing service into discrete levels
CPE	Customer-premise equipment
CSMA	Carrier-sense multiple access
CTI	Computer-telephony integration, typically describing a system with both data and audio interfaces
DEN	Directory-enabled networks, an ad hoc industry group working to define a schema for information on networking devices
DF	Default, the standard DiffServ value similar to best effort
DHCP	Dynamic Host Configuration Protocol
DiffServ	Differentiated Services, an initiative to re-use the IPTOS information in the IP header as a set of values to signal service handling
DIT	Directory Information Tree
DLCI	Data Link Connection Identifier, used in Frame Relay to identify a particular circuit
DLSw	Data Link Switching
DMTF	Desktop Management Task Force
DN	Distinguished name, a unique name in a directory system

Term	Meaning
DNS	Domain name service
DSBM	Designated subnet bandwidth manager, the router chosen to represent a media subnet for bandwidth reservations
DSL	Digital subscriber loop, the copper pair between a normal telephone installation and a central site
DVCP	Dynamic VLAN configuration protocol
DWDM	Dense wave-division multiplexing
EF	Expedited Forwarding, a DiffServ codepoint indicating that a packet should be handled preferentially over the default PHB
EGP	External Gateway Protocol
ERP	Enterprise Requirements Planning, a family of applications that manage processes for large companies
Extranet	A network that leverages Internet technologies to exchange information with a limited set of outside organizations
Failover	The ability to shift services to an alternate fulfillment node without interrupting service
FDDI	Fiber Distributed Data Interface
FECN	Forward error- correction notification
Flowspec	An outbound message from a sender in RSVP that describes the flow the sender will introduce into the network
FRAD	Frame Relay access device
FRED	Flow-based random early discard, a discard algorithm that targets greedy applications' traffic when congestion occurs
GARP	Generic Attribute Registration Protocol
Gbps	Gigabits per second
GBps	Gigabytes per second
GIF	Graphics Interchange Format

Term	Meaning
GMRP	GARP Multicast Registration Protocol
GRE	Generic Routing Encapsulation
Groupware	Applications that are designed to share information among users, either through messaging or in real-time
HDLC	High-level data link control
ICMP	Internet control message protocol
ICP	Internet cache protocol
IETF	Internet Engineering Task Force, the standards body for the Internet
IFMP	Ipsilon Flow Management Protocol, a precursor to MPLS
IGMP	Internet Group Management Protocol, the protocol by which routers manage multicast sessions
IGP	Internet Gateway Protocol
IntServ	The Integrated Services initiative that aims to define explicit reservations of fine-grained network capacity on a per-session basis
IPCP	The IP control protocol by which dial-up or VPN users have their addresses allocated; similar to DHCP for point-to-point links
IPFEP	An IP front-end processor, our term for an edge device that performs additional network functions such as caching, load balancing, encryption, and so on, on behalf of a service
IPG	Inter-packet gap
IPSEC	IP security, including interoperability of encryption mechanisms and key exchange
IPTOS	IP Type-of-service
Isochronous	Time-based
ISSLL	Integrated Services over Specific Link Layers

Term	Meaning
JNDI	Java Naming and Directory Interface
Kbit	Kilobit
Kbps	Kilobits per second
Keyframe	A frame of information transmitted intermittently that contains all of the information needed to display something properly. Between keyframes, differential frames are used to make transmission more efficient.
LCP	Link Control Protocol
LDAP	Lightweight Directory Access Protocol
LDP	Local Decision Point
Loopback	A simple response mechanism used to test a particular level of the network.
MAN	Municipal Area Network
MBps	Megabytes per second
Mbps	Megabits per second
MByte	Megabyte, or million bytes
MBZ	Must be zero, reserved bits in a byte
MIB	Management Information Base
MLPPP	Multi-link point-to-point protocol, a way of aggregating point-to-point links for more bandwidth. Similar to trunking.
MPLS	Multi-protocol label switching, a switching method that places fixed-length labels in front of IP datagrams and switches them across circuits according to routing information.
mSec	Millisecond
MTU	Maximum transmit unit
NAS	Network access server, also known as an access concentrator
NNTP	Network News Transport Protocol

Term	Meaning
NOS	Network Operating System
OSI	Open Systems Interconnection
OSPF	Open Shortest Path First
Outsourced	Said of a function that has been assigned to an outside organization
Overengineering	Creating a network in which the peak load is less than the carrying capacity of the network
Overprovisioning	Creating a network in which the carrying capacity exceeds the average load
Oversubscription	Occurs when more traffic enters a network or device than can exit the network or device on average. Bursty traffic may congest a device on occasion, but will eventually clear; by contrast, oversubscribed links are subject to chronic congestion.
Packetization	The act of putting streams of information into discrete chunks through sampling or digitization.
Pathspec	An RSVP message that describes the path from the RSVP initiator to the server
PCR	Peak Cell Rate, the maximum rate at which a device will introduce cells into an ATM network
PDA	Personal Digital Assistant
PDP	Policy Decision Point, a policy server charged with making decisions for devices that must enforce policies
PEP	Policy Enforcement Point, a device that will carry out a policy
PHB	Per-hop Behavior, the way in which a packet will be treated as it crosses a device
POP	Point of presence, a location into which dial-up users connect
PPTP	Point-to-point tunneling protocol
Proxy	A device that acts on behalf of another for security or control

Term	Meaning
PSTN	Public Switched Telephone Network, the standard voice telephone network
PVC	Permanent Virtual Circuit
QOS	Quality of Service
RED	Random Early Discard
resv	A reservation message sent from the receiving node to the transmitting node in an RSVP negotiation
RFC	Request for Comments
RMON	Remote Monitor protocol that allows a management station to obtain network statistics from afar
RSVP	Resource Reservation Protocol
RTSP	Real-time Streaming Protocol
RTT	Round-trip time, the time it takes for traffic to travel from the sender to the receiver and back
SBM	Subnet Bandwidth Manager
SCR	Sustainable Cell Rate, the rate of cells that an ATM switch can tolerate over a sustained period of time
SLA	Service Level Agreement, a contract between a service provider and an organization that agrees to deliver a specific level of performance or capacity
SLP	Service Location Protocol
SMTP	Simple Mail Transport Protocol
SNA	Structured Network Architecture
Sniffer	A device that intercepts and displays traffic as it passes by a connection, often with facilities for decoding and interpreting the meaning of packets
SNMP	Simple Network Management Protocol
SONET	Synchronous Optical Network

Term	Meaning
SSL	Secure sockets used by Web browsers to ensure confidential Web transactions
Statefulness	A property of systems that change their behavior depending on the condition of other factors.
STP	Shielded Twisted Pair
SVC	Switched Virtual Circuit
SYN	A message transmitted during the establishment of a TCP session
TDM	Time-division multiplexing
Teardown	The termination of a session or connection
Telelearning	Systems for teaching classes over distance using videoconferencing and shared applications
TFTP	Trivial File Transfer Protocol, a simple file-transfer mechanism often used by network devices to obtain their configurations at boot time
Thresholding	Setting a set of tolerances on a device or within a network to ensure that when unacceptable levels of service occur, network managers are notified
Throbers	Blinking icons that demonstrate an application is still functioning despite a lack of other activity
TOS	Type of service. IPTOS is the name of the type-of-service byte in the IP header; within this byte, there are four bits devoted to type-of-service handling.
Traceroute	A diagnostic tool that determines the path across an internetwork and displays all routers in the path
Trunking	Linking two or more circuits to function as a single circuit for increased capacity or higher availability
TTL	Time-to-live, used in caching systems and some network protocols to avoid stale messages or estimate when traffic has been lost
UBR	Unspecified bit rate, an ATM "best effort" service level

Term	Meaning
UDP	User datagram protocol, TCP's connectionless cousin
Unicast	A communications system that associates a unique sender with a unique receiver. Contrast with multicast (one sender, many receivers) and broadcast (one sender, all receivers)
UTP	Unshielded Twisted Pair
VBR	Variable bit rate, an ATM service level that offers committed handling in the network but assumes that the rate at which the sender will introduce traffic will vary over time. May be *real-time*, meaning that synchronization of sender and receiver is important, or *non-real-time*.
VLAN	Virtual LAN
VLL	Virtual Leased Line, a point-to-point virtual private network
VoIP	Voice-over-IP, a set of technologies for packetizing, compressing, and transmitting voice over internetworks
VPN	Virtual Private Network
WAN	Wide Area Network
WCCP	Web Cache Control Protocol (from Cisco Systems)
WDM	Wave Division Multiplexing
WFQ	Weighted Fair Queuing, a method of assigning traffic to queues according to a specific ratio
Whiteboarding	A system of sharing a workspace among geographically separate users for collaboration
WRED	Weighted Random Early Discard, an algorithm that discards traffic according to relative weights among classes.

Bibliography and references

Texts

Black, Ulysses: *TCP/IP and Related Protocols*, McGraw-Hill, 1995

Blommers, John: *Practical Planning for Network Growth*, Hewlett-Packard Professional Books, Prentice-Hall PTR, 1996

Clemente, Peter: *State of the Net*, McGraw-Hill, 1998

Fluckiger, François, *Understanding Networked Multimedia*, Prentice-Hall, 1995

Kaufman, Perlman, and Speciner, *Network Security: Private Communication in a Public World*, Prentice-Hall, 1995

Magedanz and Popescu-Zeletin, *Intelligent Networks: Basic Technology, Standards, and Evolution*, Thomson Computer Press, 1996

Mok, Clement, *Designing Business: Multiple Media, Multiple Disciplines*, Adobe Press, 1996

Motorola Codex, *The Basics Book of Frame Relay*, Addison-Wesley Publishing, 1993

Motorola Codex, *The Basics Book of X.25 Packet Switching*, 2d ed., 1992

Naugle, Matthew, *Network Protocol Handbook*, McGraw-Hill, 1994

Normal, Donald A., *The Design of Everyday Things*, Doubleday, 1989

Perlman, Radia: *Interconnections: Bridges and Routers*, Addison-Wesley, 1992

Sherman, Kenneth: *Data Communications: A User's Guide*, Reston Publishing Company, Prentice-Hall, 1985

Web sites

Coffman, K. G., and Andrew Odlyzko, *The size and growth rate of the Internet*, (1997)	`http://www.firstmonday.dk/issues/issue3_10/coffman/index.html`
802.1D draft specifications	`http://grouper.ieee.org/groups/802/1/vlan.html.`
Access, Searching and Indexing of Directories (asid) Working Group	`http://www.ietf.cnri.reston.va.us/html.charters/asid-charter.html.`
Critical Angle's LDAP World Web Page	`http://www.critical-angle.com/ldapworld/`
Data Communications magazine's roundup of SLA monitoring tools	`http://www.data.com/issue/99027/sla_table1.html`
Desktop Management Task Force (DMTF) Home Page	`http://www.dmtf.org/`
Directory Enabled Networks (DEN) Home Page	`http://www.universe.digex.net/~murchiso/den/`
Hodges, Jeff, *An LDAP Roadmap & FAQ: A Tutorial Aid to Navigating Various LDAP and X.500 Resources on the Internet*	`http://www.kingsmountain.com/ldapRoadmap.shtml`
Integrated Directory Services (ids) Working Group	`http://www.ietf.cnri.reston.va.us/html.charters/ids-charter.html`

LDAP and X.500 Resources	`http://andrew2.andrew.cmu.edu/ cyrus/email/standards-X500.html`
LDAP/X.500 Client, Server, and General Resource Repository	`http://www.umich.edu/~dirsvcs/ ldap/index.html`
Lucent Technologies, *Impact and Performance of Lucent's Internet Telephony Server (ITS) Over IP Networks*	`http://www.lucent.com/enterprise/ internet/its-e/documenta- tion.html#white`
Microsoft Exchange Directory Service (LDAP)	`http://www.microsoft.com/ exchange/guide/ldap.asp`
Netscape's Internet Approach to Directories	`http://developer.netscape.com/ docs/manuals/ldap/index.html`
Nortel Networks, *Voice/Fax over IP*	`http://www.micom.com/WhitePapers/ index.html`
Novell Directory Services Home Page	`http://www.novell.com/ products/ nds/).`
Stardust's QOS forum	`http://www.stardust.com/qosforum`
Zoomit Corporation's white paper on directories	`http://www.zoomit.com/info/ paper1.htm`

Requests for Comments (RFCs) and Internet Drafts

Draft:	Boyle J., R. Cohen, D. Durham, S. Herzog, R. Rajan, and A. Sastry, "The COPS (Common Open Policy Service) Protocol," March 1998
Draft:	Calhoun, P., and A. Rubens, "DIAMETER Base Protocol," March 1998
Draft:	Calhoun, P., A. Rubens, and B. Aboba, "DIAMETER: Extensible Authentication Protocol Extensions," March 1998
Draft:	Calhoun, P., "DIAMETER: User Authentication Extensions," <draft-calhoun-diameter-authent-02.txt>, March 1998
Draft:	Herzog, S., "RSVP Extensions for Policy Control," April 1998
Draft:	Moats, R, "LDAP Clients Finding LDAP Servers," January 1998
Draft:	Moats, R, "LDAP Servers Finding Other LDAP Servers," January 1998

Draft:	Reichmeyer, F. et al., "COPS usage for differentiated services," August 1998
RFC 792	J. Postel, "Internet Control Message Protocol," September 1981
RFC 1122	R. Braden, "Requirements for Internet Hosts—Communication Layers," October 1989
RFC 1349	P. Almquist, "Type of Service in the Internet Protocol Suite," July 1992
RFC 1455	D. Eastlake, III, "Physical Link Security Type of Service," May 1993
RFC 1700	J. Reynolds and J. Postel, "Assigned Numbers," October 1994
RFC 1777	Yeong W., T. Howes, and S. Kille, "Lightweight Directory Access Protocol," March 1995
RFC 1812	Baker, F., ed., "Requirements for IP Version 4 Routers," June 1995
RFC 2165	Veizades J., E. Guttman, C. Perkins, and S. Kaplan, "Service Location Protocol," June 1997
RFC 2205	R. Braden, ed., L. Zhang, S. Berson, S. Herzog, and S. Jamin "Resource ReSerVation Protocol (RSVP)—Version 1 Functional Specification," September 1997
RFC 2206	F. Baker, J. Krawczyk, and A. Sastry, "RSVP Management Information Base using SMIv2," September 1997
RFC 2208	A. Mankin, ed., F. Baker, B. Braden, S. Bradner, M. O`Dell, A. Romanow, A. Weinrib, and L. Zhang, "Resource ReSerVation Protocol (RSVP)—Version 1 Applicability Statement," September 1997
RFC 2210	Wroclawski, J., "The Use of RSVP with IETF Integrated Services," September 1997
RFC 2211	Wroclawski, J., "Specification of the Controlled-Load Network Element Service," September 1997
RFC 2212	Shenker, S., C. Partridge, and R. Guerin, "Specification of Guaranteed Quality of Service,, September 1997
RFC 2215	Shenker, S., and J. Wroclawski, "General Characterization Parameters for Integrated Service Network Elements," September 1997
RFC 2216	Shenker, S., and J. Wroclawski, "Network Element Service Specification Template," September 1997

RFC 2251	Wahl M., T. Howes, and S. Kille, "Lightweight Directory Access Protocol (v3)," December 1997
RFC 2380	Berger, L., "RSVP over ATM Implementation Requirements," August 1998
RFC 2382	Crawley, E., L. Berger, S. Berson, F. Baker, M. Borden, and J. Krawczyk "A Framework for Integrated Services and RSVP over ATM," August 1998
RFC 2386	Crawley, E., R. Nair, B. Rajagopalan, and H. Sandick, "A Framework for QoS-based Routing in the Internet," August 1998
RFC 2430	Li, T., and Y. Rekhter, "A Provider Architecture for Differentiated Services and Traffic Engineering (PASTE)," October 1998
RFC 2474	Nichols K., S. Blake, F. Baker, and D. Black "Definition of the Differentiated Services Field (DS Field) in the IPv4 and IPv6 Headers," December 1998
Draft:	Strassner, J., "Terminology for Describing Network Policy and Services," August, 1998

Index